Admissions, Academic Records, and Registrar Services

◨ ◨ ◨ ◨ ◨ ◨ ◨ ◨ ◨ ◨ ◨ ◨ ◨ ◨ ◨ ◨ ◨ ◨

A Handbook of Policies and Procedures

C. James Quann
and Associates

Foreword by Kenneth E. Young

Admissions, Academic Records, and Registrar Services

Jossey-Bass Publishers

San Francisco • Washington • London • 1979

ADMISSIONS, ACADEMIC RECORDS, AND REGISTRAR SERVICES
A Handbook of Policies and Procedures
   by C. James Quann and Associates

Copyright © 1979 by: Jossey-Bass, Inc., Publishers
                      433 California Street
                      San Francisco, California 94104
                             &
                      Jossey-Bass Limited
                      28 Banner Street
                      London EC1Y 8QE

Library of Congress Cataloging in Publication Data

Main entry under title:

Admissions, academic records, and registrar services.
   (Jossey-Bass series in higher education)
   Includes bibliographies and index.
   1. Universities and colleges—United States—
Admissions—Handbooks, manuals, etc.   I.   Quann, C. James
LB2351.A35   378.1'05'60973   79-88109
ISBN 0-87589-419-4

Manufactured in the United States of America

JACKET DESIGN BY WILLI BAUM

FIRST EDITION

Code 7925

*The Jossey-Bass Series
in Higher Education*

In memory of
Marty J. Quann
1963–1976

Foreword

This handbook fills a noticeable void in the literature on administration in higher education. The role and function of registrars and admissions officers can be traced back as far as the Middle Ages, as Chapter One explains, but until now no comprehensive textbook or reference has been published concerning these key administrative positions. Only fleeting glimpses of their important functions can be found in the many existing volumes on college and university administration. Some contain a paragraph here or a chapter there, but their coverage is inadequate. This handbook covers in detail all the functional responsibilities of registrars and admissions officers, including the interpretation and enforcement of academic policies and standards.

Within each institution, the persons most concerned with carrying out this vital responsibility for quality control are the registrar and the admissions officer. These professionals work with and advise the faculty in the development of academic policies and then interpret and apply these policies on a day-to-day, case-by-case basis. The questions they deal with are almost endless: What students should be admitted under what provisions? What previous educational experiences should be accepted and applied toward what requirements? What conditions must apply in which situations to assure that prior learning can be evaluated and properly translated? What constitutes a "college-level" course? Cumulative and consistent answers to these pragmatic, operational questions help ensure educational quality.

In this respect, registrars and their colleagues in admissions play an important role in quality assurance within the institution; complementing that of the various accrediting agencies. Indeed, accrediting agencies themselves rely heavily on educational institutions and their administrative officers to participate in the development and application of generally accepted standards. And because registrars and admissions officers play such an important, central role in this system of educational quality assurance, I am pleased to have the opportunity to introduce this handbook. It represents one more significant contribution by the American Association of Collegiate Registrars and Admissions Officers toward the increasing professionalization of its members. Like accreditation, it is a tool which, when properly used, will strengthen and protect the independent governance and self-regulation of our nation's colleges and schools.

Washington, D.C.   Kenneth E. Young
August 1979   *President*
                              Council on Postsecondary Accreditation

Preface

As early as 1930, the membership of the American Association of Collegiate Registrars and Admissions Officers (AACRAO) asked for a source of reliable information defining the functions and duties of registrars and admissions officers. In 1949 AACRAO commissioned a committee on special projects to study a handbook proposal, and in 1950 an AACRAO committee recommended a three-step approach to the development of a National Standard Practice Book for the Association (Fellows, 1950). In 1953 an abbreviated guide titled *AACRAO Policies and Procedures* was published. Since that time numerous committees and subcommittees have been formed to amplify this earlier work. The 1975–76 executive committee authorized the funds; and in the late spring of 1976 AACRAO president Garland G. Parker appointed a handbook editor and editorial committee, charging them with the preparation of a sourcebook for prospective, new, and experienced professionals in the registrar-admissions field. Their charge stated that the handbook should cover subjects and procedures including both philosophical and how-to information. Further, the editorial committee was urged to ensure that handbook content covered procedures and practices in two-year, four-year, public, and private institutions.

The editorial committee, after reviewing the attempts of previous committees and commissions, concluded that earlier efforts had failed due to the breadth of the projected publications. The committee set as its task, therefore, the development and publication of a basic introduction to the central responsibilities of members of the profession—a handbook that would serve as the definitive source for the profession. An additional goal was to make the publication useful to academic deans, department and program chairpersons, and student personnel administrators as they continue to define and develop policies and procedures related to academic programs and student services.

The handbook represents a cooperative effort on the part of the American Association of Collegiate Registrars and Admissions Officers, the handbook editorial committee, the editor, and the publisher. Preparation of the handbook involved careful planning and work with experts from all areas of the profession. The authors invited to write and edit the various chapters were chosen because of their extensive experience, and they in turn contacted and worked closely with many other experts representing all sizes and types of colleges and universities. Chapters Two and Three cover the field of admissions, and Chapters Four, Five, Six, and Seven deal with the registrar and related subjects. These two main branches of the profession, often with overlapping duties and shared responsibilities, have recently experienced phenomenal growth and expansion in computer-related systems and services. Chapters Eight and Nine deal extensively with computer automated systems, including examples, of both admissions and records systems that illustrate a variety of successfully functioning systems rather than any one theoretically ideal or "model" system.

The remaining chapters—on the academic calendar, institutional research, commencement and academic attire, and the

American Association of Collegiate Registrars and Admissions Officers itself—cover topics of importance for the profession at large, and the appendices reproduce basic policy statements of AACRAO and other organizations for use by all professionals in the field.

I am deeply indebted to the authors of these chapters and resource documents, just as all of us are indebted to the American Association of Collegiate Registrars and Admissions Officers for sponsoring this handbook. AACRAO's executive secretary, J. Douglas Conner, and his staff have provided helpful resources and direction, and the Association's executive officers have supplied helpful suggestions, moral support, and that most important ingredient—incentive—to push this project toward completion. Special appreciation goes to the chapter authors, identified in "The Authors" section; to E. M. Gerritz, dean of admissions and records, Kansas State University, for assistance with Chapter One; and to the editorial committee: Richard Eastop, director of admissions, University of Toledo, E. M. Gerritz; and Evelyn Schroedl, registrar, Goucher College. Nelson Parkhurst, registrar, Purdue University; James Scriven, dean of admissions and records, Youngstown State University; Frederick Sperry, executive associate in student services, University of Wisconsin-Milwaukee; and Donn Stansbury, director of admissions and records, William Rainey Harper College are acknowledged for their contributions to the section in Chapter Nine on "sample systems."

Many additional obligations have been incurred during the preparation of this book; some are as impossible to identify as they are to repay. We are grateful to the late Truman Pouncey, chairperson of an AACRAO handbook committee in 1968, and his colleagues, who broke fresh ground in identifying the need, by subject, for what eventually became this handbook. We also acknowledge the contributions of the 1972 committee, headed by James Schoemer, that developed the concept of a "primer" for registrars and admissions officers; Kenneth E. Young of the Council on Postsecondary Accreditation (COPA), who provided the foreword and information on accreditation for Appendix C; and Hugh M. Jenkins, executive vice-president of the National Association of Foreign Student Affairs, for Appendix E on international education exchange and Carolyn R. Smith, Department of Health,

Education and Welfare, National Center for Education Statistics, who made available the updated information on higher education associations. We also recognize the contribution of the registrar's staff of Washington State University, whose help and forbearance allowed this publication to be completed. Preparation of this book has spread over a three-year period, drawing upon the work of several committees and many individuals. One problem of extending such work over time is the possibility of failing to acknowledge primary authorship of bits and pieces from a larger work. Jencks and Riesman (1969, p. xx) refer to this as unconscious plagiarism, whereby a concept or idea, barely noticed at first, may reappear later and be considered original. If we have acquired material in this way without giving credit, we beg forgiveness.

Finally, we hope that our colleagues will view this volume as the first of several that will cover in depth all the philosophical and functional responsibilities of registrars and admissions officers. Important but more peripheral tasks, such as academic orientation and advising and space utilization and planning, could well be covered in later volumes; we welcome suggestions and information for future publications.

Pullman, Washington   C. JAMES QUANN
August 1979

Contents

▣ ▣ ▣ ▣ ▣ ▣ ▣ ▣ ▣ ▣ ▣ ▣ ▣ ▣ ▣

xv

Tables, Figures, and Exhibits

▣ ▣ ▣ ▣ ▣ ▣ ▣ ▣ ▣ ▣ ▣ ▣ ▣ ▣ ▣ ▣ ▣ ▣

The Authors

C. JAMES QUANN is registrar and editor of the catalog at Washington State University, where he also chairs the student records committee and serves as secretary to the faculty, to the academic affairs committee, and to the catalog committee.

Quann was born in Cle Elum, Washington, in 1933; he was awarded the B.S. degree in animal sciences from Washington State College (1954), and the M.A. degree in agricultural economics and the Ed.D. degree in higher education from Washington State University (1960 and 1971, respectively). He served as an International Farm Youth Exchange student to Uruguay in the early 1950s, followed by service as a first lieutenant in the U.S. Army in Korea. He was dean of men and director of housing at Eastern New Mexico University (1959–1962), dean of men and director of student activities at Central Washington State College (1962–1966), and then joined the staff of Washington State University in 1966. He is president of the Pacific Association of Collegiate Registrars and Admissions Officers, the western regional branch of the American Association of Collegiate Registrars and Admissions Officers (AACRAO). In addition to teaching on a part-time basis, Quann is involved in research on grading and calendar systems and frequently contributes articles to several professional journals. He has many years of service on various AACRAO committees, including new developments and techniques, nominations and elections, and the ad hoc committee on system design and programming for the AACRAO data base. He currently serves as a member of the AACRAO editorial board.

Quann and his wife Barbara have two sons attending Washington State University and a daughter in high school.

JAMES FLINN BLAKESLEY, administrative coordinator, Office of Schedules and Space, Purdue University, West Lafeyette, Indiana.

J. DOUGLAS CONNER, executive secretary, American Association of Collegiate Registrars and Admissions Officers, Washington, D.C.

LOYD C. OLESON, registrar, Doane College, Crete, Nebraska.

E. EUGENE OLIVER, director, University Office of School and College Relations, University of Illinois, Urbana, Illinois.

MARGARET RUTHVEN PERRY, registrar, Wake Forest University, Winston-Salem, North Carolina.

WILLIAM C. PRICE, director of admissions and records, University of Illinois at Chicago Circle, Chicago, Illinois.

HANS WAGNER, former dean of records and institutional research, University of the Pacific, Stockton, California.

Admissions, Academic Records, and Registrar Services

■ ■ ■ ■ ■ ■ ■ ■ ■ ■ ■ ■ ■ ■ ■ ■ ■ ■

A Handbook of Policies and Procedures

1

Understanding the Profession

C. James Quann

Higher education has been a part of American life since the founding of Harvard in 1636, but until recently access to college has been viewed as a privilege rather than as a virtual necessity or a nearly unalienable right. Until World War II, admissions requirements were minimal or unknown in all but the most exclusive institutions, and registration and records systems were designed for small numbers of usually nonperipatetic and docile students. Since then, traditional approaches to admissions, registration, and records have disintegrated under the stress of numbers. Educators have realized that simply placing one amorphous group of individuals (the students) in close proximity to another group (the faculty) does not necessarily result in education. Some selection and ranking of students is required to bring order to the process, and a system is needed to match students with professors and courses in ways that will stimulate teaching and learning. College and university presidents have learned that the business of recruiting and admitting students, analyzing their curricular needs, establishing schedules of classes to meet these needs, and recording the academic progress of students requires expertise, dedication, and plain hard work. More than ever before, registrars and admissions officers have come to be recognized as professional educators analogous with classroom teachers and deans. If the educational missions of seeking truth and transmitting knowledge are to be met, academic institutions need not only good students, an educated faculty, and reasonable classroom facilities but also adequate supporting services to admit, enroll, and keep records for students. The need for these special supporting services forms the genesis of this book. To do the job at hand, good admissions officers, registrars, and records administrators must be selected and trained, and professional resources must be made available to them and to other administrators to assist in this educational process.

Origins and Growth of the Profession

The registrar's role and function can be traced into educational antiquity to at least the end of the twelfth century and the emergence of the office of *bedel* or *beadle*[1] (from German *Butil* and *Büttel* and Old English *bydel,* a herald) at the three great archetypal universities, Bologna in Italy, Paris in France, and Oxford in England. Like other medieval institutions, such as the Church and courts of law, these universities required an official to proclaim messages and execute the mandates of their authorities; and, like all more recent academic institutions, they needed specialized administrative officers to assure their academic operations, whether maintaining institutional records, finances, facilities, or simply institutional order. At Bologna the registrar's title *bidelli generale,* and the duties included preceding the rectors on public occasions, collecting the votes in congregation, visiting the schools to read statutes and decrees, announcing lectures by students, and distributing lists of books which the *stationarii* (keepers of book stalls) or individual students had on sale. The *bidelli generale* or *general bedel* also served as a catalyst for research and publications, ensuring a

[1]Hastings Rashdall (1895), the foremost authority on the medieval universities, uses the spelling *bedel,* from *bedellus* or *pedellus.* Edward Stout (1954), writing on the origins of the registrar's office, uses *beadle* but inadvertently credits the University of Paris with developments that actually took place at Bologna.

continual supply of scholastic literature by enforcing the requirement that each doctor, after holding his *disputatio* or *repetitio,* write
out his argument or thesis for submission to the general bedel.
Failure to comply resulted in a fine. The general bedel, presumably
after carefully checking the doctor's work, delivered it to the
stationers for publication. There was one *bidelli generale* for each
university, and each doctor had a *special bidelli* who looked after the
doctor's classes and saw to it that the classroom or school, usually a
rented apartment or private house, was kept clean and in order
(Rashdall, 1895, pp. 190–195).

At the University of Paris, the rector served as head of the
institution, being elected by the proctors (regional heads) of the
four "nations" or associations of students from particular regions
of Europe. This relationship of the rector to the proctors appeared
in 1249, along with the bedels or "common servants of the scholars"
(Rashdall, 1895, pp. 315–316). The duties of the bedels, although
much the same as those of the bedels of Bologna, are translated
from *Chartularium Universitatus Parisiensis I* in the language of the
Middle Ages (Thorndike, 1944, pp. 72–73):

These are the statutes which the bedells of the University of Paris
obligate themselves faithfully to observe, giving personal security. They
ought to attend the opening lecture of each person incepting, poor or
otherwise, from beginning to end, unless it is well known that they have
been sent by the person incepting or the proctor of his nation on some
special errand or for some special common examination of the nation, or
unless they have to attend funeral obsequies, or unless their own bodily
infirmity prevents them, or unless they are detained by some other legitimate and notorious occasion, if there can be any other than those
specified. If, however, they absent themselves unexcused by any of the said
occasions, they ought to forfeit their portion of that purse which he gives
who incepts, which portion, I say, should go to the proctor of the said
bedell who forfeits it. Also, if it is enjoined upon any bedell to call a
meeting either special or general, and it can be proved by three or four
masters that he has not cited them, he should know that he will similarly
forfeit a portion of each purse, two solidi, which portion likewise will go to
the proctor of that nation. Also, if he ought to announce a course and it
can be proved that he has failed to go to all classes, he should know that he
will incur the same penalty and same loss in the same manner as aforesaid.
Also, each bedell ought early in the morning on each day to visit the classes
not only of the rector or his own proctor but also of every proctor of every

nation, which if he does not do, let him know that he will incur the same loss in the same manner. Also, if he shall fail to attend the common examination of anyone of his nation or shall be proved to have betrayed the university's secrets, let him know that he shall forfeit one purse as has been said. Also, if he is absent on Friday at the vespers of his nation, he shall lose two pence and for mass two. Also, if he does not have a calendar and is deficient in announcing to individuals a Feast which is not well known, or even in not preventing disputation when he should, for each such offense he shall forfeit four pence, all which pence the proctor of the nation of the delinquent bedell should keep for the use of his nation.

Higher education was developing along similar lines at Oxford. The university was headed by a chancellor, two proctors, and six bedels. The bedels were elected annually to serve the university and to execute its orders and maintain its state. In writing the history of Oxford, Charles Mallet (1924, p. 176) described the duties of these bedels:

They figured in all ceremonies, funerals included. They published proclamations, generally in Latin. They went round the Schools, giving out University announcements. They collected the votes in Congregation. They served writs, exacted fines, and escorted evil-doers to prison when they consented to go. Their dues and perquisites were settled by Statutes, which had to be repeated when the "charity of the students grew cold." Three of them, who came to be known as Gentlemen or Esquire Bedels, were superior to the others in standing. They were expected to provide their inferior colleagues with food and with ten shillings a year for shoes. And these superior posts were evidently in demand. We find great personages interfering in the nominations. In days of corruption it was alleged that the posts were sold. In 1433 the four Superior Faculties attempted to nominate a Bedel, asserting that they were the "senior and saner part of the electors." But the Masters of Arts resisted and carried their candidate in. Later on, Henry VI and Edward IV recommended candidates of their own. Henry demanded the punishment of two Bedels, who had "outrageously uttered" libels against himself, his "wyf" and his son. And later still, in 1501, the election of an Oxford Bedel caused a sharp division in Royal circles. The Prince of Wales and the Bishop of Lincoln supported one candidate. The Prince's grandmother, the illustrious Lady Margaret, preferred another. The King and Queen encouraged a third. The Lady Margaret's candidate won, and the Bishop, who was also Chancellor of the University, was respectfully reminded that even Caesar, Cicero, and Pompey had sometimes proved unable to oblige their friends.

By 1446 the responsibilities of the bedel began to change, and the registrar's office first emerged officially when an academic officer with the title of "registrar" was appointed at Oxford. This officer's duties were to give form and permanence to the university's public acts, to draft its letters, to make copies of its documents, and to register the names of its graduates and their "examinatory sermons" (Mallet, 1924, p. 327). In 1506 Robert Hobbs was appointed as "registrary" of Cambridge. Hobbs was chiefly responsible for regulating and coordinating university ceremonies, but in 1544 his successor was assigned the responsibility, by the vice-chancellor of the university, of reviewing all applicants for matriculation. Later, at Cambridge as well as at Oxford and then at other British universities, the registrar came to act as the secretary for all academic bodies. Even today, British registrars continue to serve primarily as their institutions' secretariat—preparing agenda for official meetings, keeping minutes, conducting correspondence, and, at some universities, collecting fees (Johnston, 1949).

Elsewhere in the British empire, the registrar's and bedel's office was also institutionalized. In Australia, for instance, the University of Sydney opened in 1850 with a registrar on duty from the beginning, and even today it maintains an esquire bedel and a yeoman bedel as well as a registrar.

In America the registrar's academic record-keeping functions—apart from the financial record duties of the college steward concerning students' bills—remained at Harvard a part-time faculty duty into the mid-nineteenth century. Thus, during the 1820s its Hollis Professor of Divinity, the Reverend Henry Ware, was supplementing his professor's salary by $150 a year for his work as Harvard's registrar, plus another $150 for conducting its chapel services, just as its Professor of Logick and Metaphysics, Levi Hedge, was receiving an extra $150 as its "Inspector of College Buildings" (Harvard University, 1824). And from 1880 to 1888, Harvard's professor of mathematics, Charles Joyce White, performed both teaching and registrar functions.

Unlike Harvard, America's second college, Yale, adopted the bedel tradition. Thus, at commencement in 1778—in the midst of the Revolutionary War—Yale's new president, the Reverend Ezra

Stiles, called on the "vice bedellus" and the junior tutor to convene the ceremony and oversee the examination of the thirty-six candidates in Greek, Latin, and the sciences. Afterward, the vice bedellus read the *Diploma Examinatorium* on Stiles' behalf to the examiners and candidates and, following a recess, to the ladies and gentlemen assembled in the college chapel, before returning it to Stiles for deposit in the college archives (Dexter, 1901, pp. 287–288).

At other American colleges, professors continued to serve as registrars during the latter part of the nineteenth century. Thus, when Cornell opened in 1868, its first Professor of Moral and Intellectual Philosophy and Religion, W. D. Wilson, doubled as its registrar. But the end of the century saw the evolution of the registrar's role as an increasingly professional, specialized, and full-time administrative task. For example, when Stanford opened in 1891, Orrin Elliott joined its staff as full-time registrar and administrative officer second only to its president. Edith D. Cockins, a clerk in the recorder's office, became the first registrar at Ohio State University in 1897. And Howard Tibbits of the class of 1900 became acting registrar at Dartmouth in 1902 and permanent registrar in 1908.

This trend toward full-time administrative duty is illustrated by a representative sample of thirty-two colleges and universities. As of 1880, 85 percent of the registrars at these institutions also taught. In contrast, as of 1933 only some 20 percent continued to teach; nearly 80 percent had become full-time administrative specialists (McGrath, 1938, p. 129).

Apart from the college president, the treasurer, and the librarian, the registrar was among the first administrative officers to become a specialist. Among these thirty-two institutions, for example, the registrar's position was created, on the average, in 1887; in contrast, the office of dean was created in 1891, dean of women in 1896, chief business officer in 1906, and dean of men in 1920 (McGrath, 1938, p. 192). Among another sample of twenty-five liberal arts colleges, the registrars also predated the deans and business officers. All twenty-five colleges created the registrar's position between 1881 and 1920, with the median year being 1896 (Partridge, 1934, p. 77). And among colleges accredited by the Association of American Universities, less than 10 percent had registrars as of 1880, but 25 percent had designated them by 1890, as had 42 percent by 1900, 76 percent by 1910 (the founding year of the American Association of Collegiate Registrars—AACR; now the American Association of Collegiate Registrars and Admissions Officers), over 90 percent by 1920, and all of them by 1930 (Jarman, 1947).

The need for full-time professional aid for accurate records and efficient enrollment procedures became increasingly evident in the early decades of the twentieth century, as institutions grew in size and their curricular offerings and electives burgeoned. Registration procedures alone illustrated the need: by the 1920s at the University of Michigan, students had to be in line by 4 A.M. to be sure of getting registered by the end of the day; as late as 1937, students at Michigan State College were spending an average of seven hours in line at each registration period; and stories of registration confusion were common at many institutions. At Tulane, for instance, the tale circulated of one preengineering student who, after receiving and completing the wrong registration forms and waiting in the premed line, decided that it would be too much trouble to reregister in engineering and entered medicine instead.

Registration was only one area of the registrar's responsibility. Among the information and clerical services performed by most registrars during the 1920s were those, for example, at Stanford, where the registrar "cared for student records, handled official communication between students and academic committees, prepared all official publications, and acted as a central bureau of information about the academic work of the university" (Walker, 1964, p. 97). But during the 1920s the registrar's office was assuming an increasing variety of other student personnel services as well—ranging, in one observer's view, "from janitorial to journalistic" (Smerling, 1960, p. 182). They often corresponded with prospective students, conducted high school visitations, sent and received application forms, oversaw scholarship and financial aid awards, greeted freshmen and transfer students, conducted their orientation, advised them on programs and courses, counseled them on vocations and careers, scheduled classes, forecast enrollments, predicted tuition income, analyzed teaching loads, responded to questionnaires, conducted other institutional research, suggested curriculum revisions to the faculty, signed diplomas, and even shook hands with graduating seniors at commencement. This expanded role of the registrar's office was epitomized in 1925 with the publication of "A Code of Ethics for Registrars," developed by a committee of the American Association of Collegiate Registrars. "The everyday details of duties performed by my office are secondary to the opportunity to add my influence in the building of character through personal contact outside my official capacity," the Code proclaimed on behalf of registrars, "and to this end the door to my office shall ever swing inward to students seeking advice and encouragement" (Committee on Code of Ethics, 1925, p. 259).

Later in the twentieth century, the inward-swinging door of the registrar's office was less frequently used by students seeking advice and encouragement, since many student services began to be provided by separate and independent offices—among them admissions, counseling, placement, and academic advising. With the growth of these other administrative specialties, registrars have assumed their present role of managers of data. That is, they now serve as the center of an information system controlling the input of data into the academic system and the output of data to various individuals and agencies; they also serve as a major source of institutional facts that can and should provide the raw material for effective academic decision making (Corson, 1975, p. 152). Ezra Gillis—long-time registrar at the University of Kentucky—put it more succinctly: "I have seen the status of the registrar change from that of a clerk to an administrator who is recognized not only in the councils of the universities but also in the educational councils of the nation" (Gillis, 1939, p. 114).

Although private colleges and universities had employed field representatives and admissions counselors before World War I, and Columbia University opened its Office of Admissions in 1915, separate admissions offices and officers were largely a product of later decades. Perry (1970) reports that admissions developed as a specialization in college and university administration after World War II. The enactment of the first "GI Bill of Rights" (the Servicemen's Readjustment Act) in 1946 accelerated the change of higher education from a privilege to a necessity and right, and also increased the importance of the admissions staff. The rapid influx of students that resulted from it created a dilemma, since the extremely limited physical and educational resources could not accommodate all the prospective students requesting access to these resources. The nation, recovering both from world war and the Great Depression, looked to education for solutions to the problems facing mankind, but few institutions, large or small, had sufficient teaching staff, classroom space, or laboratory equipment to meet the needs of potential students. While junior or community colleges developed as largely "open-door" institutions to meet some of the demand, most existing colleges and universities moved toward selective admissions and increased responsibility of admissions officers for screening applicants.

Two events—both centered around professional associations—marked the emergence of admissions as a specialized field: in 1937 the Association of College Admissions Counselors (now the National Association of College Admissions Counselors) was founded, and in 1949 the American Association of Collegiate Registrars added "and Admissions Officers" to its title. By 1952—when Harvard University created its Office of Dean of Admissions—admissions had become centralized in its own separate office, coordinate with that of the registrar or recorder, and was itself involved in "recruitment, interviewing, testing, counseling, evaluation and placement, orientation, research, and publication" (Gerritz and Thomas, 1953, p. 68). At some institutions the registrar oversaw the director of admissions, and at a few schools the director of admissions oversaw the registrar's office; but increasingly these two officers were separate and equal, reporting either to a dean of admissions and records or to central administrators.

The relationship between the registrar's office and the admissions office is now largely resolved, but disagreement about the organizational placement of the offices continues. Should they be academic offices under the provost or vice-president for academic affairs, or should they be student service offices under the dean of students or the vice-president for student services? The first consolidated administration under one dean occurred in 1870, when Harvard—then the largest college in the country—created the first deanship in any American college. The Harvard dean assumed among other duties a responsibility "to keep the records of admission and matriculation . . . and preserve the records of conduct and attendance" (Wert, 1955, p. 84). Differences of opinion about affiliating the registrar with academic affairs or with student services have not abated during the intervening 109 years.

Despite this continued question of desirable organizational arrangements, little disagreement remains about the roles of the registrar and admissions officer in providing accurate information and timely assistance to everyone connected with the institution. They serve both prospective and enrolled students, they respond to faculty and administrative needs for facts, and they provide the basis for informed educational policies and procedures.

Modern Organizational Patterns

Since the roles of registrars and admission officers are both operational and academic, the modern alignment of the offices may differ, especially between two- and four-year institutions. Variations in organizational alignment will occur on a regional basis, between states, and even among sister institutions. However, two main organizational arrangements, with many variations, exist nationally. In the larger colleges and universities, registrars and admissions officers are increasingly viewed as academic officers reporting to the academic vice-president or provost. In these instances, the registrar generally has many responsibilities outside of registration and records, including but not limited to editing the catalog and serving as secretary to the faculty and various academic policymaking committees. Similarly, admissions officers not only admit students but evaluate academic credentials, supervise orientation programs, coordinate relations with high schools and colleges, and advise students. This organizational pattern is illustrated in Figure 1. In some institutions an executive dean or director of admissions and records coordinates and supervises both functions, as in Figure 2.

Some four-year colleges and most community colleges place registrars and admissions personnel in the role of student personnel administrators reporting to a dean of students or vice-president for student affairs. In these instances, as shown in Figure 3, they

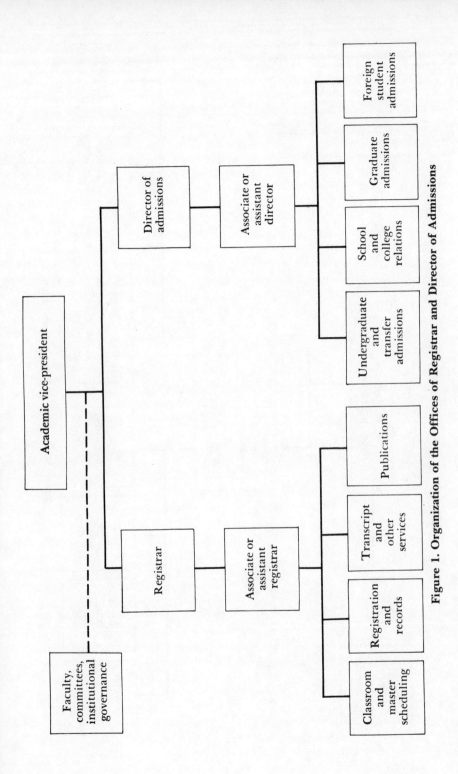

Figure 1. Organization of the Offices of Registrar and Director of Admissions

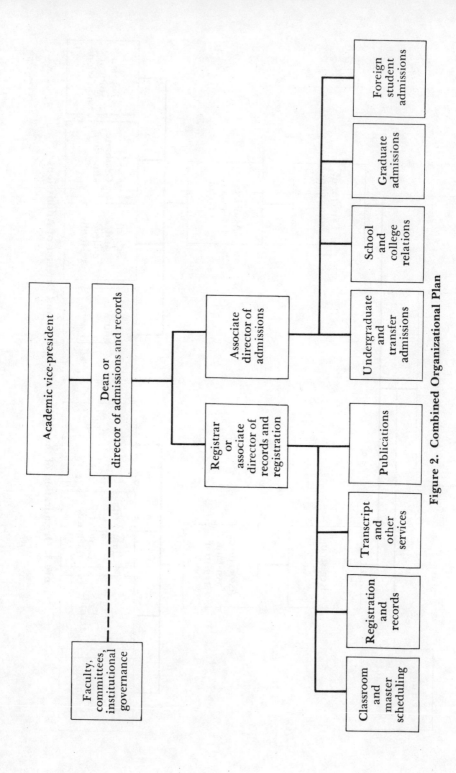

Figure 2. Combined Organizational Plan

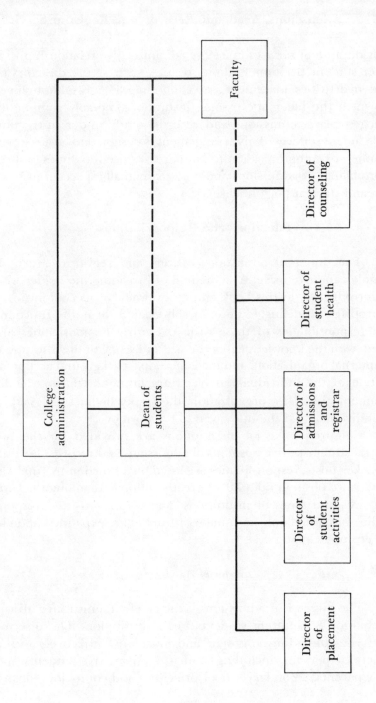

Figure 3. Organizational Arrangement Through Student Services

provide student services in a close administrative relationship with other student personnel administrators, such as the directors of student activities, placement, and counseling. Finally (although not shown in the schematics), some institutions, notably community colleges, place admissions and records jointly under instruction and student services. This arrangement is designed to ensure open channels of communication to both areas, since the duties and responsibilities of admissions and records span all aspects of instruction and student personnel services.

Functions and Responsibilities

The duties of admissions officers and registrars are both complex and extensive. As a method of providing the reader with an introduction to this book and an overview of its contents, it is appropriate to delineate here, in abbreviated form, the functions and responsibilities of these offices. Central responsibilities are listed, with the knowledge that the size and scope of the institution, its internal organization, and the educational background and preparation of the individuals involved are important factors in determining the office organization, the responsibilities assigned to an individual, and the title given to the position.

Comprehensive job descriptions are provided for the two central administrative positions in admissions and records. Beyond these key posts, responsibilities are listed on a function-by-function basis, since position titles differ greatly within and among the various sizes and types of institutions. Major functions and responsibilities are listed only in summary form but are expanded upon in the ensuing chapters.

Director of Admissions

The director of admissions is the chief administrative officer in charge of admitting students to the institution. The director supervises the admissions staff and must work effectively with a variety of persons, including students, prospective students and their parents, secondary school principals and counselors, deans, department heads and individual faculty, and alumni and friends of the college or university. Normally this individual reports to a dean of admissions and records or to an academic dean or vice-president.

The duties of the director of admissions are broad and detailed. In a small institution they will be centered in a very few individuals but may be dispersed among a dozen or more in a larger university. The director is responsible for the organizational pattern used within the division and for the assignment of specific responsibilities to individuals. The packaging of these assignments will be influenced by the size of the institution, its resources, the individual employees currently employed, and the ones to be attracted to positions there. The director will do well to maximize the potential of each employee by allocating authority and responsibility judiciously and by providing opportunities for individual professional growth.

All of the following responsibilities and duties and more are in the province of the director of admissions. In some instances, activities that are similar or related are listed separately. In a large institution these groups of duties could well be organized under one person or head, with an appropriate staff, reporting to the director.

1. Supervises the staff of the office of admissions in the administration of the various admissions policies, including all undergraduate, graduate, and foreign student admissions.
2. Administers the institutional (or state) policy on residency.
3. Maintains an admissions records system in accordance with policies recommended by the American Association of Collegiate Registrars and Admissions Officers.
4. Has responsibility for the printing and distribution of the various recruiting brochures and publications.
5. Provides advice and recommendations to the admissions committee and faculty senate or other governing unit.
6. Seeks ways to improve admissions procedures, materials, and data systems in order to achieve a more effective and efficient admissions process.

7. Works with faculty, deans, and academic staff in ensuring that the admissions office is properly and efficiently serving both the students and the institution.
8. Represents the office of admissions on a variety of institutional committees.
9. Maintains and improves relationships with high schools and colleges.
10. Participates actively in state, regional, and national professional admissions associations (such as the American Association of Collegiate Registrars and Admissions Officers, the American College Testing Program, the College Entrance Examination Board, and the National Association of College Admissions Counselors).
11. Conducts appropriate research.
12. Prepares the budget of the office of admissions or for the admissions portion of the office if it is combined with records and registrar.

Transfer Admissions. It is relatively easy for students to transfer from one institution to another within the United States. Some universities report that one third of their current undergraduates have had a college experience elsewhere. The equating of the previous academic work against degree requirements of the institution is a complex process. It is further complicated by the presentation of nontraditional achievement, experiential summaries, and military records. These responsibilities of the office of admissions are summarized as follows:

1. Evaluation of transfer records of applicants from all four-year United States colleges and universities, as well as military credit, nontraditional achievement, and experiential summaries.
2. Evaluation of transcripts of applicants from all United States community colleges.
3. Liaison with all academic departments.
4. Supervision of the processing and evaluation of applicants to institutional professional schools (if any).
5. Maintenance of a catalog library.

6. Counseling of students planning enrollment at other institutions for transfer of credit to institutional degree programs.
7. Supervision of the staff of credentials evaluators.
8. Completion of various studies and development of statistics concerning transfer students' performance by institution.

Minority Admissions. The recruitment of minority and disadvantaged students has expanded greatly in the last decade. This processing of applications, recruitment, and provision of financial aid, where necessary, may include both undergraduate and graduate students. The total effort involves these responsibilities:

1. Evaluation, selection, processing, and placement of all minority and disadvantaged student applicants.
2. Coordination and liaison with other campus offices (such as dean of students, financial aid, registrar, minority programs, housing, and academic departments).
3. Liaison with off-campus support programs such as League of United Latin American Citizens, Trio Programs, and Bureau of Indian Affairs.
4. Conduct of research related to minority and/or disadvantaged student admissions.
5. Development and maintenance of appropriate statistics.
6. Development of informational materials related to minority recruitment.

Foreign Admissions. The admission of students from foreign countries is a unique responsibility that may include the admission of both undergraduate and graduate students. Advisement of foreign students may also be lodged in the admissions office. Specific responsibilities follow:

1. Evaluation, placement, and processing of all graduate and undergraduate foreign student applicants.
2. Response to initial inquiries of foreign applicants, requests for information and application forms, and follow-up correspondence.

3. Maintenance of a library of foreign educational resource materials in addition to files of information on respective countries.
4. Assistance with the development of application forms, information brochures, and office procedures relating to foreign admissions.
5. Conduct of research related to foreign student admission and placement and the academic success of foreign enrollees.
6. Liaison with other campus offices (such as deans, academic departments, graduate school, registrar, office of international programs, program in English for foreign students, and the U.S. Immigration Service) with respect to foreign admissions and adjustment to campus life.
7. Cooperation with the institutional advisory program serving as academic adviser to newly admitted foreign students.

School-College Relations. The coordination of school-college relations is a specific responsibility, generally under the director of admissions, and includes the coordination of recruitment and other activities listed below:

1. Planning and organization of high school and college visitations.
2. Visitation of high schools to meet with interested students and their counselors.
3. Arrangement of on-campus visitations for prospective students and their parents and counselors.
4. Planning and organization of conferences, newsletters, and direct telephone communications for school and college personnel.
5. Assistance with the preparation and dissemination of publications related to admissions, financial aid, academic programs, housing, and student activities.
6. Assistance with the preparation and dissemination of planning guides for transfer students.
7. Preparation and dissemination of follow-up data on freshman and transfer student progress, reporting of appropriate data to feeder schools and colleges, and preparation of special reports as needed.

8. Assistance in research to determine recruitment objectives, target areas, and procedures.
9. Participation in admissions office budget planning and personnel supervision.
10. Supervision of related office operations, including the scheduling of travel and visitation follow-up.

Registrar or Director of Student Records

As is true of the office of admissions, certain groups of activities and responsibilities of the registrar or director of records can be grouped together under a division head whenever resources of staff and finances permit. These may include, but are not necessarily limited to, registration and scheduling, grade reporting and record keeping, transcript preparation and certification, catalog and brochure preparation, veterans affairs, data processing, and research and reporting. Even these can be divided further as an institution grows and work becomes more specialized.

The registrar, or director of student records, one of the chief administrative officers of the institution, is responsible for all aspects of student registration and records. The registrar is custodian of the institution's official seal and may serve as editor of the catalog and as a member of the curriculum and other related committees. Normally this individual reports to the academic vice-president or dean, but in some institutions various duties that are normally thought of as the responsibility of the registrar are assigned to the dean of instruction or the dean of students. The primary duties and responsibilities of the registrar are indicated below (followed by a listing of some of the functional responsibilities often found within the registrar's jurisdiction):

1. Plans and conducts academic registration and postregistration systems. In this regard, it is the registrar's responsibility to ensure, insofar as possible, that the academic offerings of the institution are adequate to meet the needs of students.
2. Maintains and updates an efficient student records system in accordance with the policies of the American Association of Collegiate Registrars and Admissions Officers.

3. Is responsible for the interpretation and application of academic rules and regulations.
4. Is responsible for the publication and distribution of the schedule of classes, the catalog, and related academic literature.
5. Certifies baccalaureate and advanced degrees.
6. Administers the Veterans Affairs and Selective Service programs (when applicable).
7. Schedules all classes and classroom facilities and compiles class and final examination schedules.
8. Certifies student eligibility for honors, participation in intercollegiate athletics, and student body offices.
9. Provides academic departments and faculty advisers with student data, including class schedules, grades, and transcript and other resource information.
10. Maintains (for security reasons) a duplicate set of student records on microfilm, updating these microfilmed records at the end of each term and summer session or when appropriate.
11. Establishes and maintains a student identification system and produces and distributes student, staff, and faculty identification cards.
12. Provides transcript service for all students and alumni.
13. Provides enrollment statistics (students, credits, majors, degrees, etc.) to appropriate state or federal offices.
14. Is custodian of the official institutional seal.
15. Conducts research as appropriate.
16. Prepares budget requests for the office of registrar or for the registrar's portion of the office if it is combined with admissions.
17. Establishes the office organization and selects appropriately trained personnel; provides a program of in-service training.

Class Scheduling, Registration, and Grade Reporting and Recording. These four activities form the core of the registrar's work. Once admitted to the institution, the student must be brought face to face with the instructional staff, and records must be kept of the progress made. In some institutions these responsibilities could be placed under one division with some or all of the following duties:

1. Responsibility for student registration and postregistration systems.
2. Responsibility for the hiring and supervision of the staff, provision of in-service training, and maintenance of personnel files and reports.
3. Preparation and distribution of the schedule of classes, in cooperation with deans and department heads.
4. Scheduling of classrooms for classes, special events, workshops, and conventions.
5. Assistance with the development of the final examination schedule.
6. Responsibility for all special and "in absentia" enrollments, including internships, fellowships, and other off-campus programs.
7. Cooperation with the state office of fiscal management in matters relating to enrollment reporting.
8. Maintenance of an efficient student record system in accordance with the policies of the American Association of Collegiate Registrars and Admissions Officers.
9. Supervision and processing of all changes of enrollment, including withdrawals from the university.
10. Providing academic departments and individual faculty advisers with student data, including class schedules, grades, transcripts, and other resource information.
11. Assistance with the interpretation and application of academic rules and regulations.
12. Administration of the institutional policy concerning confidentiality of student records.

Research and Reporting. Most research concerning students, grading, or enrollment involves the office of student records. And this office should initiate much research of its own in order to better serve the students, faculty, and administration. In those offices that can support a research analyst or statistician, duties can be assigned as follows:

1. Preparation and distribution of enrollment, scholastic, census, geographical distribution, academic major, degree, and matriculation reports.

2. Development of research criteria and determination of procedures for editing, coding, summarizing, tabulating, analyzing, and ensuring completeness and accuracy of data.
3. Compilation of rank-in-class reports.
4. Liaison with the director of institutional research.
5. Auditing of lists for approved scholastic honoraries and student activities.
6. Maintenance of close liaison with those responsible for the institutional student information system.

Publications. Catalog and brochure preparation responsibilities are sufficiently complex and different from other activities to be placed in the hands of specialists. General duties include:

1. Responsibility for publication of the institution's catalog and summer session bulletin, including consultation with departmental offices, compilation of data, editing, and proofing. Assistance with publication of the schedule of classes and related publications that list courses, majors, degrees, departments, academic policies, and registration information.
2. Thorough knowledge of catalog policies and procedures, including those applicable to the overall curriculum as well as individual courses; processing of petitions for course changes from departments through appropriate committees for action; responsibility for current and historical documentation on all approved courses, including the master catalog and master course file (computer file).
3. Responsibility for determining and assigning the official codes for courses, course prefixes, titles, departments, majors, fields of interest; maintenance of the official "code book" for the institution.
4. Cooperation with other appropriate administrators and academic units developing the calendar.

Veterans Affairs. Although the number of veterans enrolled in colleges and universities is declining, the accountability of the institution for reporting enrollments and progress to the Veterans Administration (VA) has not abated. Someone in the office must maintain close liaison with the Veterans Administration Regional Office and submit appropriate reports to the VA. Specific duties include:

1. Responsibility for enrolling eligible students with the VA Regional Office for benefits under the following chapters of Title 38 of the U.S. Code: Chapter 31 (Vocational Rehabilitation), Chapter 32 (Post-Vietnam Era Veterans), Chapter 34 (Vietnam Era Veterans), and Chapter 35 (Survivors' and Dependents' Educational Assistance).
2. Preparation and submission of enrollment reports to the VA on each student receiving benefits each term and summer session; reporting of cancellations, drops or adds, and other changes that affect the pay status of students receiving VA benefits. Submission, on behalf of new applicants, of forms or copies of records on change of program or place of training, Report of Separation from Active Duty (DD 214), marriage licenses, birth certificates for dependents, claim numbers, and related documents required for certification of eligibility for benefits.
3. Preparation and distribution of credit cards; submission of billings for tuition, fees, and supplies; and providing the VA with class schedules and grade reports for disabled veterans under Vocational Rehabilitation.
4. Distribution of current information on VA policies and regulations, eligibility, academic programs, and benefits available to eligible students. Maintenance of continual liaison with the VA Regional Office.
5. Advising veterans of availability of tutorial assistance, determination of eligibility, and processing of claims for reimbursement for tutoring.
6. Participation in workshops sponsored by the VA Regional Office for veterans coordinators and related personnel.
7. Assisting veterans in securing special veterans benefits made available through individual state resources.

Systems Analysis. The extremely rapid growth of computer services and the application of computer technology to the admission of students, record keeping, and research have made the work of the offices of admissions and records both easier and more complex. Human error can now be multiplied a thousandfold and more in microseconds. The failure of computer systems to produce the desired results can usually be traced to a lack of precise communication between the users (those in the offices of admissions and records) and the producer (the computing center). To prevent breakdowns in this communication, an experienced and knowledgeable computer-oriented person must be assigned as liaison between the two units. Some admissions and records units have their own computing capabilities; others do not. Some have computer specialists on the admissions and records staff; others use a service bureau approach, with computer personnel assigned to student records. Regardless of the organizational arrangement, there must be a close and meticulous working relationship between the two to avoid costly and embarrassing errors.

The liaison person usually has the title of systems analyst or systems analyst programmer. Specific duties include:

1. Analysis, evaluation, and preparation of cost studies relative to student records systems (offices of registrar, admissions, advisement, etc.).
2. Supervision of systems analyses and programming related to student records systems.
3. Coordination of assignments among programmers and supervision of the implementation of new programs and systems.
4. Preparation of detailed work-schedule assignments and supervision of the programmers.
5. Evaluation of user requests for system enhancements and development of priorities.
6. Continual analysis of operational computer procedures and programs to determine modifications required by changes in computer configuration and techniques.
7. Responsibility for user training in computer systems.

Job and Functional Descriptions Summarized

Well-conceived and well-written job or functional descriptions can improve the efficiency and, in some instances, the morale of an office staff in several ways:

1. The descriptions can be an invaluable tool for use in the orientation and training of staff, providing new employees with a ready reference which spells out, in summary form, the responsibilities and expectations of the job.
2. A set of descriptions can provide the employer or supervisor with an excellent method of staying abreast of the responsibilities and functions of individual staff members or the staff as a collective unit.
3. The circulation of abbreviated descriptions among the total staff provides an ideal method for introducing individuals in a large office to the unique responsibilities of their colleagues.

While job or function descriptions can enhance understanding within an office and contribute to a more effective and efficient operation, it is understood that no description, regardless of how well written, will completely describe a specific position in any single office or institution. The job and functional summaries presented in the foregoing are offered as guides to follow. It is hoped that, by choosing a sentence here and a paragraph there, the central administrator can easily construct an adequate description for any position in the offices of admissions or registrar.

Further Reading and Study

For interesting reading on the development of the profession, see "The Evolution and Development of the Registrar's Office" by Ezra Gillis (1939). The topic is expanded in "The Genesis of a Registrar" by Alfred Parrott (1946) and "The Origin, Background, and Philosophy of the Office of Admissions and Records" by Fred Thomason (1953). Less specific references are Rudolph's (1962) *The American College and University* and *The Academic Revolution* by Jencks and Riesman (1969). Harold Temmer (1970), in "A Manager's Bill of Rights," provides a modern view of the rights and responsibilities of registrars and admissions officers with respect to automated information systems.

Establishing Admissions Policy

□ □ □ □ □ □ □ □ □ □ □ □ □ □ □ □ □

E. Eugene Oliver

This chapter describes some of the functions of the college admissions office—those involving the philosophy, goals, and objectives of college admissions; the development of admissions policies and requirements; and the observance of various federal and state laws. Chapter Three deals in turn with recruitment, admissions procedures, office staffing and organization, financial aid, and internal institutional relations. Specific functions of the office are detailed in the chapter summaries.

Philosophy, Goals, and Objectives of Admissions

Admissions is a social process (Thresher, 1966), and the philosophy of admissions—the broad principles and concepts that underlie this human activity—will vary according to time and place. For the United States in the last half of the 1970s, the philosophy embraces the belief that opportunities for education beyond high school should be readily available to all. Economic, social, and cultural forces express this philosophy in a variety of ways that affect admissions: by funding the expansion of higher education facilities and programs, by providing financial aid to more and more students, by creating laws and regulations that seek to end discrimination in any form, and by supporting a growing consumer advocacy movement. At the same time, higher education is strongly pluralistic, and colleges and universities—both public and private—enjoy a considerable degree of autonomy in determining which students they will accept. Thus, although society may endorse the principle of postsecondary education for all, society also accepts different roles for different institutions. Not every institution, for example, is required to admit all applicants or to offer programs that will benefit every prospective student.

The following influences on admissions goals and objectives help to explain the differences among institutions:

1. *Type of Control.* Public institutions, with a higher proportion of their costs met by public tax dollars, usually are less selective in their admissions policies than independent institutions. Even relatively nonselective institutions, however, may have some highly selective programs with a surplus of applicants.
2. *Type of Institution.* Among the major types of institutions (two-year, four-year, four-year plus graduate, and graduate/professional only), those that serve graduate students are generally most selective. Thus, "four-year plus graduate" and "graduate/professional" institutions will generally be more selective than "two-year" or "four-year" institutions. And four-year institutions are usually more selective than two-year institutions.
3. *Institutional History, Tradition, or Location.* Selectivity also is influenced by certain historical events or long-standing traditions, such as the terms of the endowment that established the college, the strong views of early faculty members, a particular religious affiliation, an "open-door" or a selective tradition, or a particular geographical location.
4. *Economic and Social Pressures.* Most institutions have a strong instinct for survival, and if a particular admissions policy restricts an institution's enrollment to a dangerously low level, the policy probably will be changed. Thus, selective institutions

tend to increase requirements when there is an ample supply of applicants and to reduce them when the supply decreases. Social pressures also influence admissions goals. For example, in the late 1960s most colleges and universities developed special programs to recruit low-income and minority students.

The admissions officer must assume a major responsibility for the development of recommended admissions goals and objectives. The stakes are high, since the outcome of the admissions program will determine the size and characteristics of the student body, which to a considerable extent will determine the size and characteristics of the faculty, the staff, the academic program, and, in some cases, the survival of the institution. However, admissions officers alone cannot—and should not be expected to—determine the goals or the objectives of the program; nor can they be held solely responsible if the objectives are not met. The responsibility, in short, is a shared one.

In any discussion of admissions philosophy, goals, and objectives, the question of ethical conduct must be included. In admissions, as in all other areas of human activity, opportunities for unethical conduct abound. Fortunately, the professional associations have developed statements of ethics to help guide admissions officers toward the standards of conduct that should prevail. The most comprehensive of these is the joint statement developed by the National Association of College Admissions Counselors (NACAC), the College Entrance Examination Board (CEEB), and the American Association of Collegiate Registrars and Admissions Officers (AACRAO). The statement (reprinted in Appendix D of this volume) includes recommended principles for schools, colleges, and community agencies related to admissions promotion and recruitment, application procedures, and financial assistance. A separate code stressing the general responsibilities of admissions officers and registrars was adopted by AACRAO (see Appendix G); and several regional associations within AACRAO, such as the Kansas ACRAO, have also adopted more specific statements. Guidelines for international student admissions officers are included in a statement formulated by the National Association for Foreign Student Affairs (see Appendix E). The College Scholarship Service (CSS) of the College Entrance Examination Board has developed two statements as a guide to financial aid standards: *Principles of Student Financial Aid Administration* and *Practices of Student Financial Aid Administration* (College Scholarship Service, 1976a, 1976b), and the National Association of Student Financial Aid Administrators (n.d.) has adopted a *Statement of Good Practices*. The ethics statements have several themes in common: service to students, honesty and accuracy in the presentation of information, and avoidance of unprofessional promotional tactics.

As the college-age population declines and competition for students increases, admissions officers may confront a growing number of situations in which ethical judgments are required. Many of these situations concern promotional tactics. For example, the temptation to make invidious comparisons with other institutions may be strong. In commercial advertising such comparisons between products are common; but in higher education they are detrimental and usually counterproductive. It is far better—both ethically and pragmatically—to stress the advantages of one's own institution and not the weaknesses of another. Admissions officers need to work closely with their public information offices to assure that ads and news releases do not exaggerate the attractions of the campus in such a way as to mislead prospective students. Disillusioned students can do far more damage to future recruitment than any advertising campaign can overcome.

In some situations, of course, ethical choices are clear. Admissions officers in selective institutions (or working with selective programs in relatively open institutions) have been offered bribes in the hope that admission can be obtained. A tactful refusal is the best policy; for some applicants or their parents, such offers may be an accepted way of approaching authority figures. Gifts extended following admission should be returned—again, with a tactful message. The practice of reimbursing recruiters on the basis of the number of contacts, or the number that result in enrollments, is deplorable, opening the possibility for a variety of unethical practices, ranging from exaggerated claims on behalf of the institution to the encouragement of poorly qualified applicants. Sending recruiters from one four-year college to another seeking transfers—or to a two-year college to encourage students to transfer prior to completion of their program—is an unprofessional tactic. In some circumstances—for instance, where particular programs are involved that require early transfer—visits or mailings to students already enrolled in another institution may be acceptable, but these practices require full interinstitutional agreement. Generous offers of college credit by examination to high school students, which are honored only for those who later enroll in the institution, are likewise regarded as unethical. Admissions officers may also receive offers of cash or gifts in return for providing mailing lists of students, and there is no ethical justification for such a transaction.

Most situations in which ethical questions arise are not black and white, however; they are in that grey area where sincere differences may exist. Should the four-year college place ads in the student newspaper of surrounding community colleges? Should the college stress opportunities for credit by examination, or credit based on life experience, without indicating that such credit may not be accepted elsewhere? Should the college's promotional literature emphasize the superior quality of its academic programs when such claims may not be supported by the facts? Should the institution join a consortium for overseas recruiting without maintaining close control over the selection, training, and evaluation of the recruiter?

One of the concerns of college admissions officers today is that, with the anticipated increase in level and intensity of recruiting, a number of new staff members will be assigned recruiting responsibilities without adequate training or supervision. Those responsible for the admissions function must assure that the training and supervision are thorough, including careful coverage of ethical standards.

Admissions Policies

"Admissions policy is not only a very significant aspect of how higher institutions function; it also has serious social consequences and tells us a good deal about our culture and how we judge our fellows" (Willingham, 1978, p. 52). Only in a new college or university will the opportunity arise to create a complete set of admissions policies. For existing institutions, only revisions to policies are possible, and there is a historical pattern and tradition to consider in making such changes. The pressures must be considerable before substantive changes are made. Such pressures might result from a strong sense of social injustice, a marked change in the institution's finances, or a change in state or federal laws or regulations. Minor adjustments in the specific requirements that implement general admissions policies may be made frequently.

It should be noted that the courts have consistently upheld the "four academic freedoms" of colleges and universities: freedom to determine who shall teach, what shall be taught, how it shall be taught, and who shall be taught. In the June 1978 U.S. Supreme Court decision in *Regents of the University of California* v. *Bakke,* these freedoms were again emphasized and reaffirmed. Thus, institutions have broad discretion in developing and implementing admissions policies and requirements.

The Carnegie Council on Policy Studies in Higher Education (1977) identifies three different types of admissions policies: (1) nonselective admissions, occurring at most community colleges and at a number of liberal arts colleges and comprehensive colleges and universities, representing an estimated 40 percent of total admissions (see Willingham's (1970) comprehensive report on the accessibility of inexpensive, nonselective higher education in each of the states); (2) selective admissions, varying from highly to moderately selective, occurring at all levels of higher education, and representing about 50 percent of all admissions; and (3) selective admissions at graduate and professional schools that control entrance to a profession, representing about 10 percent of all admissions.

The general policies of the institution for the admission of students should be clearly stated. For example, at the University of Illinois the following policy, adopted by the board of trustees in 1970, was developed to resolve the problem of the basis for selection when the numbers of qualified applicants exceeded the number of spaces in a given program: "If, by the beginning date for action on applications, the number of qualified applicants exceeds the number that can be approved, those best qualified (academically) will be approved." This action replaced an earlier policy specifying the use of random selection under such circumstances. Regarding out-of-state applicants, the Oregon State System of Higher Education (1977) proposed the following policy statement: "Admission standards for out-of-state undergraduate students entering . . . from high school should be set at a higher level than for in-state students, but not sufficiently high as effectively to exclude out-of-state students. The level should be such as to give a reasonable assurance that the students admitted will represent a genuine asset to the student body, both as student-citizens and as scholars." Such statements provide a foundation for the development of the more specific admissions requirements needed to implement the general policy.

Admissions policies should meet the following criteria if they are to operate successfully: they should be in concurrence with institutional philosophy; they should be realistic; they should be readily understood; and they should have widespread support. To assure that policies meet these criteria, the procedures for developing the policies should include (1) an investigation (or continual monitoring) of the outcomes of current admissions policies in terms of student numbers, levels, characteristics, academic success, and retention and graduation rates; (2) participation by those groups most affected: faculty, administrators, and students; (3) careful articulation and widespread dissemination of general policy statements. Often these procedures are assured through an active admissions committee, including student, faculty, and administrative members, charged with the responsibility for general policy formulation and review.

Admissions Requirements

General policies are given specific expression in the form of the institution's admissions requirements: those things that a student must do, or demonstrate, to qualify for admission. In a 1975 survey by the College Entrance Examination Board of 144 major private and public colleges and universities (Abernathy, 1976), evaluation and selection of applicants was cited most frequently as the primary function of the admissions office.

The most common purpose of admissions requirements is to assure the entry of students who have the capability, or promise, of completing their chosen educational program successfully. Although some institutions with minimal or no requirements for admission stress the goal of opportunity for all, regardless of capability or promise, they assume a heavy burden of responsibility for helping poorly qualified students succeed and for giving them adequate counseling, guidance, and support in selecting acceptable alternatives if they do not. All institutions must justify their selection of requirements for admission—for example, relating the requirement to some criterion of success. Most commonly, success is measured by the student's college grade point average. This criterion has been criticized as too narrow and transitory, and the criticism is often combined with a call for more long-range criteria, such as job success or community service; but these are difficult to define and even more difficult to determine. Since grades do measure and control student progress and, ultimately, completion of the college program, they are therefore valid indicators of success in college. The best single predictor of such success for the entering freshman is the student's high school grades, or rank in class (correlations generally range between .35 and .50); but this prediction can be improved (by .02 to .15) by the addition of scores on a standardized admissions test. Thus, these two factors are most often taken into consideration in determining college admissions. The predictive value of other requirements—such as interviews, recommendations, and activities records—has not been demonstrated, although some colleges rely on them for other purposes, such as obtaining diversity in the student body.

Kinds of Evidence Collected

The range of admissions requirements may best be illustrated by a description of the kinds of evidence that institutions collect from and about an applicant. Specific institutional requirements for admission are almost always written in terms of the eight types of evidence described below (although not all institutions are interested in *all* the items described; for admissions purposes, each collects only those items necessary to determine whether or not the student meets the requirements). Public institutions tend more toward objective data (specific test scores, grades, high school ranks, or a combination thereof), especially for undergraduates, while private institutions and graduate and professional programs make greater use of subjective data (from such sources as interviews, recommendations, activities records, and committee reviews) in addition to objective information (Abernathy, 1976). Community colleges and other institutions with nonselective admissions policies specify few requirements and may accept the applicant's own statement of previous education as meeting the requirements for entry to certain programs.

Educational Records. The documents most frequently required in support of an application for admission are the official transcripts of an applicant's high school and/or college work. These transcripts are used to check on the nature, amount, and quality of the academic work attempted and to determine the applicant's grade point average. In the case of the high school record, the applicant's class rank may also be secured as a part of the educational record. *Rank-in-Class* (National Association of Secondary School Principals, 1972) provides guidelines for working with grade point averages and class ranks, discusses high school performance as a predictor of college success, and reports the status of the use of class rank as an admissions requirement.

Few institutions insist on completion of a specified pattern of high school subjects for freshman admission, but many institutions recommend or suggest courses. The University of California, for example, requires specific patterns of high school subjects for admission, while the University of Michigan couches its advice in terms of recommended subjects. And some institutions require some courses and recommend others. Both the required and the recommended courses emphasize academics: English, foreign language, mathematics, science, and social science. Selective institutions that recommend, rather than require, certain high school subjects may nevertheless expect to find such subjects on the applicant's high school record, and students lacking strong academic preparation will find themselves at a disadvantage.

Studies of the relationship between patterns of high school subjects and college grades indicate little or no relationship. Yet college faculty members remain convinced that such a relationship exists, and the insistence on—or at least the preference for—

students with strong academic course patterns in high school is continuing. Nonselective institutions do not, of course, require such patterns or use high school courses as a factor in admissions.

Because the possibility of fraudulent records always exists, the admissions office must obtain an official copy of the educational records directly from the registrars of the institutions that the applicant has attended; if there are any questions, the admissions office must verify the contents with the sending institution. Recommended guidelines for high school transcripts—as well as copies of a recommended form—are published by the National Association of Secondary School Principals (1974), and essential features of the college transcript have been identified by the American Association of Collegiate Registrars and Admissions Officers (1977).

Test Scores. Commonly required of applicants for admissions are scores on one or more standardized tests of academic aptitude and/or achievement; thus, it is important for admissions officers to understand the uses, limitations, and possible abuses of testing as a factor in admissions (Hills, 1971). Two testing programs dominate the field for freshman applicants: the College Entrance Examination Board's Scholastic Aptitude Test (SAT) and the American College Testing Program's American College Test (ACT). The College Board also offers a series of achievement tests in various subject fields for use in freshman admission and placement, as well as the Advanced Placement Program (APP) tests for able and ambitious high school students to use as a basis for college placement and/or credit. The tests of General Education Development (GED) are used by some institutions to determine high school graduation equivalency for applicants who are not high school graduates. While there are no commonly used undergraduate transfer tests, admissions officers should be familiar with the College-Level Examination Program (CLEP) of the College Entrance Examination Board and the Proficiency Examination Program (PEP) of the American College Testing Program. These tests are used by many institutions as a basis for awarding credits. Applicants whose native language is other than English are generally required to submit scores on the Test of English as a Foreign Language (TOEFL) or some other English-proficiency examination. There are examinations at the professional level for admission in most fields, including the Medical College Aptitude Test (MCAT), the Law School Admission Test (LSAT), the Dental Admission Test (DAT), and the Veterinary Aptitude Test (VAT). Graduate applicants are often required to submit scores on the Graduate Record Examination (GRE) or tests in a specialized area, such as the Graduate Management Admission Test (GMAT). While testing may not be necessary in all admissions situations, scores on standardized ability or achievement examinations have consistently demonstrated their value by improving the predictability of students' academic performance and thus adding a significant dimension to the admissions process, especially for institutions that are moderately or highly selective. Probably the best single guide to information on all the examinations commonly used in the admissions process is the *Mental Measurements Yearbook* (Buros, 1972).

An important issue has been raised concerning the fairness of tests when used as a factor in the admission of racial and ethnic minorities. Several recent articles on this subject are worthy of review (Cleary and others, 1975; Fincher, 1977; Harris, Pyles, and Carter, 1976). A more recent issue in testing is the decline in national norms. A special panel was established by the College Board in 1975 to look into the decline—49 points on the SAT-Verbal test score average and 32 points on the SAT-Mathematics test, from 1963 to 1977—and assess possible reasons for it. The panel's report, *On Further Examination* (College Entrance Examination Board, 1977), contains valuable information on testing in the current social and educational context.

Recommendations. Less commonly required than educational records or tests, recommendations are still used in freshman admission to a number of colleges and are commonly required for admission to professional and graduate study. A significant impact on the use of written recommendations has resulted from the Family Educational Rights and Privacy Act of 1974, as Amended, which provides for student access to recommendations—although students may waive this right if they choose. A thorough analysis of the law and its implications for postsecondary institutions—with guidelines for implementation and compliance—has been prepared by the American Association of Collegiate Registrars and Admissions Officers (1976).

Recommendations are valued highly by some admissions officers, but there are many difficulties in their use. They generally tend to emphasize positive attributes and avoid mention of negative ones. They are almost always written by persons selected by the applicant. They are often unstructured and difficult to compare with other recommendations for the same candidate—or those for other candidates. Their effectiveness depends to a large extent on the writing skills of the person who prepared the recommendation—which, it must be assumed, is the person designated on the form. While some institutions have found methods of reducing these problems (for instance, by using standard forms or by specifying who should complete the recommendation), the best that can probably be said is that their use gives somewhat greater feelings of security to the admissions officer or committee—a belief that they have explored all avenues of information that may aid them in their final choice. Some little-known talents, interests, or characteristics may emerge from the recommendations to help in the close decisions that must be made among talented applicants for a program where the demand is high and the number of spaces is limited.

Interviews. The focus of interviews, when required, seems to be shifting from evaluation to communication. Research on the effectiveness of the interview as a predictive instrument has been largely negative (Ward, 1955; Wright, 1969), but the value of the interview as an effective and intensely personal medium for communication between the prospective student and the institutional representative remains unchallenged. Ideally, during the interview the applicant can obtain information and insight about the institution that is not available from any other source—publications, high school counselors, parents, or peers. The admissions counselor should be prepared not only to describe the program and extracurricular offerings of the institution but also to aid the applicant in understanding something of the nature of student life there. The applicant can and should be in a better position to analyze his or her probable "fit" with the institution following such an interview.

Activities Records. Especially for the admission of freshmen to selective institutions, records of student activities outside the classroom are important. They help to establish a more complete picture of the student's interest and talents and may help to determine admissibility when other factors appear equal.

Geographical Distribution. Most faculties and administrators agree on the value of cultural diversity among students and encourage, to some degree, the admission of students from across state lines and national boundaries. At the undergraduate level, public institutions are sometimes restricted in this regard by state concerns over the cost to taxpayers of subsidizing the education of nonresident students while restricting the enrollment of residents of the state, and public community colleges enroll only limited numbers of out-of-state students. Private institutions are more likely to emphasize geographical distribution, which may become a determining factor in the selection of some students.

Personal Data. Institutions sometimes request, as a part of the application, information on such factors as racial/ethnic group membership or indices of socioeconomic status (parental income and education, size of family, age and educational level of siblings, nature of the applicant's community); they may also ask whether the applicant's parents or other close relatives are graduates of the institution. Questions on the application concerning the applicant's marital status and physical or mental handicap are prohibited by federal regulations in institutions with programs or activities receiving federal financial assistance. Personal data obtained as a part of the application process may be used as factors in an admissions decision by some institutions in an effort to obtain a diversified student body. The consideration of race in admissions was upheld in the June 1978 U.S. Supreme Court decision in the *Bakke* case on this basis.

Essay. Some institutions require applicants to submit a written statement as a part of the application. The applicant is usually given some direction for writing the essay, such as reasons for selecting a particular major, significant experiences that influenced the student's decision to go to college, or especially meaningful work or travel. An essay has the advantage of requiring the student to organize and present his ideas, instead of merely responding to direct questions, and thus may provide insights into the student's maturity, personality, and thinking processes—as well as writing skills—that would not otherwise be observed. Limitations of the essay as an item in the admissions process include the obvious question of whether it was prepared by the applicant. The student's socioeconomic background may also affect the content, as well as the quality, of the essay in ways that have unintended effects on the admissions decision.

Use of Admissions Committees

In a 1964 survey Hauser and Lazarsfeld found that the conduct of admissions in most colleges is under the general surveillance of an admissions committee, whose functions may vary from general policy to a review of every candidate. Large public institutions seldom, if ever, have committees reviewing individual undergraduate applicants' files. However, small private colleges often insist on committee review of all—or all minimally qualified— applicants. In some institutions committees examine the files of only those few applicants for which the admissions staff are unable to reach a decision, and the committee's choice may be advisory or final. In any case, the admissions office is responsible for organizing and presenting applicant files to the committee.

For undergraduate admissions, the necessity for committee review of each applicant's file is questionable at best. A professional admissions staff, operating under guidelines approved in advance by the committee, can identify those applicants who are clearly inadmissible, as well as those whose outstanding qualifications assure them of an admission offer. It is only in those marginal, unique, or "average" cases that an admissions committee should be involved—with a substantial saving in time for the staff, the committee, and, in terms of notification, for most applicants as well. At the graduate and professional levels, where such subjective consideration as the quality of the undergraduate institution may be taken into account, more committee involvement may be warranted. But even at these levels, some specific guidelines for automatic admission or denial will accelerate the process.

Aside from the review of candidate folders, however, a significant role for the admissions committee should be the analysis and review of general policy and the formulating of recommendations for changes in policy when needed. Thus, in those institutions where review of individual applicant files by a committee is not the practice, an admissions committee is still needed for policy review and recommendation.

Evaluation of Requirements

Evaluation of admissions requirements must be ongoing. The admissions office should conduct validity studies—or be sure that they are conducted elsewhere in the institution—to determine the correlation between preadmission variables (such as high school grades and admissions test scores, where these are used) and college success. Assistance in developing such studies is available from both the College Entrance Examination Board and the American College Testing Program. These studies should be conducted annually, or at periodic intervals of not more than two or three years when no significant changes in admissions policies, qualifications of entering freshmen, or institutional programs or standards have occurred. Declines in the correlations between high school grades, test scores, and college grades can then be detected, reasons sought, and remedies determined. Determining the validity of other requirements is much more difficult and uncertain. Yet the admissions office, in conjunction with the admissions committee, should examine periodically whether each requirement is appropriate in content for its purpose and is doing what it is intended to do in selecting an incoming class. For example, is the requirement of two recommendations aiding the selection of a class with the desired characteristics? Should there be three recommendations? Should a different recommendation form be tried? Could the requirement be discontinued without affecting the desired character and ability of the entering class?

Other important bases for evaluating selection measures have been identified as fairness (reasonableness and relation to the requirements of the educational program), feasibility (practicality and cost effectiveness), and secondary effects (unintended effects on the college, the feeder schools, or the profession served by the educational program) (Willingham and Breland, 1977).

With regard to fairness, the question is whether the particular requirement—and the manner in which it is implemented—results in biased or prejudiced judgment. For example, if interviews are a significant element in the admissions process, can it be demonstrated that the structure of the interview and the approach of the interviewer result in unprejudiced recommendations? If activities are an important factor, do students who excel in athletics (or in a particular sport) seem to have an edge over those with equally outstanding records in debate or music? Fairness in tests has been the subject of much controversy. The position currently embodied in federal regulations is that tests or other admissions requirements may not be used if they have a "disproportionately adverse effect" on persons on the basis of specific characteristics, such as sex or handicap, unless (1) such requirements predict success in the program in question and (2) alternative requirements which do not have such effects are unavailable.

Feasibility of an admissions requirement is based on its practicality, including cost. Interviews may be considered impractical by institutions whose target population includes large numbers of out-of-state students. The cost of reviewing essays may be too great to consider requiring them. Some institutions have even decided to abandon application forms, obtaining instead all the information they need for an admissions decision from the testing company. Each institution must decide for itself the feasibility of its requirements.

The question of possible secondary effects—comparable to medicine's "side effects"—is more subtle and often overlooked. For example, concentration in the admissions requirements on academic qualifications alone may result in a lack of diversity in the entering class. Some serious consideration of this problem is occurring in a number of medical schools, where too many graduates are concentrating on research or choosing a highly specialized field. If minimum levels are specified on several variables (test score, high school rank, specific units), some who are at the very top of the applicant group in several variables may fall slightly below the minimum level on one variable and thereby be denied because of the multiple cutoff policy. In some cases, an admissions requirement may lead to unanticipated and extreme public criticism or a threatened reduction in funds. This has occurred in some public institutions when the requirements for admission of out-of-state students resulted in the enrollment of unacceptably large numbers of such students. The admissions office needs to consider in advance whether a particular requirement may produce undesirable secondary effects.

Variations in Requirements for Different Categories of Applicants

Four broad categories of applicants may be identified: undergraduate, graduate, professional, and special. Carefully developed, clearly written statements of admissions requirements must be available for each category that the institution serves. The admissions office is responsible for assuring that such statements are developed and adequately communicated.

Undergraduates. Three subdivisions of undergraduate applicants exist in most institutions: freshmen entering directly from high school, transfers from other colleges or universities, and former students. Freshman requirements are often expressed in terms of the high school record and test scores, although "open-door" institutions may specify high school graduation or the equivalent as the only requirement, and selective institutions may add recommendations, interviews, and a final review by an admissions committee. Since community colleges follow the "open-door" policy in admissions, a high school diploma or the equivalent (such as a passing score on the tests of General Educational Development) or, in some cases, a minimum age beyond the normal age at high school graduation may be the only requirement. Some selection occurs within the community college, however, for admission to specific programs. For example, students who score low on placement or achievement examinations may be required to take remedial or developmental courses before beginning a baccalaureate-oriented transfer program. And admission to programs where the demand greatly exceeds the number of spaces, such as nursing, may be very selective.

The most common requirement for transfer students is a specified pretransfer grade point average, although the number of hours of credit completed elsewhere may also be a factor. Two annual publications provide important tools in the assessment of transfer credit for admissions purposes: *Transfer Credit Practices of Selected Educational Institutions* (Wermers, 1979) and *Accredited Institutions of Postsecondary Education and Programs* (Council on Postsecondary Accreditation, 1978). Useful information and advice about transfer credit acceptance also appear in the reports of two recent AACRAO annual meeting program sessions (Van Antwerp, MacCorkle, and Wermers, 1976; Young, Oliver, and Loeb, 1977). A joint statement on the transfer and award of academic credit has been recently issued by the American Association of Collegiate Registrars and Admissions Officers, the American Council on Education/Commission on Educational Credit, and the Council on Postsecondary Accreditation. This statement, which appears in Appendix F, makes a number of recommendations for consideration by colleges in developing their transfer-of-credit policies, which often have a direct effect on the numbers and qualifications of transfer students accepted.

Community college practice may differ from that of most four-year colleges with regard to the evaluation of transfer credits. Other than recording the number of hours of credit earned elsewhere and passing the transcript(s) on to the student's adviser, the community college may make no effort to evaluate prior work until, and unless, the students indicate an intention to earn the associate degree at the community college. Many transfer students to community colleges do not earn associate degrees, and the transcript evaluation step is unnecessary for them.

Returning students (applicants for readmission) are often given priority attention. Some may be returning after institutionally approved "leaves of absence," and readmission may be almost automatic. Others may have taken courses at another institution, and those records would be considered in determining admissibility. The status of the applicant at the time of leaving the institution could also be a factor in readmission. Students who were on academic probation or who were dropped for poor scholarship are often required to submit a written petition for readmission, and their applications are individually considered.

Graduates. Admissions offices differ in the degree of their involvement with graduate admissions, ranging from complete responsibility to none at all. In the latter case, the graduate school office typically handles all admissions at that level. Often the responsibilities are shared, with the admissions office handling official communications with the applicant and other procedural details. Regardless of the division of labor between the graduate school and the admissions office, the actual admissions decisions usually are made by the individual departments. A typical pattern for graduate admissions includes the establishment of a set of minimum requirements by the graduate school (undergraduate degree, grade point average, recommendations, test scores), collection of applications and supporting documents by the admissions office, evaluation of the admissions files and decisions on admissibility by the departments, and notification of the candidates by the admissions office. Responsibility for the various stages differs from one institution to another.

Applicants for Professional Programs. Operational definitions of "professional" education vary. Insofar as admissions are concerned, the term generally includes those programs with prerequisite undergraduate preparation—often completion of an undergraduate degree. Law, medicine, veterinary medicine, dentistry, theology, optometry, osteopathic medicine, podiatry, and often nursing, pharmacy, and associated medical sciences are included. Several common elements mark professional school admissions: use of centralized application services (available now in medicine, law, and dentistry); designation of required preprofessional courses; use of scores on national, standardized examinations; use of written recommendations and interviews; and reliance on admissions committees to make final selections. The role of the admissions office is critical at the professional school level, where the pressures for admission are severe. Providing information and counseling to prospective applicants, assembling the admissions files, conducting the committee review process, notifying candidates, assuring exact enrollments, and dealing with unsuccessful applicants and their families (and, not infrequently, their attorneys)—all demand the highest levels of competence and patience.

Special Categories. While the great majority of applicants follow the regular admissions requirements for undergraduate, graduate, or professional study, the time devoted to the relatively few students entering through special admissions categories may well exceed that required for the majority. The following are some, but not necessarily all, of the special categories that may be defined in a single institution:

1. *Talented students*—those with unusual academic, athletic, musical, dramatic, or artistic ability—usually are recruited, evaluated, and admitted through procedures different from those followed for most applicants. Athletes, for instance, must meet athletic conference or National Collegiate Athletic Association eligibility requirements, which may differ from those of the institution. If the requirements are more stringent than those of the institution, which may occur in a college with an "open-door" policy, there is no admissions problem. If, however, the regular admissions requirements are more stringent than the eligibility requirements of the athletic conference, special consideration is often given to the student-athlete. For example, the athletic conference may require only a C average in high school whereas the college or university may require a higher average; in such an instance, the college may still admit the student-athlete with a C average and then make special provisions for academic support, such as tutoring, academic advising, and counseling. Similarly, special requirements usually apply to applicants with other types of talent. These may be more stringent than regular requirements (such as auditions, portfolios, or higher academic achievement), or they may incorporate waivers of some of the requirements applied to regular applicants (such as grade point average or test scores). The admissions office must be prepared to describe and, if necessary, defend the institution's rationale for exceptional admissions requirements for talented students. Selective institutions can, and do, justify such special consideration as essential to their educational programs, which are seen as benefiting from a student body with a wide variety of talents. The unstructured learning that results from contacts with other students may often be as significant as the learning that takes place in structured classes. If no consideration is given to the individual talents and characteristics of any applicant, then admissions becomes a mechanized operation with little chance of obtaining the diversity among students which is, in itself, an essential ingredient of education.

2. Many institutions grant *early admission* to a limited number of mature, academically able, ambitious students at the end of their junior year in high school. In addition to their academic qualifica-

tions, school recommendations and parental requests for early entry are often required (Babbott, 1973).

3. Special programs for the identification, recruitment, admission, and academic/financial support of educationally and socioeconomically *disadvantaged students* have become a feature of most colleges and universities (College Entrance Examination Board, 1971). These programs have succeeded in increasing minority racial and ethnic enrollments and affording educational opportunities previously denied to many students. The responsibilities of the admissions office vary from one institution to another. In some cases a separate program handles all facets, including admissions. In most institutions, however, the admissions office is involved—either centrally or at least in processing applications and handling official admission or denial notices.

Typically, factors other than the high school record and test scores—for instance, motivation, achievement outside the school setting, recommendations by teachers or community agency staff members, and academic interests—are examined in determining the admissibility of disadvantaged students. Minimum academic requirements are often waived when other factors appear to indicate a strong possibility of success. Admission to special programs for disadvantaged students requires a highly individualized process. There have been a number of court challenges to such programs, on the basis that they result in discrimination against other students, who may be better qualified academically.

On June 28, 1978, the U.S. Supreme Court announced its decision in the case of *Regents of the University of California* v. *Bakke*. By a 5–4 majority, the Court found that the special admissions program of the medical school at the University of California at Davis, in which a designated number of spaces were set aside for disadvantaged minority applicants, was invalid and directed that Bakke, a white applicant rejected for admission in 1973 and 1974, be admitted. The Court also determined, again by a 5–4 majority, that race may be taken into account in admissions decisions, along with other factors, to achieve diversity in the student body. Analysis of the *Bakke* decision, and its implications for college admissions policies and procedures, will continue for some time. It also seems certain that similar cases will reach the U.S. Supreme Court, and the decisions in those cases will refine and expand on the *Bakke* decision. Publications which appeared shortly after the decision and present useful analyses for admissions officers include *The Bakke Decision: Implications for Higher Education Admissions,* a report by the American Council on Education and the Association of American Law Schools (American Council on Education, 1978b), and *The Bakke Decision: Retrospect and Prospect,* a summary report on six seminars held by the College Board (College Entrance Examination Board, 1978). Manning (1977, pp. 45–51) has proposed a two-stage model of the admissions process for institutions or programs with more qualified applicants than they can enroll: *admissibility* (minimum level required to succeed in the program) and *selection* (of those who would make up the best available entering class, based on nonacademic as well as academic considerations). Manning urges that racial or ethnic membership be considered in the second stage. Another helpful resource is Bowen's (1977) carefully constructed analysis of the relevance of race in admission to a selective, private institution, distinguishing among three considerations in choosing applicants: basic qualifications, the composition of the student body, and the potential contributions of the applicant to society.

4. Admission of *international students* is a highly complex and demanding specialization, requiring knowledge of foreign educational systems, foreign credentials, and immigration regulations. If an institution does not enroll enough international students to justify maintaining a specialist on the staff, help with the evaluation of foreign credentials is available from regional specialists identified by the Credentials Evaluation Projects of the National Association for Foreign Student Affairs. The service, which is free, is limited to institutions enrolling fewer than fifty foreign students. A number of valuable materials for international admissions are also available. The World Education Series publications (AACRAO) provide descriptions of the educational systems and records of a number of countries, with recommendations for placement. *A Guide to the Admission of Foreign Students* (National Association for Foreign Student Affairs, 1965) provides an overview of the field and a listing of service agencies, and *A Guide to the Education of Foreign Students* (Benson and Kovach, 1974) describes the steps involved in

the planning, selection, preadmission, admission, and notification stages of the process; both guides are brief but valuable aids to the staff members charged with international admissions responsibilities.

5. With the projected decline in the size of the 18- to 24-year-old college-age population during the 1980s, interest is increasing in *older students,* especially in metropolitan commuter institutions and in community colleges. There is a great variety in the backgrounds and goals of older adults seeking college admission. They may be returning to college after a lengthy absence or attending for the first time, pursuing degrees or taking courses on a nondegree basis, attending full time or part time, "catching up" in their field or preparing for a new career, or following purely avocational interests. College programs and time schedules are often adjusted to make them more attractive to older adult students, and the waiver of some of the regular requirements for admission — particularly for those who are part-time, nondegree students — may be approved. Admissions offices in a number of institutions are assuming responsibilities for recruiting older students and for recommending and implementing special admissions requirements and procedures to accommodate their needs and interests.

6. Section 504 of the Rehabilitation Act of 1973 and the final regulations to enforce this section ("Nondiscrimination on the Basis of Handicap," 1977) prohibit discrimination against physically and mentally *handicapped students* by recipients of funds from the Department of Health, Education and Welfare. The rules prohibit quotas on the admission of handicapped persons or admissions tests that have "a disproportionate, adverse effect on handicapped persons." Colleges are also barred from asking, prior to admission, whether an applicant has a handicap, unless they plan to use this information to overcome past discrimination or to support an affirmative action program. The applicant's response to a question concerning handicaps must be voluntary. "Qualified handicapped persons," defined as those who meet "the academic or technical standards requisite to admission or participation" in the program, may not be denied admission or subjected to discrimination in admission on the basis of handicap. Assistance in determining the implications of Section 504 for an institution's admissions program

is available from three recent publications. The American Association of Collegiate Registrars and Admissions Officers and the American Council on Education (1978) have published a guide for compliance with Section 504; the National Association of Student Personnel Administrators (1977) has published guidelines for the interpretation and implementation of the regulations; and the National Association of College and University Business Officers (Biehl, 1978) has published a guide to institutional self-evaluation of conformance with the legislation and regulations.

7. Admissions requirements for *veterans* of military service are, in most cases, the same as those for regular students. Additional responsibilities for certification of registration, withdrawal, and degrees are normally assigned to the registrar's office. The admissions office may, however, be involved in special recruitment programs, in the identification of applicants who are veterans, and in the development of special procedures for counseling and advising veterans. The Servicemen's Opportunity Colleges (SOC) program, established in 1972, is a cooperative network of more than 375 colleges, jointly sponsored by the American Association of State Colleges and Universities and the American Association of Community and Junior Colleges. Member colleges—more than half of them four-year colleges—offer a variety of advantages to veterans and *military personnel.* These include flexible entrance requirements, opportunity to complete interrupted work, special counseling, credit for in-service educational experience and other noncollegiate learning, and liberal transfer credit policies. The problems faced by servicemen and women seeking college degrees—such as restrictive admissions policies; inaccessibility of courses; and inadequate, interrupted, and contradictory academic advising—can often be reduced by enrollment in a SOC-member institution.

8. In a number of institutions—primarily independent colleges and universities—special programs are established for the admission of the *children of alumni or faculty.* These may be limited to reduced fees (most often for faculty children) or, in some public institutions, the waiver of nonresident fees for sons and daughters of alumni who live out of state. In some cases such applicants may be admitted after deadlines for applications have expired. In an

admissions program where subjective judgments are allowed, the status of an applicant as the child of alumni or faculty is often an important consideration.

9. Public institutions often specify different—and usually higher—admissions requirements, in addition to higher tuition, for *nonresidents,* applicants from other states. The rationale for these requirements is that the public institutions are supported in large measure by state revenues and that their facilities should be more readily accessible to in-state applicants. The higher requirements and tuition charges may also be intended to restrict the numbers of out-of-state students, thus providing more spaces for "native" students. Differences in admissions requirements (for example, top-quarter rank in class for out-of-state applicants instead of the top half required of in-state applicants) are normally limited to the undergraduate level, with no differences existing at the graduate or professional school level, where the emphasis is placed on obtaining the best-qualified applicants, regardless of their place of residence. The requirements for admission of nonresidents to public institutions may exist in state statutes, in the policies of a multicampus system, or in an individual institution's policies.

Laws, Regulations, and Legal Issues

This has often been referred to as the "age of litigation," and colleges—including college admissions programs—are not immune. Students and parents are more likely than ever to go to court to seek redress of real or imagined wrongs, and the admissions officer must know when a legal problem exists and avoid actions or situations from which legal problems may arise. Advice of the college legal counsel should be sought when legal actions—or the possibility of such actions—occur. Periodic reports initiated in 1973 and published by the Educational Testing Service (Higher Education Admissions Law Service) provide summaries of court cases, constitutional law, administrative law, and federal and state legislation affecting the admissions process. The service provides a valuable and convenient method for keeping abreast of the status of legal issues in the field of college admissions. In addition, a recent publication by the U.S. Department of Health, Education and Welfare (1978) outlines the requirements of a number of federal laws and regulations that must be observed in the college catalog. Included are sections on student consumer information, veterans benefits, nondiscrimination, privacy, alien students, second-class and nonprofit organization mailings, and federal income tax exemptions. A *Guidebook* "to help institutions improve their presentation of information to prospective students while complying with the new federal requirements" was recently published by the National Center for Higher Education Management Systems (Lenning and Cooper, 1978). The *Guidebook* presents excellent advice on assessing student information needs and upgrading the communication of institutional information to prospective students.

Federal Laws

The primary federal laws and regulations at the time of this writing, and the areas they affect, are as follows:

Nondiscrimination on Basis of Sex. Title IX of the Education Amendments of 1972 and the regulations issued in the June 4, 1975, *Federal Register* ("Nondiscrimination on Basis of Sex," 1975) prohibit discrimination on the basis of sex in any educational program or activity receiving federal financial assistance. Aids to the interpretation of Title IX are available from the U.S. Department of Health, Education and Welfare (1977). With regard to college admissions, the regulations specify that institutions covered by the act shall not give preference on the basis of sex by ranking male and female applicants separately, shall not apply numerical limitations on the basis of sex, and shall not "administer or operate any test or other criterion for admission which has a disproportionately adverse effect on persons on the basis of sex unless the use of such test or criterion is shown to predict validly success in the education program or activity in question and alternative tests or criteria which do not have such a disproportionately adverse effect are shown to be unavailable." The regulations also prohibit (1) admissions policies related to "actual or potential parental, family, or marital status . . . which treat persons differently on the basis of sex" and (2) policies that discriminate on the basis of pregnancy, childbirth, or termination of pregnancy. In fact, institutions covered by the act are not permitted to ask an applicant his or her marital status. Recruitment activities must also be free of any form of sex discrimination, such as visiting primarily single-sex schools or colleges. Institutions covered by the act are also enjoined from providing financial aid which differs by amount or type, or which limits eligibility, on the basis of sex—except that financial aid resulting from wills or trusts limited to one sex may be given, provided "the overall effect of the award of such sex-restricted ... forms of financial assistance does not discriminate on the basis of sex." Controversy still surrounds the provisions of the regulations concerning athletic scholarships, which require "reasonable opportunities for such awards for members of each sex in proportion to the number of students of each sex participating in ... intercollegiate athletics."

Nondiscrimination on Basis of Handicap. As mentioned, Section 504 of the Rehabilitation Act of 1973 and the regulations issued in the May 4, 1977, *Federal Register* ("Nondiscrimination on the Basis of Handicap," 1977) prohibit discrimination in admissions to qualified handicapped persons. Section 504 states: "No otherwise qualified handicapped individual in the United States ... shall, solely by reason of his handicap, be excluded from participation in, be denied the benefits of, or be subjected to discrimination under any program or activity receiving federal financial assistance." The prohibition against discrimination applies not only to admissions but also to recruitment, publications (which must include a statement of compliance), admissions tests, financial aid, and orientation activities. The admissions office must review carefully its policies, requirements, procedures, and publications to assure that they do not discriminate against handicapped persons. An advisory committee on admissions and recruitment, including one or more handicapped persons, is strongly recommended. Such a committee can be of great assistance in analyzing recruitment, publications, application forms, interviews, recommendation forms, testing, financial aid, orientation, registration, and grievance procedures, to assure that both the spirit and the letter of the law are observed. One specific requirement prohibits preadmission inquiries about handicaps, unless the college is taking remedial action to correct the effects of past discrimination—and then the college must make it clear that response to the question is voluntary, will be confidential, and will be used only in connection with the remedial action.

Laws Regarding Student Information. Guaranteed Student Loan Program regulations issued in the February 20, 1975, *Federal Register* ("Guaranteed Loan Program," 1975) specify procedures required for the distribution of information to prospective students. These regulations, which are mandatory for all institutions whose students borrow funds under the Guaranteed Student Loan Program, specify that information must be presented to prospective students, prior to the time they obligate themselves to pay tuition or fees, "about the institution, its current academic or training programs, and its faculties and facilities," emphasizing those programs in which the prospective student indicates interest. For institutions with programs that prepare students for a particular vocation, trade, or career field, the regulations require additional information regarding the percent of previously enrolled students employed, and their average starting salaries, in these fields. If such information cannot, after reasonable effort, be obtained, the institution must supply prospective students with "the most recent comparable regional or national data."

The Family Educational Rights and Privacy Act of 1974, as Amended, and the regulations issued in the June 17, 1976, *Federal Register* contain sections concerning admissions recommendations, student access to applications, and the release of student information. Enrolled or former students must be given access to their application records (as well as other educational records) on request. Applicants may, however, waive their right of access to letters of recommendation. The federal Privacy Protection Study Commission (1977, pp. 434–436) has recommended broadening the student-access provisions of the law, eliminating the student's waiver rights, and extending the law to cover all applicants, not just those who are admitted and enroll. Many admissions officers oppose these recommendations—especially that concerning letters of recommendation, because they believe that the recommendation may be affected if the writer knows that the student has access to it. Even though the act specifies that failure of the applicant to waive his right of access to letters of recommendation cannot influence the admissions decision, such a prohibition is almost impossible to monitor or enforce. The net result may well be that letters of recommendation will be either discontinued or disregarded, and essential information about candidates for admission to highly selective programs will be obtained in other ways—for instance, by phone.

Title I of the Education Amendments of 1976 and final regulations issued in the December 1, 1977, *Federal Register* ("Student Consumer Information Services") require institutions receiving an administrative cost allowance under certain federal financial assistance programs to provide specified student consumer information to prospective and enrolled students who request such information. Admissions offices are normally required to provide and/or disseminate at least a portion of the information. Included in the list of required topics are information on academic programs, the percent of students completing a particular course of study (if data are available), retention rates, costs, financial assistance programs, refund policies, eligibility of students for financial aid, and criteria used in selecting financial aid recipients and determining the amount of awards. Admissions officers would be well advised to have current data on academic programs, program completion rates, general retention rates, and refund policies readily available. Summaries of such information may be included in the publications sent to prospective applicants, even though the regulations require only that they be provided on request. If financial aid and admissions are administered in the same office, information on the financial aid programs and their requirements and eligibility criteria must also be available, and should almost certainly be included with information sent to all prospective students indicating an interest in financial aid.

A useful review of "student consumerism" appears in a recent ERIC report (Shulman, 1977). The consumer movement in higher education is gaining increasing attention, as students and prospective students expect and demand full information and fair procedures. El-Khawas (1977a) has identified eight areas of institutional activity that have recently come under criticism and gives several examples of good practices in each area. Three of the areas covered are official publications (where she stresses accuracy and review by prospective students to ensure that the publications can be readily understood); admissions and recruitment (emphasizing clear explanations of requirements; efficient processing; and accurate, balanced recruitment materials); and financial assistance (involving the best possible information and advice on costs; types of aid and the advantages, limitations, and obligations of each type; and complete information on the procedures for obtaining aid). El-Khawas stresses two principles in meeting student expectations and reducing the prospects of litigation: *effective communication* and *fair practice,* defined as "the maintenance of responsible and fair procedures in all administrative matters affecting students."

State Laws

Public institutions may also be subject to state laws affecting their admissions policies. In Illinois, for example, the state's Board of Higher Education has statutory authority to "establish minimum admission standards for public junior colleges, colleges, and state universities" (Illinois Revised Statutes 144:189.9[g]). State-supported colleges and universities also must classify students as residents or nonresidents of the state for tuition purposes, and often for admissions purposes as well. Tuition rates and, in some cases, admissions requirements are higher for nonresidents. Public institutions, even in the same state, may differ in their policies for determining residency. In some states, however, the residency requirements are established on a statewide basis. Residency regulations may be specified by law, or the responsibility may be delegated to the institutions or to a state coordinating agency (Carbone, 1973). A 1973–74 survey of nonresident student practices in each state (Patrick, 1976) illustrates the complexity and variety of residency requirements and their implementation. For example, approximately two thirds of the states had twelve-month durational residency requirements, and about one fourth had six-month requirements. Community colleges have the responsibility of determining "in-district" residency, since higher fees are normally charged students who reside outside the district's boundaries. The residency classification of an applicant is most often determined initially in the admissions office, but an appeals procedure is desirable.

Summary

In this chapter, attention has been focused on the social significance of the admissions process and on the role of the admissions office in helping to shape the institution's admissions philosophy, goals, and objectives, as well as the more specific admissions policies and requirements. The various types of requirements and both the general and special categories of applicants to whom they apply were described, and the recent impact of laws and government regulations on the admissions process was considered. The eight functions of the admissions office identified in this chapter are summarized here, by major area of responsibility.

Philosophy, Goals, and Objectives
  1. To participate in the development of admissions goals and objectives for the institution and, once they are determined, to assure that they are clearly articulated, widely understood, regularly reviewed, and implemented.
  2. To comprehend and maintain professional standards of ethics in all activities of the office.

Admissions Policies
  3. To aid in the development of general admissions policies through the collection, analysis, and presentation of data on the outcome of current policies and through the involvement of faculty, administrators, and students in the policy development process.

Admissions Requirements
  4. To review and recommend changes in specific admissions requirements in response to changes in institutional policies, numbers and characteristics of applicants, and the results of continual investigation of the validity,

fairness, feasibility, and secondary effects of such requirements.

5. To communicate to prospective students and their counselors, in clear and understandable ways, the specific requirements for admission, and to apply the requirements fairly and equitably to all applicants.

6. To be sensitive to the need for different admissions requirements and procedures for different types and levels of students, to maintain careful documentation of the variety of admissions programs and the authority for their implementation, and to articulate clearly the requirements and procedures for each group.

Laws, Regulations, and Legal Issues

7. To establish and maintain effective communication and fair practice in all contacts with students and prospective students.

8. To be aware of, and to be in compliance with, all applicable laws and regulations affecting the admissions process.

Further Reading and Study

Admissions officers who are concerned about the role and function of college admissions in society, and about the development of effective admissions policies and requirements for the institution, will broaden their perspectives by becoming acquainted with certain basic resources. Listed here are several books and reports that can contribute to the admissions officer's basic professional background and knowledge. Other resources—books, periodicals, and professional organizations that relate more to the operational aspects of the field—are described at the close of the following chapter.

ACT Research Reports. Iowa City, Iowa: American College Testing Company. A series of special research reports (nearly one hundred to date) prepared by the Research and Development Division of the American College Testing Company, covering a wide variety of basic issues in admissions, testing, and financial aid, including such titles as the following: *College Student Migration; Enrollment Projection Models for Institutional Planning; Impact of Educational Development, Family Income, College Costs, and Financial Aid in Student Choice and Enrollment in College;* and *Predictors of Graduation from College.*

College Entrance Examination Board. *On Further Examination: Report of the Advisory Panel on the Scholastic Aptitude Test Score Decline.* New York: College Entrance Examination Board, 1977. While directed primarily to possible explanations for the national decline in college admissions test scores, the report and its appendices contain valuable information about the current state of the art in admissions testing and identify issues and concerns.

Carnegie Council on Policy Studies in Higher Education. *Selective Admissions in Higher Education: Comment and Recommendations and Two Reports.* San Francisco: Jossey-Bass, 1977. The "two reports" are "The Pursuit of Fairness in Admissions to Higher Education" (which was referenced in the Supreme Court decision in the *Bakke* case) and "The Status of Selective Admissions." As an analysis of the issues and a summary of the known facts, this publication should be studied carefully by anyone interested in college admissions.

National Association of College Admissions Counselors. *Statement of Principles of Good Practice.* Skokie, Ill.: National Association of College Admissions Counselors, 1976. The result of cooperative efforts of three national organizations, this statement (reprinted in Appendix D of this volume) condenses the current wisdom on what does and what does not constitute ethical practice for colleges and secondary schools in admissions promotion and recruitment, application procedures, and financial assistance.

Thresher, B. Alden. *College Admissions and the Public Interest.* New York: College Entrance Examination Board, 1966. The author, a former director of admissions, presents a broad view of the basic issues of access to higher education.

Willingham, W. W. *Free Access Higher Education.* New York: College Entrance Examination Board, 1970. The author describes features which make many institutions readily available to prospective students (low cost, nonselective, and within easy commuting distance) and emphasizes the role of these institutions in higher education in the United States.

Willingham, W. W. *The Source Book for Higher Education.* New York: College Entrance Examination Board, 1973. An excellent guide to literature and information on access to higher education, including extensive, annotated bibliographies on all aspects of the admissions process.

Implementing Admissions Policy

E. Eugene Oliver

The line between policy and implementation is often extremely narrow, yet we continue to try to distinguish between the two as a reminder that, in any successful enterprise, each depends on the other. This chapter is concerned primarily with the functions of the admissions office as they relate to the implementation of recruitment, admissions procedures, office staffing and organization, financial aid, and internal institutional relations. As in the preceding chapter, the specific functions are detailed in the chapter summary.

Student Contact and Recruitment

One of the most important functions of the admissions office is to identify prospective students; to provide them with information about the institution; and to encourage qualified students to apply and, if admitted, to attend. Fundamental to the recruitment process is a thorough knowledge of the institution and its strengths and weaknesses, and a strong interest in helping prospective students make wise decisions about their educational futures. In order to reduce conflict and overlap among the efforts of various offices in the college, the admissions office should be responsible for the coordination of all recruitment for the institution.

Use of Marketing Concepts

Much has been written about the role of the admissions officer in recruiting students—identified as the primary admissions function in private institutions and the second most important function in public institutions (Abernathy, 1976). Current literature emphasizes marketing concepts, and the admissions director and staff are advised to "analyze the market," determine the "target population," develop strategies to "promote the product" effectively, and do "market surveys" to determine what appeals to— and what discourages—prospective students. Although some admissions officers resist the term *marketing*, it represents a comprehensive—not a narrow, sales-oriented—approach to identifying, attracting, and retaining students. Its concepts and techniques should be studied and understood by admissions staff members and utilized as a long-range effort to improve the institution's position and its service to students.

Marketing for Nonprofit Organizations (Kotler, 1975), a basic text in the field, describes marketing as a managerial process with four major aspects—analysis, planning, implementation, and control—and stresses the importance of careful planning, rather than random actions. Basic marketing concepts and their application to the admissions process are described in *A Role for Marketing in College Admissions* (College Entrance Examination Board, 1976), in which six different authors present various aspects of the topic. In Kotler's chapter, "Applying Marketing Theory to College Admissions," the admissions office is assigned major responsibility for developing an applicant pool, evaluating applicants, and evaluating recruitment efforts. While the admissions director should "educate other parties in the college regarding the imperatives of the college marketing process," Kotler emphasizes that the college's administration plays as large a role as the admissions office—or even a larger role—with primary responsibility for articulating the mission of the college (institutional positioning), planning the number and kinds of programs to be offered by the college (portfolio planning), and improving student satisfaction on campus (college improvement planning).

Community colleges, nonselective in most of their programs, are also using marketing concepts in recruitment programs, with the aim of increasing inquiries, applications, and admissions.

Applicant Pools

An initial function of the admissions office in the recruitment process is the development of the applicant pool—that group of prospective students from which the next class is likely to come. Ihlanfeldt (1975) identifies three markets: one from which candidates will probably enroll if admitted (primary), another from which candidates are likely to be admitted but are also likely to attend another institution (secondary), and a market in which students differ from past applicants but are encouraged to attend (test). Ihlanfeldt also defines various stages of the market pool: prospects, candidates, applicants, accepted applicants, and matriculants. The pool must contain a required critical number in each category if an entering class of the desired size is to be obtained. For example, experience may indicate that a "prospect" pool—those with characteristics likely to suggest an interest in, and qualifications for, admission—of 10,000 will yield, following an initial contact, 2,000 interested candidates, or persons who may request further information or applications. Of this number, 1,000 may actually apply (the applicant pool), 900 may be accepted, and 500 may enroll. If 500 is the desired number of freshmen, the admissions director is delighted, the president is pleased, and the faculty members are smiling. If the target was, say, 600, then the admissions director is in trouble, and the critical size of the various stages of the market pool must be revised.

To determine what types of students the institution wishes to attract (age, academic ability, geographical location, financial level) and whether adequate numbers of such students exist, research is essential in the recruitment process. Another important step is to survey current students to see why they chose the institution and what they like about it. Equally important is contact with nonapplicants, with students who applied but did not accept an admissions offer, with those who accepted an offer but did not enroll, and with noncontinuing students, in order to learn why they "dropped out."

Recruitment Methods

With information in hand about prospective students and what is likely to appeal to them or discourage them, it is necessary to establish admissions objectives (number of students desired and number of contacts likely to yield the number of applicants that should, in turn, yield the class size desired) and to develop the student contact strategy. The methods available are numerous but often involve some combination of those discussed below. Among those discussed, a recent survey in Pennsylvania to determine the views of school counselors and college admissions officers toward various recruitment practices (Haines, 1975) gave highest marks to (1) visits to secondary schools once each year, by appointment, by an admissions staff member; and (2) on-campus programs for prospective students, parents, and secondary school counselors. Also supported by a large majority of the respondents were off-campus programs for school counselors and college fairs sponsored by professional organizations.

Not all of the recruiting strategies and techniques described below are appropriate for all types of institutions and programs. Private colleges and universities, whose financial health is dependent on tuition to a greater degree than in public institutions, normally are more energetic, use a greater variety of techniques, and conduct more studies in recruiting. Some public colleges and universities limit their "recruiting" activities to information-giving sessions for prospective students, parents, and counselors. Contact with prospective students at the graduate level is handled almost exclusively by the departments, whose practices vary from active cultivation of lists of outstanding undergraduates in a particular field to simply waiting for applications to arrive. Some coordination in the recruitment of minorities, women, or other special groups may be provided by the graduate school office, but the admissions office seldom becomes involved in the recruitment of graduate students. A greater influence on recruiting methods than type of college or program, however, is an enrollment shortfall. When enrollments drop, admissions officers scramble. But the basic principles and techniques of student contact and recruitment should be maintained regardless of the enrollment picture at any given time. Such a position will discourage complacency in good times and encourage confidence in bad times.

Visits to Schools and Community Colleges. Direct contact with prospective students and their counselors in schools and community colleges is a standard and valuable technique for most admissions offices. Advance contact with the school and/or college to be visited is essential. Some schools place restrictions on access to students by college representatives, limiting such contacts to nonclass times, such as study halls, lunch periods, and before or after school. Advance knowledge of these limitations will make the visit more productive. The representative should include a brief visit with the school or community college counselor, providing updated information and answering questions about the institution and its admissions requirements and procedures. Conferences with students (and, in some cases, with their parents as well) should be approached from the point of view of helping the student make a wise college choice—even if that choice should be another college. As enrollments decline, it will be more difficult for representatives to be objective in assessing a student's interests and abilities as they relate to college choice, but the long-range interests of the college will be better served by advising some students to consider other institutions.

The development of good working relationships with school and community college counselors is an invaluable aid to recruiting. This requires that the school or college visit be carefully planned, that local regulations be scrupulously observed, and that the follow-up on unanswered questions, reports on the status of applicants, and other types of communication be prompt and thorough. If schools do not cooperate in providing space and time for visits by college representatives, or make access to students difficult or impossible, colleges may arrange to meet students and parents in a hotel or motel in the community. These meetings require careful advance planning, and counselors at the school or schools in the area should always be informed of such programs, requested to announce the meeting to their students, and invited to attend. Some colleges have found these arrangements more effective and efficient than school visits. The programs, usually in the evening, provide an opportunity to reach interested students and parents in an informal setting, and often involve alumni from the community.

Visits to Campus by Prospective Students, Parents, and Counselors. The campus visit is almost universally recommended as a vital element in student choice. Colleges should have a carefully developed plan for visitors, including the following: well-marked routes to the campus; adequate parking; campus maps; effective signs identifying buildings, offices, and other places of interest; a centrally located and readily accessible admissions office; planned campus tours, with student guides, if possible; opportunities to meet with an admissions counselor; readiness to schedule conferences with other campus units as required, such as academic departments, financial aid, and housing; opportunities to visit a class in session; and a follow-up system to contact campus visitors at a later date, providing additional information or offering further assistance.

Some colleges set aside special days for campus visits and schedule extra events, such as exhibits, cultural or sports activities, or open-house tours of campus facilities. Arrangements may also be made to have visitors stay overnight in a student residence hall, fraternity, or sorority.

Campus visits can be very influential in determining the student's choice of an institution. They are equally valuable to the student and the institution, regardless of the ultimate choice of college, for the decision can be made on the basis of direct experience and more complete information than would otherwise have been the case. Students who select an institution they have visited will know more about what to expect, and their initial adjustment should be more successful. Admissions offices should place great emphasis on campus visits by prospective students and their parents and should do everything possible to ensure a genuine and sincere welcome for each guest.

Visits to the campus by school or community college counselors are also an effective device for assuring that prospective students receive correct information and, in most cases, a favorable impression of the college, from their counselors. Tours of the campus and meetings with admissions, financial aid, housing, student personnel services, and other administrative and academic staff members are standard features of most of these visits.

Organized programs for counselors often include opportunities for them to meet with former students. Students should be invited, in advance of the visit, to meet their counselors at a specified time and place, and the counselors should be provided with a list of all their former students on the campus. The contacts provide several advantages: the counselor hears the reactions of students to their college experience; the counselor learns of school or community college practices that were especially helpful—or harmful—in the transition process; and the students have a sense of helping to improve the chances for a "good fit" between future students and the college.

Contacts with Business and Industry. Recruitment activities are being directed increasingly toward the adult student. A number of institutions—especially community colleges and those located in metropolitan areas—have established contacts with business and industry to determine employee needs and interests, have developed special instructional programs when appropriate, and have engaged in an active program of information and recruitment among employees in their regions. Community colleges are frequently aided by the establishment of advisory committees, consisting of local business or industry representatives, for each technical or vocational field offered. Four-year colleges also often establish advisory committees for some of their specialized curricula, to aid in developing and evaluating the curriculum, placing graduates, raising funds, and recruiting students. A college can improve its program by inviting leaders of business and industry in the areas served by the institution to come to the campus for a visit, to serve as guest lecturers in their field, to review program offerings, and to meet informally with students and faculty members. These visitors may also assist in recruiting students by sharing their impressions of the college with company employees and others.

Direct Mail. Services by the College Entrance Examination

Board and the American College Testing Program provide, with the student's permission, the names and addresses of students with characteristics desired by the college. Community colleges, which serve a specified geographical area, often use direct mail for recruitment of high school graduates and adult students. Giampetro and Rooney (1977) describe a number of options and advantages in the use of direct-mail contact with prospective students. The college is wise to keep its publications and all direct-mail materials under continuing review. The use of a student review panel is especially valuable, since current students quickly detect materials that are unlikely to appeal to prospective students or that contain misleading or incomplete information.

College Days and Nights. College day/night programs, which bring a large number of college admissions officers to a school or community college to be interviewed by students and parents, continue in many regions, despite criticism of these programs by college admissions officers. Some improvements have been made recently—notably in having one program serve a number of nearby schools. Statewide or regional groups of school counselors and college admissions officers often develop a calendar of college days/nights for their state or region; such a calendar has the advantage of reducing conflicts and locating successive programs near each other geographically, thus reducing travel problems for the college representatives. These regional groups also work on guidelines for improving college day/night programs. For example, the Kentucky Association for the Promotion of College Admissions, a division of the Kentucky Personnel and Guidance Association, prepares a coordinated, statewide schedule for college day/night programs and provides a useful brochure to each school, containing suggestions for establishing a date, determining what type of program to have, preparing students for the program, administering the program, and conducting follow-up activities. Exhibit 1, an outline for presentations at college day/night programs, was prepared by the admissions office of a large state university.

Publication. Attention to the content and format of recruitment literature is increasing. Honest, readable, consumer-oriented, and attractive publications are the goal. The College Entrance

Exhibit 1. Student Contact Presentation:
College Day/Night Programs

Format: The presentation length and style will be dictated by the host high school. Giving the presentation in a separate classroom or office is preferable. However, some high schools will ask the representative to use a table in the hall or lunchroom, and on occasion the bleachers in the gymnasium will be used to accommodate a larger group. Thus, the representative must adapt the presentation to the specific requirements of the situation.

Presentation: Upon arrival at the school, the representative should check in and then proceed to the assigned location. It is a good policy to have the room or table set up 10 to 15 minutes prior to the arrival of the students. The presentation itself will usually last between 15 and 30 minutes. Four basic areas should be covered at each presentation:

I. *School Profile.* Topics needing to be covered include brief history, characteristics of the student body, campus life, residence hall life, social activities, athletic activities, and other student-oriented information.

II. *Admissions Standards and Requirements.* Students must have a clear understanding about admissions requirements; that is, whether their proposed academic major has open or selective admissions, what high school academic subjects are required, test score averages needed, and whether recommendations are necessary. Topics which must be covered include application deadlines, which entrance examinations are required, simplified admissions procedures, and high school credentials required.

III. *Expenses and Financial Aid.* Outline the estimated total cost for attending one year. This should include a breakdown showing tuition, fees, room, board, and miscellaneous expenses. Advise students of the types of financial aid available and the procedure for obtaining this aid. A distinction should be made between the federal financial aid programs in which the institution participates and the specific programs offered uniquely by the institution.

IV. *Wrap Up.* At the end of any formal presentation, sufficient time should be allowed for a question-and-answer period. This informal time should be used to invite students for campus visitation and to collect requests for further information on the reply cards. Before leaving the school, the representative should stop by the guidance counselor's office; answer any questions, drop off additional information, and update the counselor's file on the institution. This will also afford an opportunity to extend thanks for the school's hospitality. Within a few days, a follow-up letter should be sent to the school, providing additional information about unanswered questions or requests.

Exhibit 1. (Continued)
Student Contact Presentation Outline

I. Introduction
II. History
    A. Founded in 1883, Land-Grant Institution
    B. Academic Majors—Agriculture and Mechanical Engineering
    C. 273 students in 1876, Statistical Data Fall 1978 Enrollment
    D. Enrollment Trends, Academic Colleges
III. Academic Programs, Seventeen Colleges and Graduate School
    A. General
        1. 100+ Academic Majors
        2. Offering Baccalaureate Through Doctoral Degrees
    B. Nonselective Colleges
        1. Agriculture
        2. Arts and Sciences
        3. Communications
        4. Fine Arts
        5. Home Economics
        6. Social Professions
    C. Lower Division, Selective Colleges
        1. College of Allied Health
            a. Community Health
            b. Medical Technology
            c. Physical Therapy
        2. College of Architecture
        3. College of Engineering
            a. Seven Different Fields of Study Offered
            b. Co-op Optional
    D. Upper Division, Selective Colleges
        1. College of Business and Economics
            a. Accounting
            b. Business Administration
            c. Economics
        2. College of Education
            a. Elementary
            b. Junior High
            c. Secondary
            d. Special
        3. College of Nursing
        4. College of Pharmacy
    E. Graduate and Professional Schools
        1. Graduate School
            a. Master's ⎫
            b. Specialist ⎬ Degrees in a variety of areas
            c. Doctoral ⎭
        2. Professional Schools
            a. Dentistry

Exhibit 1. (Continued)

             b. Law
             c. Medicine

IV. Student Life
    A. Dormitory Life
        1. Description of Facilities
        2. Meal Plans
    B. Sports
        1. Intramural
            a. Men
            b. Women
        2. Intercollegiate
            a. Basketball and Football Major Sports
            b. Men: Baseball, Tennis, Golf, Track, Swimming, Wrestling, and Riflery
            c. Women: Field Hockey, Golf, Gymnastics, Tennis, Track, Cross Country, Volleyball, and Riflery
    C. Social Organizations
        1. Sororities
        2. Fraternities
    D. Political Organizations
        1. Student Government
        2. Young Democrats
        3. Young Republicans
    E. Religious Organizations
    F. Other Student Activities
        1. Band and Other Instrumental Groups
        2. Choral Music
        3. Student Newspaper
        4. Yearbook
        5. Theatre
        6. Debate
        7. Cheerleading

V. Financial Information
    A. Tuition
        1. In-State
        2. Out-of-State
    B. Room and Board
    C. Miscellaneous
        1. Books
        2. Personal
    D. Financial Aid Information
        1. Scholarships
        2. Grants
        3. Loans
        4. Work-Study

VI. Admissions
    A. Application Procedure
        1. Take ACT

Exhibit 1. (Continued)

Examination Board has established an annual competition for such publications and presents awards to those judged best by a panel of students and media staff. A recent national project, "Better Information for Student Choice," supported by the Fund for the Improvement of Postsecondary Education, resulted in the development of a number of innovative and comprehensive publications for students and counselors (El-Khawas, 1977b). The development of recruitment publications should be a joint project of the admissions office and the public relations office. Considerable loss in effectiveness, accuracy, or both occurs when one of the offices assumes responsibility for recruitment literature without involving the other.

Contacts by Alumni, Faculty, and Students. While primary responsibility for recruitment should rest with the admissions office staff, a number of institutions utilize alumni, faculty, and students as adjunct resources. To be effective, representatives of these groups must be carefully selected and informed about current programs and admissions requirements. Consideration should also be given to the time demands imposed on them by recruitment activities. Personal contacts between alumni and prospective students may be especially helpful at locations distant from the college.

Teaching faculty may contribute through personal contact, attendance at college day/night programs, meetings with prospective
students visiting the campus, or correspondence with prospective
or admitted students interested in the faculty member's field of
study. A corps of volunteer students may be chosen to provide a
number of services, such as acting as hosts and hostesses for campus visitors, critiquing publications, writing letters to prospective
students, and phoning students who have been admitted to offer
assistance and encouragement.

Advertising. Although not yet a common technique in most
areas, radio and television spot announcements and newspaper ads
(and an occasional billboard) are increasingly being used to attract
prospective students and their parents. Such techniques are likely
to be refined and used to a greater extent during the 1980s. Public
institutions are usually prevented, by custom or law, from using
state funds to buy advertising. They may, however, use funds from
private sources for this purpose. Ads that are effectively designed,
and placed where they are most likely to be seen or heard by prospective students, will no doubt reach some otherwise hard-to-reach
individuals, but their effectiveness in increasing enrollments is difficult to measure. Clearly, they are no substitute for personal contact, school visits, campus visits, and other recruitment techniques
described in this section.

College Fairs. Organized by the National Association of College Admissions Counselors (NACAC), college fairs are scheduled
in large metropolitan centers and attract thousands of prospective
students and parents from the city and suburbs—and hundreds of
admissions officers from around the country. Each college representative is assigned a "booth" where prospective students may
obtain information and literature about the college. College fairs
are criticized by some college representatives because they permit
little individual attention and little opportunity to determine real
student interest; however, they will probably become even more
popular as enrollments decline and colleges seek every opportunity
to meet prospective students and their parents.

Specialized Recruitment Activities. Specialized activities are
aided by the National Scholarship Service and Fund for Negro
Students (NSSFNS), which prepares lists of prospective black stu-

dents; the National Merit Scholarship Corporation (NMSC), which conducts a national competition for academically talented students; the College Entrance Examination Board's "Talented Junior College Graduate" program, which lists minority graduates of two-year colleges; and the Westinghouse Talent Search to select outstanding science students. Such lists, which identify students in special categories, are used by many colleges in their admissions programs.

Marketing Calendars

Illustrating various recruitment methods, as well as the importance of careful advance planning, Exhibit 2 is a "marketing calendar" developed by the admissions office of a liberal arts college in Illinois.

Exhibit 2. Marketing Action Plan
1978–79, Office of Admissions

Goals
1. The class of 1983, those entering in September 1979 as traditional college-age students, will number 275–300.
2. To achieve this goal, both applications and yield on admits must increase.

Assumptions
1. Our public lies primarily with middle and upper socioeconomic groups in urban/suburban areas.
2. The college has four primary marketing areas.
   a. Illinois, with emphasis on the five-county "Chicagoland" section.
   b. Selected metropolitan centers in the Midwest (St. Louis, Milwaukee, Minneapolis–St. Paul, Detroit, Indianapolis, Cedar Rapids, Des Moines, Cleveland, Cincinnati, Dayton, Columbus).
   c. Metropolitan centers in the East (Boston, Hartford-Springfield, Providence, Fairfield County, Wilmington, Baltimore, Washington, D.C., area).
   d. Metropolitan centers in the West (Denver, Tucson, Phoenix).
3. The college has two secondary marketing areas.
   a. The two thirds of Illinois that can be described as rural.
   b. The metropolitan centers in the Northwest and Florida.
4. The success of our marketing efforts rests on personal attention to and concern for the individual candidate.

Exhibit 2. (Continued)

I. Direct-Mail Campaign

   Goal: To increase number of contacts in order to stimulate more inquiries.

   A. College Board Student Search
Spring—Preliminary Scholastic Aptitude Test (PSAT) takers October '77—Mailing completed June 1, 1978.

   B. Associated Colleges of the Midwest College Board Student Search
Spring—PSAT takers October '77—Mailing conducted as responses received.

   C. Lists as received—for example, church, fraternity-sorority rush, National Council of Teachers of English, Illinois State Scholarship Commission

   D. Summary: The direct-mail campaign will reach in excess of 70,000 students at a cost of $4,560.00 for the lists. In the past years, two different searches were employed to a total of nearly 21,000 students. Last year, only one search was conducted and completed three months earlier.

II. Direct-Contact Campaign

   Goal: To personalize contacts in primary market areas.

   A. National College Fairs (NACAC)
Fall '78: Minneapolis, Baltimore, Washington, D.C., Philadelphia, New York City, Milwaukee, and Chicago.
All Student Search respondents and nonrespondents informed in advance by postcard of college attendance at the fairs.

   B. Area College Nights/Fairs
Fall '78: Rhode Island, Charleston, West Virginia, Kenosha-Racine, Rockland County (N.Y.), Denver, Colorado Springs, Phoenix-Scottsdale, Tucson, Albuquerque, Kalamazoo, Appleton, and Green Bay.
Illinois: Elgin area, Rockford area, McHenry County, plus 25 individual school and school district programs.
All Student Search respondents and nonrespondents informed in advance by postcard of college attendance.

   C. On-Campus Activities
     1. Interviews and Tours
     2. Overnights
     3. Class Visits and Faculty Appointments
     4. Financial Aid

   D. Athletic Department

   E. Summary: The direct-contact campaign gives great emphasis to primary regions, is time consuming and expensive, and ignores development of secondary markets.

III. Institutional Awareness Effort

   A. Publication A
     1. April/May 1978 issue sent to all accumulated contacts with high school juniors.

Exhibit 2. (Continued)

2. Selected issues sent to all preliminary application filers (direct-mail respondents and student-initiated contacts).
B. Publication B
  1. July issue sent to all direct-mail respondents and student-initiated contacts.
  2. August issue sent with all application material packets mailed in September.
C. College Fair, College Night, School Visit Notice
  Postcards announcing college participation sent 10 days in advance of program to all who filed preliminary application and nonrespondents to College Board Search.
IV. Special Effort and Projects
A. Target Cities Campaign
  Goal: To increase freshman applications.

Area	Applicants/ Fall '77	Goal/ Fall '78	Actual '78	Goal '79
Minneapolis	14	30	12	20
St. Louis	10	20	10	15
Phoenix/ Tucson	3	10	4	8
Milwaukee	7	15	23	30
Boston	25	50	82	90
Omaha	1	5	1	3
Kansas City	—	5	2	4
Indiana	4	10	10	20
Cleveland	6	12	15	20
Denver	25	40	20	25

  Interested alumni and/or current students have expressed a specific desire to contact prospective students. These contacts take place primarily at the Thanksgiving and Christmas holiday breaks.
B. Chicago Metropolitan Area Campaign
  Goal: To increase applications and matriculations from suburban area high schools.
  In 1977–78, we anticipated programs in 20–25 communities. We were too ambitious. Five programs were scheduled. In 1978–79, 15 schools have been identified for a special effort in December and January. Programs will involve personal invitations from alumni hosts to prospective students and parents. One to three currently enrolled college students from the target secondary school will participate.
C. Admissions Staff Follow-Up
  1. Personal letters written from December 20 to January 1 to all students interviewed on campus and to all personal contacts from school visits, college nights, and fairs.

Exhibit 2. (Continued)

D. Transfer Candidate Cultivation
Goal: To increase applications and consequently enrollment of transfer students. 100 is target for Fall 1979.
1. Student Letters
    a. General letter from a student who transferred from large public university to all inquiries from similar institutions.
    b. General letter from a student who transferred from public community college to all inquiries from same type of institution.
    c. Where possible, personal faculty letter relating to academic interest.
    d. Where possible, personal letter to transfer candidate from student who transferred to college from same institution.
2. Community College Visitation
    a. Emphasis on Chicagoland community colleges.
    b. Director of Admissions will meet with department chairpersons to seek their support, assistance, and thoughts.
3. Transfer Student Brochure
    Develop a new brochure which presents four to six "case histories" of currently enrolled transfer students. It will be sent with application materials to all who inquire about transfer.
V. "Operation 300"—Sales Effort—March 19 to May 1
A. 800-line toll-free telephone available to all admitted students (Admissions staff on duty during day; currently enrolled college students on duty during evening)
B. College Day—April 21 (all admits who could possibly attend invited)
C. Off-Campus Receptions
1. New York City Metropolitan Area
2. Boston Metropolitan Area
3. Denver
4. St. Louis
5. Minneapolis
6. Additional locales, if justified
D. Faculty Letters
E. Activity Letters (for example, athletics, campus activities and organizations)
F. Alumni Follow-Up
VI. Recruitment Progress Audit
A. Monthly Report
1. Applications and mail—comparison to prior year.
2. Direct-contact analysis—off-campus contacts.
    a. Trip reports submitted by staff to director of admissions.

Exhibit 2. (Continued)

    b. Summary and comparison to prior year by director of admissions to president.

    c. On-campus activities—summary from director of admissions to president.

B. Audit Dates

    1. October 1—Director of admissions and president review direct-mail results.

    2. January 15—Director of admissions and president review recruitment program to date. Decide to stay with Marketing Action Plan (MAP) or define new effort to generate additional prospects; if the latter, weigh costs of effort on Operation 300. Additionally, director of admissions, director of financial aid, and president meet to discuss financial aid budget.

    3. February 15—Assuming no change in "MAP" as of January 15, director of admissions and president discuss reading impressions of candidates' folders by admissions staff. Basic question to be answered is: Will there be a sufficient number of qualified candidates to be offered admission? A corollary question is: Should or can admission standards be adjusted?

    4. March 1—Repeat of above. Confirm Operation 300. Confirm financial aid budget and level of commitment.

Appendix: Admissions Timetable

June	• Complete initial mailing of Student Search.
July and August	• Personal response to search respondents with specific paragraphs for expressed academic and co-curricular interests.
September	• Mail application materials and catalogs.
September to Mid-January	• Personal-contact campaign.
January 15–March 1	• Read and evaluate files of candidates.
	• Complete personal follow-up.
March 1–March 15	• Make admissions decisions.
	• Define individual follow-up procedures.
March 18	• Initial announcement date (admissions decisions announced biweekly thereafter).
March 19–May 1	• Operation 300.

Commercial Publications and Agencies

The admissions office must be aware of, and often provide data to, a wide range of commercial publications which provide information and advice to the college bound. These include such standard works as *Lovejoy's College Guide* (Lovejoy, 1979), Cass and Birnbaum's (1977) *Comparative Guide to American Colleges,* and *Barron's Profiles of American Colleges* (Fine, 1976). A survey of Illinois counselors (Wermers, 1974) indicated that school counselors regard commercial publications as an essential resource in their counseling programs for prospective college students. Nevertheless, the number of requests for such information can become burdensome, especially when the request comes from a new or an unfamiliar agency. In such cases, the admissions officer may well decide to send the agency some questions, such as:

1. How many students did you serve during the most recent year of operation?
2. When was your service first offered?
3. What are your charges to students, schools, or colleges?
4. Do you include in your service information about colleges that do not respond to your request?
5. How often do you update the information in your system?
6. What research has been conducted to provide the basic rationale for your services?
7. Do you work with any of the professional associations at the school or college level?
8. What is the educational and experiential background of your professional staff members?

In addition to providing information to commercial publications, admissions officers will be asked to provide data to the College Entrance Examination Board's guides—*The College Handbook* and *The College Handbook Index of Majors* (Watts, 1977).

Commercial agencies that offer assistance in admissions-related activities, especially student recruitment, are increasing in number. A good discussion of the possible advantages, and of the need for careful evaluation, of such agencies may be found in an article by Rosenthal, McIvor, and Meadows (1977). The employment of an outside commercial agency, however, should be considered only as a last resort—when sincere and sustained internal efforts to improve admissions operations and results have failed. Professional consultants—successful admissions officers from other institutions—might help institutions in their efforts to improve admissions operations; the American Association of Collegiate Registrars and Admissions Officers has developed such a service. But if all else fails, and a commercial agency is being considered, an institution should obtain a list of the colleges previously served by the agency and make independent contacts with the president and the director of admissions of each college to learn their evaluations of the agency; it should also obtain and verify information concerning the agency's financial position and the qualifications of its professional staff. All who are involved in and affected by the admissions process—administrators, faculty, students, and admissions office staff—should question the promise of a "quick fix" for dwindling enrollments. Current social forces, the array and quality of academic and extracurricular programs, the reputation of the faculty, the appearance of the campus and its facilities, the opinions of present and former students—all combine to exert a greater force on enrollments than the efforts of the admissions staff, critical as they are. An institution with falling enrollments should look at all these factors—including the admissions process—in arriving at a decision on alternative courses of action. The result may well be basic changes in the institution as a whole, rather than the employment of a commercial agency which promises to streamline and strengthen recruiting.

Student Retention

Closely allied to student recruitment in maintaining desired levels of enrollment is student retention. The admissions office can play an important role in this area by drawing attention to the significance of retention and by conducting or encouraging studies which demonstrate the impact of retention on enrollment. In *Preventing Students from Dropping Out,* Astin (1975) shares the results of large-scale research on factors that influence students to leave and provides practical suggestions to reduce attrition. Many of the suggestions center on ways to increase student involvement in the life of the institution. Improving academic performance is crucial, and maintaining students' interest in their courses is one of the keys to improvement. Participation in honors programs and credit by examination are valuable in this regard. Carefully planned orientation, counseling, and advisement programs can help. The proper utilization of financial aid, including work opportunities, is also important. Living in a dormitory, sorority, or fraternity during the freshman year increases persistence. Astin provides a worksheet for predicting chances of dropping out, which may be used by or for individual students or groups of students. Improving predictions of the likelihood of dropping out is a basic step in developing a more effective retention program.

"Stopping out"—a reference to temporary withdrawal from college for travel, work, or the pursuit of some special interest, with the intention of returning—is a growing phenomenon. When prospective "stopouts" can be identified, the college may apply special policies or procedures to help assure the students' return and thus improve retention. Among these are special program advising, financial aid counseling, and the assignment of "leave" status with assurance of a readmission free of red tape or extra costs, and consideration of credit for appropriate noncollegiate experiences.

Maintaining Good Working Relationships

Throughout the process of student contact and recruitment, the admissions office must make every effort to establish and maintain good working relationships with the various institutions and agencies directly related to the admissions program: counselors and administrators in feeder schools and colleges; community agency staff and other community leaders; and business and industry leaders. Maintenance of good relationships is impossible without frequent and effective communication—in both directions. Certainly the admissions office should utilize periodic reports (newsletters, special reports, research findings) to the various groups identified above. Questions on the topics covered should be solicited and answers provided. But written communication is

never enough. Personal contacts, through visits on and off campus, are vital. To help representatives of various groups become
more than just observers of the admissions process, advising
committees—either continuing committees or committees to work
on a specific issue or problem—can be established. When these
committees include faculty members as well as representatives of
outside agencies and groups, the ties to the college are further
strengthened. For example, if the college is considering a basic
change in its admissions policy or timetable, the appointment of an
advisory committee to study the issues involved and to make recommendations could be an important step in arriving at a decision. The committee may include school counselors, key faculty
members, other community representatives, and alumni representatives. The final decision will, of course, be made by the college.
But the counsel of those with experience and a strong interest
in the outcome can do much to facilitate the process and assure
the acceptance of that decision, whatever it may be. In this as in
other areas, the admissions office carries a large share of the
responsibility—but it is a shared responsibility. The involvement
and cooperation of other college officers and officials (the president, the director of financial aid, the dean, or others) will be
required in the maintenance of good relations outside the college.

In communicating with high school and community college
counselors, reports on the admission status and academic progress
of students from that particular school or college are among the
most welcome and appreciated. Reports may include action taken
on applications and, for those students who enroll, end-of-term or
annual reports on the students' academic status, as well as comparisons between the grades earned by the students from that school
with those of entrants from other schools. Exhibit 3 (Parts 1 and 2)
contains a copy of a student progress report developed by a university for each community college in the state. The example shown in
Part 1 of the exhibit was prepared for the community college
whose data are displayed in the first column. The thirteen students
who transferred to the University of Middle America in the fall of
1978 entered with transfer GPAs of 3.17 (median) and 3.22
(mean). Their combined grade performance at the University of
Middle America, by discipline, is arrayed (starting with Agriculture

(Confidential)

Exhibit 3 (part 1). Community College Transfer Student Summary Progress Report, University of Middle America, Office of Admissions and Records

Spring 1979 Data for Students Entering Fall 1978

	(1) Community College Transfers from ___ College (N = 13)		(2) Community College Transfers at Middle America Univ (N = 665)	(3) Four-Year-College Transfers at Middle America Univ (N = 605)	(4) Native Juniors at Middle America Univ (N = 4,079)
	Community College Transfer GPA Median 3.17 Mean 3.22		*Community College Transfer GPA* Median 3.27 Mean 3.24	*Four-Year-College Transfer GPA* Median 3.18 Mean 3.17	*Lower-Div GPA* Median 3.04 Mean 3.02
	Semester GPA	No. Hours	Semester GPA	Semester GPA	Semester GPA
MEAN GPA IN:					
Agriculture	2.73	47	2.97	3.13	3.16
Biol Sciences	2.00	3	2.70	2.67	3.02
Business & Comm	3.60	15	2.72	2.93	2.96
Education	3.00	5	3.46	3.47	3.64
Engineering	2.56	54	2.71	2.95	3.09
Engl & Human			2.97	3.12	3.21
Fine & Appl Arts			3.29	3.44	3.31
Foreign Langs	2.00	4	2.91	2.97	3.07
Mathematics	3.67	20	2.38	2.48	2.74
Phys Sciences	2.00	4	2.43	2.74	2.85
Social Sciences	2.80	15	2.86	3.00	3.11
All Courses	2.73		2.77	2.97	3.08

STATUS:	Number	Number	Number	Number
Good Standing	8	528	509	3,554
Drop	1	36	15	45
Probation	3	81	44	174
Withdrawn		11	13	49
Graduated	1	9	24	257

Exhibit 3. (Part 2) Community College Transfer Student Summary Progress Report, University of Middle America, Office of Admissions and Records

Spring 1979 Data for Community College Transfer Students from Community College Entering Fall 1978

Student Name	College of Enrollment	Curriculum	Class Level
Alpha, Thomas W.	Lib Arts & Sci	Genetics & Devel	Senior
Bravo, Gerald P.	Agriculture	Agronomy	Junior
Charlie, Dean A.	Comm & Bus Admin	Finance	Junior
Delta, Terry Lynn	Engineering	Civil Engr	Junior
Echo, Stanley Frank	Agriculture	Dairy Science	Sophomore
Foxtrot, Timothy S.	Engineering	Civil Engr	Junior
Golf, David Allen	Fine & Appl Arts	Architectural St	Senior
Hotel, Harvey Rudolph	Engineering	Mechanical Engr	Junior
India, John Peter	Agriculture	Agronomy	Junior
Juliet, Erian Leigh	Lib Arts & Sci	Psychology	Sophomore
Kilo, Douglas W.	Engineering	Civil Engr	Junior
Lima, Charles W.	Agriculture	Tch Agric	Junior
Mike, Bryan Gail	Comm & Bus Admin	Finance	Senior

and ending with a 2.73 cumulative grade point average for all courses). Comparable data for all community college transfers (column 2), all four-year-college transfers (column 3), and all native juniors at the university (column 4) are also shown. The current status of the thirteen transfer students is listed at the bottom of the chart. Part 2 of the exhibit illustrates a more personalized summary progress report, which is sent to each transfer institution.

Care must be taken to avoid conflict with the Family Educational Rights and Privacy Act, which prohibits the release of certain types of individually identifiable information without the written consent of the student concerned.

Other possibilities for improving understanding and good will about an institution while providing needed services include offering summer workshops for counselors in such fields as career education and college counseling; conducting summer workshops or camps for high school students in mathematics, music, engineering, speech, and other subjects; and providing opportunities for career exploration for high school students through seminars or workshops involving school counselors, faculty members, and community leaders in business, industry, and the professions.

Menacker (1975) emphasizes the need for communication among schools and colleges, institutional cooperation, and mutual understanding. The work of the admissions officers—and of the students who enter the institution—can be aided by effective articulation among the institutions concerned.

Admissions Procedures

The admissions office must recognize, and prepare for, the several stages in the admissions process. Application forms and related materials must be developed well in advance of the admissions "season." A second stage involves the distribution of the applications, followed by the processing and evaluation of those returned. Procedures must be established for correspondence with applicants and others, to clear up questions of incomplete forms or missing credentials, and for the receipt of test scores, recommendations, and other required documents. Following the evaluation of the application and the admissions decision, the office enters the final stage: notification of the candidate and other institutional offices and the follow-up of admitted candidates to help assure their enrollment. A substantial degree of mechanization and computerization is employed by most offices, making even more evident the need for careful planning and documentation of office procedures. As an indication of the significance of admissions procedures, processing applications was ranked second in the list of admissions office activities in a survey (Vinson, 1976) of 1,267 chief admissions officers at bachelor's degree-granting institutions.

Types of Procedures

Most institutions use one—or some combination—of the procedures described below.

Rolling Admissions. The majority of both public (92 percent) and private (65 percent) institutions interviewed in a recent survey of 144 major institutions (77 public and 67 private) reported that they practice rolling admissions (Abernathy, 1976). These institutions set a beginning date for acceptance of applications for a given term, act on the applications as they arrive, and give notification of acceptance or denial to the applicant as soon as the decision is made.

Candidates' Reply Date Agreement. Sixty-three percent of the private and 25 percent of the public institutions in the Abernathy survey do not require freshmen to reply to an offer of admission before May 1. This procedure gives the applicants time to hear from all colleges they have applied to before making a commitment.

Early Decision Plan (EDP). Colleges that follow an early decision procedure agree to act promptly on fall freshman applications received by a specified date (usually November 1), under either a first-choice plan (the applicant, when accepted by the first-choice college, must withdraw applications from all other colleges to which he or she applied) or a single-choice plan (the applicant agrees to apply to only one institution until notified of that institution's decision). Since institutions subscribing to early decision plans generally notify many other applicants of their decision at about the same time that they notify EDP applicants (usually December 1),

Cashwell (1976) suggests that the plan may no longer be needed.

Common Notification Date. A few institutions hold their applications until a given date, at which time they notify all candidates. If spaces remain following the notification date, additional applications will be accepted. This procedure permits the institution to select the best qualified of those who have applied.

Deferred Admission. Some institutions permit successful applicants to defer their entry for up to one year, thus giving them the opportunity to engage in other activities without losing the security of a place in the college.

Waiting Lists. Institutions with a surplus of applicants may place students on a waiting list. While this may be preferable to a denial from the student's point of view, the primary advantage rests with the institution. Institutions can turn to their waiting lists to fill spaces if other students decline their offers of admission, or they can hold the waiting list in reserve in the hope that better-qualified applicants will apply later.

Application Deadline Date. Fewer than half of the private institutions and about one third of the public institutions in the Abernathy survey publish and adhere to a deadline for receipt of applications. For fall-term admission, the deadline may be as early as the preceding January or as late as a week prior to registration, depending on the pressure for admission to a given program or institution.

Application Fee. Application fees are required by almost all private institutions and more than two thirds of the public institutions in the Abernathy survey. The median fee was between $10 and $15, with a range from $5 to $25. Community colleges rarely charge application fees, and, as the college-age population declines, many nonselective four-year institutions probably will reduce or eliminate such fees.

Central Application Services. Centralized services have been established for applicants to colleges of law, medicine, and dentistry. The candidate files a single application and a copy of his or her educational records with the central agency, which provides an analysis of grades and forwards copies of the application to the institutions designated by the candidate. These systems provide an obvious advantage to the applicant and give the institution the advantage of receiving completed applications, usually with some standardized preliminary analyses, from a single source.

Simplified Procedures. Some institutions have drastically reduced, or eliminated, the use of institutional application forms. Biographical and test data referred to the college by the admissions testing company at the student's request are used as a basis for the admissions decision, greatly reducing the time and amount of paperwork required in the admissions process (American College Testing Program, 1975). In community colleges and other nonselective institutions, entry to some programs may be accomplished at the same time as registration. On a form provided, the applicant lists his previous educational experience and enrolls for one or more courses simultaneously. Evidence of previous education may, however, be required subsequently for confirmation and counseling. Moreover, even in nonselective institutions selective requirements and procedures may be used for admission to certain specialized programs which are oversubscribed.

Comprehensive Calendars

One of the most essential tasks is the development of comprehensive calendars to guide the admissions office staff and to assure that all steps necessary for office operations are identified and implemented in a timely fashion. Each step must be coordinated not only with the internal operation of the office but also with the activities of other offices and agencies involved. Planning for admissions to a particular term must begin far in advance—a year and a half for some operations, as illustrated in Exhibit 4, a general guide for fall-term admission developed by a private university.

Detailed calendars should be developed to assure that each step is completed at the proper time. An illustration of this kind of planning is provided in Exhibit 5.

A master office calendar is desirable—one that integrates the separate calendars for recruitment, internal operations, publications, and other activities. Typical entries in such a calendar (adapted from one in use at a public university) are shown in Exhibit 6. Although the list is illustrative, not complete, it shows some-

Exhibit 4. General Admission Calendar

February	• (18 months prior to the fall term concerned) Develop long-range plan, including numbers and characteristics of students desired (for example, geographical distribution, academic ability levels, financial ability levels, male/female ratio, special talents, cultural backgrounds, racial/ethnic characteristics).
	• Develop parameters for College Board Search Service requests
March	• Submit copy for initial recruitment brochures.
May	• First mailing to prospects.
June	• Staff reexamination of previous year's admissions experience.
	• Review of estimates of numbers of continuing students.
	• Appointment of staff planning committees.
July	• Reports of planning committees' analysis of past year's experience and recommendations for next year on each phase of the admissions plan (internal procedures, recruiting visits, on-campus visitations, involvement of alumni and students, college fairs, recruitment in specialized categories, research on student characteristics, interests, and retention, and design of forms, form letters, and so on).
	• Draft recruitment travel plan.
August	• Mail applications to prospective students.
	• Integrate travel plans with alumni and volunteer students.
September	• Begin travel.
October–	• Continue programming for recruitment.
November	• Process applications.
December	• General staff review of the past fall's admissions results and modification of plans for next fall as needed.
January	• Early notification decisions.
February	• Early notifications end and regular notices of admission begin.
March	• Regular notice decisions continue.
April	• Regular notice decisions completed.
	• Major "student day on campus" conducted.
May	• Candidate's reply date—May 1.
	• Decision made on waiting list cases.

Exhibit 5. Calendar for Internal Office
Procedures, University of _____ (October, 1978)

Monday, October 2	• Application analysis report to deans—fall quarter 1978.
Wednesday, October 4	• Last fall admission master file update prior to production of cumulative average data list.
Friday, October 6	• Test of English as a Foreign Language examination (students must apply by September 27).
	• Final GPA and address transfer for fall quarter 1978.
Saturday, October 7	• ACT National Test.
Tuesday, October 10	• Admission Control Center will begin to pull application for registered fall-quarter students from the central file.
Wednesday, October 11	• Admission Control Center transfers winter-quarter 1979 future file to admissions office shelves for processing.
Saturday, October 15	• Fall College-Level Examination Program general examination—Student Counseling Bureau.
Monday, October 16	• ACT Residual Test.
Friday, October 20	• Admissions Control Center completes the "registered fall 1978 application pull" and transfer of applications to Records for ledger preparation.
Monday, October 23	• Admissions Control Center future fall 1978 file to admissions office shelves for processing.
	• Receive selection index tables for winter, spring, summer, and fall 1979 from central office.
	• Open winter-quarter 1979 admission master file tapes.
	• Send requisition for placement test brochure (tentative).
Monday, October 30	• Final fall 1978 application analysis report to deans.
Tuesday, October 24	• Admissions officers begin to evaluate fall 1979 applications.
	• Complete the evaluation of transfer permits for fall 1978 (for those permits issued as temporary permits).
Thursday, October 26	• Fall-quarter 1978 admission master file tape closes.

Exhibit 6. Master Office Calendar

July
- Update admissions files.
- Prepare summer and fall admissions analysis reports.
- Send application material to duplicating.
- Freshman orientation and advising conference.
- Transfer students' orientation and advising conference.
- Requests for community college staff directory information.
- Obtain high school certification roster for fall-term freshmen.
- Letters to students with incomplete applications granted temporary admission to the summer session.
- Revise admission brochure for use in fall (for following year's admissions).
- Request items for newsletters to schools and community colleges.
- Letter to high school and community college counselors with revised brochures and an explanation of the contact system.
- Send office newsletter.
- Prepare posters for community colleges.

August
- Report on July mail.
- Prepare application packets (for admission next year).
- Mail letters to community college and transfer applicants with incomplete files for fall term.
- Prepare revised brochures for community college and high school counselors.
- Mail community college application packets to community colleges.
- Prepare acceptance letters.
- Application deadline for international students for spring semester.

September
- Report on August mail.
- College-career day/night programs.
- Plan admissions newsletters for the year; mail first issue.
- Mail brochures to special-category students identified by ACT and College Board.
- Mail information packets to high school counselors and principals.
- Mail posters to community colleges.
- Start spring-semester admissions analysis.

Exhibit 6. (Continued)

- Mail admissions brochure to sophomores in community college baccalaureate programs.
- Send list of National Merit semifinalists to dean of undergraduate studies.
- Send letters to National Merit semifinalists and commended students.

October
- Report on September mail and applications.
- College-career day/night programs.
- Prepare and distribute reports on applications received.
- Review new freshman-class profile reports.
- Final date to mail spring-semester application packets.
- Prepare grants-in-aid packets.
- Mail admissions newsletters to fall applicants.
- Spring-semester undergraduate application deadline.
- Copy for fall advising conference newsletter to printing office.
- Print fall admission analysis.
- Prepare copy for student information brochure.

November
- Report on October mail and applications.
- College-career day/night programs.
- Advising conferences for new spring-semester freshmen.
- Mail brochure to special-category students identified by ACT and College Board.
- Admissions newsletter to printing.

December
- Report on November mail and applications.
- College-career day/night programs.
- Application deadline for college of law for spring semester.
- Send notices to pending applicants for spring semester.
- Obtain mailing labels for fall applicants.
- Mail admissions newsletter to fall applicants.
- Prepare admissions analysis for spring semester.

January
- Deadline for fall applications for allied health professions.
- Report on December mail and applications.
- Prepare admissions analysis for spring semester.
- Begin weekly analysis of fall applications and admissions.
- Mail community college newsletter.
- Deadline for applications to pharmacy.

Exhibit 6. (Continued)

- Mail brochures to special-category students identified by ACT and College Board.
- Final spring-semester admissions analysis.
- Application deadline for international students for fall semester.
- List to deans of National Merit students who have applied.

February
- Report on January mail and applications.
- Application deadline for fall semester for college of architecture.
- Invite high school counselors to conference on minority students.
- Prepare and mail admissions newsletter.
- Start update of all brochures.
- Purge last fall's applicants from admissions processing file.
- Prepare labels for admitted students for next fall.
- Send letters to College Board upper-division scholarship semifinalists and honorable mentions.
- Revise "University and U" bulletin.

March
- Report on February mail and applications.
- Application deadline for college of law for fall.
- Architecture school aptitude test for fall.
- Deadline for portfolio for architecture applicants for fall.
- Mail notices to pending summer applicants.
- Prepare and mail community college newsletter.
- Application deadline for fall for college of nursing.
- Prepare summer admission analysis.
- Revise community college brochure.
- Revise brochures for transfer applicants, minority applicants.

April
- Report on March mail and applications.
- Undergraduate application deadline for summer.
- Minority student conference.
- Prepare summer admission analysis.
- Mail brochures to special-category students identified by ACT and College Board.
- Prepare and mail admissions newsletter.
- Circulate master calendar for next year for revisions.

Exhibit 6. (Continued)

- Advising conference for new summer students.
- Revise applications and send to printer.
- Notice to summer applicants with incomplete credentials.

May
- Report on April mail and applications.
- Prepare summer admission analysis.
- Prepare fall admission analysis.
- Fall deadline for undergraduate, allied health, and law transfer applications.

June
- Report on May mail and applications.
- Notice to fall "pending" applicants.
- Print summer admissions analysis.
- Print fall admissions analysis.
- Prepare list and labels for fall-admitted applicants; request final documents.

thing of the variety of activities in which the admissions office staff engages, the repetitive nature of some of these activities, and the need for internal and external coordination in developing the master calendar.

Specialized calendars for various groups should also be considered. For example, an annual calendar of the institution's admissions activities may be prepared for school counselors (see Exhibit 7).

Data Analysis

Data management and the design and development of systems in admissions and records offices are discussed in Chapters Eight and Nine, but certain specific data analysis requirements in admissions deserve emphasis here. Quantities of valuable data are available in the admissions office, but all too often these data are not assembled in meaningful form, maintained from year to year, analyzed, or presented. As a minimum, the admissions office should prepare periodic reports, by categories of students, on the numbers of applications received, the admissions decisions reached, the responses of students to acceptances, and, following registration, the yields. Analyses of the reports should include ratios of new student enrollments to applications, admissions, and intentions to enroll, as well as comparisons with previous years.

Exhibit 7. Calendar for School Counselors

University Admissions Office	Calendar	High School Counselors
September:		
Send catalogs, flyers, and counselor information to high schools.	22—Last day to register for October 18 ACT.	Advise students of simplified procedure for the university.
October:		
Send admissions newsletter to counselors and applicants.	15—Last day to apply for Spring 1976 admission. 18—ACT national test date.	Advise students who need financial aid to take ACT on or before December 13.
November:		
College day/night programs (Oct.–March).	17—Last day to register for December 13 ACT.	
December:		
Send admissions newsletter to counselors and applicants.	13—ACT national test date.	Advise students preparing for summer high school juniors Program to register for February ACT.
January:		
Visits to individual high schools (ongoing).	19—Last day to register for February 14 ACT.	Return graduation certification forms for students enrolling at the university, spring semester, 1976.
February:		
Send admissions newsletter to counselors and applicants. Send invitations to counselors for minority student conference participants.	1—Last day to apply for financial aid. 14—ACT national test date.	Advise students applying for fall to take April ACT.

Exhibit 7. (Continued)

University Admissions Office	*Calendar*	*High School Counselors*
March:	15—Last day to register for April 10 ACT.	Send names of participants in minority student conference to the university.
April: Send admissions newsletter to counselors and accepted students.	1—Last day to apply for summer 1976 admission. 9—Minority student conference. 10—ACT national test date.	Advise students that April 10 is last ACT test date for fall admission.
May: Personal contact, telephone, correspondence (ongoing).	17—Last day to register for June 12 ACT.	Remind students to refer Advanced Placement and CLEP scores to the university.
June:	1—Last day to apply for fall admission. 12—ACT national test date. 15—High school juniors register for 8-week session.	
July Send certification of graduation from high school procedure to counselors for students entering fall semester.	6–28—Summer advising conferences for new freshmen.	
August:		Send certification of graduation information to the university, indicating those who did not graduate.

Most admissions offices are expected to provide projections of future applications and enrollments. The admissions office should also obtain and analyze studies of student retention and graduation rates related to the characteristics of entering students.

The proper presentation of these basic kinds of data is important. Wherever possible, charts should be used in lieu of, or in addition to, numerical tables; and brief interpretive comments should be provided. The plan for distribution of the reports depends on the size and complexity of the institution, but the presentations should go to the administrative officer to whom the admissions director reports, to the offices closely related to admissions (such as housing, financial aid, records and registration, and student personnel), and to the admissions committee.

Office Organization and Staffing

The placement of the admissions office in the institution's organizational structure varies from campus to campus. In some small colleges, the admissions director reports directly to the president. More commonly, however, the director will be in the area of academic affairs or student affairs, usually reporting to a vice-president or vice-chancellor. In an AACRAO salary survey of admissions and records offices (Bruker, 1977, p. 7), about 38 percent of the 2,469 offices responding operated in the academic affairs area, and 34 percent operated in the student affairs area. It is difficult to demonstrate the superiority of one arrangement over the other, since there are excellent admissions programs operating in both areas. However, the determination of who should be admitted to the college is of such vital concern to those responsible for the instructional program that a theoretical argument in favor of the placement of admissions on the academic side of the institution can be made.

Internally, the admissions office should be organized to serve the college or university community, with emphasis on humanizing services to prospective students, faculty, and staff. Service is also the key word in relation to important external constituencies, such as alumni, school and community college counselors, and parents of prospective students. As the "front door" to the campus for most students, the admissions office projects the institution's image in ways that are both obvious and subtle. The location, appearance, and physical arrangement of the office give a good indication of the institution's support for the admissions activity. Careful attention should be given to the office environment to assure that the image projected is the image desired. Special consideration in office arrangements, facilities, and staffing is required for community colleges and four-year commuter institutions. Virtually all students are within commuting distance, and they can contact the admissions office by phone without charge. An extremely high volume of phone calls must be anticipated and provided for. Likewise, because they are accessible, commuter campuses have students in the office seeking information continuously. Adequate staffing and friendly service are paramount needs, since the manner in which these contacts are handled has a direct effect on enrollment and retention.

A recent analysis of an admissions office's organizational structure resulted in the following litany of problems:

1. Decentralization of work units, leading to overcompartmentalization.
2. Low staff morale and productivity.
3. High rate of staff turnover.
4. Administration by personality rather than by function.
5. Inadequate supervision of staff.
6. Overspecialization of job assignments.
7. Poor budget and inventory control.
8. Nonfunctional physical arrangements.
9. Lack of routine articulation between work units.
10. Ill-defined lines of authority and responsibility.
11. Little central direction of functions.
12. Overcomplicated procedures.

Any one of these twelve items represents a problem to be avoided; together they paint a devastating picture. To develop an organization that will reduce the possibilities for such problems, those responsible for organizing the office should first of all prepare a list of specific objectives. The list may include the following kinds of objectives: to maximize services to prospective students, their parents and counselors, and alumni; to control and conserve valuable resources—personnel, dollars, time, space, equipment, and supplies; to expedite processing of applications; to improve the ratio of admitted students to registered students; and to provide more accurate, comprehensible, and timely statistical reports. Each office should develop and periodically update its list of specific objectives. In addition, the development of a "procedures handbook" for the office will help promote consistency, ensure that essential actions are not omitted, and maintain continuity when staff turnover occurs.

Major Work Divisions

In all but the smallest offices, major work divisions should be established and different levels of supervision assigned. For example, major divisions may include admissions processing, school and college relations (recruitment), systems and development, and publications. Levels of supervision may include the director, associate directors, and assistant directors—depending on the size of the operation. The key functions of each major division should be identified. The following are illustrative:

School and College Relations
1. Development of a proposed marketing plan.
2. Development of lists of prospective students.
3. Coordination of college contacts with prospective students.
4. Information services to prospective students, parents, and counselors.
5. Visits to schools and colleges.
6. Preadmission counseling.
7. On-campus visits and conferences.

Admissions Processing
1. Processing actions on the admission and readmission of all applicants.
2. Evaluation of transfer credits.
3. Maintenance of admissions files.
4. Coding and control of applications.
5. Response to inquiries concerning status of applications.

Systems and Development
1. Data preparation.
2. Printing and reproduction service.
3. Documentation.
4. Liaison with data processing office.
5. Development and testing of office procedures.

Publications
1. Preparation and design of recruitment materials.
2. Preparation of form letters.
3. Preparation of admissions applications and other office forms.
4. Coordination of publications and letters to prospective students from other departments on the campus.

The Admissions Director

Professional Background. Professional preparation for admissions positions is not well defined or highly visible in American higher education. The survey by Vinson (1976) of 1,267 chief admissions officers in baccalaureate-degree institutions showed 17 percent with doctorates (11 percent in education), 59 percent with master's degrees (34 percent in education), and 24 percent with bachelor's degrees (5 percent in education). Vinson also found that most of the chief admissions officers (65 percent) had prior experience in admissions or college administration. Fewer than 25 percent came from teaching or from secondary school administration. Areas of study considered valuable by admissions officers and registrars were identified in a report on professional training (American Association of Collegiate Registrars and Admissions Officers, 1954) as history of education, higher education, curriculum development, secondary education, personnel management, office management, educational measurements, statistics, educational administration, public relations, counseling procedures, student personnel work, and communications. The subject rated most valuable by the Vinson study respondents was measurement and statistics. The correlation between courses taken and those considered valuable was very low in both the Vinson study and an earlier study by Hauser and Lazarsfeld (1964). Internship experience in an admissions office is an excellent method of preparation and should be included in the professional preservice program if at all possible.

Personal Qualities and Characteristics. Personal qualities are as important to success for an admissions officer as the subjects studied. In the language of the 1954 AACRAO report, "He should be able to speak and to write well, to organize work and supervise employees, to cooperate with faculty and other administrative officers. Coupled with these abilities should be certain qualities of character—emotional stability, perseverance, decisiveness, poise, good balance, charity under criticism, patience and objectivity with people—and, in adverse situations, fearlessness under pressure. He should also have an enthusiasm for completing tasks and an eagerness to undertake new ones. Finally, he should place service above all other means of personal satisfaction" (p. 13). The essential qualities of an effective admissions officer have been described by Chalmers (1975) as good judgment, public relations ability, administrative ability, and knowledge of the institution. In a lighter vein, a former director of admissions described the personal characteristics essential to success in that position as "The Shoulders of Babe the Blue Ox . . . The Oratorical Ability of Demosthenes . . . The Numerical Facility of the Wizard of Avis . . . The Optimism of a Presidential Press Secretary . . . The Patience of Job . . . The Prescience of Jeane Dixon . . ." and "The Pizzaz of P. T. Barnum" (Treadwell, 1977, p. 18).

Almost one fifth of the chief admissions officers in the Vinson study were under 30 years of age (more than half were under 40), and 82 percent were male. Over three fourths carried a title of either director or dean of admissions. About one third of the officers held academic rank, while two thirds felt that they should have rank. Overwhelmingly, the admissions officers regarded themselves as professionals. For those who thought of admissions as an occupation rather than a profession (23 percent), lack of formal training requirements was believed to be the chief barrier to becoming a profession.

The Admissions Staff

The admissions director should be responsible for the selection, assignment, and in-service training of his staff members, who will have come from a variety of educational and experiential backgrounds. A number of professional workshops for admissions officers are available, and most of them are reported in the calendar sections of the *Chronicle of Higher Education*. *Professional Audit for Admissions Officers* (Rowray and others, 1977) prepared jointly by NACAC and AACRAO, is valuable both as a workshop tool and as an excellent aid to self-examination, self-learning, and self-improvement. Attending professional meetings, reading, visiting other admissions offices in institutions that are similar to one's own, and participating in the activities of professional associations (chief among which are AACRAO, NACAC, and the College Entrance Examination Board) are all valuable. The director of admissions still carries the major responsibility for assuring the professional competence of the admissions office staff and must place staff orientation and development high on the list of priorities.

While professional staff positions below the level of chief admissions officer differ depending on the size and complexity of the operation, titles frequently used include associate and assistant directors, admissions counselors, and field representatives. Large institutions may designate assistant directors in such areas as admissions processing, articulation, systems development, administrative services, graduate admissions, minority admissions, publications, and foreign admissions. Institutions with graduate programs also find that part-time graduate assistants can perform valuable service in many areas, including the preparation of special reports, aiding visitors and guests, conducting research, and aiding in the preparation of publications. These positions may also be used as internships for graduate students interested in careers in admissions or other areas of higher education administration. Turnover in both the professional and clerical staff requires careful documentation of the responsibilities of each position. Detailed job descriptions will reduce the time required for the "breaking-in" period of new staff members and will provide a basis for evaluating performance and revising assignments as the need arises.

Typical Functions of Director and Staff

Key functions of the director of admissions include supervision of all division heads, long-range planning, development of budgets, selection and assignment of personnel, allocation of resources, in-service training, liaison with other departments and divisions of the colleges, representation of the office to the public, and evaluation. Hauser and Lazarsfeld (1964), after consulting experts in the field, identified nine typical functions of the admissions director and staff. Vinson (1976), using the same list of activities, determined, from his survey of 1,267 baccalaureate degree–granting institutions, the total level of activity devoted to each function. In descending order of activity, the functions were interviewing applicants, processing applications, school visitation, supervision and employee conferences, research, admissions office staff meetings, handling complaints, college administrative meetings, and faculty administrative meetings. The duties and responsibilities of the chief admissions officer were also examined by Vinson, who reported a shift in priorities, since the Hauser-Lazarsfeld study, from processing applications, interviewing students, and visiting high schools, to administrative and supervisory activities. A significant increase in research activity, a decline in financial aid and registration activities, and growing involvement in professional activities were also noted for the chief admissions officer.

Salaries

Salary surveys of admissions officers are conducted periodically by professional associations. In their salary survey of fifty-two college administrative positions, Malott, Wensel, and Royer (1976) reported that the median 1975–76 salary for directors of admissions was fortieth from the top. Higher medians were noted at public institutions, larger institutions, and two-year colleges. The National Association of College Admissions Counselors' salary survey of 3,894 college and university admissions officers (Yaw and Eyestone, 1975) indicated that the factors affecting total salary are institutional type, control, location, and size, and the individual's title, experience, and educational level. An AACRAO survey (Bruker, 1977) of more than 7,000 professional staff members in admissions and records offices at more than 2,000 institutions reported mean salaries by geographical region, size of institution, sex, and type of institution. Higher mean salaries were reported for larger institutions, public institutions, two-year institutions, offices reporting through Student Services, individuals at higher educational levels, and individuals with greater responsibilities. The mean salary level for men was substantially higher than that for women, overall as well as by educational level, geographical region, and level of responsibility.

Financial Aid

In the past, financial aid for undergraduate students was almost always administered in the college admissions office. With the phenomenal growth in size and complexity of the student financial aid enterprise, however, separate offices—and a specialized professional staff—have developed. While in some institutions financial aid remains a function of the admissions office and the position of director of admissions and financial aid still exists, in most colleges and universities the responsibilities have been separated. This does not, however, relieve the admissions officer of the responsibility of (1) understanding the various types and sources of financial aid and how they are administered, (2) understanding the methods of need analysis, and (3) keeping abreast of changes in the financial aid field. Such knowledge is essential in communicating accurate information to prospective students—a prime responsibility of the admissions officer.

There are three primary types of aid: grants, loans, and employment. Grants are nonrepayable gifts, which may be termed scholarships when academic records are considered. Most grants are based on financial need. Loans may come from a variety of sources, and employment may be either on campus or off campus, during the academic term or during vacation periods. Most financial aid awards today involve the "packaging" concept, in which a student receives a combination of the three types of aid to meet his or her need. For example, the student judged eligible to receive $2,050 in financial aid might receive a nonrepayable gift of $500, a loan of $750, and a part-time job paying $800, to meet the total need of $2,050 for the academic year.

Financial aid may come from several different sources: federal, state, institutional, or private. The federal programs include

Basic Educational Opportunity Grants (BEOG), for which the student applies directly, and three campus-based programs (Supplemental Educational Opportunity Grants, College Work-Study, and National Direct Student Loan), for which the student applies through the college financial aid office. The federal government also sponsors the Guaranteed Student Loan Program (GSL), under which a student applies directly to a GSL agency, usually a local bank. Specialized federal aid programs in the health professions include the Health Professions Loan Program, First Year Scholarships for Exceptional Financial Need Students, Health Education Act Loans, National Health Service Corps Scholarships, the Armed Forces Scholarship Program, and the Nurse Training Act Loan Program and Scholarship Program. Federal financial aid is also available to students in law enforcement training through the Law Enforcement Education Program.

State scholarship programs have increased rapidly in number and size. In 1976–77, for example, forty-six states and the District of Columbia offered scholarship/grant programs based on financial need to students attending public or private institutions, with awards totaling more than $640 million. Private sources ranging from local garden clubs to major industries supply an almost infinite variety of scholarships, prizes, grants, and loans. The financial aid office is a good source of information on those programs available locally.

Institutional programs generally include all three types of financial aid. While emphasis on need-based aid remains strong, there is some evidence of a resurgence of interest in "merit" scholarships, unrelated to financial need, as a means of enhancing the attractiveness of the institution to outstanding prospective students. Need-based aid continues to be an essential feature of the various programs of recruitment of disadvantaged, low-income students.

Determination of financial need—once the responsibility of a "director of scholarships" who attempted to base judgments on scanty, unverified data—has become a large-scale, complex enterprise engaging economists, statisticians, sociologists, government planners, and legislators. The way in which need is determined has, in fact, become an issue of public policy. The President, both houses of Congress, legislative staff members, the Office of Management and Budget, and the Department of Health, Education and Welfare were all participants in the recent struggle to determine methods and amounts of aid to students from middle-income families, and this controversy has been generated, at least in part, by the need-analysis systems now in use.

Two major need-analysis services—the College Scholarship Service of the College Entrance Examination Board and the American College Testing Program's need-analysis program—supply colleges and universities with estimates of the amounts that parents can be expected to contribute, based on information supplied by students and their parents. In addition to CSS and ACT, the federal government specifies the system to be used in determining the financial need of Basic Grant applicants, and some of the state scholarship programs have their own unique systems. Progress is being made, however, in securing agreement on a single need-analysis system, as well as a common application form, both of which will simplify the process for students and institutions alike. In all the systems, attention is given to family income and assets, the student's earnings, and special circumstances such as working mothers, siblings, and extraordinary expenses. The difference between college expenses (including room and board) and what can reasonably be expected in the way of financial support from the parents and the student is termed "unmet cost," which the financial aid office then attempts to meet through a combination of types and sources of aid. Special need-analysis systems are designed for "independent students" and married students.

The critical importance of financial aid to the admissions process is underlined by the fact that, for many students, the decision to attend an institution is dependent on the timing, amount, and type of financial aid available. Because of the complexity and rapidly changing nature of the field, some financial aid directors may be tempted to suggest that "all the admissions office needs to know about financial aid is the phone number of the financial aid office." But some financial aid background and understanding are essential in presenting the institution's program to a prospective student.

Perspective on Financial Aid, published by the College Scholarship Service (1975), supplies background information of value to admissions officers. Fourteen leaders in the field contributed essays about various financial aid topics, including reports on federal and state programs and the role and function of financial aid officers. For those admissions officers who desire more specific information, Tombaugh (1977) has written a comprehensive handbook for financial aid administrators, with an excellent bibliography and many supplementary training and reference materials; an annotated inventory of federal and other national financial aid programs; a directory of federal, regional, and state financial aid programs; and other useful resources. The American College Testing Program (1978) publishes a loose-leaf *Handbook for Financial Aid Administrators* with current information on a variety of programs, a history of financial aid, and sections on aid administration and management. The National Association of Student Financial Aid Administrators (n.d.) has issued a *Statement of Good Practices* containing guidelines for ethical conduct in this field.

In institutions with separate financial aid and admissions offices, the need for close and cordial working relationships between the two is paramount. Admissions officers must be aware of the financial aid possibilities for prospective students at all times, and financial aid officers must be informed about admissions policies, prospects, and procedures. Especially in larger institutions, regularly scheduled interoffice staff meetings or designated staff liaison positions may be desirable.

Financial aid for graduate students in the form of fellowships and research or teaching assistantships is almost universally administered by the graduate school, although loans to graduate students may be administered by the financial aid office. Financial need analysis is not normally a part of the aid process at the graduate or professional school level, where awards are made primarily on the basis of student ability and promise.

Internal Institutional Relations

The admissions office both depends on and provides services to a wide array of other offices and audiences in the institution. Careful attention to the lines of communication and the day-to-day working relationships with these offices and audiences will promote efficiency, effectiveness, and a pleasant working environment. Offices with which admissions must work very closely include (in addition to financial aid) records and registration, housing, student affairs, business affairs, athletics, data processing, public relations, academic affairs, and alumni. Contacts with the faculty (often through committee service) are essential to the maintenance of mutual understanding and support; contacts with students are essential to an understanding of their experiences and points of view, important to the recruitment process; and contacts with the academic advising system—and with the legal counsel's office—may also be necessary. To put it simply, the admissions office cannot perform any of its functions effectively if it finds itself in isolation from—or in conflict with—other offices and audiences in the institution.

Summary

In this chapter, attention has been focused on the operational functions of the college admissions office in the United States. Emphasis has been given to the substantial differences in institutional procedures, reflecting differences in type, control, size, tradition, and degree of selectivity. Nevertheless, the basic operations of an admissions office are applicable to all colleges and universities. The twelve functions identified in this chapter are listed below by major area of responsibility.

Student Contact and Recruitment
1. To understand marketing concepts and processes and help to inform others of their importance; and to know the institution, including its strengths and weaknesses, goals and objectives, programs, activities, costs, financial aids, and admissions expectations and procedures.
2. To know the prospective student market and those specific segments of the market where recruitment activities are likely to yield the best results.
3. To develop a plan for recruitment that includes those strategies and techniques found to be the most effective in serving both students and the institution.

4. To implement the recruitment plan, evaluate its effectiveness, and revise future plans accordingly.
5. To emphasize the importance of improved retention, as well as recruitment, in maintaining desired levels of enrollment.
6. To develop and maintain good communications and effective working relationships with the institutions and agencies from which prospective students come.

Admissions Procedures

7. To select those admissions procedures that will be most convenient for the student and most effective for the institution (including cost-effectiveness), to describe them clearly in all admissions materials, to implement them, and to review them carefully for changes that will improve both their convenience and effectiveness.
8. To collect, analyze, and present data on the numbers and characteristics of applicants and on the rates of attrition from applications to acceptances to enrollments; to project applications and enrollments; and to analyze follow-up data on student retention and graduation rates.

Admissions Staff and Organization

9. To assemble, orient, train, and motivate a professional and support staff adequate in qualifications and numbers to accomplish the admissions goals and objectives of the institution; and to recommend a budget and maintain an office environment that facilitate rather than impede such an accomplishment.

Financial Aid

10. To assure that all admissions officers have a working knowledge of the principles, types, and sources of financial aid and the methods of need analysis, and an ability to convey accurate information about financial aid opportunities and procedures to prospective students; further, if the admissions and financial aid offices are separate, to assure coordination and good working relationships between the two.

Internal Institutional Relations
  11.   To maintain close and cooperative working relations
        with other offices and audiences in the institution.

Further Reading and Study (see next section)
  12.   To encourage reading of professional literature, and to
        encourage participation in professional organizations,
        by all admissions officers.

Further Reading and Study

Two essential components of on-the-job learning are reading
in the professional literature and contacts with others in the field.
Some of the basic periodicals and books, and several important
professional organizations, are described below.

Publications

Chronicle of Higher Education, published weekly except for the first
      two weeks of June and the last two weeks of August and
      December, by Editorial Projects for Education, Inc., a non-
      profit corporation, contains timely, comprehensive informa-
      tion on current happenings in higher education, including a
      calendar of coming events and a "bulletin board" of position
      vacancies. (1717 Massachusetts Ave. N.W., Washington, D.C.
      20036.)
College and University, the journal of the American Association of
      Collegiate Registrars and Admissions Officers, published
      quarterly by the Association, contains articles on topics of
      interest in college admissions, records, registration, financial
      aid, and institutional research. (One Dupont Circle, Wash-
      ington, D.C. 20036).
College Board Review, published quarterly by the College Entrance
      Examination Board, contains articles on basic issues and cur-
      rent topics of interest to admissions and financial aid officers.
      (College Board Publications Order, Box 2815, Princeton,
      New Jersey 08540.)
Journal of Student Financial Aid, published three times each year
      by the National Association of Student Financial Aid Ad-

ministrators, provides issue-oriented articles by experienced
financial aid administrators. (910 Seventeenth St. N.W.,
Washington, D.C. 20006.)

National ACAC Journal, published quarterly by the National Association of College Admissions Counselors, emphasizes articles
of interest in college admissions and financial aid counseling
at both the secondary school and college levels. (9933 Lawler
Ave., Suite 500, Skokie, Illinois 60076.)

Basic references, which should be available in an admissions office (in addition to the one you are reading), include the
following:

Astin, A. W. *Preventing Students from Dropping Out.* San Francisco:
Jossey-Bass, 1975. With access to the results of nationwide
surveys of undergraduate students, the author presents an
analysis and report of why students drop out and provides a
comprehensive set of recommendations for improving
retention.

College Entrance Examination Board. *A Role for Marketing in College Admissions.* New York: College Entrance Examination
Board, 1976. The four papers constituting this report ("The
Future Market for College Education," "Applying Marketing
Theory to College Admissions," "The Positioning Era: Marketing Strategy," and "Using Research in Analyzing Student
Markets: A Case Study") provide an excellent view of the
marketing approach and include enough "how-to" information to be of direct practical use.

Knowles, A. S. (Ed.). *Handbook of College and University Administration.* Vol. 2: *Academic.* New York: McGraw-Hill, 1970. Different authors describe operating procedures and practices
in the major areas of college administration, including
admissions.

Menacker, J. *From School to College: Articulation and Transfer.*
Washington, D.C.: American Council on Education, 1975. A
comprehensive examination of the full range of school-
college articulation concerns is presented by the author, a
former coordinator of school-college relations.

Rowray, R. D., and others. *Professional Audit for Admissions Officers.* Washington, D.C.: American Association of Collegiate Registrars and Admissions Officers; Skokie, Ill.: National Association of College Admissions Counselors, 1977. Designed for use as a self-evaluation instrument for admissions officers, the *Professional Audit* provides a comprehensive checklist of the skills, knowledge, responsibilities, and current issues in admissions. It is an invaluable tool for professional personnel development.

Vinson, D. E. *The Admissions Officer: A Decade of Change.* Dissertation Copy 77–08, 122. Ann Arbor, Mich.: University Microfilms, 1976. Vinson's dissertation is especially valuable for the new admissions officer or others who wish to learn more about the current status of the field. The study updates Hauser and Lazarsfeld's 1964 report, *The Admissions Officer,* and details the changing role, function, and background of admissions officers at four-year institutions. Included are sections on the personal characteristics, education, attitudes, status, duties, and responsibilities of admissions officers; the functions and operations of the admissions office; and new developments in the field.

Professional Organizations

Participation in professional organizations is a major resource for in-service training and motivation. Attendance at professional meetings and committee service at the regional and, if possible, the national level should be encouraged and supported. The dividends are substantial in terms of interinstitutional contacts, awareness of new developments in the field, and the discovery of new solutions to common problems. There are five primary professional associations serving admissions officers:

American Association of Collegiate Registrars and Admissions Officers (AACRAO). One Dupont Circle, Suite 330, Washington, D.C. 20036. (202) 293-9161. Founded in 1910, AACRAO is comprised of nearly 2,000 colleges and universities represented by more than 6,800 active members from offices of admissions, records and registration, financial aid, and institutional research. Activities include holding an annual meeting; publishing a professional journal *(College and University)*, a newsletter, and special bulletins, pamphlets, and reports; promoting regional associations of registrars, admissions directors, and related officers; conducting research; establishing committees to give attention to current problems and concerns; and providing a placement service. The Vinson (1976) study indicated that 80 percent of the 1,267 chief admissions officers surveyed in four-year institutions hold membership in AACRAO.

College Entrance Examination Board. 888 Seventh Ave., New York, New York 10019. (212) 582-6210. The College Board, founded in 1900, is a nonprofit membership organization of more than 2,000 colleges and universities, secondary schools, school systems, and educational associations offering a wide variety of measurement, evaluation, information, and advisory services to students and institutions. Membership eligibility requirements for institutions of higher education include regular and substantial use of one or more of the board's programs. Major activities are the Admissions Testing Program (including the Scholastic Aptitude Test), the College Scholarship Service, the College-Level Examination Program, the Decision-Making Program, the Advanced Placement Program, and numerous publications and research activities.

National Association for Foreign Student Affairs (NAFSA). 1860 Nineteenth St. N.W., Washington, D.C. 20009. (202) 462-4811. NAFSA is a professional association of institutions and individuals engaged in the field of international student exchange. Founded in 1948, the association has both institutional and individual members and conducts national and regional conferences, workshops, seminars, publications, and special services. NAFSA has five professional-interest sections (admissions officers, advisers to foreign students and scholars, advisers to United States students going abroad, community programmers, and teachers of English as a second language) and is divided into twelve geographical regions.

National Association of College Admissions Counselors (NACAC).

9933 Lawler Ave., Skokie, Illinois 60076. (312) 676-0500.
NACAC was established in 1937 as an association of colleges,
secondary schools, and educational organizations concerned
with admissions and financial aid. Now numbering more than
2,200 institutions and organizations, NACAC focuses on
school-to-college articulation, interinstitutional relations, and
counseling. Publishing a professional journal *(National ACAC
Journal)* and newsletter, conducting an annual meeting, encouraging regional association activities, and sponsoring college fairs in major metropolitan areas are among the associations activities. According to Vinson (1976), 67 percent of the
1,267 chief admissions officers surveyed are members of
NACAC.

National Association of Student Financial Aid Administrators
(NASFAA). 910 Seventeenth St. N.W., Suite 228, Washington, D.C. 20006. (202) 785-0453. NASFAA is a nonprofit
corporation of postsecondary institutions and other individuals, agencies, and students promoting the effective administration of student financial aid. It was founded in 1966 as
an outgrowth of six regional associations. Activities include a
monthly newsletter, a triannual *Journal of Student Financial
Aid,* an annual meeting, a national placement service, and a
variety of training activities. The association also works with
congressional staff and federal departments and agencies on
the development of legislation, regulations, and guidelines
affecting student assistance programs.

□ □ □ □ □ □ □ 4

Administering the Office of Academic Records and Registrar

□ □ □ □ □ □ □ □ □ □ □ □ □ □ □ □ □

C. James Quann

As one of the principal administrators of any institution, the registrar is responsible for a variety of functions related to the academic program. Subsequent chapters discuss several of these responsibilities in detail, including building the master schedule (Chapter Five), conducting registration and preparing the catalog (Chapter Six), and organizing and maintaining student records (Chapter Seven). Although the specific activities of the registrar's office may vary greatly among institutions, within this wide range of responsibilities the registrar interacts with students, faculty, alumni, the governing board of the institution, and state and federal agencies. This chapter delineates the relations of the registrar to these internal groups and external agencies, with special emphasis on the

115

operation of the registrar's and records office in developing and executing the policies of the faculty. (Throughout this chapter and later chapters, the terms *registrar, registrar's office,* and *records office* are used interchangeably to refer to the same office.)

Internal Relationships and Responsibilities

The registrar provides indispensable services to students and faculty, operating under the implied contract assumed by the institution to maintain timely and accurate records of the academic progress and accomplishment of its students. Students are therefore entitled to efficient and responsive treatment in course scheduling, registration, course enrollment changes, grade reporting and transcript service, and to full and complete access to their academic records. As a corollary, the registrar's office is obligated to inform students of their rights, responsibilities, and procedures, so that they may proceed toward their academic goals without undue administrative interference. Conversely, students are responsible for acting in conformance with the information and procedures provided. Peterson (1970, p. 260) develops the concept of the institution's contractual obligations to its students and suggests that catalog statements spell out as well as limit these obligations.

The paramount goal of the registrar's office is to serve the students and faculty promptly, equitably, and courteously. Specifically, the registrar gives essential administrative support to the faculty to assist them in their instructional and advisory responsibilities, provides record-keeping services for the faculty, interprets rules and policies, furnishes factual data, and generally assists faculty in the discharge of their academic duties. In addition, the registrar is usually responsible for publishing the master schedule of classes and associated publications and may also serve as editor of the official bulletin or catalog. These responsibilities relate not only to the college or university community but to prospective students and the public at large. In a legal sense, all pertinent policies, requirements, rules, and procedures concerning academic matters should be incorporated in these publications.

As a principal administrative officer, the registrar advises the vice-president or president and other chief officers of the institution, providing reports, analyses, and recommendations and assisting with policy formulation. To ensure compatibility, the registrar should also provide a link between the faculty governing unit and the central administration in the development of administrative and academic policies. Academic policies are set by the faculty or whatever governance structure is in operation, and it is the registrar's role to facilitate or implement those policies. The registrar's authority is derived principally by delegation from the vice-president or dean, although other sources of authority apply in specific areas. Establishment of fees, granting of degrees, and other major policies usually require final approval through the board of regents or trustees. Academic rules, regulations, and the instructional calendar are usually recommended by the faculty and approved by the president and board. Since the registrar is usually responsible for the interpretation and enforcement of the academic rules and regulations of the institution, the registrar usually advises the faculty and administration and assists in the research and development of the various academic policies and statutes. The registrar often serves as executive secretary or secretary to the key academic and instructional committees and commissions of the institution. As an adjunct to the lines of authority within the college or university, the registrar is guided by the ethical standards and policies of the American Association of Collegiate Registrars and Admissions Officers (AACRAO). Through the publications of this organization and its regional affiliates, the registrar keeps up to date with national norms and practices in the conduct of office affairs.

Because the registrar's office as an administrative post lies at the heart of a complex academic enterprise, the registrar is in an excellent position to provide academic support services to the faculty and central administration. The registrar should serve on those institutional committees that are concerned with academic policies and procedures, and, as mentioned earlier, the registrar may also serve as secretary of the faculty. The position of secretary—or "scribe," as it was called in medieval universities—carries with it the duty of preparing and maintaining the official minutes or proceedings of faculty or other deliberative bodies. The registrar also normally serves as a member of the institution's cur-

riculum committee. These multifaceted responsibilities are beneficial to the college or university and the faculty, since the registrar
also has responsibilities in other related areas, such as the interpretation and enforcement of academic rules and regulations. Thus, as
items are discussed in faculty or committee meetings, the registrar,
with broad-ranging experience in academic and faculty matters,
can provide the necessary background information to "brief"
faculty and students on the issues at hand, and thereby prevent the
reinvention of the academic wheel each time a subject comes up.

Serving as a member of the curriculum committee, or as an
academic screening agent before curricular items are considered,
the registrar can make sure that curricular requests are submitted
properly and do not duplicate course work already being offered
by other departments. For instance, when evaluating a petition for
approval of a new course, the registrar will check to see that some
or all of the following are indicated in the prescribed manner: (1)
department identification (prefix) and course number, (2) course
title and title abbreviation for catalog entry, (3) course description
(usually limited to a set number of words), (4) rationale submitted
in support of the course petition, (5) semester(s) or quarter(s) the
course is to be offered, (6) course prerequisites (if any), (7) identification of instructor, (8) credit- and contact-hour ratio.

Proper credit- and contact-hour ratios are crucial to the
maintenance of academic standards, and the registrar—serving as
an academic officer, editor of the catalog, and/or custodian of the
course master file—must ensure that all courses meet the requirements of the institution.

Because of their experience in and responsibility for academic
affairs, registrars also provide services to other academic units, and
they should and often do hold membership in or serve as resource
people for standing committees or ad hoc groups with jurisdiction
over matters pertaining to the registrar's function. Certainly the
registrar should serve on any committee or group studying
academic standards, grading systems, scheduling, retention requirements, or commencement. And it would be foolhardy, if not
dangerous, to make calendar decisions without involving the registrar. Similarly, institutions are constantly involved in self-study, and

the registrar can and should provide much of the data for analysis of academic departments and programs. Simply put, registrars are usually responsible for the institution's academic records as well as students' records, and their knowledge, experience, and expertise make them invaluable resource people.

External Relationships and Responsibilities

Beyond relations with other institutions and with former students regarding transcripts (discussed in Chapter Seven), primary external relationships of the registrar's office involve accrediting agencies and state and federal agencies.

Accrediting Agencies

Accreditation, the process of evaluating the academic qualifications or standards of an institution or a program of study, is a service provided largely through nongovernmental voluntary institutional or professional associations. These associations establish criteria, visit and evaluate institutions and programs, and approve those that meet the established criteria. Institutional accreditation is provided by one of the regional accrediting commissions of the various associations of schools and colleges or by an appropriate national association. Specialized or programmatic accreditation is performed by a number of national organizations, each representing a professional or specialized area or discipline. A complete list of the various accrediting agencies recognized by the Council on Postsecondary Education (COPE) is contained in Appendix B.

When visiting an institution, an accreditation team will wish to review key records maintained by the registrar and will also evaluate the registrar's standard record-keeping procedures and practices. Typical procedures and records subject to review include, but are not limited to, the following:

1. Permanent academic records of students. (Reviewers normally check a sample group of these records for uniform and consistent record-keeping practices and procedures.)

2. The institution's academic rules and policies. (The responsibility for interpreting these academic rules and regulations usually resides with the registrar.)
3. Statistical reports issued each term, including enrollment by term and year for each department and program, summer session enrollment by department and class, enrollment information for the extension or continuing education division, and the number of graduating students by department and level.
4. Official minutes of the faculty and other units of governance, including the minutes of key curriculum committees and commissions.

State, Federal, and Professional
Data Gathering Agencies

State appropriations for public institutions often depend on official enrollment statistics provided by the registrar; similarly, regional and federal allocation programs are often based on data provided by registrars of both private and public institutions of postsecondary education. Local and state reports should be scheduled on a monthly or term basis. Various federal reports, such as those required by the Department of Health, Education and Welfare under the aegis of the annual Higher Education General Information Survey (HEGIS), are due each year at precise time intervals and may be scheduled in advance. Other reports are occasional in nature and are more difficult to anticipate. To help registrars plan in advance to meet the various federal reporting commitments, an abbreviated schedule of national and federal reports due annually is listed in Table 1.

Selective Service. Prior to 1972 the registrar's office normally processed Selective Service forms for male students seeking to maintain deferments for college attendance. While the drafting or conscription of students into the military service is inactive at this writing, readers should keep in mind that the Selective Service Act has not been repealed but is merely lying dormant. If the draft is reinstated, registrars should be prepared to reinstate Selective Service procedures: preparing and filing Selective Service forms with the various agencies (draft boards); serving as the institutional liaison for Selective Service; and notifying students of regulations, dates and locations for physical examinations, and related information.

Veterans Administration. In 1966 the United States Congress enacted the Veterans Readjustment Benefits Act of 1966 (Public Law 89-358), popularly known as the "Vietnam GI Bill." This law was further amplified on October 15, 1976, by passage of the Veterans Education and Employment Assistance Act of 1976 (Public Law 94-502), and again in 1977 with approval of the GI Bill Improvement Act of 1977 (Public Law 95-202). These public laws, together with other existing legislation, were established to provide educational benefits to veterans and to the children and spouses of totally disabled or deceased veterans. These benefits are administered under the following chapters of Title 38 of the U.S. Code: Chapter 31 covers those on the VA Vocational Rehabilitation program, Chapter 32 governs post-Vietnam veterans (those who initially entered military service on or after January 1, 1977), Chapter 34 pertains to Vietnam veterans (those who initially entered the service on or before December 31, 1976), and Chapter 35 covers the Survivors' and Dependents' Educational Assistance program (formerly termed War Orphans' and Widows' Educational Assistance).

Congress has established a final cutoff date of December 31, 1989, for Vietnam-era veterans to use Chapter 34 benefits. Chapter 32 benefits (for post-Vietnam veterans) are provided through a voluntary contributory-matching program, whereby the serviceperson contributes to his or her educational benefit fund while on active duty and these contributions are then matched 2 to 1 by the federal government. Details of implementing disbursal of these funds after the veteran's release from active duty and enrollment in a postsecondary institution are not yet available but should be forthcoming from the VA in the future.

Since the registrar's office serves as the custodian of student records, and is normally the only office that can certify enrollments, the registrar is frequently assigned responsibility for veterans affairs. When this occurs, the duties are usually delegated to a supervisor or coordinator, who serves on behalf of the registrar. As the primary intermediary between the Veterans Administration

Table 1. National and Federal Reports Due Annually

Report Title	Date Due	Requesting Agency	Address of Agency
ACT special report, annual article on enrollment	Oct. 15	Office for Enrollment Policy and Educational Research	University of Cincinnati Cincinnati, Ohio 45221
Fall enrollment in institutions of higher education (HEGIS 2300–2.3)[a]	Oct. 15	Department of Health, Education and Welfare	Education Division Washington, D.C. 20202
Upper-division and postbaccalaureate enrollment by degree field (HEGIS 2300–2.9)	Nov. 30	Department of Health, Education and Welfare	Education Division Washington, D.C. 20202
Opening fall enrollment	Dec. 8	National Association of State Universities and Land-Grant Colleges	Office of Research and Information Suite 710, 1 Dupont Circle, NW Washington, D.C. 20036
Fall enrollment and compliance report at institutions of higher education (HEGIS 2300–2.3, alternate years)	Dec. 15	Department of Health, Education and Welfare	Education Division Washington, D.C. 20202
Survey of scientific activities of institutions of higher education, current and capital expenditures for research, development, and instruction in science and engineering	Jan. 15	National Science Foundation	Division of Science Resources Studies Washington, D.C. 20550
Survey of science and engineering personnel employed at universities and colleges	March 1	National Science Foundation	Division of Science Resources Studies Washington, D.C. 20550
Degrees and other formal awards conferred between July 1 and June 30 (HEGIS 2300–2.1)	Aug. 15	Department of Health, Education and Welfare	Education Division Washington, D.C. 20202

Summer sessions joint questionnaire and statistical report	Oct. 14	North American Association of Summer Sessions (NAASS) and others	Division of Computer Services Alfred University Alfred, N.Y. 14802
Estimated total enrollment	June 1	National Association of College Stores	528 E. Lorain St. Oberlin, Ohio 44074
Institutional characteristics (HEGIS 2300–1)	July 15	Department of Health, Education and Welfare	Education Division Washington, D.C. 20202

aHigher Education General Information Survey.

(VA) and students eligible to receive VA educational benefits, the coordinator of veterans affairs has the twofold responsibility of (1) providing the information and services required for students to receive these benefits and (2) making timely and accurate reports to the Veterans Administration concerning these students as required by law.

The VA coordinator must have a thorough understanding of both the institution's academic rules and policies and the regulations of the VA, so that he or she can integrate the two into a cohesive set of standards for implementation. Clear and concise explanations of the VA regulations as they are applied at the institution should be made available to the students, since they must understand that it is their responsibility to keep the institution's VA office informed of any changes in their status.

In order for the institution to meet the reporting requirements of the VA, the VA coordinator must have access to the following types of information:

Student identification data:
  Name
  Address
  Phone
  Student ID Number
  Social Security Number

Admission data:
  Degree program for which the student has been admitted
  Credit granted for previous training or schooling to be applied toward graduation

Enrollment data:
  Course schedule
  Credit hours to be earned per class
  Repeat course work, if any
  Changes in student status and the effective date of the change:
    Additions to course schedule
    Withdrawals from course work
    Changes in credit load, such as a change from credit to audit

> Cancellations of enrollment, both voluntary and administrative
>
> Changes in the student's academic major

Final grades:
> Term and cumulative grade point averages
>
> Identification of VA students receiving failing and incomplete grades
>
> Identification of VA students placed on academic probation or academically dismissed

Enrollment statistics for each term:
> Overall statistics:
>> Total number of students enrolled who are receiving VA benefits
>>
>> Total student body enrollment
>
> By major:
>> Number of VA students enrolled, by academic major
>>
>> Total number of students enrolled, by academic major

Starting in 1976, the Veterans Administration initiated new procedures designed to curb the growing problem of overpayments made to veterans enrolled in postsecondary education. These procedures surfaced in the form of directives from the Department of Veterans Benefits (DVB) requiring educational institutions to tighten policies affecting students receiving VA benefits. Examples include Unsatisfactory Progress (DVB·Circular 20-76-84, Appendix O, Public Law 94-502) and Reporting of Nonpunitive Grades (DVB Circular 20-76-84, Appendix M). Educational institutions are now required to review individual student records to determine whether the student will finish his or her course of study within the approved length of the student's academic program; they must also keep records of previous education and training, projected graduation dates, credit hours of enrollment as they relate to clock hours of attendance, withdrawals (including last dates of attendance), and reenrollment for any course previously taken. Institutions must also promptly notify the Veterans Administration of changes in credit hours and terminations which may affect benefits.

Institutions are also required to monitor the number of veteran students enrolled in any given course of study in relation to the number of nonveterans enrolled in the same course or program. This stipulation is set forth in Extended 85-15 Percent Ratio Requirements (DVB Circular 20-76-84, Appendix H). Different types of training (such as undergraduate resident training, graduate resident courses, research in absentia, independent study, cooperative training, and other practical training) must also be determined and reported.

The Veterans Administration has also changed the payment procedures. Previous VA policy allowed individual prepayments and advance payments to make it easier for the veteran to begin training. This liberal policy resulted in vast amounts of overpayments to students who collected advance or prepayments but failed to remain enrolled. Therefore, in June 1977 prepayments were eliminated and restricted advance payments were begun for those veterans specifically requesting them. To qualify to receive an advance payment, the eligible recipient must make his or her request by signing an "advance-pay" request. This advance payment represents one month's benefits paid at the beginning of the month rather than at the end of the month, which is now customary. After the initial advance payment has been received, the student then receives payments at the end of each month. Thus, because of poor record-keeping practices by some institutions and abuse by some veterans, all institutions and all veterans are now under very strict VA regulations with respect to academic progress and payment procedures.

Office Management

Every organization operates toward achieving certain goals or objectives. One of the major responsibilities of a registrar, in addition to meeting the overall objectives of the college or university, is to manage the office in an efficient and effective manner. In this connection, several imperatives are worth mentioning.

A well-trained staff is an effective staff. Techniques and procedures employed by registrars differ even more than their duties and responsibilities. What worked for one's predecessor may not work for the newcomer. Although tremendously important, the techniques utilized are secondary to the principle of service that must dominate every activity of the registrar's office (Mahn, 1949, p. 241). Often the first and perhaps the only contact a parent or concerned citizen has with the institution is with the registrar's office. In the public's view—students, faculty, alumni, taxpayers—the staff "speak" for the institution. The total staff should be *trained* as representatives of, or spokesmen for, the college or university.

The effective manager holds frequent but short staff meetings as a method of in-service training, to solicit ideas and suggestions from the staff, and to keep the office apprised of faculty actions, new developments, and professional topics. The registrar should see that staff members are adequately motivated and know what is expected of them—including a basic understanding of the duties and responsibilities of their office colleagues and those of the management. This is best achieved through the development of comprehensive job descriptions and manuals or workbooks for each position in the office. The job descriptions should list major responsibilities in summary form, much like those listed in Chapter One, and proceed to cover in detail the duties and expectations of each position. These might be listed in procedural form in chronological order in each workbook, starting with the opening of fall term. Flow diagrams, routing procedures, and required forms should also be included, so that a new employee can perform an appropriate task with minimal supervision. The office or area supervisor should see that the information in each staff member's workbook is current and accurate. This updating procedure is helpful in several ways: it ensures accuracy in day-to-day operations and encourages evaluation of procedures; it promotes in-service training for the clerical staff; and it keeps the professional staff and supervisors abreast of the duties and responsibilities of their subordinates.

Registraring, like farming, requires the performance of continuing as well as repetitive tasks, and the effective manager recognizes the value of prior planning and job scheduling. Well-planned and organized office calendars or schedules provide advance notice of impending deadlines and completion dates. Sharing schedules with service groups, such as systems and computing or the printing office, is crucial. These supporting agencies often complete or partially complete a job process which is the prime responsibility of the registrar. Helping other involved offices plan and meet their commitments in turn assures timely output and on-schedule operations for the registrar.

Unlike many administrative officers of colleges and universities, the registrar has major duties and tasks to perform that cannot be delayed or tabled. A registration that fails paralyzes the entire institution. Grades or transcripts not released on time may prevent subsequent enrollments, financial aid dispersal, admission to graduate or professional schools, and employment. Without well-developed office procedures and schedules, the registrar's role becomes a series of reactions to crises and deadlines imposed from outside. Since good planning is a critical ingredient in effective management, a "sample" office schedule is provided here. The schedule, shown in Exhibit 1, is designed on the early semester calendar, the most popular academic calendar in use today. The examples are illustrative only, and can be adjusted to fit into any calendar scheme. Summer schedules are omitted due to the great variety in summer session calendars.

Exhibit 1. Office Schedule, Early Semester Calendar
Fall Semester

July:
1. Conduct registration for new freshmen, graduate students, transfer students, and returning former students.
2. Prepare demand analysis report for distribution to chairpersons for revision before scheduling.
3. Coordinate scheduling and billing of students for fall semester.
4. Call a registration planning meeting to set the stage for fall registration. Key supervisors from the office as well as systems personnel meet to establish the various registration schedules, assign work loads, and coordinate the start of a new academic year. Arrangements are made with Physical Plant for necessary support services.

August:
1. Arrange for part-time registration workers and submit necessary personnel action forms through proper channels.
2. Send a memo to deans and department and program chairpersons and advisers regarding fall registration procedures and deadlines. Emphasize deadline for final time schedule (schedule of classes) updates to be sent to the registrar.

3. Distribute appropriate drop/add and other registration and post-registration materials to the departments and deans as necessary. If formats have been changed, request that departments destroy old materials. (Note: if formats change on an annual basis, be sure that new cards or forms carry the appropriate dates in bold type.)
4. Update class schedule and order printing of class schedule supplement for distribution to students and faculty.
5. Conduct registration and fee collection according to prearranged plan. Distribute student class schedules prior to the start of classes.
6. Send preliminary class enrollment figures to departments.
7. Classes start; and registration adjustment period begins (drop/add). Late registration begins.
8. Conduct registration for off-campus satellite programs as required. Continue in September as necessary.
9. Complete evaluation check for summer session graduates, post degrees, and mail diplomas.
10. Request that Administrative Services purge student information system files for previous academic year and summer session for inactive students who have not attended in the last two semesters.
11. Prepare and distribute night examination schedule and send copy to Physical Plant for night classroom use.

September:
1. Prepare fall enrollment reports for local and state distribution. (In many states legislative funding is based on these reports.)
2. Prepare and distribute class rosters to departments and programs following close of late registration and end of enrollment adjustment period (drop/add).
3. Produce internal set of student schedules for daily updating. (No attempt was made to hand-post enrollment changes made by students during the first two weeks of the term; now that the bulk of the activity is over, one up-to-date set of schedules is printed, with all subsequent drops and adds and other enrollment changes hand-posted to internal schedules before computer processing.) If computer output to microfilm (COM) is available, update the registration files daily or weekly and produce microfilm copies for the users of the registration course file each week. Also produce a registration transaction report, listing all changes to student registrations for internal use.
4. Edit computer printouts of ineligible pass/fail enrollments, unpaid fees, and other exceptional enrollments as necessary, and take appropriate action.
5. Send overload notices to departments and programs, listing all students enrolled for credit hours in excess of institutional limit. Send students notification of excess hours of registration.
6. Edit records of all currently enrolled students for grade changes and necessary record updates. Change incompletes to "F" according to institutional policy on the removal of incomplete grades; notify students and departments as appropriate.

7. Update academic record files (transcript), removing inactive records from active files.
8. Prepare academic records for all newly enrolled students; post personal and academic data either manually or by computer.
9. Prepare computer printout of students from previous term who did not enroll for current term. Send copy to cognizant departments for purging of departmental record files.
10. Request determination of summer teaching allocations in preparation of the next summer schedule.

October:
1. Send notices and/or grade cards or sheets for midterm grades if appropriate.
2. Microfilm current academic record file for security purposes and store film off campus.
3. Process midterm grade reports if applicable. Send deficiency warnings to students and faculty advisers.
4. Prepare fall-term census report, listing course enrollments within departments and programs by sex, total, percent of total, total student credit hours, and summary information (statistical report).
5. Prepare and distribute academic majors report, listing enrolled students by department and program, class, and total (statistical report).
6. Graduations officer prepares graduation evaluation forms for all degree applicants for mailing and sends to those students attempting to graduate at the end of the fall term.
7. Advance register students for second semester and prepare demand and conflict analysis report for department heads and deans.
8. After adjustments are made to courses, schedule students into courses for second semester.
9. Distribute "Call for Summer Session Catalog" to all departments and deans, listing all directions and deadlines.
10. Remind president or committee head to select and invite commencement speaker for spring commencement ceremony.

November:
1. Inventory all paper supplies, cards, and printed forms and prepare purchase orders as needed to replace these expendable supplies. Some forms, such as enrollment and drop/add cards, should not be ordered until late in the spring, since card formats are subject to rule changes promulgated through normal faculty channels.
2. Prepare listing of all prospective graduates for fall term. Edit listing and order diplomas for distribution following completion of term. (In order to save time, order diplomas for all students who meet the graduation checks, even though final grades will later indicate that some have not completed all degree requirements.)
3. Publish final examination schedule.
4. Send notice to all departments regarding deadline for petitions for "new" courses to be offered in the spring or summer.
5. Have change-of-schedule week for second semester and conduct continuous registration for new and former students.

December:

1. Prepare and send end-of-term grading sheets or cards to instructional staff with cover letter from registrar indicating grading procedures and deadlines.
2. Notify mailing department of expected number of grades to be mailed, so that mailing and postage arrangements can be completed in advance.
3. Process grades; print and distribute grade sheets to students, academic divisions, departments, student affairs office, and others as needed. Send letters to students who have been academically suspended or dismissed.
4. Post fall-term grades to academic records; microfilm records while they are in precise order for posting.
5. Using end-of-term grade reports, make final graduation check, post degrees earned, mail diplomas.
6. Publish notices and dates for spring registration.
7. Confirm employment of part-time assistants for spring registration.
8. Microfilm grade sheets for retention. If some grade sheets have not been submitted, microfilm them later and splice into the original roll.
9. Prepare instructions and worksheets for the next academic year's annual time schedule (course planning guide or class schedule) and distribute to department heads with deadline dates for late January and early February.
10. Hold registration planning meeting to set the stage for spring registration. Key supervisors from the office as well as systems personnel meet to establish the various registration schedules, assign work loads, and coordinate the start of the new semester. Arrangements are made with physical plant for necessary support services.
11. Notify deans and department and program chairpersons and advisers regarding spring registration procedures and deadlines. Emphasize deadline for final time schedule (schedule of classes) updates to be sent to the registrar.

Spring Semester

January:

1. Update class schedule and order printing of class schedule supplement if necessary for distribution to students and faculty.
2. Conduct delayed and late registration and fee collection according to prearranged plan. Distribute student class schedule prior to the start of classes.
3. Conduct registration for off-campus satellite programs as required. Continue in February as necessary.
4. Conduct change of schedule (add/drop) session for spring semester the first few days of classes.
5. Send preliminary class rosters and enrollment data to departments.
6. Classes start, and registration adjustment period begins (drop/add). Late registration begins.
7. Prepare and distribute night examination schedule and send copy to physical plant for night classroom use.

8. Send follow-up letter to undergraduate and graduate students who have not applied for May graduation.

February:
1. Prepare spring enrollment reports for local and state distribution. (In many states legislative funding is based on these reports.)
2. Prepare and distribute official class rosters to departments and programs following close of late registration and end of enrollment adjustment period (drop/add).
3. Produce internal set of student schedules for daily updating (see schedule for September).
4. Edit computer printouts for ineligible pass/fail enrollments, unpaid fees, and other exceptional enrollments as necessary, and take appropriate action.
5. Send overload notices to departments and programs, listing all students enrolled for credit hours in excess of institutional limit. Send students notification of excess hours of registration.
6. Edit records of all currently enrolled students for grade changes and necessary record updates. Change incompletes to "F" according to institutional policy on the removal of incomplete grades; notify students and departments as appropriate.
7. Update academic record files (transcript), removing inactive records from active files.
8. Prepare academic records for all newly enrolled students; post personal and academic data either manually or by computer. Microfilm active file for security purposes.
9. Prepare computer printout of students from previous term who did not enroll for current term. Send copy to cognizant departments for purging of departmental record files.
10. Publish summer session catalog based on information received from departments (received in December and updated in January). Distribute catalog according to institutional instructions.
11. Prepare and distribute academic majors report, listing enrolled students by department and program, class, and total.

March:
1. Send notices and/or grade cards or sheets for midterm grades if appropriate.
2. Process midterm grade reports if applicable. Send deficiency warnings to students and faculty advisers.
3. Prepare spring-term census report, listing course enrollments within departments and programs by sex, total, percent of total, total student credit hours, and summary information.
4. Call commencement committee meeting to set plans for commencement exercises.
5. Graduations officer completes graduation evaluation forms for all degree applicants for mailing to students attempting to graduate at the end of the spring term.
6. Make appropriate announcements concerning spring vacation (if any).

7. Publish final examination schedule.
8. Send notice to all departments regarding deadline for petitions for "new" courses to be offered during the next academic year.

April:
1. Prepare listing of all prospective graduates for spring term. Edit listing and order diplomas and commencement programs for distribution following completion of term.
2. Inventory all paper supplies, cards, and printed forms and prepare purchase orders for those materials not ordered in the fall (see November schedule).
3. Publish notices and dates for fall- and summer-term registration.
4. Confirm employment of part-time assistants for fall registration.
5. Hold final planning meeting for end-of-term commencement ceremony; coordinate facility use, physical arrangements, flowers, etc., with appropriate units.
6. Begin processing applications for summer session.
7. Advance register students for fall semester and prepare demand and conflict analysis report for department heads and deans. After adjustments are made to courses, schedule students into courses for fall semester. Advance registration for summer begins and continues through summer.

May:
1. Prepare and send end-of-term grading sheets or cards to instructional staff with cover letter from registrar indicating grading procedures and deadlines.
2. Notify mailing department of expected number of grades to be mailed, so that mailing and postage arrangements can be completed in advance.
3. Hold planning meeting for registration for summer session; send out appropriate publicity, schedule facilities, and send notices to physical plant.
4. Process grades; print and distribute grade sheets to students, academic divisions, departments, student affairs office, and others as needed. Send letters to students who have been academically suspended or dismissed.
5. Conduct commencement ceremony.
6. Post spring-term grades to academic records; microfilm records while they are in precise order after posting.
7. Using end-of-term grade reports, make final graduation check, post degrees earned, and mail diplomas.

Further Reading and Study

For basic principles regarding the registrar's responsibilities, see the AACRAO Code of Ethics, reproduced as Appendix G later in this volume. A helpful reference for registrars and other academic or student service administrators is Rosemary Shield's (1970) chapter, "Registration, Scheduling, and Student Records," in the *Handbook of College and University Administration* (A. S. Knowles, editor). Other more generalized sources are Corson's (1975) *The Governance of Colleges and Universities* and Salmen's (1971) *Duties of Administrators in Higher Education* (1971). Professor X (1973) provides a less serious look at grading and other aspects of higher education in *This Beats Working for a Living. Recruitment, Admissions and Handicapped Students,* published by the American Association of Collegiate Registrars and Admissions Officers and the American Council on Education (1978), provides an extensive overview of requirements for compliance with Section 504 of the Rehabilitation Act of 1973.

□ □ □ □ □ □ □ 5

Building
the Master Schedule

□ □ □ □ □ □ □ □ □ □ □ □ □ □ □ □ □ □

James Flinn Blakesley

The construction of an institution's master schedule of classes is an intricate, time-consuming process. It is the process by which the academic resources of the institution and the students' course needs are linked into a time-pattern relationship that enables instruction to be conducted in an orderly manner. The method by which the master schedule is constructed varies greatly from institution to institution. Approaches to this function might be categorized as centralization, decentralization, and coordination.

Centralization denotes complete control and authority in one office. This approach assumes that one office knows the course needs of all students, the teaching capabilities of every member of the staff, and the facilities most suitable for each course, together with class size policies and other pedagogical requirements. In small institutions with a closely knit faculty and administration, such a system can function well and to the best advantage of all concerned.

Decentralization, in various forms, becomes the operating mode as institutions grow. As programs expand and faculties grow in size and become increasingly specialized, budgets as well as other resources tend to be subdivided into reasonably sized operating units. Thus, schools and departments become "cost centers" which are responsible for their own operation, and scheduling of academic resources becomes their responsibility. A central scheduling office often functions only in the role of a deadline setter and arbitrator, acting solely as the recorder of the various agreements made between departments, faculty, and students.

Coordination is an operational mode under which the central office assumes a higher level of authority and responsibility and makes use of a representative organizational structure involving both the academic entities that set curricula (the faculty of the schools) and those that administer the resources of the departments (the department heads). Centrally, policies are set that apply equally to all. In this mode of operation, the central office functions in a dual role: it coordinates the necessary exchange of information between school advisement areas and the departments offering the courses; and it administers various operating policies—such as the use of consistent time patterns, definition of the academic week, and classroom allocation procedures—to which all units are expected to adhere. The job of actually constructing the schedule is left to each of the departments or cost centers, but the procedure is monitored by the central coordinating office.

Many large institutions attempt to build a portion of the master schedule centrally by retaining control of the general-purpose classroom facilities, with a central administrator making room assignments. This splits the scheduling function, with space being handled separately from the other resource components of scheduling. In such instances there is usually a need for more classrooms, since no one is willing to change his or her class times to fit the available rooms. To handle these situations, the central scheduling office at some institutions temporarily allocates classrooms each term to each department, depending on the projected need. Departments then choose the meeting times within the rooms allocated to them and assign the staff before returning the control of the rooms to the central office. This provides an effective procedure only when there is a definite understanding that (1) no additional rooms may be obtained until all available periods have been used and (2) all unused periods within those rooms assigned will revert to the central office at the time the tentative schedule is forwarded. This procedure permits, within policy limits, total departmental responsibility for the initial schedule and ultimately provides for central review and adjustment before the schedule becomes final.

In using this kind of procedure, the central office should anticipate certain special situations: (1) Large auditorium or lecture rooms and small seminar rooms typically are not well utilized by a single department. Therefore, either specific hours should be allocated to a department, or select departments must share rooms of this type. (2) Course offerings of some departments may be too small to justify the assignment of even one room. In this instance, space for their courses may come from the use of reserve rooms or from a shared use of a room with other departments having similar limited needs. (3) In assigning rooms, care should be taken to provide the right mixture of room sizes in conveniently located buildings. (4) As in any budgeting or allocative process, last-minute changes should be anticipated by keeping a reserve of rooms on hand for the unexpected, but normal, emergencies. In essence, the guiding principle is to give each department the opportunity for self-determination of its schedule within available resources.

Elements of the Schedule

The development of a master class schedule deals primarily with resource allocation and can be posed in very general terms as follows:

Given:

S, a set of students with varied curricular requirements

C, a set of courses with specified resource and pedagogical requirements

F, a set of faculty members with specific course capabilities (and possibly some external time constraints)

R, a set of physical facilities of given size, capacity, and geographical location

T, a set of time periods which define the academic week

Then: Superimposing C onto $F \times R \times T$ provides a class schedule with the probability that all students will be able to fill their curricular needs.

The set or group of students is usually defined by grade level, curriculum, and plan of study. Consideration of the curricular requirements and the number of students in each of these categories provides an indication of the types and number of *course patterns* necessary for the proper planning of the master schedule. The more "regular" the students' progress is, the fewer course-pattern variations are required, and the easier it is to build a nonconflicting schedule.

A set of courses is defined as a grouping of courses that could be offered together with a high probability that no student would choose to enroll in more than one of the courses in the set. For example, English 101, Pharmacy 210, Mechanical Engineering 320, and a senior-level course in business administration would fall into the same set, since these courses are designed for students with different class levels and majors. Grouping courses into sets is accomplished by identifying all the known patterns of courses that students normally require and arranging them into the fewest number of sets of nonconflicting schedules. The number of sets can be further reduced by identifying those courses that will be subdivided into sections and redistributing the sections among the remaining sets of courses. This provides identification of the sets of courses that may be scheduled together and those that must be kept separate. If faculty or facility constraints require more flexibility, the minimum number of sets may be expanded by subdividing one or more of the existing sets.

The set of faculty is defined by name and the courses that each member plans to teach. Greater flexibility in class assignments can be achieved if all the courses that each faculty member is capable of teaching, not just the preferred ones, are identified.

The set of facilities is usually defined by building, room number, type of room, and special equipment available in each room. Except for reallocations between courses within departments or between departments, early commitments to specific courses should be made.

There is obviously a long list of constraints that any master schedule must satisfy, such as nonconflicting staff and space schedules and known limits of available resources, especially in certain courses. Likewise, there is the need to honor special time requests from faculty and students for various reasons, such as research and competing teaching assignments for faculty, and rehearsal and athletics for students. These external requirements need to be identified and weighted in order of priority, so that they may be given their proper relationship in arranging the master schedule.

The Academic Week and Scheduling Time Patterns

The length of the academic week and variations in time patterns used in developing a schedule play vital roles in the effectiveness of the schedule. The academic week may be considered the boundary condition limiting the daily starting and ending times for normal instruction. It may include the noon hour or exclude Saturdays. For some campuses it includes the evening hours. For others those hours are considered separately from the academic week—for adult education classes. In other words, the academic week is the framework of days and hours within which a set of classes may be offered.

Time patterns are the configurations of hours to be used in setting up the master schedule of classes. If specific or standardized time patterns are used (for example, if beginning and ending times are the same for each class period), the schedules of all component elements (staff, space, students, and courses) will fit together with much greater ease. If the patterns are dissimilar, the time frame will have to be expanded to keep course offerings from conflicting. Standardization of class times for classes, therefore, helps to minimize conflicts and lessens the need for extending the academic week.

Patterns of hours for laboratory classes vary greatly from those of lecture and recitations but should still be chosen wisely to fit together with one another in the best possible manner. Curricula that require many laboratory hours of instruction have space and time frameworks that are more complex and require an academic week with more time frames than do curricula without laboratory classes.

Most institutions have a maximum class break of five to ten minutes, but many have found it necessary to use fifteen- to twenty-minute periods between classes. The effect is a major reduction in instructional time. If an institution operates an 8 to 5 schedule Monday through Friday and utilizes the noon hour, the academic week is forty-five hours in length; if the last period each day is disregarded, there are forty periods, each lasting sixty minutes. Therefore, for every additional five-minute period added to the class break, 200 minutes of class time are lost each week. Institutions should therefore carefully examine each reason behind such broad policy decisions. Isolated lateness to classes should not result in campus-wide policies when relocating a class might solve the problem. Planning of the campus buildings should include ground-floor and first-floor centrally located classrooms as a partial means of minimizing the time between classes. Core courses should be centrally scheduled with the specialized curricula on the perimeter.

Estimating Future Course Enrollments

When one is planning a master schedule for a given term, reasonable estimates should be obtained regarding the numbers of students expected in each course to be offered. These numbers may be estimated or determined from historical enrollment records. Changes in the master schedule should be expected, so that the master schedule should be modified when necessary; such modification should become a normal operating procedure.

Faculty advisers can provide one estimate of the needs of their students. These estimates tend to reflect the advisers' best guesses and usually are somewhat optimistic in terms of expected enrollments in any given course. They are, however, an important source of information when new programs or revisions in curricula are being planned.

Data received from department heads, faculty advisers, and the registrar's historical files provide good preliminary course limits during initial planning. No matter how potential enrollments are estimated, each academic department must determine the initial course limits that will be utilized for planning the schedule of classes.

Scheduling Rationale

While it may be the goal to build the "perfect schedule," there is a tendency for all to avoid the unpopular hours and to collapse the schedule into as few hours as possible, preferably Monday, Wednesday, and Friday mornings at 9, 10, and 11 A.M. This individual preference for hours should be redirected toward satisfying diverse course needs of the total group and away from the tendency to queue at prime times, since such a schedule is neither academically sound nor economically appropriate. For example, if all courses were taught at one time (9:00 A.M. on Mondays), students' choice of courses would be limited to one course per term; consequently, the students' ability to progress rapidly toward their degree requirements would be severely hampered. In addition, the staff and facility requirements would be at a maximum, since a different staff member and room would be required for each course and section offered. At the other extreme, if all courses were taught at different times, then students could select any set of courses offered, since there would be no conflicts in hours. Their ability to progress would be limited only by their own capabilities. In addition, staff and facility resources could be minimized. Theoretically, since there would be no time conflicts, only one multitalented professor would need to be assigned to teach all courses; similarly, if one room were suitable for all the courses offered, only one room would be required. (See Figure 1.)

In general, an institution that operates on a twenty-hour week is much more restrictive in its course selectivity and less effective in its use of staff and space than an institution that operates on a forty-hour week. That is, the effectiveness of the master schedule of classes is dependent on the distribution of classes over as broad a weekly time base as institutional policy will permit. The more usable hours in the academic week, the most effective the system. Such a schedule will provide a greater selectivity of courses and more utilization of staff and space resources.

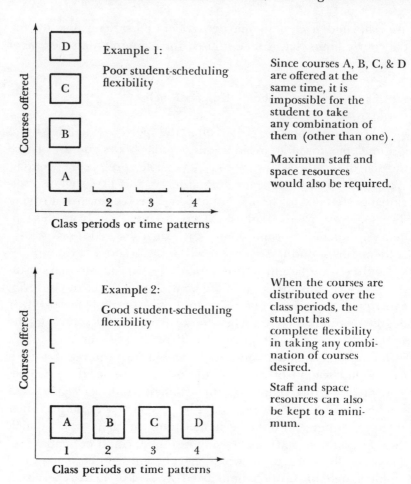

Figure 1. A Scheduling Philosophy

Obviously, neither of these extremes is a viable plan for scheduling. Even the "distributed" extreme is limited by the number of hours in the academic week as compared to the number of courses offered. There must certainly be more than one course per period if there are more than forty one-hour courses in a forty-hour academic week. If there are, say, two hundred courses, at best there will be five courses per period. If each course is actually a three-hour course and the time patterns fit together properly, then perhaps twelve patterns of three-hour classes could be scheduled within the forty-hour week. The forty-hour week is now reduced to twelve time patterns per week, requiring that sixteen to seventeen courses be offered each pattern of hours and thus increasing the probability of conflicts between courses. Further, as the time patterns become more varied and complex, such as required for a chemistry course with a one-hour lecture, two separate one-hour recitation sessions, and one three-hour laboratory, it becomes quite apparent that even sixteen to seventeen courses per time pattern are a bare minimum, and more than likely many more courses will need to be offered at a given period, again increasing the probability of conflicts.

The interrelationship of time patterns, length of academic week, and number of course offerings becomes more apparent as the complexity increases. A liberal arts curriculum with very limited numbers of laboratory periods and many regular class periods can operate with a much greater potential for a wider selection of courses within a given academic week than can a curriculum that has relatively more complex time patterns, such as those found in the scientific and technical fields. Curricula with complex time patterns require a longer academic week to obtain the same flexibility of course selection as less complicated curricula.

Large single-section courses—especially those required by students from many curricula, such as a basic freshman course— must be scheduled with great care. The time selection for such a course will influence the freshman schedules for all associated curricula and will preclude other freshman courses from utilizing the selected time pattern. The unit cost for the course may be low, but the resultant idle facilities in other areas might make the course prohibitively expensive. One rule of thumb is to encourage at least two time periods for such a course, thus providing scheduling alternatives and fuller use of other facilities, since single-section courses, especially those with large enrollments, tend to restrict course selection.

Multisectioned courses offer more opportunities for nonconflicting schedules than do the large single-section courses. Scheduling officers should offer as many different standard time patterns as possible for multisectioned courses. In most cases, if enrollments in the sections are kept balanced, hour conflicts in student schedules due to such courses will be minimized. Multi-sectioned courses, in effect, increase the potential for greater course selectivity.

The planning of the master schedule and the ultimate scheduling or sectioning of students are interdependent. A well-conceived master schedule can fail if the more popular sections of multisectioned courses are allowed to fill up and close prematurely before all students are registered. As sections close, the flexibility offered by multisectioned courses is reduced; and as registration proceeds, more and more students find fewer patterns of courses that will fit together to make an acceptable schedule of classes. In practice, therefore, all sections of multisectioned courses should be kept open as long as possible by balancing student course requests among all the sections. When this procedure is used, the last student to register will have essentially the same choice of courses as was afforded the first student to register. The penalty for not observing this practice is to deny certain students their choice of courses.

Theoretical Considerations

To further illustrate the importance of the relationship between the academic week and the time patterns, it is useful to examine the probabilities of developing nonconflicting schedules, assuming a uniform distribution of courses with random selection. Questions are frequently raised about the length of the academic week and just what effect a nonuniform distribution of hour patterns has on the probability of obtaining a nonconflicting schedule. In answer to the first question, assume a simplified situation in which the academic week is divided into disjoint patterns of uniform length (not necessarily contiguous; for example, MWF 9 could be a period) and where each course meets for exactly one pattern per week. The actual length of a period is immaterial; but if, for example, it were assumed to be three hours and the total number of such nonconflicting three-hour periods were thirteen, the academic week would be approaching forty hours. In this example: let K = number of periods in the academic week, let N = total number of courses offered by the institution, and let M =

average number of courses taken by each student. If it is assumed that the N courses are uniformly distributed over the K periods, it is reasonable to ask what the probability would be for a student to randomly select M courses without a conflict. Using the formula for conditional probabilities

$$P_{no\ conflict} = \prod_{i=1}^{M} \frac{N - \frac{N}{K}(i-1)}{N - i + 1}$$

some representative values may be derived, as shown in Table 1.

A review of these values indicates that the *number of courses offered* has less influence on conflicts than does the *number of time patterns selected* by the students. If there are thirteen time patterns available and the student is choosing six time patterns (courses) from an array of 100 courses, then the probability is .30. If the student chooses from an array of 3,200 courses, the probability only drops to .26. However, if the *number of courses selected* from a set of 100 courses increases from six to eight, the probability of no conflicts drops significantly, from .30 to .08. A drop of the same

Table 1. Probabilities of Developing Nonconflicting Schedules[a]

Time Patterns Available	Time Patterns to Be Scheduled						
	6	7	8	6	7	8	
10	.18	.07	.02	.15	.06	.02	
11	.22	.11	.04	.19	.09	.03	
12	.26	.14	.06	.22	.11	.05	
13 - - - -	.30	.17	.08	.26	.14	.06	◄—— 40-hour week
14	.33	.20	.11	.29	.17	.08	
15	.37	.24	.13	.32	.19	.10	
16	.40	.27	.16	.35	.22	.12	
17	.43	.30	.19	.37	.24	.14	
18 - - - -	.46	.32	.21	.39	.26	.16	◄—— 55-hour week
19	.48	.35	.24	.42	.29	.18	
20	.51	.38	.26	.44	.31	.20	
	100 Courses Offered			3,200 Courses Offered			

[a] Assuming an even distribution of courses with random selection.

magnitude occurs for the example where the array of courses is 3,200.

These data reaffirm that it is much more difficult to schedule students with "full academic" loads than it is to schedule part-time students within a given academic week. The data also suggest that planning the master schedule is only somewhat more difficult for institutions with many courses than for those with few courses. In each instance, the complexity remains virtually unchanged, but the volume of work increases.

Within a well-constructed master schedule, the courses are not randomly arranged, nor do the students randomly select their courses. The probability of obtaining a conflict-free schedule should be greatly increased when the courses are distributed throughout the hours of the day and the days of the week. In addition, as the number of nonconflicting time patterns increases from ten to twenty, the probability of no conflict improves significantly and in an exponential fashion.

Figure 2 shows the significant increase in possible course-time combinations that occurs as the number of time patterns or hours (N courses) in the academic week increases. For example, if there were only twelve discrete periods in the academic week, a student taking five courses would have only 792 possible course-time combinations. If the academic week were increased to eighteen discrete periods, nearly 9,000 possible combinations would exist for the same student. While calculated for theoretical situations, these data serve to highlight the point that the length of the academic week and the time patterns of hours have a direct and significant impact upon the institution's ability to plan a master schedule which meets as nearly as possible the diverse course requirements of students.

The effects of skewing the distribution of courses over the available class periods are also worthy of study. As the skew (or noneven distribution) increases, the probability of conflicting schedules will also increase; as the number of available class periods is decreased, the probability of conflicts increases even further. Therefore, from a course selectivity standpoint, it is highly desirable to distribute courses evenly over an academic week, thus providing for the largest number of nonconflicting time patterns. If

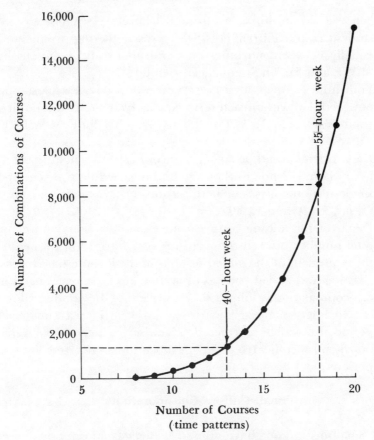

Figure 2. Increases in Course-Time Combinations
(Combinations of N Courses Taken Five at a Time)

choices must be made, courses that are to be taken in sequence (through enrollment a subsequent term) and/or should not be taken during the same term may be scheduled at the same time whereas courses that must or may be taken during the same term must be scheduled at different times.

Some Practical Suggestions

Some possible scheduling strategies that can be employed to accomplish these theoretical objectives include the following:

1. Schedule all multiple lecture and laboratory sections so that student course enrollments will be distributed approximately equally between mornings and afternoons and between the M,W,F and Tu,Th,S sequences each term.
2. Four-hour lecture courses which meet four days a week should be scheduled within each term equally over the five following combinations: M,Tu,W,Th; M,Tu,W,F; M,Tu,Th,F; M,W,Th,F; Tu,W,Th,F.
3. Departments could be strongly encouraged to schedule noon-hour classes, although they should not schedule two required single-section courses or both sections of a two-section course at, say, 11:30 and 12:30.
4. Departments adding lecture courses and sections above the total number offered the previous year (term) must schedule the equivalent of the added sections in the low-use time blocks. Existing and added courses or sections may be rearranged in any combination as long as the equivalent of the number added is scheduled in these low-use periods. No increase in peak-period use will be permitted. Likewise, reductions (cancellations) must come from the peak periods—not the low-use periods.

Small-College Considerations

Small institutions have unique challenges and opportunities with respect to building the master schedule of classes. The lines of communications are short; the needs of the campus can be observed on a personal basis; and the curriculum can be viewed as a single entity rather than a mixture of diverse curricula. As a result, the scheduling officer should have fewer sets of courses competing for the popular class hours, and scheduling conflicts should be fewer than on a large campus. Conversely, centralization of authority to make time and space assignments as they relate to faculty, courses, and student requirements is even more important in the smaller school because there may be less scheduling flexibility due to the existence of fewer multiple-section courses.

The primary consideration or first step in building the master schedule for a small college involves partitioning the proposed course offerings into sets of courses, independent of hours, and determining the number of sets which minimize conflicts between courses required to satisfy the various curricular needs of the students. For this purpose, a set is defined in the same way that it was earlier in this chapter. After the sets of courses have been determined, time patterns (class hours) should then be established with beginning and ending times that will fit together properly within the established academic week for the institution. Care must be taken to coordinate laboratory (for example, Tue. 1–4) time blocks as well as lecture or recitation (8 Daily) hour patterns. Again, the fewer the hours in the academic week, the fewer the number of patterns that will be possible and the more difficult it will be to accommodate the number of sets of courses within the available time patterns. Moreover, if the total hours available for scheduling courses are severely restricted, it will not be possible to schedule students into certain patterns of courses without expanding the academic week.

The next step is to have the scheduling officer assign specific times to each course and section within the available classroom space. In order to do this, the scheduling officer or registrar must be familiar with the inventory of facilities, including classrooms, laboratories, seminar rooms, and other assignable space; and the schedules for each must be set forth.

Required single-section courses with large enrollments need to be assigned their times and places first, especially those whose student populations are drawn from freshman through senior class levels and are required of all majors. Examples of these types of courses might include an institution's weekly convocation, religious services, great issues courses, and military drill. When selecting these class periods, one should be careful to avoid imposing major time and space restrictions on subsequently scheduled courses.

The next group of courses to be scheduled should include the lecture-laboratory type of course work generally geared to a particular group of students. The laboratory periods must be carefully scheduled due to their typical multiperiod (for example, Tue. 2–5) time patterns and the need for specialized facilities. Such courses may introduce many conflicts with the single-period multiday (for example, Daily or MWF 2) time patterns if they are not carefully considered in the planning process. Multiperiod laboratory classes should be assigned in a way that will provide maximum use of limited and expensive laboratory facilities. For instance, assigning a three-hour laboratory to a 1–4 time block uses up the entire half day, and the additional one hour (4–5) is usually wasted. Better utilization of space and equipment can be obtained if two laboratories are scheduled in a single half-day, such as 12 noon–2:30 and 2:40–5, provided the short break between classes allows sufficient preparation time for laboratory experiments. Similarly, scheduling efficiency is enhanced if one three-hour laboratory is scheduled in the afternoon from 2 to 5 rather than from 1 to 4, since the later time block allows students to schedule a single-period multiday class at the prime one o'clock hour (classes scheduled from 4 to 5 are generally unpopular).

Lecture or recitation courses, which are generally taught in multisectioned small classes, are assigned to specific time periods by fitting them into the master schedule around the previously scheduled single-section courses. This provides the flexibility needed for better course assignment at registration. In addition, to allow for better course selectivity, multiple sections of a course should be assigned to as many different normal time periods as possible. As discussed earlier in this chapter, it is also wise to attempt to assign multiple sections of a single course, so that student course enrollments will be distributed approximately equally between mornings and afternoons. This precaution will help to reduce student scheduling conflicts. Care, however, should be exercised to keep the enrollments in the sections balanced, thus providing equitable teaching loads for the faculty while ensuring that the more popular time patterns (sections) do not close prematurely —thereby reducing the scheduling options for students enrolling toward the end of the registration period. Faculty schedules must also be developed, and teaching assignments adjusted for obvious conflicts. The scheduling officer in a smaller institution has an advantage here too, since he or she is dealing with a smaller faculty and decisions may be made on a more personal basis. For instance, a faculty member with a health problem may be assigned to a classroom next to his or her office or within the same building; some can be assigned to requested facilities, while still others are given class periods that dovetail with other important assignments.

Finally, arranging or plotting classes into the various class-rooms within the approved class hours and days is accomplished through the use of a simple "scheduling map" or board. Such a map might be a simple matrix listing, along the left side for example, the various buildings and rooms, classroom capacities, and special equipment provided in each room. The days of the week and class periods within each day form the other side of the matrix, with Monday and its various class periods shown at the top left, followed on the right by Tuesday, and so on through Friday or Saturday. To increase its readability and durability, the "map" might be mounted on standard 30″ × 36″ posterboard. The scheduling officer, observing the various sets of courses mentioned earlier, as well as the intended size of each class (or estimated class size based on historical enrollment trends), plots each course into an appropriate classroom within a designated time and class-day sequence (e.g., Daily, MWF, TuThs). With this system, conflicts in classroom assignment are easily avoided, since it is visually impossible to schedule two classes into a given room during the same class period. After the classes have been plotted on the scheduling map, one can quickly determine the remaining available hours in each room that can be used for scheduling low-priority curricular activities such as tutorial hours, quiz sections, and study halls. The sample scheduling map shown in Exhibit 1 illustrates one hand-scheduling technique.

Other than taking into account these special considerations, small institutions can apply the material in this chapter as will large institutions: using the same scheduling principles; understanding resource availability; and properly relating time considerations to the curriculum requirements of students and the institution.

Publication Considerations

The pamphlet, newspaper, or booklet distributed to students and faculty detailing and publicizing the course and section offerings for a given session may vary greatly in content, quantity, and cost. There are perhaps as many different ways of presenting and distributing this information as there are institutions of higher

Exhibit 1. Sample Scheduling Map, College of Middle America

Bld & Room		Capacity	Equip[a]	Monday 8	9	10	11	12	1	2	3	4	5	Friday 8	9	10	11	12	1	2	3	4	5	Room & Bld	
OLD	101	25	TAC																					101	OLD
MAIN	105	35	TAC																					105	MAIN
	110	35	TAC																					110	
	115	50	FTA																					115	
College	103	25	TCH																					103	College
	106	30	TCH																					106	
	110	50	FTA																					110	
	203	60	FTA																					203	
	206	60	FTA																					206	
Kennedy	100	150	ATA																					100	Kennedy
	102	100	ATA																					102	
	104	60	FTA																					104	
	200.	60	FTA																					200	
	202	60	TCH																					202	
	204	60																						204	
CAMPUS	110	45	TAC																					110	CAMPUS
CENTER	120	45	TAC																					120	CENTER

140			140
210			210
220			220
240			240

140	25	TAC
210	15	TCH
220	45	TAC
240	60	FTA

[a]EQUIPMENT CODE: ATA, Auditorium Tablet Arm Seats;
FTA, Filed Tablet Arm Chairs;
TAC, Tablet Arm Chairs;
TCH, Tables and Chairs.

education. Generally, the document produced is of a temporary and changing nature and need not be elaborate, just factual. Some institutions list only the minimal essential scheduling elements—departmental abbreviation, course number, abbreviated course title, and credit hours—and then, after obtaining each student's course selections, assign each student to classes, and then provide each student with a computer-printed schedule listing the assigned courses and their meeting times and locations.

Other institutions develop and print advance copies of the schedule of classes to aid in the scheduling process. In addition to the data elements noted above, proposed times for sections would also be included, but buildings and room numbers might be excluded, so that changes in location could be made prior to printing the student schedules. Many institutions also include the building and room number and the name of the instructor for each course. Examination requirements and restrictions as to who may be admitted to the various courses or sections may also be listed. As content grows, there is more chance for change and more need for addenda, and the schedule tends to become more definitive and restrictive. Those institutions operating in a manual (noncomputer) mode for registration must be very specific about class scheduling details, since the student at the time of registration will have to know the time and place of all classes. Those institutions operating in a computer mode can delay, if they choose, the final printing of the student schedules until necessary alterations and adjustments are made to the master schedule.

Some institutions provide printed time or class schedules only to faculty advisers and thereby limit the quantity to be distributed. The concept behind this plan is that students need and should see an adviser each session; therefore, only the advisory offices need copies, and this procedure helps ensure student-advisory contacts. Others print a copy for each student enrolled, and some print multiple copies per student enrolled (because of the tendency for students to misplace these materials).

Institutions must also decide whether to publish a class schedule for more than one session at a time. The advantage, of course, is that advising and course selection can be accomplished for more than one term at a time. The disadvantage is that there will be more errors and changes due to curricular revisions by the faculty.

All institutions should periodically examine their practices to determine the effectiveness of their procedures as they relate to class selection and sectioning. As a result of computer-aided scheduling, many operations can be sequenced to eliminate the need for many proofreaders and checkers, and student schedules, staff schedules, room schedules, and the schedule of classes can be printed from the same master schedule file stored in the computer.

Final Examination Scheduling

The philosophy and rationale used in preparing the master schedule of classes are also relevant to building the final examination schedule. Therefore, it is appropriate to close this chapter with a brief discussion of final examination scheduling. The institution's final examination schedule is usually determined by the registrar, based on local practice, action by the academic governing body, or the registrar's experience in these matters. Policies governing examination procedures, the number of examinations a student may have in one day, and the length of the examination period, (whether it is several days or weeks) are usually developed through faculty action. One week reserved for final examinations is standard practice. The final examination schedule may be determined and printed in advance by listing it in the master schedule of classes. When this is done, the student essentially determines his or her own final examination schedule through selection of courses. If the schedule is not published until after registration, the registrar must arrange the schedule in such a manner that students will have no more than the maximum number of examinations per day, as determined by institutional policy.

Some institutions with sophisticated computer equipment have developed computerized final examination schedules based on the actual course enrollment of each student; in these instances, examination scheduling conflicts are reduced to a minimum. Several commercial firms have final examination scheduling packages available to customers at a cost of a few cents per student.

Regardless of the method used to develop the schedule,

specific examination periods or "blocks" of time are usually set aside for each class-hour sequence. For instance, all classes that meet at 10:10 A.M. on Mondays, Wednesdays, and Fridays will take examinations in the same block of time. For classes that meet for two or more consecutive hours, the time of the first hour of the class meeting determines the time of the final examination. For example, classes that meet from 10:10 A.M. to 12 noon on Mondays, Wednesdays, and Fridays would also take their final exams in the same block as the 10:10 A.M. M,W,F group. Classes that meet in split blocks of time, such as 9:10 A.M. to 10:25 A.M. on Tuesdays and Thursdays, take their exams with the 9:10 Tuesday-Thursday block, and it is not uncommon to award large multiple-sectioned courses special time blocks, so that all the students taking the course, regardless of class meeting times, may take the exam together. This is a most convenient service for faculty, since it allows them to give a single final test rather than multiple versions of the same exam. To avoid conflicts in scheduling examination room assignments, the registrar should remind the teaching faculty that all exams must be given according to the time blocks assigned in the official final examination schedule, and that exams will be held in the same room in which the class normally meets for instruction. Rotation of the exam blocks from term to term is recommended. In this way, no single class or instructor will always have the last examination. Rotation is particularly helpful to professors who teach large classes or sections and need more time for grading. An example of a typical final examination schedule is illustrated in Exhibit 2.

Further Reading and Study

For an extended coverage of this topic see *Building The Master Schedule Of Classes* by John Miller (1968). This booklet is designed as a reference manual covering the total process of building a master schedule, and procedural examples and forms are provided. "Facilities Utilization Analysis, Classroom Allocation, and Course Scheduling" by Harold Temmer (1972) explores the process of course scheduling in detail, delving into the subject of classroom utilization as well. "Maximal Utilization of Instructional Time" by

Exhibit 2. Sample Final Examination Schedule
Fall Semester

Final examinations for the three-hour lecture courses scheduled for two 75-minute periods on Tuesday and Thursday must be given during the time blocks as follows: 7:45–9:00 at the 8:00 block, Tu, Th; 9:10–10:25 at the 9:00 block, Tu, Th; 10:45–12:00 at the 11:00 block, Tu, Th; 12:45–2:00 at the 1:00 block, Tu, Th; 2:10–3:25 at the 2:00 block, Tu, Th; 3:45–5:00 at the 4:00 block, Tu, Th.

7:00 am to 10:00 am, 3:10 pm to 6:00 pm, and 7:00 pm to 10:00 pm schedules apply only to four- and five-hour courses.

All other courses are scheduled for a two-hour period.

Final examinations for all sections of a course approved for a mass examination must be given during the assigned time block.

Exam Times / Days	7:00–10:00 am or 8:00–10:00 am	10:10 am to 12:00 pm	1:00 pm to 3:00 pm	3:10–5:00 pm or 3:10–6:00 pm	Evenings 7:00–9:00 pm or 7:00–10:00 pm
MON	4 Daily 4 M, W, F	9 Tu, Th	Math 101, 107	11, Tu, Th 12 Daily 12 M, W, F	Geol 101
TUES	10 Daily 10 M, W, F	8 Tu, Th	Pol S 101, 102	11 Daily 11 M, W, F	Bio S 102, 103
WEDS	9 Daily 9 M, W, F	2 Tu, Th	Psych 101	Chem 101, 102, 105, 106	3 Daily 3 M, W, F
THUR	2 Daily 2 M, W, F	10 Tu, Th	3 Tu, Th	8 Daily 8 M, W, F	Econ 102, 201, 203, 301
FRI	1 Daily 1 M, W, F	1 Tu, Th	4 Tu, Th	Spe 101	Genet 301
SAT	Special Exams	Special Exams			

Unless announced by the instructor, the examination will be held in the classroom where the class meets for instruction.

Franz Fredenburgh (1968) expands on the concept of the proper utilization of instructional time. Those interested in a computer approach to planning the schedule of classes and assigning facilities should read "Building a Class Schedule and Space Assignment: A Computer Assisted System" by Kenneth Bogard, Robert Patterson, and James Scriven (1977). Finally, D. Kent Halstead (1974) provides a thorough analysis of class scheduling and space management and projection in *Statewide Planning in Higher Education*.

6

Conducting Registration and Preparing the Catalog

C. James Quann

Two separate but related responsibilities of most registrars are analyzed in this chapter: producing the institution's general catalog or bulletin and organizing course registration.

Registration

Registration in the broadest sense normally includes the development of a well-balanced curriculum, with classes distributed equally throughout the hours of the day and days of the week; faculty advising; collection of personal data elements, such as the student's local address; assignment of students to sections and classes; and payment of fees. The techniques used will vary by institution, as will the type and variety of students being served. Four-year institutions whose student bodies consist mostly of full-time day students will normally develop highly structured registration systems that involve such things as placement testing, faculty advising, course selection, and fee payment. Admission precedes registration by many weeks or months, allowing sufficient time to evaluate credentials, determine admissibility, and create appropriate records. Other institutions, such as community and junior colleges, with large percentages of part-time and night students, must combine admission and registration into a quick and easy one-step operation. These types of institutions, operating under an open-door policy, must gear their systems to students who vary greatly in age and skill and who may simply mail in a form or appear unannounced to be admitted and registered. Thus, the procedure used must be very flexible and must accomplish the task with minimal effort in no more than fifteen to twenty minutes.

Although there are various approaches to the registration of students, these approaches share many common elements and have similar objectives. These objectives should include at least the following, regardless of the procedures used:

1. Provide each student with a conflict-free class schedule.
2. Section maximum numbers of students into their requested courses while optimizing the use of available time (clock hours) and classroom space.
3. Reduce or eliminate prematurely closed classes by allowing academic departments to adjust their offerings to meet the actual course requests of the students.
4. Achieve and maintain course section balance, thus ensuring minimum class size and equitable teaching loads.
5. Minimize the time and effort expended on the part of students, faculty, and staff at registration.
6. Collect tuition and fees according to prescribed institutional or state policies.

Alternative Registration Systems

Preregistration. Preregistration techniques vary widely but normally include the selection of courses and full or partial payment of fees during the term preceding the specified enrollment period. The registration system selected may not be affected by the academic calendar; however, due to the reduction in time available for classes and registration, institutions operating on the quarter calendar frequently utilize preregistration. Methodology includes systems as simple as having the student pick up the enrollment master card or form, receive faculty advisement, and return later at a specified date to pay fees and pick up class cards. The more complex preadvisement and preregistration systems generally call for students to enroll for classes according to a prearranged alphabetical or numerical (based on student ID number) sequence in May for the fall term, early December for winter, and February or March for the spring quarter. On the semester basis, preregistrants are processed in May for the fall semester and in November or December for spring.

Regardless of the system in use, it is generally impossible to preregister all students. Thus, it is the general custom to hold a miniregistration just prior to the start of classes each term. This last-minute clean-up process generally includes the adjustment of schedules for preregistered students who have changed their minds or academic objectives, students admitted after the close of preregistration, and current students who were unwilling or unable to register early. The sectioning of early registrants also varies; most institutions section preregistrants into classes at the close of the preregistration period; others may hold course input information, so that all students are sectioned at one time—following the termination of the miniregistration conducted just prior to the start of the subsequent term. (Specific hand and computer system details, such as sectioning algorithms, student information systems, and course files, are omitted from this discussion, since these areas are covered in other chapters.)

Mass Registration. The mass or arena-type registration normally takes place several days immediately preceding the first day of classes each term. It normally includes the distribution of enrollment packets, faculty advisement of students, payment of fees, and collection of all cards or forms commonly associated with registration. Under the quarter calendar, mass registration would take place during a one- or two-day period in September for fall quarter, in January for winter, and in March for the spring term. Under the semester calendar, mass registration takes place in September for fall and in January or February for the spring semester. Classes normally start after a one- or two-day (usually a weekend) processing period following registration. At some institutions faculty representatives from each department conduct and control the assignment of classes, with students essentially hand-sectioning themselves through the process of obtaining the various class cards. At other institutions departmental representatives and faculty generally absent themselves from the scene while a computer system makes the course assignments based on the student's preferences as submitted on machinable cards or forms. Fee payment may take place on site or in an adjacent facility or at a later time based on a postbilling or deferred-payment arrangement. Institutions with more sophisticated computer hardware may use the direct-access approach, with registration information input to a computer through high-speed terminal systems.

Advantages and Disadvantages of Alternative Systems. The registration approach selected by an institution should be based on a careful study of the objectives of the system; the unique needs of the faculty and students; and the time, space, and finances available. There are advantages and disadvantages to each approach, however, and these are listed here for the benefit of those who anticipate a change in their registration system.

Advantages of Preregistration

1. An early inventory of course and section enrollments is made possible.
2. The registration work load is spread over a longer period of time.
3. The advance date of registration allows time for subsequent adjustment of section size.
4. Students are saved the cost of arriving on campus several days before classes start.
5. Since advance planning is required of departments and faculty, the resulting schedule of offerings should meet the needs of the students.

Disadvantages of Preregistration

1. Departments cannot accurately predict section numbers and sizes, since a significant number of students will not

be registered until the clean-up period held just prior to the subsequent term.

2. The need for a mop-up registration just prior to the start of the subsequent term is not eliminated.

3. The number of drops and adds is increased significantly due to mind changing and registration prior to the receipt of grades from the previous term.

4. Academically deficient students must be readvised and enrolled in different courses at the start of the term.

5. Information provided to deans and departments is less than satisfactory, due to items 2 and 4 above.

6. The office staff must meet regular obligations and responsibilities during preregistration. Thus, an adjunct staff must be hired, increasing the overall cost of registration.

Advantages of Mass Registration

1. Departments and faculty can make last-minute changes in the schedule of offerings to meet the anticipated needs of students.

2. Since classes are not in session during registration, faculty, staff, and students can devote their complete attention and energy to registration.

3. Information provided to deans and departments following registration is complete and accurate, since all students are registered at one time.

4. The number of drops and adds is minimized, since students are registering after grades have been received and academic goals have been clarified.

Disadvantages of Mass Registration

1. Students must come to the campus several days before the start of each term. The period from the end of registration to the start of classes is "lost time" for students.

2. Registrants are processed in mass, leading to possible frustration of standing in line, accusations of benign neglect on the part of the institution, and a feeling of loss of identity by students.

3. Cash on-the-barrelhead fee collection procedures will lengthen the registration process.
4. Postbilling fee systems result in extended administrative effort to collect fees.

Registration Instructions and Sectioning

A well-constructed schedule of classes (the master schedule) and a well-planned set of registration instructions for students and faculty are necessary to a smoothly functioning system. So, too, is a commitment from faculty and the central administration to the development of an effective and efficient registration system. Faculty involvement may require physical presence in the case of arena-type programs, or cooperation and moral support for a computerized system. Some faculty will view the registration process as disruptive, while others look forward to the change of pace it provides (see Higham, 1974). In either case, a wise registrar, wishing to ensure full support from the faculty, will keep them posted on the system, since an informed and involved faculty will be a supportive faculty.

Traditionally, the academic departments have the primary responsibility for planning the master schedule (discussed in detail in Chapter Five). Once information for the master schedule has been compiled, it is reproduced and made available to students and faculty, preferably well before the start of registration. Almost without exception, detailed registration instructions for students and faculty are printed in the master schedule.

The generation of registration packets, whether by hand or computer, is a routine function which should be planned well in advance of the day of distribution. To even the flow of students throughout the registration period, enrollment packets are often distributed on a prearranged alphabetical basis over a series of time blocks. Effective control of the distribution of packets will control the length of registration lines, whether they form in front of the registrar's office, the adviser's office, or the fee payment station. A well-controlled pack handout schedule can effectively eliminate long lines and provide for an efficient and effective registration process.

The next step in the registration process is initiated by the students. The sequence commences when a student receives an enrollment packet—a set of plain or prepunched cards or forms including an enrollment master card and a fee card and sometimes such items as automobile registration and optional health insurance. These cards or forms may be mailed or distributed to the student, on an alphabetical (or numerical) hand-out arrangement, or sent to academic departments for distribution. Distribution by department is not normally recommended, since it may increase the incidence of lost or mislaid packets. The method of collecting or inputing course requests varies from a decentralized department-based system to a centralized registrar-controlled facility. (For a discussion of cross-registration between two colleges, see Martorana and Kuhns, 1975, pp. 123–130). Decentralization forces the student to traverse the campus several times in order to obtain course enrollment cards. With a centralized system, whether it is a hand operation involving departmental representatives and prepunched cards or a computerized course selection system, the student can complete the process without leaving the building. Many institutions utilize a computer to schedule or section the student into courses, based on a complex set of priorities. In these instances, the student often has the opportunity to indicate preferred sections and to set aside open time for approved work or cocurricular activities. Some sectioning programs even identify alternative course choices in case one or more of the requested courses are unavailable. Computer sectioning algorithms may section students into courses and sections class by class or on a student-by-student basis. A typical set of computer sectioning priorities is as follows:

1. Free time for employment or approved cocurricular activities such as band or athletics.
2. Single-section courses.
3. Preferred sections of multiple-sectioned courses when indicated.
4. Other requests for multiple-sectioned courses.
5. Physical education activity courses.
6. Laboratory assignments.
7. Alternative courses if one or more of the original requests are denied.

With computer sectioning, all course requests are processed in this manner until each student is given a conflict-free schedule. If there are conflicts which the computer cannot resolve, an appropriate message is printed on the student's class schedule, indicating why the course request was not honored.

In some institutions departments control section size by limiting the number of prepunched class cards; in other institutions departments attempt to seat all students who have requested a course. In both instances, adjustments in section size are difficult to make, since at any given point the department may not know exactly how many students have requested a course. Some institutions utilizing the computer sectioning technique have a built-in flexibility that allows curricular adjustments to be made after the enrollment phase of registration has been completed. In these cases, deans and department chairpersons meet with registrar personnel, prior to sectioning, and review a summary of total student course requests. This summary report lists all courses by section and seats available, as well as total student requests by course and section. After the course requests have been reviewed and compared with the respective departmental master schedules, the department heads are allowed to make the adjustments that may be required in order to honor as many student requests as possible. Departments are permitted to increase or decrease the maximum number of students permitted to enroll in a course or section; drop courses or sections; change times, rooms, or buildings; or open "blind" sections that have been held in contingency status. This built-in flexibility is unique in that, although student requests are almost always in variance with the schedule of offerings, departmental personnel are able to adjust the supply to meet the demand, and the end result is that maximum numbers of students receive the courses they request.

Collection of Tuition and Fees

A crucial step in any registration system is the collection of tuition and fees. Fee collection is usually the responsibility of the institution's comptroller or director of student accounts. However, since payment of fees is an integral part of any registration system, the registrar must also assume some responsibility for the development of an effective fee collection system. Fees are collected by one or a combination of several of the following methods:

1. Partial or complete payment of tuition and fees during preregistration. The student normally makes a partial payment (retainer fee) when preregistering, and the remainder is due at a specified time. The partial prepayment approach is favored over advance payment of full fees, since many students, especially in the spring of the year, do not have sufficient funds to make full payment. Federal, state, and local financial aid policies may also preclude advance release of aid to meet tuition and fee obligations.

2. Full fee payment at registration. The collection of full tuition and fees at the time of registration has been the usual procedure, at least in small to medium-sized institutions. This type of fee collection may prolong the registration process, however, and registrars should urge personnel in the student accounts section to employ sufficient personnel to prevent the collection stations from becoming a bottleneck in the system.

3. Postbilling. The size of some institutions make it difficult to collect full fees at the time of registration without creating unmanageable lines and mass confusion. In those instances, some form of late fee collection or postbilling is utilized. Students enroll in classes, and fee statements are generated after the fact. The statements are distributed or mailed to the students, and a reasonable time is allotted for the students to pay by mail or in case of errors or discrepancies in fee and/or financial aid calculations, to report to the finance section for payment. The number of institutions utilizing the postbilling technique is growing each year, although statutes in some states prevent the extension of credit necessary in this approach to fee payment.

4. Installment plan. If local or state laws permit installment paying, an institution may allow payment of fees over a period of weeks or months. This concept usually requires a substantial down payment at registration, with the remaining amount paid in several installments. This technique, although not allowed in many state-supported systems, is based on the need for stu-

dents or their parents to use the payroll deduction plan to distribute payments over time.

Regardless of the procedure used, registrars must be certain that the system of fee collection is efficient and equitable. From the point of view of the academic consumer, the registrar should see that tuition, fees, and other charges are properly listed in all current publications, including, but not limited to, the institution's catalog and schedule of classes. Special fees (such as those for supplies in fine arts courses, private lessons in music, green fees in golf, and required field trips), penalties for failure to meet fee obligations, acceptable methods of payment (for example, an increasing number of institutions, mostly private, now allow payment of tuition and fees through a nationally recognized credit card), and refund policies should also be published and accessible to students.

Some institutions require an earnest-money deposit at the time of admission to reserve a place in the student body. This deposit is usually kept as insurance that the student will register for subsequent semesters or quarters. Students who withdraw during the term and those who notify the institution (before the appropriate deadline) that they are not returning receive their deposit back. The same is true for those who graduate, provided they do not owe debts to the institution.

The Registration Processing Schedule

Regardless of the type or size of the institution or the level of sophistication of its computer hardware, the registrar must closely supervise the preparation and use of a registration processing schedule. This schedule, prepared well in advance of registration, should list all the hand and machine steps in registration processing and is prepared for the convenience and guidance of those personnel responsible for processing. Normally, the responsibilities of these computer or systems personnel lie outside the registrar's office; thus, it is of primary importance that the processing schedule be developed early and well, since it provides the processors with a "road map" of systems and required services. The sample processing schedule shown in Exhibit 1 illustrates some of the data elements that should be contained in such a schedule.

Registration Output

Materials and reports provided to students and faculty following registration may vary in format and design, but commonalities exist regardless of the institution. These common reports, or registration output, should include at least the following:

1. *Student class schedules.* A class schedule is produced for each student, listing the student's name, ID number, assigned classes by departmental prefix and course and section number or other identifying number, class meeting times and locations (buildings and rooms), credits per class, and total credit enrollment. The schedule might also list related information concerning special grading options, such as pass/fail or credit/no credit; the student's class, major, and faculty adviser; and the student's local address. The schedule should also indicate the academic year and term. If the class meets for a regular class period, its starting time should be listed; both starting and ending times should be indicated for classes that extend through more than one class period. Carbon copies of the student's schedule of classes may be made available to the academic advisers, departments, and the dean of students. The registrar's office should keep an official copy of the class schedules.

2. *Student fee statement.* In those institutions using some form of late fee collection or postbilling, an itemized fee statement must be prepared and given or mailed to each student. The statement, which may be combined with the schedule of classes or issued separately, should list the tuition owed; prepayments recorded, including financial aid granted (if any); special fees or charges, such as course fees, laboratory fees, and optional insurance fees; a balance due; and the required deadline dates for payment. Students who do not meet the payment deadline,

Exhibit 1

Registration Processing Schedule, Fall 1978

	Name	Process Number	Date	Time	Comments
1.	Time schedule update	RES834	Sept. 6–8	8:30 am	Dept. updates to registrar by 9-5-78
2.	Time schedule listing 2-part (decollate only)	RES836	Sept. 11	After update run	Copy for each dept.; master for registrar
3.	Time schedule update cards & related preparation for sectioning	RES837	Sept. 11		Interpret the time schedule update cards
4.	Build and test course request files	RER820	Sept. 12	7:00 pm	Final system test before registration
5.	Print list of packs prepared	REP820	Sept. 13	8:00 pm	Due to registrar with 4th enrollment pack run
6.	Mass registration	RER910	Sept. 14–15	All Day	
7.	EAM processing of pack cards	RER821	Sept. 14	All Day	Hourly basis
8.	Edit student requests	RER822	Sept. 14	All Day	Edit report to registrar following each batch run
9.	Back-up course request files (first day)	RER823	Sept. 14	6:00 pm	Secure back-up tape (disc) in vault
10.	Test sectioning program	RER826	Sept. 14	8:00 pm	Registrar will check test results
11.	Print preliminary course request report	RER824	Sept. 15	7:00 am	Report provides depts. with first-day registration data
12.	Preliminary enrollment count	RER840	Sept. 15	7:00 am	
13.	EAM processing of pack	RER821	Sept. 15	All Day	Hourly basis
14.	Edit student requests	RER822	Sept. 15	All Day	Edit report to registrar following each batch run
15.	Back-up course request files (second day)	RER823	Sept. 15	3:30 pm	Secure back-up tape (disc) in vault

16. Print course request reports	RER824	Sept. 15	5:30 pm	For review by depts. and deans
17. Preliminary enrollment count (mass registration)	RER840	Sept. 15	6:00 pm	List by class and sex, new and continuing
18. Address & student information system file up-dates		Sept. 15	6:00 pm	Continual processing
19. Final update of time schedule before sectioning	RES835	Sept. 15	10:00 pm	Deadline 11 pm
20. Registration sectioning	RER826	Sept. 15	10:30 pm to Midnight	Process following input of depts. updates
21. Print status of sections reports (6 copies, 3-part, narrow-decollate only)	RER831	Sept. 16	1:30 am	3 copies; depts., deans, registrar
22. Print student schedules (copy on microfiche)	RER828	Sept. 16	6:00 am	Original for student; copies to advisers, dean of students, student accounts, registrar
23. Decollate & burst student schedules		Sept. 16	6:30 am (start)	As printed
24. Temporary class lists (2 part)	RER834	Sept. 16	1:00 pm	Decollate only; original to dept.; copy to registrar
25. Select enrollment, pass/fail, and repeat cards (sort in alpha sequence)		Sept. 16	2:00 pm	
26. Pass/fail enrollment count	RPF815	Sept. 16	ASAP	To registrar
27. Repeat course count & alpha listings	RER836	Sept. 17	ASAP	To registrar
28. Sort enrollment cards (alpha seq.)		Sept. 17	4:00 pm	To registrar

Notes: 1. Deliver course request and enrollment cards to computing center on hourly basis.

2. Deliver address and personal information cards to Administrative Services on hourly basis.

3. Computing Center personnel are responsible for arranging back-up computing services with neighboring college.

plus a reasonable grace period, are subject to enrollment cancellation.

3. *Class lists.* A class roster must be made available to each instructor, preferably before the state of class. Since most enrollment changes take place in the first week or two of classes, many institutions prepare a temporary class list for the start of classes and issue a permanent or official class list several weeks into each term, after most of the enrollment changes have been processed. Class lists are sent to the respective instructors with a cover memo from the registrar that asks the instructor to read the list in class and report discrepancies to the registrar's office or direct students in attendance who are not on the list to report directly to the same office. Copies of all class lists should be kept on file in the registrar's office.

4. *Enrollment report.* This report—summarizing enrollments by class, sex, part-time/full-time enrollment status, and total enrollment—is usually issued at the end of registration (preliminary report) and again at the close of late registration (official enrollment report). These reports are normally given directly to the president and other top-level administrators and are usually released to the press. Care must be taken to ensure that the data being released are absolutely accurate because the institution's integrity and, in some cases, potential funding are based on the accuracy of these figures.

5. *Course enrollment summary report.* This report, issued to deans and department heads at the close of registration and again at the end of late registration, summarizes the enrollments in each course and section by department, division or college, and the institution as a whole. This printout, sometimes called a status of sections report, lists each course and section by department prefix, course and section number, meeting time(s), building and room, students enrolled, and seats remaining (if any). Official copies of this report are kept in the registrar's office for historical planning.

6. *Enrollment analysis report.* This study is usually prepared at the close of late registration and after drop/add activity is essentially complete. The report summarizes student course

enrollments and student credit hours (SCH) by department, division or college, and the total institution. Additional summary data on lecture, laboratory, and studio contact hours (clock hours) may also be included. The enrollment analysis report, sometimes referred to as the census report, is issued to the central administration and all deans and department heads.

7. *Closed class list.* This listing is normally a staff report prepared from the course enrollment summary report or the enrollment analysis report. The listing is made available to late registrants as well as deans and department heads.

8. *Entitlement reports.* Entitlement reports (a single report or a series of reports), usually prepared by state-supported colleges and universities for funding purposes, combine the data elements in 5 and 6 above, detailing student contact hours by department and/or cost categories according to varying state funding formulas. These reports are usually based on net enrollment each term and may be combined to indicate average annual enrollment.

Change of Enrollment

Although institutional policies vary widely regarding changes of enrollment, in general the student's official enrollment is recorded at registration, and procedures are made available for students to change their enrollment just prior to (in the case of pre-registration) or after instruction begins. The student is normally made responsible for initiating enrollment changes (such as dropping or adding a course or changing sections, credits, or grading options), and the enrollment change is effective upon receipt of the appropriate form by the registrar's office. Internal processing of enrollment change forms involves several of the following basic functions: (1) noting the change on the office copy of the student's record or class schedule; (2) transmitting the change to the computerized student record file; (3) notifying the instructor or department; (4) notifying other administrative or academic offices as appropriate; and (5) forwarding information on the enrollment changes to the accounting or financial section for adjustment of student fees in those cases where the changes create refunds or additional charges.

Enrollment changes are recorded on the official academic record according to institutional policy, and the original instrument by which the student submitted the enrollment change is retained to support the entry on the academic record at least through the current academic term.

Late Registration

The late-registration process—for students who, for reasons beyond their control, cannot register on time—should parallel regular registration, although more responsibility may be asked of the students. For instance, while preregistration or mass registration systems may make it possible to complete the registration process in one location, the registrar's office may require that late registrants seek course enrollment approval from each academic department offering the courses requested. In this way, the student is essentially hand-sectioned into class as negotiations take place with each department. If a class at the required time is closed or filled, the student must select an alternate class and proceed until all course enrollments have been approved by the respective departments. The student then reports back to the registrar's office to complete late registration and pay fees. Since the late process may coalesce several registration procedures into a single process, several steps may be eliminated. For instance, a late-registration enrollment card when completed may replace the printed class schedule. The form may be prepared in several parts, with the student keeping a copy of the late-registration enrollment card after it has been approved by the registrar. Late-enrolling students are usually placed into courses through the same process as regularly enrolled students who are adding or dropping during the first few days of class.

Late registrants are usually assessed a penalty fee that varies from a few dollars to twenty-five or fifty dollars. Some institutions use a graduated scale—one or more dollars the first day and a maximum fee at the end of the late registration. If the institution does not have a stated late-registration period or penalty fee, the registrar must accept the responsibility of requesting such a rule through the central administration or faculty governing body. Care should be taken to ensure that the late-registration period ends prior to the cutoff date for enrollment reporting for funding purposes.

Reregistration

Students who meet the published academic standards of the college or university are permitted to register term after term without reapplying, as long as their registration is continuous. Students who do not meet institutional standards are usually not allowed to reenroll without the permission and approval of a faculty-student hearing board, often referred to as an academic standards committee. Reregistration or reinstatement is the process of clearing the way for the registration of those who have been dropped from the institution. This clearance may have conditions imposed, in which case the student is given conditional registration. A student may be dropped from the institution because of low scholarship, health problems, or disciplinary problems. Health policies are the province of the health center administrators, and disciplinary problems are handled by the dean of students. Enforcement of academic retention rules and policies is usually the responsibility of the registrar.

Institutional admissions policies directly affect scholarship levels and academic retention; therefore, one might assume that few problems will develop with regard to retention policies and academic dropouts if entrance requirements are sufficiently high. This, however, is usually not the case, since academic performance is based on a complicated set of variables—including but not limited to admissions standards, problems of adjustment, ability of the teaching faculty, institutional resources, grading standards, and the health of the student. In addition, community colleges and other institutions with an open-door policy generally admit all students, regardless of their academic preparation; thus, administration of the academic retention program makes up a vital portion of student academic services.

Policies concerning the types of students to be attracted to the institution are covered in Chapters Two and Three. In most institutions scholarship standards are already established and in effect, and implementation of those standards and requirements is a primary responsibility of the registrar. If scholarship standards have not been set, the registrar should develop a rationale and recommended policy at both ends of the scholarship scale. Students whose performance is academically outstanding should be nominated to an honor roll or a dean's or president's list. Conversely, students who are performing below institutional expectations should be notified of their unacceptable academic behavior. Such notification should outline corrective procedures. Since most institutions already have such policies in effect, the registrar must ensure that the policies are being followed with precision and that the data generated are accurate. The registrar must also see that appropriate data—including basic profile information, test scores, grade performance in the most recent term (and overall), and related data—are provided to students who do not meet minimum retention requirements and to the administrative body in charge of retention decisions. Academically deficient students are normally notified that their academic records are unacceptable at the time that grades are reported. Such notification generally takes one of two forms: (1) students whose performance is less than desirable are notified that they are being placed on academic probation and, if they are to remain as students, must obtain a specified grade point average at the end of the next term; (2) students whose performance is below acceptable standards are informed that they have been dropped from the institution and may not reenroll (reregister) without the permission and consent of the office or committee in charge of academic standards.

The registrar must also ensure that institutional standards are listed in prominent publications, including the general bulletin or catalog, the master schedule, and any student handbook that might be in circulation. To make certain that the deficient student is notified of his or her deficiency at the same time that grade slips are distributed, many institutions have a deficiency message printed on the grade slip. Computer messages must be short and succinct, and references to the printed rules are helpful. For instance, a computer-printed message on the grade slip of a deficient student might simply state, "Academically deficient, see Rule ___."

With the advent of the Family Educational Rights and Privacy Act of 1974 and other state and local statutes that protect the privacy of the student, most institutions no longer send copies of grade slips to parents. However, the registrar concerned with good public relations will see that feature articles regularly appear in the student press, the alumni newspaper, and other bulletins that may be seen by parents, so that the public at large is informed of the scholarship standards of the institution. The registrar should also see that local news media are informed of the names of those students who achieve honor ratings. This is permissible under the Family Educational Rights and Privacy Act and is an excellent public relations effort on the part of the institution.

Processing of appeals from academically deficient students who petition for reregistration must rank high on the priority lists following distribution of grades. The procedures for appeal and the forthcoming decisions should be communicated to the student as early as possible. The registrar, by processing grade reports and applying retention standards, can expedite notification to students and academic officials simultaneously. Directions issued to the student should include the process of appeal, the office or agency to which the appeals should be addressed, and the deadlines to be observed. Students should also be informed of their right to appear in person before the committee or agency involved. When appeals are denied, the student should be informed of the time period involved before a new petition for reregistration or reinstatement will be accepted. Students whose petitions are granted with conditions must also be officially informed of those conditions—for instance, that they must repeat certain courses or that they may take only a limited number of courses. In these instances, the standards committee or the office charged with the responsibility for implementation should, as a follow-up procedure, check the student's record with the registrar to see that the proper conditions are being met.

A statement describing the retention standards and reinstatement procedures should be listed in the catalog. This statement in summary form might be somewhat as follows:

Academic Deficiency:

Undergraduate students are expected to maintain at least a 2.00 cumulative grade point average during their academic career at Central State. A student who falls below a 2.00 cumulative gpa is considered academically deficient, and special action is required for continued enrollment.

A student who is deficient for the first time is normally reinstated for a second semester. If the student is a certified major, reinstatement is the decision of the student's academic department. If denied reinstatement by the academic department, a student may appeal to the Office of Academic Standing for continued enrollment in another department. A student who is deficient for two consecutive semesters is normally dropped. A student who feels there are important extenuating circumstances can appeal to Academic Standing. A student whose work is improving (semester gpa of 2.00 or better), even though the cumulative gpa is below a 2.00 for two semesters, is usually reinstated.

The Catalog

Since registrars are deeply involved in curricular matters and are usually responsible for publication of the master class schedule, they are often assigned the task of editing the institution's general bulletin or catalog. This assignment helps to ensure the continuity and accuracy of printed curricular materials, since one office maintains the official course master file, curricular committee actions pertaining to courses and programs, and the master catalog.

Editing and publishing the catalog is a very time-consuming task involving many procedural steps as well as the cooperation of staff and faculty. Assuming that catalog style and size and the method and place of printing have been decided, minimal steps toward publication are as follows:

1. A "call for catalog material" is released to cognizant deans, department heads, and administrators. The call includes special instructions for preparing printer's copy, procedures, deadlines, and a copy of the addressee's portion of the most recent catalog for updating (the appropriate pages are usually removed from the previous publication and pasted on 8½" × 11" white bond). Instructions should indicate that *new or revised (or ALL)* information is to be typed, double-spaced, on white bond and submitted in duplicate to the catalog editor. Units with no changes in catalog material should

be instructed to return the paged material unchanged, with their signature or stamp indicating approval without changes.

2. When the first deadline has been met and the new and revised copy received, the editor compiles the materials, checking for accuracy, readability, and duplication, and forwards one copy of the edited material to the typist, typesetter, or, when a computer is being used, to the computing office for preparation of catalog galleys. This assumes that the editor has full authority for catalog changes or has had the appropriate changes approved by the central administration.

3. Catalog galley is returned to the editor in three copies. One copy is sent to the respective departments and administrative offices for proofing, with instructions and deadlines indicated. Cooperating authors are advised that all corrections and changes are to be made at the galley stage of publication, since changes at the page proof stage are troublesome and expensive. The second set of galleys is kept as the editor's official or office copy. As departmental galleys are received, corrections and changes are proofed and edited and consolidated on the editor's copy. When completed, the editor transfers all corrections to the third galley copy, which is sent back to the printer for updating and production of page proofs.

4. Page proofs are returned to the editor in two copies. Corrections made on galleys are checked against the page proofs, and pagination is added by the editor. Care is taken to read the lines just above and below each final correction, since they could have been altered when the typesetter made the corrections. The top and bottom lines of each column are also proofed for possible deletions during pagination. These instructions will differ somewhat for those using a computer or some other advanced form of typesetting. Changes at this stage of publication should be limited to typesetting errors that have occurred between galley and page proof. Additions at this stage are forbidden. The editor transposes all corrections to the second copy of page proofs, adding such last-minute items as the table of contents or index, cover material, and instructions, and sends the complete edited page proofs back to the printer.

5. The printer makes the necessary corrections to page

proofs, sets the index and cover, and prepares catalog blueprint. Based on time restrictions, the blueprint or final catalog copy is returned to the editor, or the editor may go to the publication office for final proofing.

Although the steps outlined above may be oversimplified, if they are followed carefully and if enough lead time is built into the publication schedule, the catalog should be ready for distribution on time.

United States postal regulations allow certain publications, such as periodicals and catalogs, to be mailed at the second-class postage rate if they are published at least four times annually. The second-class rate provides impressive savings, but the editor must be extremely careful to follow the postal regulations and meet mailing deadlines. Failure to meet these obligations may result in a fine or loss of the second-class mailing permit. Copies of publications mailed under the second-class rate must have an identification statement, listed in type no smaller than that of the normal text, on one of the first five pages of the publication or in the masthead on the editorial page. The statement must include the name of the publication; the date, issue number, and frequency of issue; the subscription price (if any); the name of the office of publication and zip code; and the second-class imprint and publication number. Mailing wrappers must show a notice of entry in the upper right corner. The upper left corner must list the name of the publication and the address to which undeliverable mail or change-of-address notices can be sent.

Contents of Catalog

The editor's responsibility goes beyond simple organization and editing of clerical errors in the catalog. The contents of the publication are vitally important. For instance, the catalog must clearly and precisely describe the student's academic rights and the institution's obligation to deliver the education promised in the catalog. What happens if a degree program is discontinued after the student is admitted? This must be spelled out for prospective students to read before they decide to attend the institution. Which set of degree or graduation requirements does the student meet:

those in effect at the time of admission or those in effect at graduation? This too must be stated, but the policy need not be over-restrictive. For example, the following statement or variation thereof might suffice:

Requirements for Graduation:
The graduation requirements of the college as published in the *Catalog* in effect at the time of the student's initial enrollment are those which must be met for completion of an undergraduate degree program. For transfer students the initial enrollment date shall be that upon which the student entered postsecondary education. Subsequent changes in degree requirements, as published in the *Catalog* or amended by the college senate, may be substituted at the option of the student.

Undergraduates who will not graduate within the normal degree time frame (four years for a four-year baccalaureate program and five years for a five-year program) must meet the requirements for graduation as published in the *Catalog* four years prior to the date of graduation.

Departmental requirements for graduation are those in effect at the time the student certifies the major. Changes in departmental requirements after certification will apply provided they do not require a student to enroll in more than a normal complement of credit hours in any term or do not prolong the time required to complete degree requirements. Department and program chairpersons have authority to waive or provide substitute course work for departmental requirements.

Since the institution's curriculum is under constant review and subject to change, catalogs are often at least partially out of date when they come off the press. Therefore, to avoid misunderstandings and to prevent consumer suits, the catalog might carry a caveat in the section preceding the course listings: "Courses listed in this catalog are subject to change through normal academic channels. New courses and changes in existing course work are initiated by the cognizant departments or programs, approved by the appropriate academic dean, the academic vice-president, the curriculum committees, and the senate. Additions to the curriculum for the ensuing year are published each fall in the *Catalog Supplement.*"

Course Prerequisites. Course descriptions in catalogs usually list prerequisites (specific courses or levels of performance or competence) for each course. The catalog also should indicate whether the prerequisites must be met or are merely guidelines for the student, whether students have alternatives, whether they can take a chance on passing even though they have not met the prerequisites and whether prerequisites can be waived. A simple policy statement, perhaps somewhat as follows, should solve the problem:

When applicable, prerequisites are listed in this catalog with the specific course description, preceded by the abbreviation "prereq." Prerequisites may be levels of competence or courses which a student must have completed before enrolling for a specific course. For example, the description for Calculus (Math 171) lists a prerequisite of Precalculus (Math 107), meaning that students may not enroll for Calculus until they have successfully completed Math 107. Prerequisites may also be general, such as "one semester of chemistry or concurrent enrollment," or they may specify a certain level of expertise or class standing (for example, "Students may not enroll in Spanish 324 without first being fluent in Spanish" or "Students may not enroll in an advanced seminar before achieving senior standing in the major"). Questions concerning prerequisites should be referred to the instructor of the course. Students who have not met all prerequisites may be excluded from the course, or the instructor may waive the prerequisite based on demonstrated competence or equivalent academic experience.

Names of Faculty. The listing of the names of the instructional faculty by the courses they teach is a practice that may have outlived its usefulness. Instructors resign, go on leave, and opt to teach new and more exciting courses; thus, the listing of faculty names by courses tends to be incorrect and a potential source for consumer action. Why not delete the names or carry them in the master class schedule, a publication that can be published each term, allowing for greater accuracy?

Statements of Nondiscrimination.[1] Catalog editors should also be aware of emerging developments with respect to federal legislation. As a result of the Civil Rights Act of 1964, institutions of postsecondary education who are recipients of federal assistance in any form are required to list in their catalogs and other pertinent publications a statement indicating that the institution does not discriminate on the basis of race, creed, color, or national origin. Title

[1]For more extensive coverage of this and related legislation, see the monograph titled *Keeping Your School or College Catalog in Compliance with Federal Laws and Regulations,* published by the U.S. Department of Health, Education and Welfare (1978).

IX of the Education Amendments of 1972 mandates that all applicants for admission and employment must be notified that the institution does not discriminate on the basis of sex and that it is required by Title IX not to discriminate in this manner. Section 504 of the Rehabilitation Act of 1973 specifies that institutions must publish their policies on nondiscrimination on the basis of handicap in admission or employment. Since all three of these statements on nondiscrimination must appear in college and university catalogs and related publications, the catalog editor might combine them into one comprehensive statement. All three are combined in the following example:

> The College of Middle America subscribes to the principles and laws of the state of _____ and the federal government pertaining to civil rights and equal opportunity, including Title IX of the 1972 Education Amendments. College of Middle America policy prohibits discrimination on the basis of race, sex, religion, age, color, creed, national or ethnic origin, marital status, or handicap in the recruitment and admission of students and the employment of faculty, staff, and students and in the operation of all college programs, activities, and services. Evidence of practices which are inconsistent with this policy should be reported to the office of the executive vice-president.

Policies Concerning Access to Records. Based on the requirements of the Family Educational Rights and Privacy Act of 1974 (FERPA), the catalog and similar publications must list students' rights and procedures with respect to access to records. These requirements are well defined, and examples are listed in the publication *A Guide to Postsecondary Institutions for Implementation of the Family Educational Rights and Privacy Act of 1974, as Amended* (American Association of Collegiate Registrars and Admissions Officers, 1976).

Student Consumer Information. The final regulations for implementation of Title I of the Education Amendments of 1976 (as listed in the December 1, 1977, *Federal Register*) require that catalogs and similar publications of postsecondary education which receive administrative payments under Title IV of the Higher Education Act of 1965, as Amended, contain information relative to financial aid and retention rates. Analysis of job market and employment data is recommended for inclusion if such information is available. Section 178.4 further specifies that the following information be prepared for dissemination (on request) to enrolled or prospective students:

1. A description of all financial aid programs available to students who are enrolled at the institution, including programs authorized under Title IV of the Higher Education Act and all institutional and state financial aid programs. The institution must describe for these programs the procedures and forms available for applying for such aid, student eligibility requirements, the criteria for selecting recipients from the group of eligible candidates, and the criteria for determining the amount of the award given to individual recipients.
2. A statement of the rights and responsibilities of students receiving financial aid under the Basic Educational Opportunity Grants, Supplemental Educational Opportunity Grants, College Work-Study, National Direct Student Loan, or Guaranteed Student Loan programs. This information must include the criteria for continued eligibility for each program, the criteria for determining that a student is in good standing and maintaining satisfactory progress, the criteria by which a student who has failed to maintain satisfactory progress or good standing may reestablish eligibility for payment, the means by which payment of awards will be made to students and the frequency of payments, the terms of any loan received by a student, and the general conditions and terms applicable to any employment provided to a student as part of his or her financial aid package.
3. The cost of attending the institution, including tuitions and fees; books and supplies; typical room and board and transportation costs for students living on campus, off campus, or at home; and any additional cost for the program in which the student is enrolled or expresses a specific interest.
4. The refund policy of the institution for the return of unearned tuition and fees or other refundable costs paid to the institution.
5. The academic program of the institution, including the current degree programs and other educational and training pro-

grams; the instructional, laboratory, and other physical facilities which relate to academic programs; and the faculty and other instructional personnel.

6. Data regarding student retention at the institution and, if such data are available, the number and percentage of students completing the program in which the student is enrolled or expresses interest.

7. The titles and locations of employees available to assist students or prospective students in obtaining the information specified in items 1–6 above.

Veterans Assistance. In accordance with Public Law 94–502 (as outlined in DVB [Department of Veterans Benefits] Circular 20-76-84, Appendix P, dated February 1, 1977), institutions must submit to the state approving agency a certification that the school's catalog is true and correct in content and policy. This certification must be made by an authorized official of the institution, such as the registrar or the catalog editor. The example below is offered for illustration only. Although the DVB Circular does not recommend that the statement refer directly to the appropriate federal law or the communication from the Department of Veterans Benefits, these citations are recommended because they add necessary specificity to what would otherwise be a rather general statement that could easily be misunderstood.

Information contained in this publication is hereby certified as true and correct in content and policy as of the date of publication, in compliance with the Veterans Administration DVB Circular 20-76-84 and Public Law 94-502.

Signature _____

Title _____

The Veterans Administration also requires that the catalog or bulletin list the following information:

1. The institution's policy and regulations relative to standards of progress required of the student by the institution (this policy will define the institution's grading system).

2. The minimum grades considered satisfactory.

3. The conditions for interruption for unsatisfactory grades or progress and a description of the probationary period, if any, allowed by the institution.
4. The conditions of reentrance of those students dismissed for unsatisfactory progress.
5. A statement regarding the progress records maintained by the institution and furnished to the student.
6. The institution's policy and regulations relating to student conduct and conditions for dismissal for unsatisfactory conduct.

Cost Cutting

The shortage of paper, the rising cost of printing, and the ever increasing expense of postage mandate a change in catalog style and format. The editor should consider reducing catalog bulk through the elimination of unnecessary information, use of lighter paper or newsprint, elimination of multicolored layouts, and possibly even a reduction of the number of photographs. If the catalog is being produced on an annual basis, consideration might be given to conversion to a biennial catalog; or, if institutional policy requires annual printing, the editor might consider distributing the catalog to libraries and out-of-state and federal users on a biennial basis. One sure method of reducing printing costs and postage is through the use of microfiche. Several vendors, including the National Microfilm Library, will contract to reproduce a catalog on microfiche for pennies per copy. Editors might propose to the central administration a reduction of total catalogs printed, restricting the hard copy to local patrons only and using microfiche for all out-of-state and federal mailings. Most catalogs can be totally reproduced on only six to eight microfiche, which can be mailed in a small envelope for a tremendous savings in postage. Obviously, the profession is years away from complete use of microfiche or microform technology, since most individual users do not have access to viewing equipment. However, most major libraries and certainly state and federal government offices do have such equipment, and thus the use of this new technology should be seriously considered. Volkmann (1977, p. 421) suggests other practical ways of reducing the cost of publications. Finally, catalog editors might band together on a local, regional, or national basis to seek methods of reducing catalog size and weight. Most catalogs seem to be reproductions of previous publications. Perhaps editors, working together, could propose a list of catalog elements that might be deleted from future publications.

Further Reading and Study

The subject of registration appears throughout the literature, especially in *College and University,* the professional journal of the American Association of Collegiate Registrars and Admissions Officers. Of special interest is J. D. Hopperton's (1975) "Registration Can Be Fun: A Small Computer Can Do It All." Also helpful is Rosemary Shield's (1970) chapter, "Registration, Scheduling, and Student Records," in the *Handbook of College and University Administration* (A. S. Knowles, editor). The handbook *Registration Roulette* by Bernard Hoffman and Edwin Smith (1967) is recommended reading. Helpful hints are also provided in the *Self-Audit Manual for Registrars* (second edition), published by the Kentucky Association of Collegiate Registrars and Admissions Officers (1975). A good survey of machine registration procedures and forms will be found in *Optical Scanning Applications in Higher Education,* published by the American Association of Collegiate Registrars and Admissions Officers (1972).

Regarding the catalog, useful readings include the chapter on "Cost-Saving Devices" (Volkmann, 1977) and the chapter on "Publications for Key Audiences" (Crawford, 1977) in the *Handbook of Institutional Advancement* (A. W. Rowland, editor). These chapters contain, among other things, an excellent overview of college and university publications and suggestions for consolidation of various brochures and catalogs for cost savings. Similarly, *Keeping Your School or College Catalog in Compliance with Federal Laws and Regulations,* issued by the U.S. Department Of Health, Education and Welfare (1978), is recommended reading for all catalog editors.

7

Organizing and Maintaining Academic Records

C. James Quann

Student records include those of a permanent nature (normally the permanent academic record and certain initial source and supporting documents) and various transitory records used for input to or revision of the permanent academic record. Comments herein pertaining to the permanent academic record are not comprehensive, since a detailed description is found in Appendix A (the AACRO *Academic Record and Transcript Guide.*

The permanent academic record should be designed so as to be durable, easily corrected, readily copied, yet difficult to produce in facsimile (by forging an original). The format should be logical and professional in design, conveying a positive image of the institution. All entries should be neat, readable, and, perhaps most important, readily and completely understandable. These requirements are based on the basic purpose of the permanent record: to provide a record of academic progress and achievement to be transferred from the institution to prospective employers, other institutions, and others to whom the student presents his or her records. The permanent academic record provides a complete accounting of all work attempted at the institution, unless institutional policies permit deletions or omissions, in which case the policy should be clearly explained. All corrected entries or revisions should be annotated to explain the reasons for such corrections or changes. Essential portions of the permanent record are the complete identification of the institution, including zip code; identification of the student; the basis for admission; record of work taken; the major field of study (if any); and a complete explanation and description of all entries in the record of work taken. (Records managers should note that the 1977 edition of the *Academic Record and Transcript Guide* no longer lists sex and marital status as an essential element of the academic record.)

The record of work taken should be arranged chronologically by term and year, with an identifying departmental or academic unit prefix, catalog number, and descriptive title (avoiding misleading or undecipherable abbreviations). The credit granted and grades for each course completed round out the list of essential items. Termination status is normally essential to the record. However, indications of suspension or dismissal for academic reasons are little used in current practice, and such entries for nonacademic reasons are no longer appropriate under the Family Educational Rights and Privacy Act of 1974; therefore, the recorder usually indicates only what degree (if any) the student received and whether the student terminated in good standing.

Perhaps the most prevalent shortcoming of permanent records or transcripts is the portion on institutional policies. Although the length of term, definition of credit unit, column headings for credits and grades, designation of sources of credit, and explanation of the grading system are minimum essential elements, they seldom provide complete information to the evaluator without additional explanation. Examples of desirable information include the institutional course-numbering system, policy on the repeat of course work, requirements for graduation, graduation honors, and a description of the official method of validation and seal. This and other explanatory and identifying information can be printed on the reverse side of the stock paper used for photoreproduction and thus will always appear on the reverse side of a transcript of the student's academic record.

Other important types of student records include the student's original application for admission and accompanying documents such as the high school transcript, transfer records from other institutions, the advanced standing report or the record of credit accepted on transfer, and results of entrance examinations or scores on national or statewide standardized tests. Transitory records consist of such items as grade cards or sheets, student class schedules, and change of enrollment cards or forms. The contents of such records are ultimately reflected on the permanent academic record or grade report; hence, they serve only to substantiate entries on the permanent record. Transitory records are treated as official student records during the academic term, but their usefulness declines sharply after the end of the term or the student's graduation, and their preservation beyond a limited period is questionable. The institution is obligated to maintain the official academic record of all students in perpetuity, but many of the supporting records need not be kept beyond the student's date of graduation.

Student educational records stored on magnetic tape or disk must be stored and protected in the same manner as hard-copy records. Care should be taken to see that important magnetic tape or disk records are prepared in duplicate (backed up), so that there will be an alternative means of performing critical record-keeping operations if data processing facilities or equipment are damaged or destroyed.

Ideally, the registrar's office should make the official academic record or transcript and its supporting personnel folder available to the student on request. Indeed, the Family Educational Rights and Privacy Act of 1974 mandates that these records be open and available to the student within a reasonable time following the student's request. Except during rush periods, such as registration and grade reporting, a student ordinarily should have immediate access to the requested records as a continuing service. Procedures must also be established to allow students to appeal or challenge information (not including grades) in their educational records that they feel is incorrect or inaccurate. A standing committee should be appointed to hear these appeals, with membership including representatives from the registrar's office, the faculty, and the office of student affairs. If the institution has a graduate school, a representative of that body should also serve on the appeals group. The representative of the office of student affairs is included in case appeals concerning disciplinary matters recorded on educational records kept in other than the registrar's office.

Definition of the Credit Unit

The credit hour (or unit of credit) is universally used to denote a standard unit for measuring a student's accomplishment and progress, but quantitative definitions of the term are neither uniform nor widely published. A precise definition is important within each institution to promote uniformity in credit assigned to each course, with respect to contact and clock hours devoted to the course, and as a guide for faculty teaching regular course work and for those responsible for evaluating independent study, summer reading, and other nonstructured courses.

One of the more authoritative definitions of the credit hour appears in a publication of the National Center for Education Statistics (1968, p. 15):

Credit Hour. The unit by which an institution may measure its course work. The number of credit hours assigned to a course is usually defined by the number of hours per week in class and the number of weeks in the session. One credit hour is usually assigned to a class that meets fifty minutes a week over a period of a semester, quarter, or term; in laboratory, fieldwork, drawing, music, practical arts, physical education, or similar type of instruction, one credit hour is assigned for a session that meets two or three hours a week for a semester, quarter, or term. Quarter credit hours and semester credit hours are the two most common systems of measuring course work. Institutions on the trimester plan generally use the semester credit-hour system. Courses offered in a calendar other than semester or quarter, including summer sessions, may be measured in term credit hours or stated in semester credit hours or quarter credit hours.

In the above definition, the credit hour is a simple function of the number of hours a student devotes to class during the semester or quarter. Under the semester scheme, a lecture course meeting fifty minutes a week for sixteen weeks is assigned one semester credit hour, and a laboratory course that meets for two or three fifty-minute periods a week for sixteen weeks also is assigned one credit hour. Studio, the form of instruction not totally lecture or laboratory but a combination of both, such as oil painting or music recital, may have a special credit-hour ratio set midway between the two primary types of instruction. The foregoing definitions recognize two components of the time-to-credit ratio: lecture and non-lecture class work. A third component of credit-hour measurement is the outside preparation or other work related to the class. All three components can be indicated in one comprehensive definition as follows:

Credit Ratios. Academic credit is a measure of the total time commitment required of a typical student in a particular course of study. Total time consists of three components: (1) time spent in class; (2) time spent in laboratory, studio, fieldwork, or other scheduled activity; (3) time devoted to reading, studying, problem solving, writing, or preparation. One quarter or semester credit hour is assigned in the following ratio of *component hours per week* devoted to the course of study: (1) lecture courses—one contact hour for each credit hour, two hours of outside work implied); (2) laboratory or studio course—at least two contact hours for each credit hour, (one hour of outside preparation implied); (3) independent study— at least three hours of work per week for each credit hour.

The credit-hour ratios above are the same whether for quarter- or semester-hour computation. Thus, the hour earned over a ten-week quarter is equivalent to two thirds of an hour earned over a sixteen-week semester. The above formulas can also be used to calculate the credit ratios for workshops and special sessions of less than term duration. For example, a one- or two-day workshop would normally not qualify as a one-credit offering unless there were sufficient required preworkshop study or postworkshop follow-up assignments equivalent to the additional hours of outside preparation implied in the above credit ratios.

Impact of Recent Developments

During the past decade, higher education has experienced some revolutionary changes, especially in the area of nontraditional or alternative educational programs. Prior to these changes, academe had been virtually "locked in" to the concepts of traditional on-campus lecture classes, course credits, and alphabetical grading. During the turbulent 1960s and early 1970s, many of these time-honored practices were challenged and some exciting new educational concepts were developed.

New Grading Options

In the late 1960s pass/fail, credit/no credit, and similar innovations became popular alternatives to traditional letter grading. Although many of these less competitive forms of grading are referred to under the umbrella term *pass/fail,* the pass/fail option itself may be dying out more quickly than some of the other fail-safe methods of grading. For instance, credit/no credit and other nonfailure grading schemes remain popular in the community colleges, especially within vocational-technical education.

Regardless of the type of nontraditional grading used, registrars should ensure that the grading options are clearly spelled out in the catalog and are well identified on student transcripts. Transcript marginalia or legends should specify which nontraditional options are available as well as the meaning of nontraditional marks. For instance, the transcript legend might specify the quality of performance indicated by passing grades; for instance, "P = A, B, and C" or "P = A–D." If the grading option calls for the posting of only A, B, and C grades, with no indication (expungement) of enrollments in course work graded D or F, this too should be explained in legend information. Similarly, credit/no credit options, which allow the awarding of withdrawal passing grades in lieu of failure, should be indicated. If nontraditional marking is used extensively, other evaluative measures, such as narrative evaluations and test scores, should be reflected on each student's official record. Limitations on pass/fail and similar grading options should also be indicated in catalogs and transcript legends.

Noncollege Experiential Learning

The practice of awarding academic credit for noncollege experiential or life learning is not new, having been used at colleges such as Antioch and Sarah Lawrence for many years. The practice, based at least in part on John Dewey's (1938) philosophy of the intimate and necessary relationship between the processes of actual experience and education, received added stimulus when several federal and national agencies encouraged development of procedures for awarding educational credit for work accomplished outside the formal classroom. In 1971 a Carnegie Commission on Higher Education report titled *Less Time, More Options* urged development of these modes of nontraditional credit. In 1972, in a report titled *The More Effective Use of Resources,* The Carnegie Commission further developed the need and rationale for such innovations. Leadership from the Office of Educational Credit of the American Council on Education (ACE) and the Cooperative Assessment of Experiential Learning (CAEL), a Carnegie Corporation–funded project of the Educational Testing Service (ETS), further accelerated this movement.

Currently, some form of experiential credit is offered at most colleges and universities. These forms include, in addition to credit for life or work experiences, such variations as advanced placement based on superior high school performance or high scores on local or national placement tests; credit for standardized examinations through the College-Level Examination Program (CLEP), the College Entrance Examination Board's Advanced Placement Program (APP), and the American College Testing Program's Proficiency Examination Program (PEP); military credit as recommended in the *Guide to the Evaluation of Educational Experiences in the Armed Services,* published by the American Council on Education (1976); and credit earned through challenge examinations administered by the college or university in which the student is enrolled.

An official cumulative permanent record must be established and maintained for each student, regardless of the type of program or system of evaluation. Institutions awarding credit for experiential learning are obligated to see that academically sound evaluations are made and properly documented on these student records. Specifically, institutions awarding experiential credit must develop and publish clearly stated policies and procedures regarding assessment methods and criteria, student eligibility, and recording practices. Furthermore, the substance and meaning of the experiential credits awarded must be clearly indicated. (The record might state, for instance, that a particular experience is recognized as equivalent to a specific regular course or to a certain number of units or credits of English composition.) Finally, experiential credit must be evaluated by qualified and experienced departmentally based faculty; admissions and records personnel should assist in these evaluations, but final decisions should rest with subject matter specialists in the academic disciplines under consideration.

The concept of noncollege experiential learning is both broad and challenging, and it is not possible to adequately cover all the issues here. An overview of the subject has been published by the American Council on Education (1978a) in a monograph titled *Recommendations on Credentialing Educational Accomplishments.* This publication provides an excellent summary of the problems, offering fifteen recommended changes in credit and credentialing systems.

The Continuing Education Unit[1]

In 1968 the American Association of Collegiate Registrars and Admissions Officers, the National University Extension Association, the U.S. Office of Education, and the U.S. Civil Service Commission sponsored a national conference and a task force (see National Task Force on the Continuing Education Unit, 1974) on the creation of a uniform unit of measurement for noncredit continuing education offerings. Subsequently, the Continuing Education Unit (CEU) concept was adopted by the Southern Association of Colleges and Schools and by colleges and universities in other parts of the United States.

The CEU *is not in any sense credit per se.* It is designed to provide a systematic method of measuring and recognizing partici-

---

[1] This section is based largely on *The Continuing Education Unit: Guidelines and Other Information* (Southern Association of Colleges and Schools, 1973) and *The Continuing Education Unit: Criteria and Guidelines* (National Task Force on the Continuing Education Unit, 1974). It was prepared with the assistance of Keith E. Glancy, Director of Special Projects, Johns Hopkins University; Lloyd Joyner, Registrar and Director of Admissions, Georgia Southern College; and John Rhodes, Vice-President for Public Services and Continuing Education, Memphis State University.

pation in professional and continuing education, vocational re-training, adult education, and in-service training. Ordinarily this recognition is achieved through the issuance of a hard-copy CEU report similar to standard grade reports. Based on an official copy of this report or a CEU transcript, current or prospective employers may hire, promote, or grant salary increases as they currently do with "credit" records. The CEU serves as a unit of measure to give recognition to an individual's participation in *non-credit educational activities* that meet the appropriate criteria. One Continuing Education Unit is defined as ten contact hours of participation in an organized continuing education experience—under responsible sponsorship, capable direction, and qualified instruction. *Continuing education* is noncredit learning experience in organized formats that impart education to postsecondary learners. *Organized* means scheduled and approved in advance, with delineated objectives, content, and instruction processes. *Experience* includes, but is not limited to, noncredit courses and classes, workshops, conferences, institutes, symposia, seminars, and short courses. Although departmental or agency names vary within colleges and universities, *sponsorship* means offered by an academic or other appropriate department or program through an Office of Continuing Education or a similar agency.

The CEU is a relatively new addition to the taxonomy of higher education. Some institutions will award CEUs; others will not. In institutions that do award them, CEU records should be officially filed in and available from institutional records offices. However, CEUs must always be kept separate from regular credit records to avoid pressure from students to develop formulas for the conversion of noncredit CEUs into usable credits that will meet degree requirements.

Criteria for Awarding Continuing Education Units. In order for the Continuing Education Unit to become the basic unit of measurement for an individual's participation in qualified noncredit classes, courses, and programs, the following criteria are required before CEUs can be awarded to a course or program.

1. The noncredit activity is planned in response to an assessment of educational need for a specific target population.

2. There is a statement of objectives and rationale.
3. Content is selected and organized in a sequential manner.
4. There is evidence of preplanning, including opportunity for input by representatives of the target group to be served, the faculty area having content expertise, and continuing education or extension personnel.
5. The activity is of an instructional nature and is sponsored or approved by the academic or administrative unit best qualified to assure the quality of the program content and to approve the resource personnel utilized.
6. There are provisions for registration of individual participants and for providing data for permanent records and for institutional reporting.
7. Appropriate evaluation procedures are utilized and criteria are established for awarding CEUs to individual students prior to the beginning of the activity. These may include the evaluation of student performance, instructional procedures, and course effectiveness, and/or the taking and recording of student attendance.

Continuing Education Units may be awarded for the following types of activities:

1. Intensive courses and workshops in technical and professional areas (such as accounting, engineering, nursing, pharmacy, social work, teaching, or veterinary work).
2. In-service training programs on new techniques or in technical areas.
3. Programs that may be used in partial fulfillment of certification or licensing requirements.
4. Programs, cosponsored by the institution and technical or industrial societies, designed to upgrade the performance of members in occupational or technical areas.
5. Training or refresher courses for paraprofessionals and subprofessionals.
6. Liberal education programs for the general public.

The following types of programs *would not be awarded* Continuing Education Units:

1. Courses or programs carrying academic credit.
2. Programs leading to high school equivalency certificates or diplomas.
3. Orientation programs.
4. Programs only casually related to any specific college-level upgrading purpose or goal.
5. Entertainment, social, or athletic events.
6. Activities conducted prior to the adoption of the CEU by the institution.

The *number of units awarded* is determined by the number of contact hours of organized learning (classes, organized discussions, laboratories, field trips, or independent projects). CEUs are awarded in whole units or portions of units; for example, a 35-hour activity normally provides 3.5 CEUs. Partial contact hours are not recorded. Sponsoring departments should indicate the content level of programs with the following designations: *introductory, intermediate, advanced.* The level, if designated, is recorded on the student record and appears on transcripts. Although practices may vary by institution, it is recommended that the registrar's office be given the responsibility for maintaining the necessary records and for issuing reports and transcripts associated with the recording of Continuing Education Units. Individuals who participate in CEU activities meeting the specified criteria should have individual records of their involvement submitted to and available from the institution through the registrar. A nominal fee may be charged for this transcript service.

Implementation of the CEU Program. The awarding of CEUs for participation in a program should be promised or published only after specified procedures have been followed and the necessary approvals received. The following procedures for implementation are provided only as an example; they should not be viewed as recommended or "model" situations. The ensuing assumptions underlie the procedural examples:

Procedures governing the CEU program are developed by a Committee for Continuing Education Units and approved by the dean or academic vice-president prior to implementation. Existing organizational and procedural responsibilities are retained, except for the insertion of the

Committee for Continuing Education Units reporting to the dean or academic vice-president. Specifically, the Office of Continuing Education is responsible for developing course offerings, obtaining approval of each offering through the Committee for CEUs, and, upon completion, providing notice to the registrar for maintaining permanent CEU records. The registrar creates and maintains the permanent CEU records and provides transcripts upon request for the same fee as for other academic records.

The CEU Approval Petition (Exhibit 1) is prepared by the sponsoring academic or administrative unit and forwarded through the CEU administrative unit and the Committee for CEUs to the dean or academic vice-president (or designee). The Committee for CEUs recommends approval or disapproval and determines the number of CEUs to be awarded. Upon approval by the dean or academic vice-president, copies of the form are distributed to the sponsoring unit, the CEU administrative unit, the committee, and the registrar. At the first meeting of the session, the participants complete Section I of the Enrollment and Completion Form (Exhibit 2); the forms are then collected by the instructor, who completes Section II at the close of the course. The cognizant office then forwards one copy per student to the registrar.

The cognizant sponsoring office provides a Certificate of CEUs Awarded (Exhibit 3) to each participant who is awarded CEUs upon completion of the activity. The registrar's office may create a permanent CEU record upon successful completion of a CEU activity, or it may simply accumulate and file the completed CEU Enrollment and Completion Forms by name and then prepare the permanent CEU record as transcript requests are received. Many registrars report that requests for CEU transcripts are very rare; hence, the latter procedure may save both time and expense. Also, the American College Testing Program (ACT) has established a National Registry for Continuing Education. Institutions offering CEUs may transfer to ACT the function of maintaining permanent CEU records, with the student paying for the service through transcript fees.

Grade Reporting

The grade-reporting system should be designed to provide the student with a complete report of grades earned, together with

Exhibit 1. Continuing Education Unit (CEU) Approval Petition, College of Middle America

1. Title of Activity/Course _____

2. Activity/Course Objectives _____

_____

_____

3. Brief Description _____

_____

_____

4. Planning Consultation _____

5. Target Audience _____ Format _____ Level ___ Introductory

___ Intermediate

___ Advanced

6. Estimated Attendance _____ 7. Tentative Dates _____

8. Cooperating Noninstitutional Organizations _____

9. Total Clock Hours of Instruction _____ 10. Number of CEUs Recommended _____

11. Teaching Location _____

12. Source of Revenue _____ 13. Enrollment Fee _____

14. Instructors _____

15. Evaluation Procedure _____

_____

16. Activity Director _____

APPROVED:

_____ Date _____
Sponsoring Academic or Administrative Unit

_____ Date _____
Director, CEU Administrative Unit

_____ Date _____
Vice-President—Academic (or Dean)

COMMENTS: _____

_____

_____

_____

INSTRUCTIONS:
(1) After completing the form, the activity director forwards all copies to the sponsoring academic (normally department or program) or administrative unit.
(2) The sponsoring unit retains copy 3 (pink), copy 2 (yellow) is retained by the appropriate CEU administrative unit, and copy 1 is forwarded to the academic vice-president.
(3) Upon approval, copy 1 is returned through the registrar and the CEU administrative unit to the originator.

Exhibit 2. Continuing Education Unit (CEU) Enrollment and Completion Form, College of Middle America

SECTION I (To be completed by participant)

Name _____   Highest degree or grade completed:
      Last   First   Middle Initial _____

Address _____
      Street   Male ___ Female ___

_____   Date of Birth _____
City   State   Zip Code

Home Phone (___) _____   Soc. Security No. _____
      Area Code

Activity or course in which enrolling:

    Title _____

    Dates _____

    Location _____

Have you previously earned CEUs from CMA? ☐ Yes ☐ No

SECTION II (To be completed by activity instructor)

Evaluation of participant's program completion

    ☐ Satisfactory
    ☐ Unsatisfactory
       (No CEU awarded)

Comments _____

_____   _____
Date   Instructor's Signature

SECTION III (To be completed by activity director)

This activity and the CEU awarded were offered in accordance with approved procedures for the Continuing Education Units of the College of Middle America.

    CEUs Awarded _____

_____
Activity Director's Signature

_____
Title

NOTE: At the conclusion of the activity, send this copy to the Registrar's Office.

INSTRUCTIONS:

(1) Each student completes Section I during the first class meeting and returns forms to the instructor.

(2) Upon completion of the activity the instructor completes Section II.

(3) Copy 2 (yellow) is retained by the instructor and copy 1 is routed through the activity director to the registrar.

Exhibit 3. Certificate of CEUs Awarded

College of Middle America

Awards

_____ Continuing Education Unit(s)

to

_____

For satisfactory completion of _____ hours of organized instruction in

_____

_____   _____

Program Director   Date

The instructional program represented by this certificate was provided in accordance with the criteria and standards of the National Task Force on the Continuing Education Unit.

updated cumulative grade point and credit summaries, at midterm (when applicable) and promptly after the close of each academic term. The reporting procedure typically begins with machine-printed grade sheets or cards provided to each member of the teaching faculty. These grade-reporting forms should contain the student's name and other identifying data and provide appropriate space for the instructor to mark the grade awarded to each student in longhand or in a machinable mode. Although the practice is nearly outmoded, some small colleges prepare grade slips and records by hand, typing the reports from grade rosters received from the instructional staff. Other institutions use machine-readable forms, such as mark-sense cards or scanning sheets, to automate grade processing. In this instance, the completed grade sheets or cards are returned to the registrar's office, where they are checked and then read on to computer files. Since promptness is essential in this phase of grade reporting, a firm deadline, fully supported and emphasized by the central administration and deans, must be established for receipt of grading forms. A deadline of twenty-four to forty-eight hours following the close of final examinations is feasible and can be enforced by aggressive action on the part of the registrar, acting through department heads and deans when appropriate.

After all the grades have been placed on computer files, grade reports may be produced in automated mailers concurrently with copies needed for internal purposes. The mailers are immediately dispatched to the students, with copies of the grade reports supplied to faculty advisers, department heads for certified majors, and the dean of students. Grade reports are no longer sent to parents unless they can prove the dependency status of their sons or daughters, as required by the Family Educational Rights and Privacy Act of 1974.

An essential step in automated grade processing is to determine, on a timely basis following the grade-reporting deadline, which grade reports have been returned by the faculty and which ones are outstanding. Small institutions may develop a hand-tally system to record grades when they are received. Larger colleges and universities find it more expedient to let the computer count the grades received and produce an exception report, sometimes called a "shy report," listing the grades not received. This printout can be used to call the tardy professors to request that grades be delivered immediately. It also provides a basis for determining whether the percentage of grades returned is sufficient to warrant a go-ahead signal to computing and systems to print student grade reports.

Several steps can be taken to prevent faculty from turning grades in late. First, when designing the final examination schedule, the registrar should ensure adequate time for test scoring and grading between the end of the examination period and the deadline for grade reporting. If the schedule is prepared by hand, examination periods for the largest classes can be scheduled early to maximize the time for scoring tests and awarding grades. The examination schedule should be well advertised—preferably in advance, by including it in the master class schedule, and again toward the end of the term. Enlightened registrars also know that secretaries can often be more helpful than the dean when it comes to collecting late grades. Head secretaries should be encouraged to develop grade sign-in systems at the departmental level. In this way, the secretarial staff can determine well in advance which grades are likely to be turned in late, and collection can be expedited. Faculty handbooks and, if possible, teacher contracts might carry the admonition that the instructor's commitment to teach is not fully met unless final grades are posted on time. Some institutions even suggest that pay checks might be held until grades are deposited. Registrars should note, however, that on occasion conditions occur that are beyond the control of the instructor, and arrangements must be made to process late grades. In these instances, most institutions award an "X" grade or some other recognizable symbol indicating that the grades are being withheld due to instructor sickness or absence. This course of action tells the student that the grade has been withheld for a good and sufficient reason, a procedure that helps with public relations and reduces the number of panic phone calls and letters from students.

When all grades have been received and grade slips issued to students, the registrar's staff posts the final grades and credits earned to the student's official record. Methods for accomplishing this task vary from hand typing to heat transfer, gummed labels, and generation by computer of the student's total record on transcript stock. In the late 1960s and early 1970s, due to the increasing incidence of late grades and grade changes, a few registrars developed a system whereby final grades were not posted until three to four weeks after grade reports had been issued. This delay allowed the staff to add late and corrected grades to the computer files before posting the student's official record. In this way, when records were finally posted, the grade information was complete and accurate. Urgent transcript requests received during the interim are honored by superimposing the latest grade slip on the official record and photocopying both. Instructions printed on the reverse side of the transcript describe this practice to evaluators and students.

Certification of Degrees and Other Information

The certification of graduates is one of the foremost and oldest responsibilities of the registrar. The registrar of the University of Paris in the Middle Ages certified only licentiates and masters (Stout, 1954), but his modern counterpart must certify a myriad of degrees and certificates. The president and boards of regents or trustees and the faculty actually award the degrees and certificates, but the responsibility for clearing and certifying degrees lies with the registrar. This normally involves the processing of degree applications, the careful evaluation of the academic records of each degree candidate, and determination of whether or not each candidate has completed the general education or distributive requirements as well as department or major requirements. In institutions with graduate programs, the graduate school usually assists with the evaluation and certification of graduate degrees.

Responsibility for determining whether department or major requirements have been completed is generally shared with the head of the cognizant department. The procedure usually involves preparing a graduation checklist for each candidate (sometimes referred to as a to-do list) that contains the student's name and identification number, academic major, and expected graduation date; general as well as departmental or major requirements to be completed and minimum total credits and grade points to be earned; and related information, such as the amount and payment deadlines for the degree or graduation fee. The academic department usually assists in the preparation of the checklist by supplying data relative to departmental and major requirements to be completed. After the evaluation process has been completed, normally toward the end of the student's junior year or at the beginning of the senior year, and the grades and work completed in the final term have been checked and double-checked, the registrar prepares a list, arranged by degree title, of those students who have completed all requirements for certification. After this list has been approved by the faculty or governing body, the registrar records the appropriate degree on each student's official record and distributes the degrees and certificates, which were printed earlier and held in abeyance, to the respective students. The diplomas and certificates carry the official seal of the college or university as well as the signature of the president, head of the governing board, and sometimes the registrar.

The registrar, as custodian of the college or university seal and with access to official records not available to other departments or administrators, also certifies official statements in compliance with requests from students for information that is not readily available from other sources (information such as rank in class, date of birth, hours enrolled, class status, completion of degree requirements, athletic eligibility, or qualification for student body office). Such information may be required for veterans or social security benefits, scholarships, loan deferments, applications to graduate or professional schools, admission into the United States for foreign students, or prospective employers. In addition, the registrar's office certifies student information directly to a correspondent when such requests fall within the guidelines of the Family Educational Rights and Privacy Act of 1974. Examples would include the certification of dates of attendance, degrees granted, and honors received.

Transcript Service

A transcript is a reproduction of the complete and unabridged educational record at the issuing institution and must be an effective means of prompt and accurate communication of educational information. Prompt and efficient transcript service is not only a basic responsibility of the registrar's office but is vital to public relations, since it is the primary link between the institution and its former students and alumni. Transcripts should normally be produced within one working day, and they must be legible, self-explanatory, and properly validated so as to preclude unauthorized reproduction. Requests for transcripts, with certain exceptions provided in the Family Educational Rights and Privacy Act of 1974, may be honored only when they are received from the person whose record is being requested. Students requesting access to or copies of their records must provide adequate identification (such as the student ID number, date and place of birth, and dates of attendance) before their requests are granted. Because of the difficulty involved in properly identifying the requestor, transcript requests are normally not accepted by telephone. Letters bearing the student's signature and order forms with signatures provide legal proof of identification and relieve the registrar of the burden of proof. Official transcripts furnished to educational institutions or prospective employers are marked with a statement that the "release of information from this transcript to a third party is prohibited by the Family Educational Rights and Privacy Act of 1974." Transcripts issued directly to the student should also be conspicuously marked "Issued to Student" or "Unofficial—Issued to Student."

The means of reproduction used should produce a clear, permanent copy, with provisions for reducing the probability of undetected alterations. Authentication includes the date, the official seal of the institution, and the signature and title of the certifying officer. A further measure against unauthorized reproduction of the copy is provided by validating with colored ink, with a notation in the margin or on the reverse side that without such validation the transcript is void. Unauthorized reproductions are instantly detected if the appropriately colored and embossed seal is absent.

Office procedures should include a method of recording requests, the date that the record was mailed or released, the person or institution to which it was released, and fee information when applicable. The requestor should be notified that the transcript has been mailed in accordance with his or her request. If instititional policy requires withholding a transcript for indebtedness, the requestor should be notified of the policy, the reason that the record is being held, and the charge or balance owed. The policy should also be clearly stated in all appropriate institutional publications. Requests by students for copies of their transcripts from other educational institutions are normally not honored, and the students are referred to the previous institution concerned. In exceptional cases, where another transcript is unattainable or can be secured only with the greatest difficulty, as in the case of some foreign institutions, copies may be prepared and released to the student as long as the copies are carefully marked "certified copy of a record from the student's file."

Charges for transcript service vary. Many institutions provide free service. Others provide the first transcript free and impose a standard charge thereafter—an excellent procedure from a public relations point of view, but the record keeping required to determine whether a student has received a free copy militates against this practice. Some colleges and universities charge a standard fee for the first copy and a lesser fee for additional copies ordered at the same time. Still others vary the split-fee practice by requiring the standard fee per addressee, with the lesser fee for multiple copies provided to the same address. This plan compensates for the additional clerical work necessary to make out forms, address envelopes, and pay postage. An alternate fee plan that has gained a degree of popularity is to provide what appears to be free transcript service while collecting a standardized fee from all students in some other fashion, such as a graduation fee, a matriculation fee, or a records fee. Although the latter scheme has some merit, it tends to be inequitable because heavy users are subsidized by those who never or infrequently use the transcript service.

A transcript key or legend should also be included with or incorporated into the transcript. Many institutions print such information separately and include it with all mailings. This procedure can be burdensome and is easily replaced by simply printing the legend and descriptive material on one side of the paper that is used for photoreproduction. In this way, the information always appears on the reverse side of the transcript and cannot become separated from that record. Since academic regulations and policies are changed through faculty or administrative action, the back-printing concept is desirable, since it may be readily changed without causing alterations to the permanent records. The listing of the transcript key and legend information on the margins of the transcript is not desirable, since it cannot be changed when policies and regulations are changed.

ID Systems

The fundamental purpose of a student identification system, usually a unique number or the social security number, is to positively identify students for record purposes. The additional help provided by such an ID numbering system is crucial for identifying students with identical or similar names. The identification number also allows the machine sorting of student records in institutions using unit record equipment or limited computer equipment without the capability of sorting records in name sequence.

Although the social security number affords a tailor-made identifier, the legality of its use under the Privacy Act of 1974 (Public Law 93.579) and other pending legislation is questionable. Other limitations of the social security number include the need for assigning bogus numbers to foreign students and the inability to sort records in name sequence. Thus, where the social security number is used to identify students, institutions often find it necessary also to assign each student a unique identifying number for data processing purposes.

Identifying numbering schemes vary from a five- to eight- or nine-digit system. Some institutions also use a three-digit code, as a prefix or suffix, to indicate the term and year of enrollment; for example, 771 would indicate the first term of the 1977 academic year. The assignment of ID numbers in an alphabetical sequence correlated with the student's surname is feasible, but this approach is relatively time consuming and subject to human errors, such as the assignment of duplicate ID numbers, with attendant complications. Therefore, sequential assignment of ID numbers without regard to alphabetical-name sequence may be preferable. This process is further simplified by producing computer-printed numbers in sequence for a given admissions term on adhesive label tapes, which may be affixed to the entering student's admissions papers at the appropriate point in processing.

The student identification number serves several ancillary purposes, in that it normally appears on an identification card or other official document which identifies the bearer as a student enrolled in the institution. Such cards may be validated to indicate the student's current enrollment status, and the ID card provides access to college or university facilities and to athletic, cultural, and recreational events. To preclude their unauthorized use, careful attention must be given to safeguarding the issuance, replacement, and validation of ID cards.

Records Security

Records security includes all physical measures designed to protect and preserve the records throughout their retention period; measures to reconstitute essential records in the event of fire or other natural disasters; and the protection of records from tampering, loss, illegal reproduction, and unauthorized access. Basic protection requires that confidential student records be kept in locked storage at all times when the office is not open for business and under surveillance of authorized personnel when the storage area is unlocked. All records, and especially the permanent academic records, are to be protected from damage during handling in the normal course of business, from fire, and from abnormal changes in heat and humidity. Preferably, the permanent academic records should be stored in a fireproof area. The ability to reconstitute the essential files in the event of fire or natural disaster is best provided by microfilming the records and storing the microfilm in a secure place separate from the registrar's area.

Office procedures should be designed to secure the records against tampering, loss, and unauthorized access. All registrar's records personnel should be alert when the files are open for normal usage, to preclude any unauthorized person from having access to the files and to prevent alterations by persons who are given such access. Specifically, positive measures should be taken to ensure that students have no opportunity to tamper with their own records while reviewing them in the presence of registrar's personnel. One method is to make the record available for viewing through a glass-topped table or counter or to insert the record in a transparent case, such as Plexiglas, before presenting it to the student for review. Nonetheless, the review should always take place within the view of staff members. Official academic records should under no circumstances leave the control of the registrar's staff at any time. Since employment in the office of the registrar provides the opportunity for unauthorized changes in academic records, procedures for periodic checking of the records of employees and their spouses are desirable.

Protecting the transcript of an official record from tampering or alteration after it leaves the office is a difficult matter. Several practices provide some insurance against such tampering. These include the production of transcripts of official academic records on photocopy machines with reduction capabilities. A slight reduction condenses the record, often making printed information easier to read, and the reduced type size precludes altering the record by typewriter. Another accepted practice is to place the date, the signature and title of the certifying official, and the college or university seal on the transcript with colored ink. It is also helpful if an embossing seal is used, so that transcript evaluators can actually feel the raised seal. Also, the method used to update or officially change recorded information on academic records should be noted in the margin or on the reverse side of all transcripts. In this way, if the institutional practice is to record grade changes and the like by hand in india ink, the viewer of the record will know that the record has been *officially* altered.

Retention of Records

A retention program is vital to the efficient operation of any registrar's office. Limitations of office and storage space demand that decisions be made as to which records are to be retained, and for how long, and which records can be destroyed. The sooner a systematic program is established, the easier it will be for the records manager to make these decisions. For permanent academic records, the accepted practice is to retain the records indefinitely, either in hard copy, on microfilm, or in computerized form. If the records are microfilmed or maintained on magnetic tape or disk, provisions must be made for reasonably responsive reproduction time as well as for updating the records as required. Current practice also places admissions materials—including original source documents, such as the application for admission and transcripts from previous institutions—in the category of permanent records. Retention of supporting documents such as grade reports and enrollment changes should be related to the available storage space. Because such records serve only to substantiate entries on the permanent record, they are essential for a relatively short period of time. Since challenges to permanent record entries normally occur during the course of the student's attendance or shortly thereafter, a retention period of four to five years is generally satisfactory for these types of records. However, many institutions retain microfilm copies of grade records permanently, since permanent academic records are occasionally challenged years after grades have been recorded.

The essentials of a retention-destruction program should be based on (1) the projected availability of storage space as it relates to the creation of the particular record file; (2) a systematic microform schedule, and (3) a systematic destruction program. Legal statutes in some states mandate specific retention and destruction schedules and classify documents into specific retention categories, with some records kept in perpetuity and others classified for destruction on an annual basis. Since record keeping is an extensive and expensive business, in states without such retention laws some institutions have created their own records retention and destruction program. Although some may consider such a program a bureaucratic waste of time, others will realize the value of a complete inventory of all records and the development of a specific schedule for storing, microfilming, and destruction of records. The inventory itself, if properly and thoroughly performed, will assist the records manager in the operation of an efficient and effective office. A records inventory can also become invaluable for in-service training of new personnel and may assist in ferreting out outdated practices and procedures. A sample "Record Retention and Destruction Schedule" is provided in Exhibit 4 for those who may wish to develop their own program. The sample schedule is intended to include the more common records with their generic titles. It is provided only as an example and should not be viewed as a model for all institutions, since record-keeping practices and retention needs will vary. For instance, community colleges normally have large numbers of noncontinuing and nonmatriculated students, and the record-keeping requirements may be less severe for these kinds of students. Some two-year schools provide nonmatriculated students with grade reports but do not maintain permanent academic records for them. Also, since most community colleges operate on the open-door policy (nonselective admissions), they may not need to maintain extensive admissions files.

Further Reading and Study

A Student Records Manual, a publication sponsored by the National Association of College and University Business Officers (1970), provides a basic primer for registrars and records office

Exhibit 4. Record Retention and Destruction Schedule, Office of the Registrar

Record Title	LOCATION OF RECORDS*			Retention Schedule	Transfer to Archives	Remarks
	Original	Microfilm				
Permanent record (transcript)	RO	RO Remote		Permanent	50 years following last enrollment	Microfilm each term
Admission application and supporting source documents	RO	RO Remote		Permanent	same as above	Microfilm 5-yr. intervals; burn originals
Minutes of faculty, graduate faculty, senate	RO	Remote Library		Permanent	50 years	Microfilm every 3 years for safety; keep originals indefinitely
Enrollment reports	RO	N/A		Permanent	To be determined	
Course request reports	RO	N/A		12 years	No	
Pass/fail lists	RO	N/A		12 years	No	May be altered by senate action
Size of class lists	RO	N/A		12 years	No	
Status of section Reports	RO	N/A		12 years	No	
Scholarship reports	RO	N/A		12 years	No	
Census reports	RO	N/A		12 years	No	

Record					
Grade distribution Reports	RO	Remote	Permanent	20 years	Original to deans and academic VP
Geographical distribution reports	RO/Adm	Remote	Permanent	20 years	
Extension records (continuing educ)	RO	Remote	Permanent	50 years	Microfilm every 3 years
Correspondence transcripts	RO	Remote	Permanent	50 years	Microfilm every 3 years
CEU records	RO	Remote	Permanent	50 years	Microfilm every 3 years
Enrollment cards (Forms)	RO		4 years	No	
Student class Schedule	RO		4 years	No	
Grade cards or sheets	RO		4 years	No	
Pass/fail grade cards	RO		4 years	No	
Drop-add cards	RO		4 years	No	
Student grade reports	RO		1 Academic Term	No	
Class books (Rosters)	RO		4 years	No	Original to instructor; copy to RO
General correspondence	RO		4 years	Partial	Materials selected by archivist

Exhibit 4. (Continued)

| Record Title | LOCATION OF RECORDS | | Retention Schedule | Transfer to Archives | Remarks |
	Original	Microfilm			
Marriage file (cross-index of names)	RO	Remote	Permanent		Microfilm 5-yr. intervals; burn originals
General catalog (bulletin)	RO	N/A	Permanent	12 years	
Master schedule of classes	RO	No	Permanent	12 years	
Commencement programs	RO	Remote	Permanent	To be determined	Microfilm annually
Diploma books (listing of degrees awarded)	RO	Remote	Permanent	To be determined	Microfilm annually

*Adm = the admissions office
RO = the registrar's office
Remote = a location outside the registrar's office, preferably a separate building

personnel. This manual, prepared under a grant provided by the Esso Education Foundation, covers the usual responsibilities of registrars and includes brief outlines of procedures and examples of various general and computer forms.

The subject of awarding credit for nontraditional learning is thoroughly discussed in *Awarding College Credit for Non-College Learning,* by Peter Meyer (1975). Meyer outlines an academic rationale for experiential learning and provides guidelines and recommendations for the assessment and award of such credit.

In 1960 the American Association of Collegiate Registrars and Admissions Officers published *Retention of Records: A Guide for Registrars and Admissions Officers in Collegiate Institutions.* The *Guide* is currently being updated by a national task force, and AACRAO published a revised *Guide* in 1979.

8

Creating and Using Information Systems

□ □ □ □ □ □ □ □ □ □ □ □ □ □ □ □ □ □

William C. Price

This chapter highlights important information systems definitions and concepts. Chapter Nine then describes new information systems tools and techniques that are important to those who manage data for students on college and university campuses; it also contains examples of how information technology is being used effectively in support of admissions and records work at five different colleges and universities.

Historical Background

The interest of college registrars and admissions officers in the use of machines and systems to aid them in their work is not new. As early as 1930, they were using Hollerith punched-card machines to support such basic administrative functions as admissions, registration, tuition assessment and collection, and the preparation of student directories, student class lists, and institutional statistical reports. Registrars at New York University, the University of Iowa, the University of Michigan, the University of Texas, and the University of Oregon were nationally recognized as leaders in the use of punched-card methods in colleges and universities. As is the situation today, these registrars were seeking ways to process student information accurately, rapidly, and flexibly before it became outdated and useless.

Despite the early and effective use of punched-card methods by a few registrars and business officers in large universities, however, interest in administrative data processing did not become widespread nationally until after World War II. The world's first all-electronic computer, named ENIAC, went into operation in 1946 at the University of Pennsylvania (Spencer, 1974). The International Business Machines (IBM) Corporation introduced its first general-purpose electronic digital computer (the IBM 604) in 1948. The IBM 604 was much slower than today's computers, and all input-output functions were performed on punched cards. In 1951 Universal Automatic Computer (UNIVAC) produced the first large-scale business data processing system for the government. This first UNIVAC computer included some important new input-output equipment common today, electric typewriters and magnetic tape units. Soon after the UNIVAC I computer was operational, programming techniques were developed to help people better utilize the machines.

In 1952 the American Association of Collegiate Registrars and Admissions Officers (AACRAO) sponsored a series of punched-card workshops for its members. Not until the 1960s, however, did registrars, admissions officers, and other college administrators begin seriously to consider the potential for totally new techniques and achievements made possible by the development of high-speed computers and improved data processing technology. The role of administrative data processing in all types of colleges and universities grew dramatically in importance and scope during the 1960s. "Computers on Campus" (Caffery and Mosmann, 1967) became the subject of much study and debate.

In 1959 IBM introduced the IBM 1401 data processing system. The phrase *first-generation computer* was associated with this event. The IBM 1401 became the workhorse computer of administrative data processing on many college campuses for the next five years. Printers for the 1401 system ran at 600 lines per minute. The

IBM 360 computer was introduced in 1964. Printing was up to 1,100 lines per minute. By the middle 1960s other computer manufacturers—such as Burroughs, Control Data, Honeywell, and UNIVAC—had also developed computers that colleges and universities were using. But throughout the 1960s the most common types of computers found on college campuses continued to be manufactured by IBM.

Computer-based student data systems grew quickly during this period. Indeed, by 1963 the University of Illinois, Purdue University, Massachusetts Institute of Technology, Pennsylvania State University, the University of Massachusetts, the University of Iowa, and the University of California at Davis had developed national reputations for using computers effectively to support essential admissions and records work (Price, 1966). During the late 1960s, community colleges and some smaller public and private senior colleges also began to make effective and significant use of computers to manage admissions and records activities.

In 1964–65 the American Association of Collegiate Registrars and Admissions Officers appointed a special subcommittee on electronic data processing to conduct its first national survey on the status of administrative computer operations and facilities in colleges and universities. (AACRAO sponsored similar surveys again in 1965–66, in 1968–69, and in 1978–79.) In 1967 AACRAO sponsored its first Management of Data for Students (MODS) seminar at Colorado State University for college administrators interested in the development and management of student information systems, and since 1967 over thirty national and regional MODS seminars have been held on college campuses throughout America.

In 1970 IBM introduced the IBM 370 computer, and IBM printers at that time were printing at 2,000 lines per minute. Because of engineering breakthroughs in the areas of transistors and microminiature circuits, many computer manufacturers besides IBM were marketing machines that were smaller, faster, and much more reliable than the first-generation computers. New types of equipment and computer technology that focused on the input-output needs of computer users began to appear on campuses. Registrars and admissions officers were quick to capitalize on these new developments. College administrators and computer specialists began to design and implement new information systems using optical scanning devices, computer output to microfilm, and word processing equipment. Today an IBM 370/3032 computer equipped with the newest IBM 3800 printing system using laser and electrophotographic technologies can print at 13,360 lines per minute. Even more important, today's computers are now capable of receiving and processing millions of instructions per second at reduced costs. The central factor in planning new computer systems is no longer the cost of equipment. The biggest cost is for personnel to test, maintain, and change these systems.

Key Definitions

Many people, including some who have been operating computers and programming them for some time, have no formal training in the subject. This lack of training has contributed to the basic problem of communication between those who operate and manage computers and those who wish to use them. Misunderstandings have resulted from the lack of standard agreement on definitions. Even the term *data processing system* evokes a variety of responses from those who are asked to define it. Therefore, it is essential that some definitions be set forth and agreed on at the outset.

Space limitations do not permit an exhaustive listing of key terms and their meanings here, and so the reader may wish to procure copies of the dictionaries and glossaries mentioned in the section on Further Reading and Study at the end of this chapter. But the following definitions are fundamental to the vocabulary of effective college users of computers and information systems technology:

> *Administrative data processing.* The processing of data by electrical machines or electronic computers with little human assistance. In a college or university, administrative data processing is usually accomplished in a single, central location; processing of data is limited to that which is needed to manage the institution; and processing is characterized by a systematic approach, a sequencing of activities, and precise rules.

The term is used synonymously with *automatic data processing* (ADP) and *electronic data processing* (EDP) by some college administrators.

Alphanumeric code. A code consisting of letters, digits, and associated characters such as those found on typewriters. Early punched-card methods featured alphanumeric codes for the unique identification of students and to expedite alphabetizing operations.

Analyst, systems. A person skilled in defining problems and in developing techniques for solving problems, especially those associated with computers and information systems technology. Not necessarily a person with programming abilities. There is no agreed-upon body of knowledge about computers or computer programming that one must possess to be called a systems analyst.

Back-up. Alternate means to permit performance of critical operations in case of significant damage or destruction to data processing facility or equipment (National Bureau of Standards, 1974).

Batch processing. Mode of processing whereby transactions are "saved up" and then grouped for processing during the same machine run.

Cathode-ray tube (CRT). An electronic vacuum tube, such as a television picture tube, that can be used to display graphic images.

Coding. Representation of data or a computer program in a symbolic form that can be accepted by a computer. Synonymous with *coding scheme.*

Computer. A device capable of accepting information, applying prescribed processes to the information, and supplying the results of these processes. Typically, a computer consists of input and output devices; storage, arithmetic, and logical units; and a control unit. Synonymous with *hardware configuration* (Bureau of the Budget, 1962).

Computer output to microfilm (COM). A system whereby a computer-produced magnetic tape is sent through a microfilm processor that converts the information on the tape onto microfilm. Systems have been developed at a number of colleges and universities to convert tapes to microfiche. Various sizes of microfiche and different types of film can be used; a photoreduction process is involved. For example, a microfiche might be a 4-inch by 6-inch sheet of 105-millimeter film exposed at a 42 to 1 reduction.

Computer specialists. Personnel (programmers, operators, or administrators) with expertise in the management, operation, and control of computers.

Computerized system. A system that includes some processes which are executed by a computer or equipment controlled by a computer.

Common data base. A collection of data that are central or fundamental to the administration of a college or university. A file cabinet, a card file, computer files, and human memory are all forms of a data base.

Central processing unit (CPU). The unit in a computer system that includes the circuits controlling the interpretation and execution of instructions. Synonymous with *main frame.* Also referred to as *hardware.*

Data. Raw statistics and facts, to which meaning may or may not be ascribed.

Data processing system. "A network of machine components capable of accepting information, processing it according to a plan, and producing the desired results" (International Business Machines Corporation, 1972).

Disk, magnetic. A rotating disk with a magnetizable surface, on which information is recorded and stored. A magnetic disk storage system is an array of such devices.

Documentation. The supplying of documents or supporting references to describe how a system works. Documentation may include flowcharts, descriptions, reports, and matrix charts showing inputs and outputs of a system as well as how information is collected, filed, maintained, and retrieved.

Drum, magnetic. A rotating cylinder having a surface coating of magnetic material, on which binary information is stored. The binary system of computation, which uses the numbers 0 and 1, is used by most computers.

Flowchart. A symbolic representation of the major steps in the processing and flow of information within a system.

Information. The knowledge acquired from data when they

have been processed. (The terms *information* and *data* are sometimes used synonymously and erroneously by college administrators.)

Input. A device, process, or channel involved in the transfer of data into a system. In the case of computing, inputs of data may be entered into a system by punched cards, magnetic tape, terminals, or some other method. Applications for admission and registration forms may be referred to as "inputs" into a system.

Input-output (I/O). A general term for the equipment used to communicate with a computer and the data involved in the communication.

Job control language (JCL). A programming language used to code job-control statements or to identify the requirements to a computer's operating system.

Language. A set of representatives, conventions, or rules used to convey information. The terms *machine language, algorithmic language,* and *programming language* are all used in computing (American National Standards Institute, 1970).

Magnetic tape. A recording of bits of information sent from a computer central processing unit in patterns onto a tape.

Management information system (MIS). Management performed with the aid of automatic data processing (American National Standards Institute, 1970). Sometimes referred to as the use of centralized information systems designed around decision requirements (Murdick and Ross, 1971).

Master file. Frequently referred to in administrative data processing as the *history file* or *file of authority* for a particular job; as, for example, a permanent student "master file" that contains data for all students enrolled in a college during a specific term (Awad, 1966).

Minicomputers. A small computer system that enables operators to create and utilize information files. Like all computers, minicomputers are built as systems containing data-entry and output devices. Software for such systems may be developed or purchased. A typical system might include a terminal device that can be used to create, store, retrieve, change, print, communicate, and eliminate records (Green, 1977).

Objective. Something toward which effort is directed; an aim or end of action. Objectives and goals are words frequently used and associated with information systems developments. Unfortunately, the objective of a computerized system is sometimes forgotten in the process of developing such a system.

On-line system. A mode of processing data whereby input data enter the computer directly from the point of origin or output data are transmitted directly to the place where individual action may be taken; for example, a computer terminal located in an admissions and records office.

Optical character recognition (OCR). Machine identification of printed characters through use of light-sensitive devices.

Optical scanning. A device that scans printed or written data and usually generates an analog (continuous) or digital (numerical) signal. Scanning may be done by an optical mark reader (OMR) or by an optical character reader (OCR) (American Association of Collegiate Registrars and Admissions Officers, 1972).

Output. The product of a system, usually resulting from a response to input. Outputs may take the form of computer-generated messages, punched cards, magnetic tapes, pictures, graphs, visual displays, or reports.

Programming, computer. The act of designing, writing, and testing a computer program. Programs are written in a variety of programming languages. For example, COBOL is the acronym for *CO*mmon *B*usiness-*O*riented *L*anguage, a language frequently used by programmers working with college and university administrative data processing systems.

Punched cards. A card with a pattern of holes used to represent data. Sometimes referred to as a *tabulating card* (because of early use of such cards in machine accounting operations) or as a *Hollerith card* (because Dr. Herman Hollerith devised an alphanumeric system for encoding cards). Often mistakenly referred to as IBM cards (many companies besides IBM produce them).

Real time processing. The processing of data in a sufficiently rapid manner so that the information obtained is available in time to influence the activity being monitored or controlled

(Bureau of the Budget, 1962). Synonymous with *real time system.*

Software. A set of programs, procedures, and documents used in a computer system; for example, compilers, library routines, manuals, circuit diagrams, and administrative application programs.

Student information system. A plan of procedures for the systematic collection, processing, maintenance, and retrieval of information about students. Usually the use of a computer is associated with the development of a student information system. However, the term is intended to be less restrictive and to encompass the use of a variety of information tools (such as word processing equipment, microforms, telecommunication devices, closed-circuit television, files, and publications) not necessarily connected to a computer.

Terminal, computer. A device, usually equipped with a keyboard and some kind of display, capable of sending and receiving information over a communication channel (International Business Machines Corporation, 1972).

Unit record equipment. Electromechanical data processing equipment including the following punched-card devices: keypunch, verifier, sorter, collator, interpreter, calculator, reproducer, and accounting machine. Synonymous with *punched-card equipment* and *punched-card methods.*

User. One who is primarily responsible for an information system or procedure that is dependent on data processing support but who is not a computer specialist.

Virtual memory storage (VMS). A computer storage-allocation technique which allows the size of programs and data to exceed the memory space available, by bringing into memory (from disk storage) only the parts of programs and data needed for processing. In VMS the computer hardware and software move information into main memory when and only when it is required for processing, and change the virtual storage address to the real address during execution (Bradley, 1973). Even when a computer with limited memory is used, VMS gives programmers the illusion that they have a very large main memory at their disposal.

Important Management Concepts

Is college A's computerized arena registration a good one? Is it better than college B's on-line advance registration? Should college C computerize its manual registration? Which registration alternative is the most efficient and effective? Answers to these questions are not easily obtained. No national standards exist to aid in the evaluation of student information systems in colleges and universities. It is as difficult to determine the quality of a registration activity as it is to judge the excellence of mathematics instruction. However, experience has led professionals in the field to conclude that some techniques and procedures do work better than others, especially when certain concepts are understood and appreciated.

Importance of User Involvement. The success of a computer-based data system is measured by the extent to which students, faculty, and staff can use the system to increase their effectiveness. "User involvement" in defining the problem to be solved through automation is central to achieving successful information systems (Price, 1968). Unfortunately, in the brief history of data processing in colleges and universities, the major users of automated systems have learned this lesson the hard way. Naturally, the ultimate objective is to design and install a successful system. Why, then, have so many systems failed on campuses throughout the country? There is no single, quick, and easy answer to this question, but perhaps part of the answer can be found by assessing typical comments from both users and computer specialists who have had to live and work with unsuccessful systems. Let us examine *user comments* first:

"The system was designed by the data processing staff, and it is not responsive to the real needs of the campus or this office."

"I kept telling the systems analyst what our objectives were, and he kept redefining them for me."

"The director of the data processing center tells me we have a successful automated system. The students, faculty, and my own staff tell me we are doing a poorer job than before the system was installed."

"The system was designed to fit the machine and not to solve the problem we asked the DP people to help us with. Computer specialists look upon the hardware and installation of the system as being *the system.*"

"The labor costs and work involved at both the input and output points in the system were underestimated by the systems designers. They simply focused on the computer and neglected two extraordinarily important aspects of any system: the administrative processing resources required to maintain the system, and the people who must work with the system, clerks, students, faculty, etc."

What do *computer specialists* have to say about systems that have been perceived as failure on campus?

"The user group is very difficult to determine on a college campus. I tried to get the top campus administrators and leaders involved in defining the problem. But they kept saying, 'That's what we hired you to do.' It was only after the system was operating that they got interested in the objectives we had set."

"The registrar is an old-time administrator who doesn't like computers. He resisted involvement all along the way. He thinks change will be forced on him by computer people. Our working relationship is just not good."

"Users want the benefit of advanced information systems, but they won't take enough time to learn about the complexities of these systems."

"I told the deans and the director of admissions that we might have some problems and slippage along the way. Nevertheless, they approved the project with enthusiasm. When we experienced some delays because of programming problems, they became disillusioned. Then, when the system was implemented, we had some set-up problems: missing functions, bad data, limited documentation, etc. The next thing I knew they were complaining about the cost of the system and that the system was not doing what they expected it to do. It's a no-win situation!"

"The vice-president thought our staff could not do the job alone, so the university set up a contract with this outside consulting firm. The outside firm did not try to study the old student system, which contributed to a major problem during the initial design phase. In my opinion, the design of the new student information system will never be satisfactory in meeting reporting deadlines and in providing timely student information that is needed by the university. Top administrators would not act to make important decisions or get involved until we had problems. This definitely led to delays in getting ready for the new system. I am indeed sorry to resign. But because of administrative conditions which cannot be tolerated, I must leave the university."

While the preceding comments do not represent the situation on most collegiate campuses, systems failures have occurred frequently enough to be of significant concern to colleges and universities. The lesson to be learned from these experiences is that the ultimate responsibility for establishing a hierarchy of objectives is with the user and not the computer specialist. Admissions officers, registrars, and top campus administrators must be involved in the design of any computer-based student information system: "To achieve successful infosystems installations, DP people must subordinate themselves to the user. The user is the source of information and, often, the man (or woman) who pays the bills. . . . It is the user, and only the user, who makes the system work. . . . Lack of understanding is the primary cause of user resistance" (Ainsworth, 1977, p. 46).

The more specific a user can be about the problems to be solved, the more help he can expect from a computer specialist in solving the problems. Of course, some developments have been stopped dead by computer specialists who have not attempted to assist the user in defining a problem. Experienced data processing personnel call this ploy "paralysis by analysis." They know that most users have difficulty in defining exactly what is required when advanced technologies offer new solutions to old problems. Therefore, a sharing of technical skills and knowledge and a sound working relationship between users and computer specialists are really the keys to successful systems development. Managers of student data (users) must interact continously with computer specialists to ensure the development of systems that yield accurate, timely information in a usable form.

Technicians tend to concentrate on the technical beauty of a system and to assume that nontechnical personnel will somehow be able to figure out how to use it in solving problems (Alter, 1976). In many ways, college administrators and nontechnical staff have only themselves to blame for this situation. Some college administrators have resisted almost any efforts to advance administrative data processing capabilities on campus, and others have completely defaulted in their responsibilities as users to "define the problem." As a result, computer specialists are permitted to make basic decisions about systems goals and objectives that will significantly affect students and faculty, or to make changes in campus administrative structure. The expert knowledge of computer specialists can be valuable, but their judgments may be narrow and technically parochial at times. The management of data for students is a sensitive process, not an event. Successful college teachers and administrators are cognizant of this fact. Some computer specialists are not.

Student Information as an Institutional Resource. There was a time in the history of higher education when college registrars and their staffs were the only persons who had direct access to student files. Now, however, users of individual student data with a "legitimate educational interest" may have direct access to computer files with or without the knowledge of the registrar. The pros and cons of this development have been hotly debated by some registrars, campus leaders, and citizens in recent years. Some contend that automated student data systems present a serious threat to the individual rights of a student, including the potential for infringement on some basic liberties. Others argue that the potential for abuse and misuse of student information has existed since the first manual files or student records were established. They are optimistic about the use of technical innovations, such as access-control devices, to prevent substantial problems for the student, faculty, and staff who rely on computer-based systems to do the work of the academy.

A useful report entitled *Records, Computers and the Rights of Citizens* (U.S. Department of Health, Education and Welfare, 1973) sets forth the issues involved in this debate in much greater detail and recommends safeguards for automated data systems. Without such safeguards, there could be an increase in violations of campus policies pertaining to the release of student information. Admissions officers, registrars, and student personnel administrators have always been sensitive to the need for colleges and universities to have written policies that protect the rights of students and the privacy of student records. But the increased use of automation on campus and the enactment of the Family Educational Rights and Privacy Act of 1974, as Amended (the "Buckley Amendment"), have heightened the need for such policies.

The purpose of the Act is to require educational institutions and agencies to conform to fair information practices; that is, persons who are subjects of data systems must be informed of the existence of such systems, be able to learn what data about themselves are on record, be assured that data are used only for intended purposes, be able to correct or amend records, and be assured that those responsible for data systems take reasonable precautions to prevent misuse of the data. Information about individuals should be retained only so long as it is valid and useful, and those responsible for data systems have an obligation to destroy information when conditions under which it was collected no longer prevail. [American Association of Collegiate Registrars and Admissions Officers, 1976, p. 1].

Regardless of the potential problems associated with automation and technological change in student record keeping, computers have made it possible to improve services to many more legitimate users of student information: individual students, faculty, and college administrators with critical academic and student-support roles. College administrators recognize that student information is a valuable institutional resource; it does not belong exclusively to the registrar and his or her staff. And the computer age is here to stay.

Documentation as Communication. Experience has also taught us that failure to document can lead to disaster and "management by crisis." In numerous instances computerized systems have failed because knowledgeable computer personnel (operators, programmers, systems analysts) have stopped working for the college or university. Similarly, systems have broken down in user offices because an assistant registrar, who acted as the liaison between a computer center and a records office, left the job for greener pastures and took with him (in his head) user knowledge of the system.

Administrative data processing systems are usually complex. Few humans, even the most able and intelligent, can remember how a system works without written documentation. Since documentation is a form of communication, it should not be neglected when managing systems, especially computerized systems. Interested readers are advised to obtain the MODS2 syllabus (Ekstrom and others, 1972) for specific information on documentation tools, methods, and procedures.

Three points about documentation efforts deserve emphasis here. First, college registrars and admissions officers should develop a sensitivity to the fundamental importance of documentation. Second, documentation should be maintained on a continuing basis. Constant surveillance over documentation files and references is required to accomplish this goal. As changes in an information system occur in daily operations, these changes should be written and recorded routinely, or documentation of the system can quickly deteriorate; the so-called "little changes in the system" are often those that cause major difficulties when they are not documented. Finally, documentation should be written in the language style of its audience.

Importance of Planning for an Automated System.   Edwin D. Smith, former registrar at Syracuse University and now deceased, was an early advocate of the notion that users of computer technology in higher education should prepare detailed plans before any new data system project is approved and funded. His way of alerting admissions officers and registrars to this important concept was to say, "Do it once. Do it right. Do it right the first time." Today this expression is referred to as "Smith's Law" by some professional colleagues in AACRAO who recognize the value of his counsel. He predicted, quite accurately, that many of the new systems he saw being installed in colleges and universities during the early 1960s were doomed to failure because of unrealistic and slipshod planning. With uncanny accuracy, he forecast what today is referred to as the classic sequence of "what went wrong": (1) a superficial approach to computer purchase and installation of hardware, (2) overdelegation by top campus administrators, (3) confusion of objectives, (4) cost escalation.

Persons interested in an excellent in-depth discussion of what went wrong in a significant number of computer projects in business and industry will want to read *The Effective Computer* (Grindley and Humble, 1974). Similarly, far too many student information systems have failed, and often these failures grew out of unfulfilled expectations and unrealistic planning activities (Price and others, 1973). Valuable resources (people, time, money, space, and equipment) have been misused on many campuses because goals, objectives, and important cost-benefit questions were not considered in the planning process.

A planning document should answer the questions "what, when, where, how, who, and why?" More specifically, an automation project proposal ought to include at least the following:

1.   A *budget* based on realistic cost estimates and including user costs as well as computer software and hardware costs.

2. *Scheduling information* showing critical development dates and deadlines.
3. *Assumptions* fundamental to the success of the project.
4. *Personnel assignments* indicating who will be responsible for ensuring that the tasks are accomplished correctly and on time. As Drucker (1977) and other management specialists remind us, and as successful professionals in higher education administration know, the performance and competence of people will correlate quite highly with the success of any system. Consequently, the project plan or proposal should spell out who will be in charge of the project and what the person's qualifications are, unless they are already well known to those who must approve the project.

Users are looking forward to the day when project proposals are clearly and precisely written to answer these critical questions: What will the new system do? What must be done to get the new system? How much time will it take? What will it cost? What effect will the new system have on present policies and procedures? A project plan that does not answer these questions to a user's satisfaction should be returned for clarification.

Computer Systems Analysis and Design

The Systems Analyst. As mentioned earlier, there is no agreed-upon body of knowledge that one must possess to be called a systems analyst. Although thousands of persons are employed as "systems analysts" in business, government, and higher education, their qualifications and competencies differ widely. Some were trained on the job as data processing operators and programmers and then became so-called analysts. Some became systems analysts on the basis of completing one or two computer programming courses. A few simply took a short standardized test and were appointed as analysts because of their deductive reasoning skills, as measured by the test. Still others had no computer programming skills or experience but were hired because they had a mathematics or engineering background. Only in recent years have systems analysts been able to receive formal education in data processing and computer science. But even among colleges and universities, there is no agreement about the subject matter or curriculum needed to train a prospective analyst. Indeed, there has been so much confusion about the job specifications and qualifications of the systems analyst that one computer manufacturer abolished the use of this title in its corporation.

Higher education has been equally confused about the role of the systems analyst. Some college administrators and teachers assume erroneously that all systems analysts have computer programming skills. In the midst of such confusion and disagreement, what can be said to aid registrars and admissions officers in understanding the systems analyst's role in higher education? Are there any expectations about the work of a systems analyst to guide us? The answer is "yes." Generally speaking, a systems analyst should be able to define and develop techniques for solving problems, especially those associated with computers and information systems. Additionally, a competent systems analyst should be able to identify the critical elements of a plan for a systems study. He or she will usually have a knowledge of data gathering techniques and will also be able to analyze document flow to determine the usefulness of forms and files. Finally, a good systems analyst will be able to monitor information flow and conduct feasibility studies to determine whether projects can or should be automated.

Let us examine a *sample* description of a senior systems analyst job in order to provide further information on what work an analyst might be expected to do.

Senior Systems Analyst

Summary of Position. Perform complex systems analysis, usually involving a number of interrelated computer programs. Develop or supervise development of general and detailed specifications for a project. Code instructions from prepared specifications. Test and correct coded programs. Provide documentation to ensure successful operations and maintenance of a new system.

Nature and Scope of Work. Assist project managers in the evaluation of a system or subsystem. Confer with users to define the problem and identify research areas. Analyze needs of users and conduct feasibility studies to aid in the preparation of project proposals. Prepare systems design and program specifications, and test, document, and implement a project.

May plan and coordinate the work of other analysts, programmers, and technical writers. Should have experience and enough programming expertise to trouble-shoot systems, to solve programming problems, and to evaluate the work of programmers. This position is the primary contact with users concerning technical questions or problems related to a project.

Qualifications. A baccalaureate degree in mathematics or computer science or equivalent experience. One to two years of supervisory experience. Two to three years of programming experience (COBOL required) and a thorough knowledge of computer concepts, IBM operating systems, and the use of utilities and IBM *Job Control Language* (JCL). Proficiency in both verbal and written communication activities. Experience in college or university administrative data processing highly desirable.

Note that a candidate for this position would be required to have a thorough knowledge of programming, in order to supervise other programmers, evaluate their work, and solve programming problems. The most critical aspect of a systems development may very well be the accuracy of the design phase and the definitions of requirements for the project. Unfortunately, systems analysts in colleges and universities often have little or no experience in programming or knowledge of the *specific language* being used to develop software for a project. Some argue that it is not important to know computer programming languages at all. But a wise admissions officer and registrar will look for employees who are technically qualified and will carefully examine the credentials and experience of these persons before an important student information systems project is entrusted to their care.

The Systems Project. There are many ways to characterize system development, but the following eight phases provide a good basis for discussing the importance of initial design considerations and user involvement in critical project development (Freeman, 1977):

Phase 1: *Needs Analysis.* Consideration of existing conditions, current systems, user hopes, and system requirements; identification of major functions and constraints.

Phase 2: *Specifications.* Development of functional descriptions, including economic constraints. Sometimes this stage is combined with needs analysis. It should result in a clear statement of specifications and refinement of the design concept.

Phase 3: *Architectural Design.* Design of the system from specifications. At this point plans are not necessarily detailed; however, the parts of the system and the relationships should be determined. For example, if a new registration system that includes computer sectioning is being planned, the basic algorithm that the system will use should be known.

Phase 4: *Detailed Design*. Determination of precise algorithms and data structures. This phase is primarily in the hands of technical experts. Decisions are made about hardware and software, but not all program details are spelled out.

Phase 5: *Coding*. Representation of data or initial computer programming.

Phase 6: *Testing*. Testing and correction of programs.

Phase 7: *System Integration*. User testing of hardware and software. In an on-line admissions system, for example, an admissions officer might be asked to see whether the cathode-ray tube display is correct and useful.

Phase 8: *Maintenance*. Location of programming errors, modification of existing functions as users begin to operate the system, addition of features originally planned for but never implemented. Everything that happens after the system is "finished" is termed maintenance.

In many organizations every system is analyzed, designed, coded, and implemented differently (Yourdon, 1976). This lack of a formalized approach to development is of increasing concern to campus leaders. There is nothing new about the concept of a formalized approach. Several well-known systems are being marketed today, but only a few are being used by colleges and universities. Only the future will tell whether computer specialists in collegiate institutions will develop or adopt standardized guidelines for EDP project management and control.

Many student information systems to date have had two unfortunate characteristics: (1) they were not completed on schedule, and (2) there were significant cost overruns. More often than not, operational failures and cost overruns have resulted from people problems and not equipment problems. One recognized authority in the computer industry suggests that 90 percent of the maintenance work after a system is operational is systems development work that could have been avoided had the system been designed properly in the first place (Barnett, 1971). Another tells us that 75 percent of all DP personnel are involved in maintenance, as a result of inadequate design. The implications of this situation should be clear to those who wish to see new student information systems implemented on time and within budget. Extraordinary attention and consideration should be given to recruiting and retaining technically qualified systems analysts on campus. Employing persons who lack technical training and expecting them to design efficient and successful computer-based systems is sheer folly and a waste of valuable resources.

Planning for a New System: A Sample Project

As indicated earlier, there are no standards or cookbook recipes to show us how to go about the task of developing new systems. Colleges and universities, like business, industry, and government, are struggling with these questions: What is the best way to develop a new system? Where are the models for development? Aren't there carefully documented ways in which to approach large-scale systems projects, especially those involving computers and related technologies? Answers to all these questions are in an evolutionary form today. There are about as many different ways to go about developing new systems as there are people who wish to develop them. There are commercial packages for sale to guide those who undertake large-scale projects. One such package is called PRIDE, an acronym for *PR*ofitable *I*nformation by *DE*sign— through phase planning and control. More specifically, PRIDE is a proprietary system design and implementation methodology (developed by M. Bryce and Associates, Incorporated, Cincinnati, Ohio) that has been used by a few collegiate institutions. A growing number of colleges and universities are hiring private consulting firms to help design and implement new systems. One of these is the Systems and Computer Technology Corporation, which specializes in designing computer-based systems for colleges and universities. And, of course, some help is always available from computer manufacturers such as IBM. In the main, though, most large-scale computer projects on college campuses have been developed, implemented, and managed by full-time college and university staff without assistance from outside consultants or the use of commercially packaged planning methodologies.

Despite the uncertainties and differences, new systems projects are being undertaken almost daily in colleges and universities. Many will be successful while others will fail. Recognizing that there are no universally acceptable project standards, we present here a major system development project at the University of Illinois at Chicago Circle (UICC) merely to illustrate how the Office of Admissions and Records (OAR) and the Office of Administrative Information Systems and Services (OAISS) at that university recently undertook the business of developing and implementing an on-line admissions system.

As an aid to the planning process, personnel from OAR and OAISS visited Youngstown State University and Syracuse University, among other schools with on-line admissions systems, to discuss implementation. They also studied literature and technical developments elsewhere. This kind of research is helpful in providing an understanding of what a system can and should accomplish, as well as giving a reasonable time frame for expectations.

Getting Started. As a first step, the OAR systems staff became thoroughly familiar with the existing (old) system and current objectives of admissions. They concluded that current and future goals might best be accomplished by a new system in an on-line environment. After the familiarization period, a detailed proposal was prepared (Zoars and others, 1977) for preliminary review by the directors of OAR and OAISS, respectively. The proposal outlined and evaluated the current system and provided an overview of the proposed system from these points of view:

Technical Considerations
Policy Considerations
Processing Flow
Screen Formats
Output/Reports/Documents
Unresolved Issues
Data Base Requirements

The written proposal was 229 pages in length and took approximately seven months to complete, at an estimated cost of $12,000. The proposal was next presented to various campus units, including the Committee of Associate and Assistant Deans (CAAD), for comment and review. Response from CAAD and other units was generally favorable, and comments and suggestions from those consulted led to improvements and revisions in the proposal. It should be noted that a top-down management commitment was being sought. At this point in the planning process, the directors of OAR and OAISS jointly presented the proposal to the chancellor and briefed him on objectives, costs, and the schedule for implementation. During this final review activity, the chancellor appeared most concerned about two aspects of the proposal: budget estimates, including annual as well as initial implementation expenses, and the length of time it would take to implement the system.

Personnel. After final approvals were received, a systems team composed of trained computer specialists from OAR and OAISS began the implementation process. It was clear from the outset that the new system had to have a dual role: the capability of making admission decisions and the capability of providing information to the campus administration. Also, since university policy and needs are not static, it was necessary to design a system flexible enough to accommodate itself to changing admissions criteria.

Within a few weeks after the implementation process began, the director of the Office of Admissions and Records added to the development team a liaison person who was intimately familiar with UICC admissions policies and procedures from an operational viewpoint. The person appointed was a veteran admissions officer with a superior work record. Assigned to work full time for one year on the project, she served as a contact person for the technical analysts/programmers and the regular admissions staff. Additionally, she was assigned the tasks of preparing user documentation and training manuals for terminal operations.

Project Progress. A redefinition of some goals and a rethinking of the means for achieving them took place soon after full-time work on the new system began. As both users and technical staffs got more familiar with new equipment capabilities and limitations, there were numerous mutually agreed-on revisions to the original proposal. Originally, the implementation schedule called for the project to be completed within one year. However, delays, primarily attributable to people (software) problems rather than equipment (hardware) problems, were encountered, and implementation fell six months behind schedule. There were three major reasons for the delays. First, as some specific programming tasks were completed and tested by user personnel, there was a demonstrated need for additional changes and refinements to the system. Second, some campus-wide and admissions office priorities shifted because of other work commitments and university needs. Third, there was a shortage of trained programmers capable of programming in IBM's teleprocessing software package (Customer Information Control Service [CICS]) to work on the project. In short, the original implementation schedule had to be altered because of people problems, not equipment problems; and the modifications to the system could not have been forecast, because the world of campus work changed significantly during the one-year period when the system was to have been implemented.

System Characteristics. The development of the UICC on-line admissions system was characterized as a major, large-scale computer project. UICC is an urban commuter institution of over 20,000 students, who move in and out of the institution frequently within a quarter system. Each fall, over 14,000 undergraduates apply for admission as new, transfer, or readmission students. The system was designed to support not only domestic undergraduate applicants but graduate and foreign applicants as well. Some academic programs have stringent admissions criteria, while others are not as selective; some of the colleges and departments maintain a tight control on the spaces available in certain programs, while others delegate this responsibility to the admissions staff.

The on-line admissions system accepts data about applicants and prospective students for up to five quarters in advance of a new term. There could be data on approximately 45,000 individuals at one time. There are nineteen IBM 3278 terminals in the system, used in nine different campus locations. Some terminals are for inquiry only, while others are used for both inquiry and update activities. There are twenty-five screens in the system, and statistical reporting modules (screens as well as paper output) were part of the development. Recruitment information and management reporting requirements were also considered in designing the system to aid campus planners in projecting future enrollments. In short, the system concept is complex and comprehensive, and only time and the users will tell whether it is effective and successful.

The "Total Systems" Controversy

Not all registrars and admissions officers agree that a single, integrated system can be devised to meet basic student information needs on a college campus. Those who do believe that such a system is feasible might be called advocates of a "total systems approach" to solving management information problems — specifically, those associated with the collection, processing, maintenance, and retrieval of information about students. Proponents of student information systems (SIS) believe that it is technically possible and desirable for colleges and universities to develop and manage a single, unified information system. Some veteran admissions officers and registrars, however, believe that SIS concepts are unworkable and impractical. They often ask supporters of a total systems approach, "Where are the model systems?" It is important to recognize that student information systems are in an early stage of development in higher education. Few proponents of SIS contend that the colleges and universities where they work are completely satisfied with all aspects of their student information systems. At the same time, the student information systems at institutions such as Brigham Young University, Harper Community College, Indiana University, Syracuse University, Tulsa Junior College, and Youngstown State University have gained national recognition. Arguments for and against a total systems approach might be summarized as follows:

Against SIS
1. Student information is not homogeneous. No one expert or team of experts can possibly know the basic information requirements of an entire collegiate institution.
2. It is not practical or consistent with college and university tradition to centralize the control over student information systems.
3. It is a fallacy to believe that if different subsystems involving student information are developed separately, they will necessarily lack coordination and therefore be inefficient and unsatisfactory. Coordinated student informa-

tion systems can be devised *without* a single, integrated approach.

4. The true SIS expert cannot and does not exist. A student information system is so complex and dynamic on most campuses that no person possesses broad enough knowledge or skills to lead such a development.
5. SIS is merely an elaborate phrase for good management.

For SIS

1. Traditional methods of developing student information systems on campus have been inadequate. They have led to bureaucratic, redundant, and inefficient subsystems in which "everyone is doing his or her own thing."
2. The lifeblood of a college or university is the enrollment of students, and information or "intelligence" about them. A centralized approach to the development of a student information system will help ensure that student information requirements are met more effectively and efficiently.
3. Early EDP techniques have resulted in numerous patchwork subsystems on many college campuses. An integrated systems approach offers hope that new student information systems will be more consistent, coordinated, dynamic, and humanistic.
4. In the climate of diminishing resources faced by some colleges and universities today, it is vital to be able to retrieve timely and complete data about students. The SIS approach calls for a determination of information needs from the top down.

Further Reading and Study

Confusing jargon, acronyms, and ambiguous language are commonly encountered by college administrators who become involved in the world of administrative data processing. For help in understanding this computer-talk, the reader is referred to *Automatic Data Processing,* a glossary published by the Bureau of the

Budget (1962), and *Data Processing Glossary,* by the International Business Machines Corporation (1972). These glossaries define basic terminology and provide authoritative references for the industry. Another volume of special importance to designers of information systems in higher education is the *Data Element Dictionary* (Goddard, Martin, and Romney, 1973), published by the National Center for Higher Education Management Systems (NCHEMS). The dictionary's five main sections cover course, facility, finance, staff, and student-related data elements for internal management and information exchange purposes. The elements contained in the dictionary are set forth as NCHEMS recommendations rather than national standards. Another useful reference is the 1977 *American National Dictionary for Information Processing,* published by the American National Standards Committee and the Computer and Business Equipment Manufacturers Association. This dictionary has been adopted for federal government use as a basic reference document to promote a common understanding of information processing terminology.

An excellent overview of higher education and the computer phenomenon is found in Caffery and Mosmann's *Computers on Campus* (1967). This reference work, published by the American Council on Education, is a nontechnical report designed to supply the basic knowledge needed by those who make computer policy and management decisions.

☐☐☐☐☐☐☐ 9

Using New Tools and Techniques in Systems Development

☐ ☐ ☐ ☐ ☐ ☐ ☐ ☐ ☐ ☐ ☐ ☐ ☐ ☐ ☐

William C. Price

There are many promising new tools and techniques to aid in the work of the admissions officer and registrar. New office products—including improved typewriters, dictation and copying equipment, micrographics, microfiche, and a marriage of these technologies to computers—are quite impressive. Phototypesetting equipment and publication processes are improving, as are telecommunication and television tools and techniques—all of which can be used to support better student information systems on collegiate campuses. "The office of tomorrow will not result from a sudden revolution. It will be an evolution. And it is evolving right now" (Jass, 1978).

General Areas

Only a few of the more promising areas of systems development will be discussed here. Consequently, further readings and continual professional study (see the last section of this chapter for specific suggestions) are encouraged for both veteran and new admissions and records staff. Those areas to be briefly reviewed include on-line systems, optical scanning technology, minicomputers and distributive data processing, and microfilm and micrographics. Other significant developments and topics that may be useful to admissions officers and registrars are the following:

1. The use of outside consultants and business firms to design, develop, and implement new student information systems.
2. Telephone registration techniques and telecommunication alternatives.
3. Closed-circuit television to support admissions and records work.
4. Student identification alternatives, including new data-entry techniques.
5. The training and education of office personnel who must work in a computer-related environment.
6. The growing cost of information systems technology in a period of diminishing resources.
7. The changing role of admissions and records personnel as a result of automation and technology advances.

On-Line Systems. On-line computer systems are not new to colleges and universities, but increasing attention is being given to these systems. Two samples of on-line systems—one an on-line registration system at William Rainey Harper College, the other an on-line admissions system at Youngstown State University—are described in the next section of this chapter. A complete listing of colleges and universities with operational on-line systems would contain over one hundred names. The following partial list should suffice, however, to make the point that on-line systems have been developed in institutions of varying sizes, types, and characters:

Brigham Young University (Provo, Utah)
Central State University (Edmond, Oklahoma)
Florida Technological University (Orlando)
Indiana University (Bloomington)
Michigan State University (East Lansing)

Purdue University (Lafayette, Indiana)
Regis College (Denver, Colorado)
State University of New York (Albany)
Syracuse University (Syracuse, New York)
Tarrant County Junior College (Fort Worth, Texas)
Tulsa Junior College (Tulsa, Oklahoma)
United States Air Force Academy (Colorado)
University of California (Irvine)
University of Iowa (Iowa City)
University of Illinois (Chicago Circle)
University of Maryland (College Park)
University of Michigan (Ann Arbor)
University of Wisconsin (Oshkosh)
William Rainey Harper College (Palatine, Illinois)
Youngstown State University (Youngstown, Ohio)

Those who wish to learn more about on-line systems developments may consult admissions officers, registrars, and computer specialists at the above schools. Those interested in reading more about on-line systems should be aware that *College and University* has carried many articles about on-line admissions and registration in recent years (see, for example, Bell, Melott, and Wooley, 1977). Additionally, it might also be pertinent to note that AACRAO's Data Management and Research Committee (E. Wagner, 1977) is conducting a national survey on uses of computer equipment and applications in membership schools. Undoubtedly, survey findings will identify many more colleges and universities that have designed and implemented on-line systems.

Because of the growing interest of colleges and universities in on-line systems, more and more seminars and workshops on this topic are being held. Some are sponsored by computer manufacturers, others by governmental agencies, and still others by professional educational associations such as AACRAO. One such seminar hopes to teach its participants the following procedures (Peterson and Spencer, 1978):

• Determine your needs for computer-based and on-line admissions and registration systems.

- Identify your limitations for implementation of on-line admissions and registration systems.
- Compare alternative on-line systems.
- Design specifications for your own on-line system.
- Implement an on-line system.
- Evaluate an on-line system after it is installed and running.

A word of warning about on-line systems needs to be sounded. On-line systems are not a panacea for all the admissions, registration, records, and financial aid problems faced by colleges and universities today. The installation of an on-line system is neither necessary nor desirable for some colleges and universities. Each institution needs to weigh carefully the costs and benefits of the various tools and procedures available. There are advantages and disadvantages to manual, semiautomated, *and* computerized student information systems. On-line systems show promise for helping some schools not now using them, but they require a substantial commitment to the computer. Therefore, the prudent manager of data for students will be careful not to endorse on-line systems for his or her campus simply because colleagues are doing it elsewhere. Without specific and satisfactory answers to cost-benefit, technical, and educational policy questions of critical importance to a college or university, an on-line system could be expensive and disappointing.

Optical Scanning Technology. One of the most promising new technologies currently being investigated by admissions officers and registrars is optical character recognition (OCR). Optical scanning of applications using mark reading equipment has been done effectively in colleges and universities for over ten years. But more recent technological breakthroughs in character recognition equipment and computers promise significant potential for solving data-entry problems. OCR offers an alternative to the on-line system. There are cases where on-line systems are not possible or desirable, and OCR offers a better solution of data-entry problems than on-line keying would. Experienced admissions officers and registrars in large universities and colleges have long been plagued with the problem of "the keypunch bottleneck." They have looked for means other than those involving keying operations to process voluminous amounts of student data in a short period of time.

What is OCR? Huffman (1977, p. 15) explains that OCR is a system, not a device: "OCR can be defined as a data-entry method whereby material which has been captured on specifically designed paper forms by typewriters, pencils, and/or high-speed computer printers can be scanned and recognized (read) directly by a machine without intervening human translation steps. OCR systems usually include the capability of processing and editing this material in conjunction with the data capture, and also are instrumental in aiding error correction for good-quality data output."

Cleveland State University, Ohio State University, Tulsa Junior College, and a handful of other colleges and universities are already using OCR systems effectively, and it is probable that many more colleges and universities will use OCR to support student information systems in the future. Ohio State University uses OCR for what the university calls "change ticket" activities (add/drops) during registration cycles. Because Ohio State is one of the largest universities in America, and is on a quarter system, an extraordinary number of adds and drops must be processed in a short period of time to serve the student body and faculty there. The OCR system permits the university to keep add and drop records current for a student body of over 40,000. Perhaps the most extensive use of OCR equipment in support of student information system requirements is taking place at Cleveland State University, an urban institution of about 20,000 students. Cleveland State University uses an OCR system to support a mail registration option for its student body, and does this effectively in a quarter system.

Another type of scanning activity of interest to admissions officers uses student activity cards and bar codes as data-entry devices. At Brigham Young University scanners are tied to a minicomputer and other equipment to form a computer-assisted, on-line testing system (Kozachok, 1977). The system is called SCOUT—System for Computer-Assisted, On-Line, University-wide Testing. SCOUT operates as follows: To take a test, a student presents his activity card. A bar code label is then read. The system makes sure he is registered for the class and is taking the test within the allotted time span. If it's a retake, the system makes sure the new test is completely new and not the one the student took previously. It also checks back for any fees owed and then gives the student any message from the teacher—or even from home.

Scanning systems, like on-line systems, are not the answer to all college management problems. There is a constant danger that college administrators, teachers, and students will be too quick to think that a new exciting machine or scientific advancement will solve all campus information systems problems. OCR and optical mark reading (OMR) systems may help colleges and universities, but they are only management tools and should be treated as such.

Minicomputers. Certainly one of the more exciting new developments in the world of computers is the minicomputer. Some admissions officers and registrars see great potential for these new, smaller, faster, and less expensive computers. What many persons are really talking about when they discuss minicomputers is a concept known as distributed data processing—or using minicomputers and a data base. The primary goal of distributed data processing is to improve service through efficiency. With the recent advances in minicomputers—and taking into account the economies of scale—minicomputers, data communications, and data-base development are now feasible.

Generally speaking, minicomputers can supply computing power to a variety of users and satisfy user needs at many different locations. If developed properly, a distributed data processing system can do two other things of importance for admissions officers and registrars. First, such a system can provide back-up support by use of another computer within the system in case of machine failure. Second, it will enable a small-sized location to use the power of a large-scale computer when needed. New Mexico State University is one of several collegiate institutions beginning to take full advantage of the minicomputer's potential in the area of admissions and records. Similarly, the University of California at Berkeley recently procured a minicomputer for use by the office of admissions and records (Benedict and O'Connell, 1978).

The presence of a smaller computer on campus holds promise for improving systems in both large and small colleges and universities. Perhaps the most attractive aspect of using a minicomputer is that transaction processing may occur at the point of origin. This adds the dimension of user control of his or her own data and decreases the potential for transaction errors, because the user is familiar with the data base being used. A good example of how a small computer helps support a registration system can be found at the United States International University. Hopperton (1975) says that the usual objections a hard-pressed private college might raise to using a computer are these:

1. Such a computer would have to be huge; we simply can't afford it.
2. If we tied all our operations into one computer, a failure would literally shut us down. We can't afford to support the maintenance staff needed to keep this from happening.
3. No one has a software operating system that could handle all these functions.
4. Our people aren't computer experts; mistakes made by admission clerks or payroll clerks would really foul up our operations.
5. Our people aren't trained programmers either; we'd spend years and countless dollars getting the system optimized for the unique requirements of college administration.

In spite of these preliminary concerns, the United States International University went on to develop a successful comprehensive system involving time sharing, a minicomputer, disk storage, terminal controllers, CRT terminals, and printers. Hopperton now calls the objections listed above "phantom concerns." Indeed, minicomputers offer great potential for improved student information systems, especially for smaller colleges and universities with limited resources.

Microfilm and Micrographics. No discussion of modern information systems technology would be complete without mentioning the growing significance of the microfilm and micrographics industry to registrars and admissions officers. The National Microfilm Association is the organization to contact for more complete information in the micrographic/microfilm area. Only one form of microfilm technology—computer output to microfilm (COM)—will be discussed here. Some experts in automation consider COM one of the most significant technological breakthroughs of the 1970s.

The National Microfilm Association defines COM in three ways: "(1) *Computer Output Microfilm:* microfilm containing data produced by a recorder from computer-generated signals. (2)- *Computer Output Microfilmer:* a recorder which converts data from a computer into human readable language and records [them] on microfilm. (3) *Computer Output Microfilming*: a method of converting data from a computer into human readable language onto microfilm" (Avedon, 1971, p. 41). The development of COM has made significant achievements in information retrieval possible. A user can bypass production of the most common form of output—paper. COM can be thought of as a marriage between the computer and the camera. A COM camera (recorder) converts data from a computer tape into alphanumeric characters or even graphics (such as engineering drawings) and records them on microfilm.

In 1969 the University of Wisconsin at Milwaukee pioneered in the use of COM systems to support admissions and records operations (Allison, Schmidt, and Sperry, 1970). Since then, many other collegiate institutions, including the University of Illinois at Chicago Circle (Price, 1972) and Temple University, have adopted COM systems to support critical administrative functions. A detailed description of the University of Wisconsin at Milwaukee COM system can be found in the next section of this chapter. Analysis of the system will show that there are many advantages to using microfilm as an information system tool. Most notably, COM provides a low-cost solution to the problem of retrieving student information before it becomes outdated and useless. When student data retrieval and display are of serious concern but daily updates are not a critical requirement, a COM system can be developed at a fraction of the cost of an on-line computer system.

COM has already had a significant impact on record-keeping operations in government and industry. It is just a question of time until higher education discovers its potential. Colleges and universities will find it economical and desirable to place microfiche reader stations in hundreds of different campus locations. Totally new student record retrieval and storage systems will be produced through microfilm technology. Major manufacturers are working on new readers, reader-printers, and other equipment. All signs point to a rosy future for the microfilm industry. Collegiate registrars and admissions officers would be wise to watch COM developments closely in the next few years. This new and powerful management tool has been proven successful and should continue to provide data managers with new methods of improving services.

Other Developments. Many other significant developments are taking place as a result of new technology and experience. "Database management" is beginning to take on importance at some colleges and universities. Suggested readings on data bases include a paper presented at the nineteenth annual College and University Machine Records Conference (CUMREC), "Data Base—The Solution to the Impossible Dream" (Ehrensberger, 1974) and two articles that appeared in the *Harvard Business Review:* "Computer Data Bases: The Future Is Now" (Nolan, 1973) and "Cost and Benefits of a Data Base System" (McFadden and Suver, 1978).

Another topic demanding attention in both industry and higher education is the management of data services and information costs. Two excellent articles on this topic are "Controlling the Costs of Data Services" (Nolan, 1977) and "Managing the Costs of Information" (Strassmann, 1976).

Sample Systems

There are literally hundreds of examples of how information systems technology is helping college administrators do a better job of serving students, faculty, and staff. Five will be described here: the on-line registration system at William Rainey Harper College (Palatine, Illinois), the on-line admissions system at Youngstown State University (Youngstown, Ohio), the mass registration and computer sectioning program at Washington State University (Pullman), the registration system at Purdue University (Bloomington, Indiana), and the computer output microfilm system at University of Wisconsin-Milwaukee. At the end of each systems description, two consultants are listed for additional information regarding technical and user problems. Officials at these institutions have agreed to assist those who wish to obtain more detailed information about their systems.

On-Line Registration System, William Rainey Harper College

Harper College is a public community college with 20,000 students. It operates on the semester system.

Purpose of System. The Harper College on-line student registration and accounting system makes it possible to develop the course schedule on-line. A course master file can be used to control which classes can be added. On-line registration involves capturing the necessary information about the student and performing adds and drops to the student's schedule. Following the registration process, the student receivables are matched with the student payments.

The on-line student registration and accounting system was designed to meet the following application objectives:

1. Use a common methodology to handle both traditional credit and continuing education courses.
2. Provide for multiple-campus processing without limitations.
3. Provide for a multiple-semester capability without restriction.
4. Parallel course development and approval with that of outside agencies to provide more accurate data reporting.
5. Use the student master file for both registration and student accounts receivable.

The system also meets the following technical objectives:

1. On-line capability for all file updating.
2. All file activity be logged sequentially as it occurs, regardless of the type of activity.
3. Any terminal be able to access, from the master files, data from any semester or campus.
4. Coded data be set up and maintained by the users on a separate file to reduce program maintenance.
5. The design of terminal functions requires that the operator complete a given task before going to the next task.

Student Registration. Student registration includes all the steps necessary to register a student into a requested class (credit, non-credit, continuing education unit, etc.), to update the student and class file, and to determine the student's fees. When students approach the registration area, they present a student course request form, containing their anticipated schedule and any required approvals. The student keeps one copy to verify the actual schedule, and one copy remains in the registration area to provide a hard-copy audit trail.

Building the Student's Schedule. Keying in the class identification (course number plus section number) of the requested courses allows the system to build the student's schedule. The system also requires that an indicator be entered to determine whether the class is taken for credit or audit purposes, or whether the class is to be dropped.

After all classes are entered, the system responds with a line of class information for each class requested. Completing the registration process produces a screen showing the student's related fees.

If the student's schedule contains time conflicts or the required prerequisites are not met, a message will appear on the screen informing the operator which item contains the conflict. When adds and drops take place in building the student's schedule, the student's fee is continuously updated and is displayed after a conflict-free schedule is developed.

Student and Class Files. At the end of a registration, the student file contains the students' records, the courses in which they have been registered, and their current fee information. The class file contains the students' identification in every class where a registration occurred. Data can be reported from either file or from a combination of both files.

Contacts for Additional Information

Technical Expertise

Director of Computer Serivces
Harper College
Palatine, Illinois 60067

User Expertise

Director of Admissions and
  Records
Harper College
Palatine, Illinois 60067

On-Line Admissions System, Youngstown State University

Youngstown State University is a public university with 15,600 students; it operates on the quarter system.

The Master File. The student information process is initiated when a student first applies for admission to the university. The data-entry operator creates a student master record for that student by using an entry function on a television terminal. Once the master file is created, it may be displayed and updated through any television terminal in the system. Any information originally entered in encoded form is displayed in a decoded fashion. If errors are found, or if other student data changes are necessary, corrections are made on the student master file by means of a change function.

The admission file is supplemented with data received on magnetic tape from the American College Testing Program (ACT) for all students who indicate Youngstown State University as one of their college choices. These test scores are placed onto the student master file directly from this tape for any student who has already applied. A prospect record is created for all those who have not applied.

Data Entry. When an application for admission is received, the data-entry operator checks the master file to see whether the data are already available. If they are, the master record is revised without unnecessary reentry of data from the application. If the data are not on file, the operator enters all data from the application.

All data entered are edited against code files to verify their accuracy. The terminal function interacts with the terminal operator to correct any errors before a master record is created.

When a master record is to be changed, the terminal operator enters the student's number. The name of the student appears on the television screen, so that the operator can be assured that the proper student's record is being changed. The operator may enter the names of the items to be changed or may choose the names of the items from a list available on the terminal. When the items to be changed have been identified, they are displayed on the television screen and the operator enters the correct data. As with the initial entry of data, the computer interacts with the data-entry operator to correct any errors, and the changes are visually verified before the master record is changed. Changes are instantaneously made to the file and are immediately available for display.

In this admissions system, the data are entered only once by the terminal operator. At any subsequent time, changes or corrections may be made instantaneously, so that the information on file is always current and correct.

The Prospect File. Youngstown State University is now augmenting the prospect function presently in its system. The prospect file created with data from the ACT tape will be used for the provisional admission of all eligible prospects who have not yet applied. The records of those who have not applied will go through a computer selection process. Since Youngstown State University is an open-admissions university for all high school graduates from the state of Ohio, it may provisionally accept all prospects from Ohio. Out-of-state students must be in the upper two thirds of their graduating class.

Confirmation Procedures. All students who are provisionally accepted will be sent a confirmation-of-application form. The student needs only to verify the data and return the form with an application fee. When the confirmation form is returned, the data-entry operator will change the status of the prospect from provisional status to confirmed applicant without reentering the available data. At this time, additional data not on the prospect file may be added and existing data may be revised.

Admissions Materials. When a regular application has been entered or a provisional admission has been confirmed on the student master file, a set of admissions materials is immediately printed on a computer terminal in the admissions office. These materials consist of an acknowledgment card, file control cards, a decision card, a fee receipt card, and a set of labels.

The acknowledgment card is immediately sent to the applicant to acknowledge that the application has been received. The acknowledgment card asks the applicant to verify that the information has been correctly entered onto the master file. The fee receipt card is used by the bursar's office to verify payment of the application fee. One label is used to create a student folder, and the remainder of the materials are placed in the student's folder, to be used by the admissions office or distributed to other offices for their use as the need arises in the admissions and registration processes.

Service to Others. The admissions system also provides other services to admissions, the registrar, and other offices on campus. A general request program provides names and addresses for lists, or labels for specific categories of applicants, to assist in university promotional activities. Printed permits to register are used by the registrar's office in the registration process.

Contacts for Additional Information

Technical Expertise	*User Expertise*
Director of Planning	Dean of Admissions and Records
Youngstown State University	Youngstown State University
Youngstown, Ohio 44555	Youngstown, Ohio 44555

Mass Registration and Computer Sectioning, Washington State University

Washington State University is a public residential four-year institution operating on the semester system. Enrollment is 16,500.

Background. The sectioning program is the basic component of the Washington State University registration system. Since the major objective of the sectioning program is to develop a conflict-free schedule for maximum numbers of students, the curriculum must be well balanced, with classes distributed equally throughout the hours of the day and the days of the week. To ensure this, department heads, through the various deans, are required to follow prescribed formats and procedures when they set up their time schedules. For example, department offerings must be scheduled within standardized time limits; multiple lecture and laboratory sections must be distributed equally between mornings and afternoons and, insofar as possible, between Monday/Wednesday/Friday and Tuesday/Thursday; new offerings must make use of the 12:00 noon, 3:00 to 4:00 P.M., and 4:00 to 5:00 P.M. time blocks; and four-hour courses and sections that meet four days a week must be scheduled to distribute the off-day equally throughout the week.

Academic Registration. Student enrollment packets are prepared from student information system (SIS) files. Enrollment packs are distributed according to a rotated alphabetical sequence at thirty-minute time intervals to control the flow of students to advisers and department heads. In addition to the enrollment card, the pack contains transaction cards including health insurance, *Chinook* (yearbook), and address cards. Academic advisers are assigned to all undergraduates, and adviser approval of course selection is required for registration. Adviser/student contact is facilitated through the use of an undergraduate enrollment advisory form that carries the advisory signature and may be completed any time during the semester. At registration, the student transfers the course selection information from this advisory form to the enrollment card and reports to the registration center to complete registration. Students who do not elect to use the advisory form pick up their enrollment packets and then report to their academic adviser or department head for counseling and guidance before proceeding.

Blank course request cards and electrographic pencils are made available to students as they enter the registration area. The student completes one course request card for each course listed on the enrollment card, marking each request by section number (optional), department prefix, course number, and credit. Requests for pass/fail or "repeat" enrollment are also marked on the course request card. The student arranges the course request cards in the same order as the requests appear on the enrollment card and reports to one of the thirty registrar's check-out tables to complete the academic portion of registration. An important advantage of this in-person routine is that it allows the registrar's staff to double-check for errors while the source is at hand. If a student wishes to keep certain times free for work or approved cocurricular activities, the student submits the request prior to registration and, if approved, receives a coded blocked-free-time request card that is filed with the student's course request cards. The blocked-free-time request card is premarked with a code that will allow the time block to be preserved in the student's schedule.

Machine Processing. The enrollment and course request cards are collected and batched for processing periodically throughout the sixteen-hour registration period. In the first processing step, the marked cards are read through an IBM 514 Reproducer, and the course-identifying information is punched into each card. In this same process, the student identification number is gang punched into each course request card from its respective enrollment card. The cards are taken to the computer center for a card-to-disk run using a 3350 Disk Pack. The card-to-disk program does extensive editing, checking every field in the enrollment card and the course request cards for invalid information. If an error is found, the student's requests are rejected, and an on-line message indicating the nature of the error is printed. The cards are processed in batches, allowing a skilled registrar's crew to locate errors and make on-the-spot corrections. In this way, more than 90 percent of the errors are corrected before sectioning. Once corrected, the student's requests are resubmitted during the next card-to-disk pass. Common errors corrected through this editing process include marking too lightly on the course request cards, selecting courses from the wrong semester, or using the wrong abbreviation (such as Geol instead of Geog). A preliminary course request report is prepared at the end of the first day of mass registration and is distributed to department heads the following morning. This report lists, by number and section, the first day's total of courses requested and provides advance notice of enrollment patterns and trends, so that department heads may begin planning the necessary curricular adjustments.

Departmental Adjustment Session. At the close of mass registration and after all errors have been corrected and all requests added to the file, a course request report is printed for review by department heads and deans at the 6:30 P.M. meeting. This report lists all courses by section, seats available, seats remaining (if any), and total student requests by course and section. The department heads, deans, and the academic vice-president meet with the registrar's staff to review the course request report and make the necessary adjustments before students are sectioned. After the course requests have been reviewed and compared with the respective departmental time schedules, department heads are allowed to make adjustments in order to honor as many student requests as possible. Departments are permitted to increase or decrease the maximum number of students permitted to enroll in a course or section; drop courses or sections; change times, room numbers, or buildings; or open "blind" sections that have been held in contingency.

This adjustment session is one of the finest aspects of the WSU system and is unique in that, although student requests almost always vary from the schedule of courses that departments plan to teach, the department heads are able to adjust the supply to meet the demand, and *maximum* numbers of students receive the courses they request. After the adjustments have been keypunched and added to the computer time schedule file, the sectioning process begins.

Sectioning. In processing each course request, the sectioning program first tests for each of the following error contradictions: no course requests, duplicate course requests, invalid course requests, more than fifteen course requests, and all sections of a course closed. If any of these conditions exist, the exception is noted and the request search continues. The sectioning program will attempt up to 9,999 scheduling combinations in an effort to build a conflict-free schedule for each student. The sectioning routine places students into classes and sections according to the following priorities: (1) blocked-free-time requests for approved work or cocurricular activities, (2) single-section courses, (3) preferred sections of multiple section courses when indicated, (4) other requests for multiple-section courses, (5) physical education activity courses, (6) laboratory assignments.

Seniors are sectioned first in order, to ensure placement into courses required for graduation. All others are sectioned according to the time they completed registration. Classified staff employees who enroll as part-time students under the fee waiver option are sectioned last on a space-available basis. If there are conflicts that the computer could not resolve, a message is printed on the student's schedule, telling the student why the course requests were not honored.

Postbilling Routine. During the editing of academic course requests and the departmental adjustment session, controller personnel are processing various student fee inputs generated by previous balances; tuition and incidental fees; hospital insurance requests; yearbook purchases; damage deposits; and special fees, such as nonresident tuition and outstanding library and parking fines. Credits from student loans, scholarships, prepaid deposits, and grants are also calculated; and the resulting balances are prepared for printing, along with an itemized list of the various sources and amounts of credits and debits. The data from sectioning and postbilling files are merged to print a Schedule/Statement for each student.

Schedule/Statements are printed on two IBM 1403 High-Speed Printers at 1,100 lines per minute (taking about four hours for 16,700 students). After decollating and bursting, the Schedule/Statements are hand-sorted for distribution on a prearranged schedule the day following the close of registration. Virtually all the Schedule/Statements are handed out in a two-hour period at fifty-six pick-up stations located in the three largest facilities on campus. The Schedule/Statement has a self-addressed envelope encouraging students to pay by mail. The deadline for payment of fees without penalty is five days following the start of classes. Subsequent month-end statements are mailed to the student's local address. In cases of balances due the student, checks are printed through the postbilling system and are available to be picked up at the same time the Schedule/Statements are disbursed. Discrepancies in individual student accounts are resolved through batch processing or on-line, using cathode-ray tube (CRT) terminal units. Mistakes can be corrected and changes made in resident status, special fee eligibility, and fee waivers through this system. Fees that change due to enrollment changes (drops and adds) can also be adjusted through the on-line terminal.

Concurrent with the printing of the Schedule/Statement, a six-part student schedule is also produced for use by department heads, the dean of students, the graduate school, the curriculum advisory program, and the registrar's office.

Other reports produced at this time include temporary class lists, pass/fail enrollment report, the repeat course report, and a status of sections report. Temporary class lists and a status of sections report are issued immediately to departments. Departments utilize the status of sections report as a control ledger for approving subsequent drops and adds after the start of classes.

Contacts for Additional Information

Technical Expertise	*User Expertise*
Director of Administrative Services	Registrar
Washington State University	Washington State University
Pullman, Washington 99164	Pullman, Washington 99164

Registration, Purdue University

Purdue is a public, state university with 30,000 students. It operates on the semester system.

Schedule of Classes. The university schedule of classes is prepared early each semester for the succeeding semester. The Office of Schedules and Space, working with school and departmental schedule deputies, prepares the schedule for distribution to academic advisers. The summer session schedule is distributed in January, the fall schedule in March, and the spring schedule in October.

Course Requests. Students initiate registration by reporting to their academic adviser. The courses to be taken are determined and listed, along with other pertinent data, on a course request form. Only the subject matter or departmental abbreviation and the course number are listed for each course the student plans to take. The academic adviser retains the course request and forwards it to registration headquarters. Students have nothing more to do until they receive fee statements in the mail.

When course requests are received at registration headquarters, each request is checked for completeness and placed in a ready-to-scan container. When a sizable number of forms have been accumulated, they are transferred to the data processing center, where they are scanned by an IBM computer that transfers the information to tape or disk for further processing.

At the data processing center, each student's request is checked against an "eligible to register" file. This file contains the names of continuing students and newly admitted graduate and undergraduate students. The request is also checked against the encumbrance file, which contains the names of those not permitted to complete a registration until some obligation has been met. If the student is eligible to register, even if encumbered for financial reasons, the request is placed in a file for transmission to the Office of Schedules and Space.

Course Subscription and Scheduling. The Office of Schedules and Space receives each batch of course requests. These are transmitted from the administrative data processing center by the IBM computer via direct link to a computer in the computing center. The Office of Schedules and Space loads the entire schedule of classes into the CDC, and each course request is matched with the semester schedule to determine whether the course is offered and whether space is available. If available, a space in the course is reserved for the student. After space is reserved, the student's request is held in a computer file called "ready to schedule." This process is called a subscription run. It assures the student space in each course but does not provide a specific section.

The ready-to-schedule files are held until several thousand course requests have been received; then a scheduling run is made. In this run, a workable schedule is made if possible; if not, a status note is prepared to tell the academic adviser and the student why the request could not be filled. Those schedules that are complete are transmitted by the link back to the administrative data processing center for billing.

Fee Assessment, Billing, and Payment. The bursar's system is used at the administrative data processing center to assess fees and prepare fee statements. In addition to the fee statement, a general-information form (including addresses and telephone numbers) is printed for each student. The bursar mails the fee statement, the information form, and instructions to the student. On receipt of the fee statement, the student is responsible for checking the information form and making any correction necessary. In addition, blank spaces calling for specific information are to be completed. In an envelope provided, the student returns to the bursar the fee statement, the information form, and a check or money order in the amount of fees.

End of Registration for Student—the Receipted Schedule. Upon receipt of payment and information forms, the bursar forwards the information forms to the registrar and mails students their receipted schedules. The student is then ready to go to class on the opening day of the semester or session.

Delayed Registration and Schedule Revision. The week prior to each semester or session is a period for delayed registration and schedule revision. During this period, students who for one reason or another did not register when they should have may do so. The procedure is basically the same except that students must hand-carry their course requests to registration headquarters. There they receive a claim notice to go to the bursar's office the following day and pick up a fee statement. The student puts a check or money order and the fee statement in an envelope and places it in a drop-box at the bursar's office. Per the option checked by the student, the bursar will place the student's receipted schedule in a hold file or mail it to the student at the address provided.

The schedule revision process is very similar except that the fee assessment and payment steps are omitted. Students get a schedule revision form approved by the adviser and take it and their receipted schedule to registration headquarters. There they receive a claim form that indicates when and where a revised schedule can be picked up.

Scheduling and schedule revision runs are made each night during the delayed registration period and during a late registration period that ends with the first week of classes.

Record Rosters and Reports. After the end of the first week of each semester, the file of student schedules is transferred into the academic records file and shown as work in progress in each student's record. The file of student schedules is also used to produce a class roster for each section of each course. In addition, enrollment reports are produced.

Contacts for Additional Information

Technical Expertise

Director of Administrative
  Data Processing Center
Purdue University
Lafayette, Indiana 47907

User Expertise

Registrar
Purdue University
Lafayette, Indiana 47907

Computer Output Microfilm, University of Wisconsin-Milwaukee

The University of Wisconsin-Milwaukee is a public, state university with 24,500 students. It operates on the semester system.

The first computer output microfilm (COM) file at UWM was the administrative student study list. In its hard-copy form, this file consists of one computer-produced form for each student enrolled in the university. In 1969, when COM was introduced here, this file contained about 20,000 of the IBM-size forms. The study list contains biographical and academic data about the students, including their schedule of courses for the current semester, the time and location of the courses, and courses added or dropped since the original registration. In addition to student number, the study list also contains the students' classification, year, adviser, major, residence, entry status, sex, employer, number of hours worked, birthdate, local and permanent address, telephone number, name of person to be notified in case of emergency, and date of update.

Originally, copies of this file in hard-copy form were sent to seven other campus offices. This particular file took about seven hours of computer print-time to produce. Every week, updates of the file were run. Staff in admissions and records and in the seven other offices receiving this file were to pull the old forms and insert the updated forms when applicable. The first update each semester was particularly large because of the early semester add/drop activity. The admissions and records staff were forced into keeping the file up to date simply because they were responsible for the records. But the other offices, usually staffed by one secretary, began to store the updates separately because of lack of time. After a few weeks of updates, the other offices became totally dependent on the records area for up-to-date information. With COM and the completely updated file, problems of hard-copy records filing or information dependency were eliminated.

Through COM, the University of Wisconsin-Milwaukee was able to maintain the type of information, both in quantity and quality, that it had previously intended to maintain; at the same time, the handling and use of this information became more economical. With COM, the information contained on the study list became available on the first day of classes instead of the third or fourth week, as had been the case with the hard-copy study list. The file became much more accessible, especially for answering telephone inquiries. The task of interfiling updates was eliminated, since the entire file is updated on microfilm at least biweekly.

COM allowed admissions and records to disperse an important working document within the office. Where previously the office had one study list file, it now has twenty in various locations. The accessibility and convenience of these files led to work and time savings throughout the office. The full study list file is now also available to seventy other offices on campus. These offices have also realized time savings. The need to call or visit admissions and records for certain data has been eliminated. Data are now available to these offices after hours and on weekends. Because of the sharp decrease in telephone inquiries from other offices, the records area has been able to reassign one clerk-typist.

Contacts for Additional Information

Technical Expertise

Programming Manager
Computer Services Division
University of Wisconsin-
  Milwaukee
P.O. Box 413
Milwaukee, Wisconsin 53201

User Expertise

Director of Admissions
University of Wisconsin-
  Milwaukee
P.O. Box 749
Milwaukee, Wisconsin 53201

Further Reading and Study

Computing and information systems technology is changing and expanding at a rapid pace. To stay abreast of recent developments in this dynamic area is an extraordinary challenge for college administrators and requires continuing study. Because knowledge in the field is quickly outdated due to new technical discoveries, knowing where to go for expert help and what to read is critical to the educational process. Therefore, basic sources for additional information and further study are recommended.

Educational Organizations

The list of associations and organizations that follow are not the only good sources for further study of information systems developments. There are numerous public and private organizations that might have been mentioned, including the National Microfilm Association, the National Association of College Admissions Counselors, the American College Testing Program, the Educational Testing Service, and the American Institutional Research Association. However, those listed have a special and central interest in information systems technologies and developments that seem to be especially pertinent to the work of admissions officers and registrars in the office of tomorrow.

American Association of Collegiate Registrars and Admissions Officers (AACRAO). AACRAO remains the best single source for further study of information systems of special interest to admissions and records personnel. Annual programs typically feature many presentations on new information systems developments, and AACRAO is in continuous contact with other postsecondary educational associations and government agencies with mutual interests in data management and research. One of the major divisions of AACRAO, Group IV, is organized into four standing committees that have a common interest in data management and research: Electronic Computers, Institutional Studies and Operational Analysis, New Developments and Techniques, and Systems Development. Through the years AACRAO has sponsored MODS seminars (mentioned in Chapter Eight), conducted workshops and surveys on the uses of electronic computers, and published monographs on information systems. For example, in the summer of 1978 three new monographs were made available to members, providing information on a computer-assisted registration and enrollment system, an academic record information and edit system, and a computer-based activity and event system for assigning rooms (see AACRAO *Newsletter,* Summer 1978).

Perhaps the richest source of new information emanating from AACRAO, though, can be traced to individual members who have shared their new systems experiences, good and bad, with other AACRAOans through presentations and papers published in AACRAO's house organ, *College and University;* via campus visits; and by acting as individual consultants to those who have asked for help. For further details about AACRAO's involvement in information systems developments in higher education, contact AACRAO, One Dupont Circle, Suite 330, Washington, D.C. 20036.

CAUSE. Formerly, CAUSE was an acronym for the College and University Software Exchange. Now incorporated as a nonprofit educational association under the name CAUSE, this organization is another excellent source of current information about information systems developments in higher education. For example, as a result of a recent National Science Foundation (NSF) study, CAUSE is currently working on a joint project with AACRAO to produce an update of administrative systems utilized by higher education.

The objectives of CAUSE are to provide a professional association for individuals and institutions engaged in the development, use, and management of information systems in higher education; to enhance the effectiveness of college and university administration through the use of computer-based information systems and related management techniques; to serve as an interchange for promoting effective development, use, and management of information systems in higher education; and to anticipate, clarify, and communicate the concepts, issues, and problems related to computer-based information systems in college and university administration.

Two major activities are part of the CAUSE program. First, there is an annual conference held each year late in November or early December. Second, CAUSE has a library of nonproprietary computer software and systems documentation available to its members. CAUSE also publishes a bimonthly magazine called *Cause/Effect* and a bimonthly newsletter called *Cause Information*.

CAUSE has a central office located at 737 29th Street, Boulder, Colorado 80303. Membership is open to all colleges and universities.

College and University Machine Records Conference (CUMREC). CUMREC is a nonprofit educational organization of data processing administrators and another good source of current information about new college and university systems. The purposes of CUMREC are to conduct an annual conference of administrators in higher education for the purpose of exchanging and disseminating information of mutual interest and value relative to administrative data processing in higher education, to assist its members in the exchange of information in the development of a professional group of data processing managers in higher education, and to cooperate with the regional and national organizations in the fields of college and university administration and data processing.

The conference proceedings of CUMREC, which contain the annual program of presentations and papers, are available to the membership and cover a wide variety of data processing subjects. Typically, they are of special concern to designers, managers, and users of higher education systems. Membership in CUMREC is open to anyone who pays a registration fee at the annual conference. Although there is no permanent national office, those in-

terested in learning more about CUMREC and its annual conferences can consult the 1979 conference chairman, Ernest Jones, at
Indiana University.

International Word Processing Association (IWPA). The International Word Processing Association has chapters throughout the
world as a result of phenomenal growth in the word processing
industry during this decade. The individual chapters hold meetings to exchange information, ideas, and techniques. There are
also three-day conventions held during the year to acquaint participants with the newest technological developments and trends in
fields related to word processing. Attention is also given to managerial and supervisory skills, such as interviewing and hiring,
budgeting, personnel training, and performance appraisals. The
International Word Processing Association publishes various
books, surveys, reports, and a quarterly magazine called *WORDS*.

For further information, write to International Word Processing Association, Maryland Road, Willow Grove, Pennsylvania
19090.

*National Center for Higher Education Management Systems
(NCHEMS).* Formerly, NCHEMS was associated with the Western
Interstate Commission for Higher Education (WICHE), but now it
is a nonprofit educational association whose general mission is to
carry out research, development, and evaluation activities for the
purpose of bringing about improvements in planning and management in higher education. Many useful references have been
published by NCHEMS over the past decade. A partial listing of
these includes: *Data Element Dictionary, A Structure for the Outcomes of
Post-Secondary Education* by Oscar Lenning, *Quantitative Approaches
to Higher Education Management, A Glossary of Standard Terminology
for Post-Secondary Education,* and *A Reference Guide to Post-Secondary
Education Data Sources.* A complete listing of current NCHEMS
readings can be obtained by writing to the Publications Department, NCHEMS, P.O. Drawer P, Boulder, Colorado 80302.

NCHEMS continues to play a national leadership role in encouraging information systems developments in higher education.
For example, NCHEMS is currently working on a project concerning communications base concepts, and a publication describing
this project is scheduled. AACRAO, through its national office and
various committees, continues to work closely with NCHEMS in the

promotion of information standards and efforts to develop state-level information bases. Designers and users of information systems in higher education would be wise to watch closely the developments and programs of this important public agency.

Optical Character Recognition User Association (OCRUA). Admissions officers and registrars interested in learning more about OCR developments may wish to contact the OCR User Association (OCRUA), 10 Banta Place, Hackensack, New Jersey 07601. This is a small but rapidly growing national organization whose main objective is to advance the techniques and application of optical character recognition as a means of capturing data. Members of the organization have access to a "member information service" and can seek answers to questions involving OCR technology. Conferences are held twice a year, and transcripts and papers from past OCRUA conferences are available. Periodically, OCRUA sponsors comprehensive expositions on OCR equipment, supplies, and services. Only a few colleges and universities—including Cleveland State University, Ohio State University, and Tulsa Junior College—are pioneering in using OCR systems, but many more will be using OCR systems in the future. OCR offers new alternative solutions to old input bottleneck problems associated with keying operations.

OCRUA publishes a quarterly magazine called *OCR Today,* which is aimed at directors of data processing, managers, and administrative and technical personnel concerned with the application, design, or purchase of OCR equipment, supplies, and services.

Publications

The list of publications that provide information on new technologies of interest to registrars and admissions officers is growing annually. The following commercial publications typically feature articles and stories on the very latest systems, equipment, and technological developments in the area of information systems. But the listing is by no means exhaustive, and one can find many other excellent sources for further reading (for example, *EDUCOM Bulletins, Educational Technology, Educational Media,* and the *Educational Record*).

Administrative Management. Published monthly by Geyer-McAllister Publications, New York, this magazine is edited for administrative executives in many fields. There are articles on a wide variety of topics of general interest to college managers. For example, a recent magazine featured stories on office security, records management, telecommunications, mail systems, OCR, the delegation of work, the *Bakke* case, and Proposition 13.

Computerworld. Published weekly by CW Communications Inc., Boston, *Computerworld* is considered to be the newsweekly for the computer community. It contains articles about new equipment, systems, and important developments within the computing industry. Persons with systems and data processing responsibilities in higher education are more likely to read this publication regularly than are other college administrators.

Computer Decisions. This magazine is published monthly by Hayden Publishing Company, Rochelle Park, New Jersey, and is issued free of charge to qualified individuals with active professional and functional responsibility in computer manufacturing or in the computer user industry. Consequently, some data processing and systems personnel in higher education receive this magazine routinely. Although the magazine is intended for a more technically oriented reader, occasionally there are excellent articles of special interest to admissions officers and registrars, on subjects such as data processing personnel, management information systems, and input/output devices.

Datamation. Published monthly by Technical Publishing Company, Barrington, Illinois, *Datamation* is circulated without charge to certain qualified individuals involved with automatic information handling equipment. Therefore, some admissions officers and registrars, as well as data processing personnel, qualify for free copies of the magazine. Although the magazine features articles most frequently aimed at business and industry, there are articles that would be of special interest to those employed as systems personnel in admissions and records offices.

Infosystems. This magazine is published monthly by the Hitchcock Publishing Company, Wheaton, Illinois, and contains relatively nontechnical articles on subjects of interest to admissions officers and registrars, as well as data processing personnel.

Planning the Academic Calendar

◙ ◙ ◙ ◙ ◙ ◙ ◙ ◙ ◙ ◙ ◙ ◙ ◙ ◙ ◙ ◙ ◙ ◙

Loyd C. Oleson

The academic calendar in many institutions of higher learning is the responsibility of the college registrar. Following a brief historical statement and a list of the definitions currently in use, this chapter presents information for the person in charge of the academic calendar.

Calendar Trends

Historical Background[1]

The first institution of higher learning in America, Harvard College (founded in colonial Massachusetts in 1636), followed the four-term academic calendar used by Oxford and Cambridge in England. The terms were Hilary, Easter, Trinity, and Michelmas. The academic year, beginning in the middle of August with the Trinity quarter, was a year-round calendar of twelve months divided into four quarters. The present quarter system, used by

[1]Information in this section is based on Oleson, 1977a.

about one fourth of the institutions in the United States, evolved from the four-term plan that Harvard followed for its first 165 years.

Other colonial colleges in America apparently were not influenced by Harvard with respect to their academic calendars. Records show that the College of William and Mary (founded in colonial Virginia in 1693) was using a three-term academic calendar in 1736. The terms were named Hilary, Easter, and Trinity. The academic year consisted of approximately ten months, starting in late September or early October with the Trinity term; Easter, the third term, closed the academic year in late June or early July. The three-term plan was the dominant academic calendar for American institutions of higher learning during the eighteenth and nineteenth centuries. The two-term or semester system first appeared in the middle of the nineteenth century, probably originating at Princeton University in 1823. The desire for articulation with the public secondary schools was a factor in the development of the two-term semester calendar. Until the middle 1960s the academic calendar used by 76 percent of institutions in the United States was the traditional semester; 16 percent of the institutions were on the quarter system. Prior to 1960 there was some experimentation with the trimester, but it was not until the late 1960s that significant changes began to take place. The 1960s saw the advent of the "new" semester, now called the "early semester"; the "4-1-4"; and "modular" calendars.

The early 1970s will probably be remembered as the period of the calendar revolution. In the four-year period 1970–71 through 1973–74, approximately 45 percent of about 2,450 institutions of higher learning made a calendar change. (A change from the "traditional" semester to the "early" semester is counted as a change.) Changes have continued to be made each year since 1973–74, but at a slower rate.

Data regarding academic calendars are available over the ten-year period 1967 through 1976–77. In that decade the usage of the traditional semester went from 64 percent to 7 percent; the early semester, from 9 percent to 48 percent; the quarter system, from 19 percent to 24 percent; and the 4-1-4, from 1 percent to 13 percent. Table 1 gives the complete report.

Table 1. Number of Institutions Using the Six Types of Calendars

	No.	(1)	(2)	(3)	(4)	(5)	(6)
				Calendar Type			
1967–68	2,378	1,517 (64%)	205 (9%)	467 (19%)	86 (4%)	39 (1%)	64 (3%)
1968–69	2,427	1,379 (57%)	308 (13%)	514 (21%)	79 (3%)	75 (3%)	72 (3%)
1969–70	2,460	1,207 (49%)	438 (18%)	535 (22%)	75 (3%)	118 (5%)	87 (3%)
1970–71	2,475	895 (36%)	680 (27%)	539 (22%)	73 (3%)	186 (8%)	102 (4%)
1971–72	2,475	637 (26%)	860 (35%)	542 (22%)	77 (3%)	236 (9%)	123 (5%)
1972–73	2,450	354 (15%)	976 (40%)	585 (24%)	81 (3%)	329 (13%)	125 (5%)
1973–74	2,722	308 (12%)	1,170 (43%)	653 (24%)	77 (3%)	393 (14%)	121 (4%)
1974–75	2,821	263 (9%)	1,269 (45%)	696 (25%)	90 (3%)	383 (14%)	120 (4%)
1975–76	2,786	242 (9%)	1,257 (45%)	675 (24%)	101 (4%)	375 (13%)	136 (5%)
1976–77	2,472	172 (7%)	1,172 (48%)	586 (24%)	86 (3%)	324 (13%)	132 (5%)

Note: In Table 1, and in all tables where applicable, percentages are shown to the unit and may have been adjusted so that totals equal 100.

Sources: Oleson, 1971; Reynolds, 1972–1976.

Current Calendar Types[2]

Six major types of academic calendars are described in this chapter. Unless otherwise stated, the academic year is considered to be nine months in length—from the last week in August to the middle of May or from the first week in September to the first of June.

Type 1. *Traditional Semester.* Fall semester begins in September and ends sometime in January; spring semester begins late in January and ends in late May or early June. Students carry fifteen semester hours each semester.

Type 2. *Early Semester.* Fall semester begins late in August and ends in December before Christmas; spring semester begins about the middle of January and ends about the middle of May. Students carry fifteen semester hours each semester.

Type 3. *Quarter.* The college year is divided into three parts of about twelve weeks each. Students carry fifteen quarter credits each quarter. (Three quarter hours equal two semester hours.)

Type 4. *Trimester.* This calendar uses more than the normal nine months that define the college year, consisting of three parts of about sixteen weeks each. Students carry fifteen semester hours each trimester.

Type 5. *4-1-4.* The college year is divided into three parts, usually four months in the fall, one month in the winter (January), and four months in the spring. The fall term ends in December before Christmas. Students carry four courses (sixteen credits) in the fall and spring terms. Students carry one course (three or four credits) in the January term.

Type 6. *Other.* All types of calendars that do not fit any of the above five types. This group includes about twenty subtypes— among them, 4-4-1, 4-0-4, 3-3-3, and modular (short terms of three-and-a-half to seven weeks each, during which the student concentrates on one or two courses).

The quarter-system calendars are sometimes divided into *standard quarters* and *early quarters,* the main distinction being that

[2]Material in this section is based on Oleson, 1971.

the fall quarter ends shortly before Thanksgiving on the "early quarter" calendar. These distinctions do not appear in any of the tables that follow.

As Table 1 shows, in 1976–77 only 5 percent of the institutions used calendars that do not fit any of the five standard types. This is type 6, referred to as "Other." The largest subtype in this group is the 3-3-3 calendar (three terms per academic, year, with students carrying three courses each term), used by about twenty-four institutions. In several cases the calendar is unique. Usually, these unique programs are based on a modular plan and, while some have roots back to the Hiram Plan of the 1930s, evolved during the late 1960s and early 1970s as a result of the desire of faculties and students to innovate. The format of the modular calendar permits teaching-learning by means of intensive courses (see Hefferlin, 1972). Due to the many variations of these "Other" types of calendars, as well as the small number of institutions involved, this chapter includes no additional information about these unusual calendars other than to list them as type 6 in all the tables that follow.

Most institutions have one or more summer sessions (see Roller, Edwards, and Bruker, 1973), not necessarily related to the calendar type used for the academic year. At some quarter-system institutions, however, the summer session is the fourth quarter; and at trimester institutions the third trimester usually runs from late April to the middle of August. Many institutions using the traditional semester and the early semester calendars schedule two five-week summer sessions. Other institutions schedule several short workshops, of two and three weeks, during the summer. Because of the varied nature of summer sessions and the lack of statistical data, this chapter includes no additional information regarding summer session calendars.

Usage and Stability[3]

Of 537 two-year colleges, 45 percent had used their present calendar for nine or more years; 24 percent had been on their

[3]Data for this discussion, based on Oleson, 1977b, were obtained in the spring of 1977 from questionnaires completed by 1,170 four-year institutions (797 private and 373 public) and by 537 two-year colleges. All results are effective 1976–77.

present calendar from one to four years. The quarter-system calendar is the most stable calendar used by the two-year institutions; 23 percent had used that calendar type for nine or more years. Of 1,170 four-year institutions, 41 percent had used their present calendars for nine or more years, while 18 percent were in the one- to four-year category. The quarter-system calendar is also the most stable with the four-year institutions, 16 percent having been on the quarter system for nine or more years. Forty-five percent of the 373 public four-year institutions had used their present calendar for nine or more years, as compared to 40 percent of the 797 private institutions. Both groups shared the one- to four-year category, with 18 percent. The quarter-system calendar was the most stable for the public institutions, with 26 percent in the nine-or-more category; 13 percent of the private institutions had used the early semester calendar for nine or more years.

Tables 2, 3, and 4 show the distribution of calendar types and years of usage for those institutions included in the 1977 Academic Calendar Survey (Oleson, 1977b).

Table 2. Calendar Types and Years of Use—Two-Year Colleges, Private and Public

Years of Use	Calendar Type						Total	%
	(1)	(2)	(3)	(4)	(5)	(6)		
1–4	11	77	12	1	13	13	127	24
5–8	11	84	42	1	19	10	167	31
9 and over	57	38	123	8	2	15	243	45
Totals	79	199	177	10	34	38	537	
%	15	37	33	2	6	7		

Table 3. Calendar Types and Years of Use—Four-Year Public Institutions

Years of Use	Calendar Type						Total	%
	(1)	(2)	(3)	(4)	(5)	(6)		
1–4	4	52	2	1	4	5	67	18
5–8	2	113	13	2	6	3	139	37
9 and over	12	37	98	10	1	9	167	45
Totals	18	202	113	13	11	17	373	
%	5	54	30	4	3	4		

Table 4. Calendar Types and Years of Use—Four-Year Private
Institutions

Calendar Types and Years of Use	(1)	(2)	(3)	(4)	(5)	(6)	Total	%
1–4	10	69	6	7	29	22	143	18
5–8	11	123	22	4	137	40	337	42
9 and over	46	102	84	12	33	40	317	40
Totals	67	294	112	23	199	102	797	
%	8	37	14	3	25	13		

Opening Dates, Vacations, and Commencement[4]

Fall-Term Opening Dates. The figures reported below are based on the range of opening dates of 2,436 institutions for the 1976 fall term from August 16 to September 30 (see Table 5).

1. *Traditional Semester* (175 institutions). Opening dates range from August 23 to September 30. The mode was Monday, September 13: 62 institutions started classes on that date. The next largest group, 30, started the day after Labor Day, Tuesday, September 7.
2. *Early Semester* (1,166 institutions). Opening dates range from August 16 to September 21. The mode was Monday, August 30: 221 institutions. The next largest group, 149, started Monday, August 23.
3. *Quarter System* (568 institutions). Opening dates range from August 23 to September 30. The mode was Monday, September 27: 94 institutions. The next largest group, 78, started one week earlier, on Monday, September 20.
4. *Trimester* (82 institutions). Opening dates range from August 23 to September 28. The mode, 18 institutions, was Tuesday, September 7, the day after Labor Day.
5. *"4-1-4"* (321 institutions). Opening dates range from August 23 to September 16. The mode, 48 institutions, was Thursday, September 9. The next largest group, 46, started on Tuesday, September 7.

[4]Information in this section is based on Oleson, 1977b, and Reynolds, 1976.

Table 5. Dates Institutions Started in 1976: August 16–September 30

	Starting Date	Calendar Type						Total
		(1)	(2)	(3)	(4)	(5)	(6)	
August	M 16	0	14	0	0	0	1	15
	T 17	0	6	0	0	0	0	6
	W 18	0	8	0	0	0	0	8
	Th 19	0	15	0	0	0	0	15
	F 20	0	7	0	0	0	1	8
	M 23	4	160	15	2	3	4	188
	T 24	0	20	2	1	1	4	28
	W 25	0	72	3	3	6	0	84
	Th 26	0	82	2	0	4	0	88
	F 27	0	17	12	1	3	1	34
	M 30	2	221	6	6	18	9	262
	T 31	0	46	2	1	10	1	60
September	W 1	8	123	11	9	44	8	203
	Th 2	0	56	5	4	27	1	93
	F 3	0	10	3	2	9	0	24
	M 6	1	24	10	3	12	5	55
	T 7	30	112	60	18	46	18	284
	W 8	9	77	38	5	45	14	188
	Th 9	6	51	30	4	48	12	151
	F 10	1	12	8	2	7	2	32

Table 5. Dates Institutions Started in 1976: August 16–September 30 (continued)

Starting Date		Calendar Type						Total
		(1)	(2)	(3)	(4)	(5)	(6)	
September	13 M	62	21	41	10	29	21	184
	14 T	4	3	8	0	3	3	21
	15 W	4	2	13	1	5	4	29
	16 Th	8	3	13	1	1	6	32
	17 F	3	0	4	0	0	0	7
	20 M	11	1	78	1	0	4	95
	21 T	4	3	18	0	0	1	26
	22 W	9	0	39	1	0	3	52
	23 Th	6	0	30	0	0	0	36
	24 F	0	0	1	0	0	0	1
	27 M	2	0	94	6	0	0	102
	28 T	0	0	7	1	0	0	8
	29 W	0	0	10	0	0	1	11
	30 Th	1	0	5	0	0	0	6
Totals		175	1,166	568	82	321	124	2,436

Source: Reynolds, 1976.

6. *Other* (124 institutions). Opening dates range from August 16 to September 29. The mode was Monday, September 13, with 21 institutions. The next largest group, 18, started on Tuesday, September 7.

Some general observations: (a) 55 institutions started classes on Labor Day; (b) a total of 1,116 institutions in the above summary were under way *before* Labor Day; (c) of the 2,436 institutions in the above summary, the Tuesday immediately following Labor Day was the most popular starting date: 284 institutions. The next most popular date was Monday, August 30: 262 institutions.

Thanksgiving Recess. Table 6 shows the number of days taken for Thanksgiving recess by 456 two-year and 1,178 four-year institutions.

The two-day Thanksgiving recess is used by 50 percent of the two-year institutions and by 42 percent of the four-year institutions; the three-day recess is used by 27 percent of the two-year and 29 percent of the four-year institutions.

October Vacations. The 1977 Academic Calendar Survey (Oleson, 1977b) revealed that sixty-four institutions, located in twenty-five states, have some type of October vacation. Of these, twenty-eight have "one-day" breaks, usually Friday. The vacation consists of a long weekend, Friday, Saturday, Sunday, and Monday, for twenty institutions. Thirteen vacations were for an entire week. The longest vacations, ten days, were enjoyed by three institutions.

Table 6. Thanksgiving Recess

Number	*Number of Institutions*	
of Days	*2-year*	*4-year*
No recess	10	36
One day	4	14
Two days	230	494
Two and a half days	9	72
Three days	121	342
Four days	27	85
Five or more	6	58
Break between terms	49	77

Source: Oleson, 1977b.

Dates of Commencement. Table 7 shows the dates of commencement from April 21 through June 30, 1977. Table 8 is a summary by months.

As the tables show, only forty-nine institutions held commencement exercises during the last ten days of April. (Twenty-one of these were on April 30.) Twenty-seven of the forty-nine were on the early semester calendar; fifteen were using the trimester calendar. The month of May accounted for 1,567 of the total of 2,188 commencements shown in Table 7. The institutions using the early semester held a total of 1,007 commencements in May; 282 institutions using the 4-1-4 calendar also had commencements in May. A total of 572 commencements were held in the first twenty days of June. The largest group was the quarter-system institutions, with 318 commencements; 116 institutions using the traditional semester held traditional June commencements.

The most popular day for commencement in 1977 was Sunday, May 15. A total of 206 institutions, including 162 on the early semester calendar and 29 on the "4-1-4," held their commencement exercises on that date. The next most popular date was a week later, on Sunday, May 22. The 203 institutions having commencements on that date included 98 on the early semester and 80 on the 4-1-4.

Twenty-five quarter-system institutions hold their commencements in August at the end of the summer quarter, in lieu of June or May commencements at the end of the spring quarter. (These dates are not included in Tables 7 and 8.)

Length of Fall Term Under Early Semester

This section (based on Reynolds, 1976) is a discussion of the fall term of the early semester calendar, which is used by 48 percent of the institutions. The distinguishing feature of the early semester is that it ends just before the Christmas holiday season. There is no problem with regard to the number of class days available in the spring term, but there is an apparent shortage of class days in the fall term. We define class days to include regular teaching days, reading or review days, and final examination days.

To establish a base for comparison, the 1976 fall-term calen-

Table 7. Dates of Commencement, 1977

			Calendar Type				Total
	(1)	(2)	(3)	(4)	(5)	(6)	
April 21	0	1	0	0	0	0	1
22	0	0	0	2	0	1	3
23	0	1	0	4	1	0	6
24	0	1	0	2	0	0	3
25	0	0	0	1	0	0	1
26	0	1	0	1	0	0	2
27	0	1	0	1	0	0	2
28	0	4	1	0	0	1	6
29	0	3	0	0	0	1	4
30	0	15	0	4	0	2	21
May 1	0	25	0	4	0	3	32
2	0	2	0	1	0	1	4
3	0	3	0	2	0	0	5
4	0	1	0	1	0	0	2
5	0	3	1	0	0	1	5
6	0	31	0	0	0	2	33
7	0	54	0	2	1	2	59
8	1	63	1	1	3	4	73
9	1	11	1	0	0	0	13
10	0	6	0	0	0	0	6
11	1	6	0	0	0	0	7
12	0	29	2	0	2	0	33

Table 7. Dates of Commencement, 1977

			Calendar Type				
	(1)	(2)	(3)	(4)	(5)	(6)	Total
May 13	0	79	1	0	2	4	86
14	0	142	2	1	12	4	161
15	2	162	7	1	29	5	206
16	1	14	1	1	2	3	22
17	0	15	1	0	0	0	16
18	1	19	3	0	0	1	24
19	0	22	3	0	1	1	27
20	2	42	15	0	9	0	68
21	1	74	11	3	48	6	143
22	1	98	13	1	80	10	203
23	0	9	3	0	1	2	15
24	1	8	1	0	1	0	11
25	1	8	2	0	3	1	15
26	0	10	10	2	2	3	27
27	5	13	20	0	12	1	51
28	3	20	18	5	28	7	81
29	6	29	25	2	45	11	118
30	3	7	4	0	1	1	16
31	0	2	3	0	0	0	5
June 1	4	8	2	0	1	0	15
2	6	4	9	1	1	2	23
3	9	9	34	0	4	0	56

4	8	2	28	6	8	6	58
5	11	19	41	5	13	5	94
6	2	3	4	0	1	0	10
7	2	1	5	0	0	0	8
8	4	2	6	0	0	0	12
9	7	1	13	0	1	0	22
10	6	2	44	2	0	0	54
11	5	3	43	1	0	7	59
12	9	1	38	2	0	4	54
13	1	0	1	0	1	2	5
14	3	0	6	0	0	0	9
15	5	1	5	0	0	0	11
16	10	2	5	0	1	0	18
17	20	1	15	0	0	0	36
18	3	1	9	1	0	2	16
19	0	1	9	0	0	0	10
20	1	0	1	0	0	0	2
Totals	146	1,095	467	60	314	106	2,188

Source: Reynolds, 1976.

Table 8. Summary of Commencement Dates, by Month

Month			Calendar Type			
	(1)	(2)	(3)	(4)	(5)	(6)	Total
April	0	27	1	15	1	5	49
May	30	1,007	148	27	282	73	1,567
June	116	61	318	18	31	28	572
Totals	146	1,095	467	60	314	106	2,188

dars of about 100 institutions using the traditional semester were examined. The range of class days was from 79 to 93, with 84 being the mode. Thus, based on actual practice, it seems that 80 is a reasonable minimum number of class days for the fall term.

The fall term for the early semester calendar is complicated in several ways: (1) some institutions are not able to start classes before Labor Day (students are involved with summer jobs that continue until or through Labor Day); (2) most institutions take a Thanksgiving recess of at least two days; and (3) students and faculty prefer that classes and final examinations end several days prior to December 25.

Table 9 shows the number of class days in a fall term as determined by the starting date. The dates are for 1976. The following assumptions are made: (1) No classes on Labor Day. (2) A three-day Thanksgiving recess. (3) If classes start *before* Labor Day, the last day of classes is December 17. (4) If classes start *after* Labor Day, the last day of classes is December 23. (5) No classes on Saturdays. (6) No October vacation. (7) Class periods are fifty minutes in length.

Some institutions, to compensate for a shortage of class days, use class periods longer than the traditional fifty minutes. The use

Table 9. Number of Class Days in a Fall Term

Starting Date	Number of Class Days	Starting Date	Number of Class Days
August 16	86	September 1	74
17	85	2	73
18	84	3	72
19	83		
20	82		
		7	75
23	81	8	74
24	80	9	73
25	79	10	72
26	78		
27	77	13	71
		14	70
30	76	15	69
31	75		

of sixty-minute periods has the effect of adding one class day every fifth day. A class meeting for sixty minutes three times a week for ten weeks is in session for 1,800 minutes. This is the "equivalent" of a class meeting for fifty minutes, three times a week for twelve weeks. Some institutions have even longer class periods—of seventy-five, eighty, or ninety minutes.

The use of sixty-minute periods necessitates a lengthening of the class day by approximately one hour if the same number of class periods is maintained. If the longer periods are obtained at the sacrifice of the number of class periods in the day, there are fewer choices for students and more schedule conflicts.

Some institutions gain a day by having one day of final examinations on Saturday. Miami University (Oxford, Ohio) did this in 1976. Its classes started August 30; Labor Day was a holiday; Thanksgiving recess was for just two days. There was a two-day reading period followed by four days of final examinations— Friday, Saturday, Monday, and Wednesday. The term ended with the last day of finals, December 22. Table 9 shows a total of 76 days. Adjusting by one less day of Thanksgiving recess and the Saturday used for finals, plus three days beyond the assumed end of the term, gave Miami University a total of eighty-one class days for the 1976 fall term.

Contingency Calendars

The complexity of operation of present-day institutions of higher learning suggests that some attention be given to the contingency calendar. Plans and procedures for the continued operation of the institution following any interruption should be on file. The energy problems faced by many institutions in the 1976–77 winter may well be encountered again in the future.

Central Michigan University's *Report of the Ad Hoc Contingency Calendar Committee to the Academic Senate* (used with Permission of Central Michigan University) illustrates the implementation of a contingency calendar. The report is dated April 1977. (Central Michigan University uses the early semester calendar. Its second semester started January 17, 1977; commencement was May 14, 1977.) The report is developed around the three charges to the committee:

1. To recommend for senate action an alternative calendar to that which is established for the winter semester of 1978. This alternate calendar is to serve as the basis of a contingency plan to be implemented if the combination of severe weather and limited energy resources mandate that the university take immediate and extreme conservation measures.
2. To recommend for senate action guidelines for the implementation procedures for the contingency calendar (i.e., by what date should the decision be made to use the alternate calendar, what criteria should be given priority in the decision, etc.).
3. To identify and direct to the attention of the university community any considerations relative to long-term energy conservation measures, including permanent calendar modification.

The committee was guided in its deliberations by the words *voluntary* and *reactive*. Potential changes in calendar which *anticipated* energy crises were viewed as voluntary adjustments.

The recommendations of the committee in response to Charges 1 and 2 are reproduced below:

Charge 1
1. The 1978 winter semester calendar not be changed by voluntary action.
2. The university be reactive to governmental or utility action rather than initiate action concerning the calendar.

Charge 2
3. (One-Week Closing) The university use the spring break of winter 1978 to make up a one-week mandated closing occurring prior to February 10; or the week between winter and summer semesters if closed after February 10.
4. (Two-Week Closing) The university use the spring break and the week between the winter and summer semesters to make up a two-week mandated closing occurring before February 10.
5. (Four-Week Closing) The university make up the time by using a combination of adjustments in class schedule, time, and format as follows:
   a. Two weeks from the spring break and break between winter and summer semesters.
   b. Two weeks by adding ten minutes to the current fifty-minute class period for ten weeks.
6. (More Than Four-Week Closing) The university make up the time by:
   a. Two weeks as in 5a.
   b. Each additional week needed by adding twenty minutes to the current fifty-minute class period for a three-week period

(i.e., six weeks under a seventy-minute class period will replace two weeks of lost time.)

7. The university immediately provide the community, after the
    mandate has been received, the following:
    a. Contingency calendar to student, faculty, staff, community.
    b. Adjusted class schedule time format to students, faculty,
        staff.
    c. Adjusted student class schedules to students.

Institutional Policies and Practices

Calendar Changes

In all cases, the calendar should be the responsibility of some
designated official. In many institutions the registrar either chairs
the calendar committee or is a member. The committee should
include representatives from the faculty, the students, and the administration. The University Calendar Committee for Ohio State
University is used as an example.

1. The University Calendar Committee is one of the standing
    committees of the University Senate and is advisory to the Coun-
    cil of Deans.
2. The University Calendar Committee consists of thirteen mem-
    bers as follows:
    a. Six members of the faculty, at least one of whom must be a
        senate member.
    b. Four members of the student body: one graduate student,
        one professional student, and two undergraduate students.
    c. The provost or a designee.
    d. A representative of the Council of Deans.
    e. The Assistant Vice-President for Registration Services or a
        designee.
3. The University Calendar Committee is responsible for making
    recommendations pertaining to:
    a. Preparation and review of the university calendar.
    b. Study of the comparative advantages and disadvantages of
        the quarter system [calendar] and alternative systems.
    c. Development of improved quarter-end validation procedures.

Either a standing committee, charged with responsibility for
the academic calendar, or an ad hoc committee can accomplish a

calendar change. The committee should have a definite charge. At Washington State University, in 1974, the charge to the committee was to "examine the characteristics of a quarter calendar as it might be used at WSU." At Northwestern University, in 1975, the charge was to examine alternative calendars to their present quarter-system calendar.

The committee should set up a methodology that includes (1) reading the literature; (2) collecting information from similar institutions; (3) using questionnaires to learn opinions of students, faculty, and administration; (4) evaluating possible calendars against criteria established by the committee; (5) listing advantages and disadvantages; (6) estimating the cost. To illustrate step 3, questionnaires used by Ohio State University and Miami University of Ohio are shown in Exhibits 1 and 2.

Exhibit 1. University Calendar Questionnaire, Ohio State University

The University Calendar Committee is attempting to obtain maximal information for planning future university calendars (1976–1980). You are invited to express your opinions by completing this questionnaire and returning it with your Registration Form to your college or regional campus office. The responses requested have necessarily been simplified to facilitate interpretation of this poll.

1. Do you favor:
   a. ____ a continuation of the present quarter system?
   b. ____ *consideration* of a semester system (two 15-week periods) such as:
          Example I : First Semester: Sept 20–Jan 15
                            Second Semester: Feb 3–June 1 (including Easter recess)
          Example II: First Semester: Sept 2–Dec 15
                            Second Semester: Jan 13–May 15 (including Easter recess)
   c. ____ *consideration* of a trimester or some other calendar?
2. What dates do you most prefer for autumn quarter?
   a. ____ classes begin in early September, end in November, and the academic year ends in May. (Features the normal quarter breaks.)
   b. ____ classes begin in mid-September, end by Thanksgiving, and the academic year ends in early June. (Features a month break between autumn and winter quarters.)
   c. ____ classes begin in late September, end in December, and the academic year ends in mid-June. (Features either normal

quarter breaks or a month break between autumn and winter quarters.)

3. Do you think the present practice of early final examinations for graduating seniors should be eliminated?

    a. ___ Yes   b. ___ No

4. If you answered "Yes" to Question 3, should there be:

    a. ___ no final exams for graduating seniors?

    b. ___ a later date for commencement so that all students can take final exams at the same time and graduates can still receive valid diplomas during the ceremonies?

    c. ___ commencement at the end of final exam week, but with all students having taken exams together, and with diplomas *mailed* at a later date?

    d. ___ only one commencement per year, say in the spring, with certification made available all quarters?

5. If modifying the academic calendar required reducing the final exam period from five to three or four days, would you be:

    a. ___ for this schedule

    b. ___ against this schedule

    c. ___ no opinion.

6. What is your present year in college (circle closest)?

    Undergraduate: 1 2 3 4   Professional School   Graduate School

7. Other suggestions, additions or comments: (Please use reverse side.)

Please return the completed questionnaire with your Registration Form to your college or regional campus office. Thank you for your cooperation.

Exhibit 2. Semester Calendar Survey of Students, Miami University (March 1975)

[Questions 1–10 dealing with demographic variables have been omitted.]

11. Given that the semesters would contain 33 weeks of instruction and examinations (this does not include vacation time), which of the following possibilities would you prefer:

    0) 15 weeks instruction; 1½ weeks of final exams per term

    1) 15½ weeks instruction; 1 week of final exams per term

    2) 15 weeks instruction; 3-day reading period (no classes); 1 week of final exams per term

    3) No preference

12. If it were possible to offer it, would you prefer a semester with 16½ weeks of instruction and all examinations being given during regular class periods; that is, a semester with no final exam week?

    0) Yes, I definitely would want this

    1) I probably would want this

    2) I probably would *not* want this

    3) I definitely would *not* want this

    4) No opinion

13. Assuming that 128 hours will be required for a baccalaureate degree, how many courses (taking into consideration separate subjects, assignments, exams) would you feel comfortable taking in a given semester?
    0) 3
    1) 4
    2) 5
    3) 6
    4) 7
    5) No opinion

14. Assuming that 128 hours will be required for a baccalaureate degree (which means an average of 16 hours a semester), in which of the following course loads do you think you could gain the most academically? We realize, of course, this would be dependent on what is offered.
    0) 5 3-hour courses
    1) 4 4-hour courses
    2) 5 courses—mixture of 3- and 4-hour courses
    3) 5 4-hour courses
    4) 6 3-hour courses
    5) No opinion

15. If you were taking a four-credit-hour course, please select from the options following the number of times you feel you would most prefer to be in class per week.
    0) Four 50-minute periods
    1) Three 65-minute periods
    2) Two 100-minute periods
    3) No opinion

16. If construction of the master schedule required including some classes in the evenings, would you
    0) Prefer to have some courses in the evening
    1) Be willing to have an occasional course in the evening
    2) Prefer not to have any evening courses
    3) Definitely not take a course in the evening
    4) No opinion

17. In the first semester, what day of the week is more practical for you to start classes, given the activities of moving into your room, buying books, changing your schedule, and the other matters associated with the beginning of the school year?
    0) I'd prefer to start on Monday
    1) I'd prefer to start on Tuesday
    2) I'd prefer to start on Wednesday
    3) I'd prefer to start on Thursday
    4) No opinion

18. There will be a Thanksgiving break of 4 days (Thursday through Sunday) in the first semester. Do you feel that an additional 4-day weekend late in October is needed, even though this would mean beginning the first semester at an earlier date or ending it later?
    0) I think it is definitely needed

1) I think it is probably needed
2) I think it is probably *not* needed
3) I think it is definitely *not* needed
4) No opinion

19. The first semester will end just prior to Christmas. What vacation option would you prefer?
    0) A short break at Christmas (14 days) with the second semester ending in early May
    1) A long break at Christmas (21 days) with the second semester ending in mid-May
    2) No opinion

20. Assuming that there would be a spring break in the second semester, would you prefer
    0) A week of vacation in March
    1) A 4-day weekend in March
    2) No spring break
    3) No opinion

21. Miami could offer a three-week intersession starting before mid-May in which probably only one course would be taken. A course offered during this term would provide credit and have requirements identical to those of the same course during a regular semester. Would you attend such an intersession?
    0) I definitely would
    1) I probably would
    2) I probably would *not*
    3) I definitely would *not*
    4) I would look for a job rather than attend an intersession
    5) No opinion

22. If you attended a 3-week intersession, would you do so because you wanted
    0) to accelerate my graduation or pick up more hours
    1) to make up hours lost during preceding terms
    2) to reduce my academic load during the regular semester
    3) Other reasons
    4) I would not attend
    5) No opinion

23. As an alternative to a 3-week intersession, Miami could offer a 5-week term ending by approximately June 10. Two courses could be carried during such a term. If you were to attend the first summer offering, would you prefer
    0) a 3-week intersession in which I could take one course
    1) a 5-week term in which I could take two courses
    2) I probably would not attend an early summer term of either 3 or 5 weeks
    3) No opinion

24. If you were to attend Miami during the summer, would you prefer to attend:
    0) 3 five-week terms beginning early May
    1) 2 five-week terms beginning mid-June
    2) 1 five-week term

3) 2 six-week terms beginning in May
4) 1 six-week term
5) I probably would not attend
6) No opinion
25. If you have any additional comments or any general questions regarding the early semester, please write them on the back of this sheet and return it with the scanner form.

Step 4 (evaluating calendars against criteria) is illustrated by the Calendar and Examination Committee of the University of Cincinnati, which considered five different calendars and evaluated each against the following criteria (the first five were considered the most important):

1. Instructional benefits
2. Accommodation of the Professional Practice Program
3. Utilization of university resources
4. Synchronization with other calendars
5. Impact on student employment
6. Instructional drawbacks
7. Faculty development opportunities
8. Student recruitment
9. Support of university activities
10. Opportunities for special events
11. Creature comforts and costs
12. Synchronization with Colleges of Law and Medicine
13. Administrative workload

Step 5 (listing advantages and disadvantages) is illustrated by two universities that contemplated a change from the quarter-system calendar to the early semester. In both instances, the advantages and disadvantages of the two systems were considered. A report, dated February 1977, by the University of Akron explained its change to the early semester. It cited the following advantages of the early semester system (two semesters):

1. Provides proportionately more out-of-class time for students for the preparation and assimilation of course materials, for in-depth study, for independent study, reading, writing, and deliberation.

2. Provides proportionately more time for faculty for class development, for reading, writing, research, rethinking courses, and for a more thorough evaluation of students.

3. Reduces the amount of faculty activity related to term endings and beginnings—grading, advising, registration—thus freeing time for instruction and other matters related to instruction.

4. Reduces the tendency toward compression and fragmentation of courses.

5. Provides ample time between all terms for various academic actions—getting out grades, notifying students of academic actions—and for open and late registration.

6. Permits a better use of textbooks, which are most frequently designed for semesters, especially in some fields, and usually reduces the yearly textbook and materials cost for students.

7. Makes it easier for students to plan an entire year's program with fewer probable changes.

8. Provides earlier summer job opportunities for students and therefore a longer period in which to earn and save.

9. Provides more time for the freshman student to secure faculty help, academic counseling, and necessary judgments before the first-term grades must be produced and judgments made as to the freshman's probable academic success.

10. Requires only two grading, registration, billing, and collection periods, resulting in substantial time and money savings to the university and staff.

11. Eliminates the "lame duck" session following the Christmas holiday.

12. Reduces the pressures on both faculty and students inherent in getting everything done in ten weeks, the need for "crisis to crisis" operations, and allows more time for planning and the evaluation and improvement of various operations.

13. Provides an opportunity to establish an "energy savings" calendar by allowing a four- to six-week break in classes from Christmas through January.

The University of Akron report listed the following advantages of the quarter system (three quarters):

1. Provides shorter learning modules, one more opportunity for course selection and program variety.
2. Makes possible a larger number of courses and therefore a narrower focus on subjects and a greater variety of choices for the student.
3. Provides for more flexibility in course and program design.
4. Provides easier scheduling in a five-week summer time frame.
5. Provides less probability for conflict between school and work or home responsibilities due to the shorter time frame (11 weeks versus 16 weeks) for scheduling activities.
6. Makes it easier for students to plan their personal schedules for a term and their schedules for a full program of study due to a greater variety of course opportunities.
7. Provides one more term for students to start their educational programs or to transfer in from another institution.
8. Provides fewer problems in planning joint programs with sister institutions which are also on the quarter system.
9. Reduces the costs both in money and time to the student who must withdraw from school during a term.
10. Provides more terms for scheduling such activities as leaves of absence, faculty exchange programs, terms of study abroad, field experience.

A report of the Academic Calendar Subcommittee to the Committee on the Improvement of Instruction at Miami University (Ohio), dated February 1973, included the recommendation that the university change from the quarter-system calendar to the early semester. It listed the following advantages of the early semester system:

1. Provides more time for students for out-of-class preparation and digestion, for independent study, reading, writing, and deliberation.
2. Provides more faculty time for reading, writing, rethinking courses, for research, and for instruction and evaluation.
3. Reduces number of faculty chores such as exams, grade assignments, advising, registration, etc., thus leaving more time for matters more closely related to instruction.

4. Provides more time for larger units of instruction, for study in depth.
5. Discourages course fragmentation and compression.
6. Provides ample time to get out grades between all terms, for the certification, evaluation, probation/suspension/petition process.
7. Permits better use of textbooks, which are most frequently arranged for semesters, especially in the social sciences, business, and the sciences.
8. Provides an improved program for student teachers.
9. Utilizes the standard credit hour.
10. Provides some acceleration possibilities.
11. Requires only two grading, registration, billing, and collection periods, thus providing substantial time and money savings.
12. Provides better student retention, thus saving present losses resulting from hall vacancies, reduced number of fee payments.
13. Provides increased revenue from longer-term investment of greater student fee amounts.
14. Permits better course enrollment planning.
15. Increases summer job opportunities for students and the length of employment time.
16. Lowers textbook and materials cost for students (savings of about $50 per student).
17. Coincides better with opening of public schools.
18. Utilized by more institutions than any other calendar, thus facilitating transfer from many institutions.
19. Permits development of an "intercession" between fall and spring terms or of a "miniterm" following the spring term.

At the same time, the Miami University report noted the following disadvantages of the early semester system:

1. Provides fewer opportunities for course selection, changing of sequences, and adjusting academic major problems.
2. Provides one fewer period for transferring in or out.
3. Creates the possibility of some students' registering late for the fall term, particularly those who have jobs at summer

camps which remain open until Labor Day and those who have not returned from family vacations.

4. Creates the possibility of the first summer term's starting before public school teachers and other potential students have completed spring terms.
5. Creates a transportation problem for some students going home in the period immediately before Christmas (December 22-23).
6. Creates possible problem in scheduling faculty-staff vacations as children in the public schools are not free in mid May.
7. Makes comparison with other state schools more difficult.

The following quarter-system advantages were listed in the Miami University report:

1. Provides more opportunities for course selection, changing of sequences, and adjustment of academic major problems.
2. Terminates before Christmas.
3. Provides more frequent evaluations of student progress.
4. Provides maximum potential for transfer in from and out to other state schools.
5. Provides one more opportunity for admissions and enrollment of new students.
6. Facilitates comparison with other state institutions.
7. Accommodates flexible vacation periods and alternative leaving opportunities.

Finally, the report noted the following quarter-system disadvantages:

1. Provides less student time for out-of-class preparation and digestion, for independent study, reading, writing, deliberation.
2. Provides insufficient time to develop a class properly and for ample instruction.
3. Provides less faculty time for reading, writing, rethinking courses, research, instruction, and evaluation.
4. Allows insufficient time for grade distribution and for

probation/suspension/petititon actions between winter and spring quarters.

5. Is too short a term as a basic academic unit, particularly in the sciences.

6. Makes use of many textbooks difficult, as most, especially in the social sciences, business, and the sciences, were made for semester use.

7. Requires an additional period of registration, change of course, grading, probation/suspension/petition procedures, housing assignments, etc., thus significantly increasing costs.

8. Results in loss of revenue due to student attrition between winter and spring quarters.

9. Results in loss of revenue from short-term investment of lesser amounts of student fees.

10. Lowers summer job opportunities for students and provides less time for summer earning.

11. Increases textbook and material cost for students (estimate about $50 per student).

The final part (step 6) of the report of the calendar committee consists of the estimated costs related to a calendar change. The cost estimates should include costs to the student, to the faculty, and to the institution.

Institutional costs divide into the one-time *conversion costs* and the increased (or decreased) *annual operating costs*. In changing from the two-semester calendar to the three-quarter calendar, the institution would experience increased cost in the registrar's office (in supplies, materials, personnel salaries and staff benefits, computer time, and postage) due to the third registration and the third grading period each year. In addition to the tangible costs, there are expenses which are not easily estimated; for example, the processing of grade changes three times per year rather than twice. Other offices would incur added expenses. The bursar's office would handle a third set of billings and collections; the financial aid office must process a third set of awards; the housing director must make residence hall assignments an extra time each academic year. Conversion costs to the institution could include the printing of new registration forms, new grade reports, new billing forms, new financial aid forms, new brochures, publicity about the change, and new or altered computer programs. A partial list of institutions that have issued calendar committee reports, with carefully estimated cost estimates, includes Washington State University, Miami University (Ohio), Northwestern University, and Grand Valley State College. (Due to their financial implications, these reports are not included in this chapter.)

The cost to the faculty would be the time and personal energy needed to rewrite lectures and redesign courses, or to prepare completely new courses, to fit the new calendar format. This could also involve actual expense for materials, typing, and duplicating. The cost of preparing a third set of final examinations also occurs.

The cost to the student would include the need to purchase textbooks three times a year rather than two. There would also be the expense of one extra round-trip home for the resident student. There might be a loss of income from summer employment if the spring quarter did not end until the early part of June.

The committee should keep all populations in the academic community informed of its progress. The University of Akron committee used a question-answer type of report. The questions, from its report dated February 1977, are listed below:

1. Why has the university decided to return to the semester system?
2. What kind of academic calendar would we have under the early semester system?
3. When will the proposed change become effective?
4. How do quarter credits convert to semester credits?
5. Will any of the conversion activities have an adverse effect on students' graduation?
6. Will the semester system cost the student more or less in actual money outlay?
7. Will there be money savings to the university?
8. What are the major arguments to support a semester system over a quarter system?
9. Will the basis for faculty salaries be different under semesters than under quarters?
10. How about salaries and load in the summer?

11. How will the change affect student enrollment?
12. Would the scheduling and housing of classes be affected by switching to semesters?
13. Where do we stand in the conversion process?

A change in type of calendar should be announced at least one year in advance, with the year immediately preceding being the transition year. The University of Akron, after having studied the matter for about three years, announced in February 1977 that the change from the quarter system to the early semester calendar would become effective with the 1978–79 academic year. Miami University (Ohio), also after considerable study, announced in April 1975 that the change from the quarter system to the early semester would become effective with the 1976–77 academic year. In each of these two cases, there was an entire year between the time of the announcement and the actual change; thus, students and faculty had a one-year transition period.

Calendar Setting and Publication

The ongoing planning and operation of the academic institution is so dependent on the calendar that careful attention should be paid to its setting and publication. The registrar, either as chairman or as a member of the calendar committee, should be the expert regarding the institution's calendar policy and should take the initiative in preparing the forthcoming year's calendar for presentation to the committee, the administrative head, and the governing body for approval. Accuracy is mandatory. One of the common errors is for last year's date (June 3) to be used for this year's corresponding event (June 2). Another common error is to use last year (1978) on the 1979 program.

Several editions of the calendar, all carefully coordinated, should be issued to publicize the events of the academic year to the various populations in the academic community. In all cases, the published calendars should include the name of the institution, the type of calendar (early semester, quarter, etc.), the date issued, and the name of the person responsible.

The *administrative calendar,* establishing the starting and ending of each term and the recesses or vacation periods, should be complete and available on request at least two years in advance and published at least one year in advance. In larger institutions, the corresponding lead times may need to be six and five years, respectively. The registrar's office is the logical place for this calendar to be on file.

The *general calendar* should be published at least twelve months prior to the opening of the fall term. This calendar usually appears in the college catalog. However, it should also be prepared for easy distribution.

The general calendar should include the following basic items for each semester, quarter, or term:

1. Dates of registration just prior to the opening of term.
2. Date classes start.
3. Last date to register.
4. Last date to pay tuition and fees.
5. Last date to add courses.
6. Last date to drop courses.
7. Dates of official holidays (national, state, and institutional).
8. Date midterm grade reports are due from the faculty.
9. Date midterm grade reports are issued to the students.
10. Dates of any midterm recesses.
11. Date of final examinations.
12. Date of the official end of the term.
13. Date final grades are due from the faculty.
14. Date grade reports will be issued to the students.
15. Dates of preregistration (if this procedure is used) for the next term.
16. Date of commencement.

Various forms of the general calendar can be issued. A *calendar for students* should include, in addition to most of the items shown above, the dates when dormitories open and close, the dates when the cafeteria opens and closes, the dates when tuition and fees are due, and the dates when seniors must file applications for graduation. If this calendar is published in the student handbook, it might also include athletic events, homecoming, and other institutional special events. A special *calendar for freshmen,* as a variation of the calendar for students, can be a useful part of the orientation process. Such a calendar can include the dates of advanced placement tests, the schedule of minicourses designed to help the teaching-learning process, and other important dates.

A *calendar for parents* is good public relations for all institutions. This calendar enables the parents to know when to expect the students home for recesses and vacations, when tuition and fees will be due, and the dates of Parents' Day, commencement, and other events of special interest to parents.

A *calendar for faculty* can include, in addition to most of the items in the general calendar, dates of faculty meetings (or faculty senate meetings), dates when pay checks are issued, and deadline dates for filing requests for leaves of absence and for submitting proposals for new courses to be added to the curriculum. A special *calendar for spouses,* as a variation of the calendar for faculty, can be good public relations for institutions of any size. This calendar can include dates of adult education seminars and special events for the entire family.

Further Reading and Study

The report of a faculty committee of Ohio State University (Cowley, 1932) includes a chapter on the history of the American college calendar for the period 1636 to 1931. This chapter is recommended for anyone making a study of academic calendars. Information regarding academic calendars has been of interest to members of AACRAO for many years. In 1961 a committee on academic calendars published *The University Calendar* (American Association of Collegiate Registrars and Admissions Officers, 1961), in which calendar trends of the late 1950s and early 1960s are discussed. In the *Fact Book on Higher Education* (American Council on Education, 1971), the types of academic calendars in use in 1971–72 are depicted graphically by region and state. An unpublished doctoral dissertation (Walz, 1972), based on a study of 904 institutions that made calendar changes during the three-year period 1969–1972, is a useful reference for anyone charged with the responsibility of making a change in the institution's academic calendar. Bouwman (1970) provides a thorough discussion of the 4-1-4 calendar, and Kuhns (1971) outlines the modular system in use at Mount Vernon Junior College. Readers are also referred to the January 16, 1978, issue of the *Chronicle of Higher Education* for a comparison, in graphic form, of the four major types of academic calendars in use in 1977.

□□□□□□□ 11

Undertaking Institutional Research

□□□□□□□□□□□□□□□□□

Hans Wagner

Many admissions and registrar personnel are reluctant to involve themselves in institutional research because they believe that it is too complex, difficult, expensive, and time consuming. That may sometimes be true, but institutional research can also be simple, fun to do, and involve modest expenditures with little extra time demands if made a part of the routine office work. It is also extremely important, since there is a continual demand for data on which to base academic and campus decisions. This is simply a fact of life, and if admissions officers and registrars do not become involved, someone else will. These offices have the data collected, and the responsibility for evaluation and dissemination of the data is clear. No greater contribution to the development of better academic programs and facilities can be made than to assume the challenge of institutional research.

While there is no clear-cut distinction, institutional research may be thought of as encompassing two areas. The first consists of responses to local, state, and federal survey requests. These are required reports (for instance, registration results showing the demographic diversity of the student body by sex, age, geographical source, class level, or major field of study) and for most offices have become a scheduled and routine part of the office procedure. The second area deals with questions that are critical to the ongoing status of the institution: Are students learning what they are presumed to be learning? How can the efficiency of the educational process be determined? Are some instructional operations more cost-effective than others? If so, why? What are the indicators of institutional effectiveness, efficiency, and economic operations? Why do students drop out? Should student retention patterns be higher? Are current grading patterns inflated? If so, should or can anything be done to change the situation? Is classroom availability in size and equipment in step with current instructional needs? Can reasonably accurate predictions be made as to future enrollments, curricular shifts, faculty needs, and facility requirements? Do graduates of the school believe that the institution met their educational needs? How can student advising be enhanced?

Much of the data to answer these surveys and questions can be found in the admissions office and the office of the registrar. Because of the immediate necessity to respond to the demographic queries, procedures have been developed to acquire this information routinely. Answering the questions indicated, and others of the same kind, is more difficult because the data are not so easily compiled or analyzed. Still, it is this area which, if answers can be developed, will contribute greatly toward future institutional decisions and directions.

Practically all institutional research data comes from three sources: (1) student characteristics and enrollment patterns, (2) faculty characteristics and assignments, and (3) space utilization of classrooms and offices. Fiscal connotations are eventually attached to these data, but policy is frequently made without direct financial association. For instance, if student interest in a course or a department is low, this lack of interest is quickly noted in the enrollment patterns and, if uncorrected, will have obvious financial implications. So the question becomes: How can these various characteristics be made available for ready analysis and summarization? The following are some suggested routines for establishing initial research efforts.

First, list the data elements—such as sex, class, home town, age, ethnic background, financial aid, matriculation date, and major—that seem to have some research significance. These items are in general those needed for regular work and also those necessary to complete many of the national survey questionnaires.

Next, find some means to capture these items so that sorting, aggregating, and cross-referencing can take place. If one has a computer available, these data can be established in the computer files. If only a manual system is available, there is the possibility of Keysort cards. These cards have appropriate data areas punched out so that, as a needle is inserted in the selected areas, the punched cards drop out and the nonpunched remain on the needle. Good research is not dependent on the device used but on the interest of the researcher, and there are many techniques that will enable the data to be manipulated without delay.

To eliminate the need for "crisis" research, make sure that data are collected, and files updated, as a part of the daily work schedule. As the staff become research conscious, new research ideas and questions will be generated.

Finally, make sure that all relevant data have been collected and are as accurate as possible. How one chooses to use these data depends on the point of interest or the kinds of research to be explored.

Areas for Research

Research can be simple or complex, inexpensive or costly; it can involve only basic mathematical skills, or it can involve sophisticated statistical techniques; it can be done with a pencil and a piece of paper or with a computer. Because it varies so widely, it can be uniquely adapted to the background of the researcher. The beginner can start with simple findings of an end-of-term report and, as experience develops, expand the research areas toward more sophisticated projects. Following are some possible areas for beginning research:

Space Utilization. If an interest has developed about space utilization, one could start with the schedule of classes being taught in a particular room throughout the hours of the day and the days of the week. This information could be arrayed in matrix form, with the days of the week indicated horizontally at the top and the hours of the day arranged vertically on the left-hand margin. Let's assume that the fire marshall has established the seating capacity of a room as 48 students (see Table 1). At 8:00 A.M. on Monday, the class using this room had an enrollment of 43 students, 90 percent of occupancy. The same computations could be done for 9:00, 10:00, 11:00, and so on, so that the total number of students using the room on Monday and the percentage of use on Monday are computed. One can then proceed similarly for the other days of the week. Summing the use of this room at 8:00 A.M. for each day provides the usage percentage for the week at 8:00 A.M. Percentages for each of the other hours could be computed similarly. High and low levels of room use can be quickly noted by day, or hour, and by week, providing a comparison with the use noted in other rooms. Recommendations for classroom use and new construction are possible results. This study is simple in design but has some interesting possibilities for rethinking old ways of doing things as well as suggesting new ways.

As Table 1 shows, classroom A was available for use during nine periods. Classes were in the room for only seven periods, for a use rate of 78 percent. Of the total seats available ($48 \times 9 = 432$) during the nine periods, occupancy was 143, or 33.1 percent. At 8:00 A.M. during the week, there was a 71.7 percent seat usage. Further summations by different groups or size of rooms could indicate what size of room is most needed on campus. One could

Table 1. Percentage of Classroom Use
Room A, Maximum Seating Capacity = 48

Hr.	Monday	Tuesday	Wednesday	Thursday	Friday	Totals
8	43 (90%)	43 (90%)	43 (90%)	— —	43 (90%)	172 (71.7%)
9	21 (44%)	21 (44%)	21 (44%)	21 (44%)	21 (44%)	105 (44%)
10	24 (50%)	— —	24 (50%)	— —	24 (50%)	72 (30 %)
11	15 (31%)					
12	— —	[Normally, additional data would be inserted, depending				
1	17 (35%)	on actual room assignments.]				
2	23 (48%)					
3	— —					
4	25 (52%)					

also determine whether large-capacity classrooms are being under-utilized with small classes. A number of interesting and informative analyses, then, can be made from such data.

Another interesting study can be made on classroom use. This study is also simple in concept, but the ramifications of the findings are highly significant. Seven columns of data are used (see Table 2). The first column (x) arrays the class sizes from lowest to highest number of students. The second column indicates the frequency (f) or the number of times each class size occurs. The third column is a running total or cumulative total of the frequencies. The fourth column (Px) establishes a percentage of each number in the third column divided by the total sum of the third column. In other words, Px is the percentage of all classes having a size less than or equal to x. In the remaining three columns, the reference is to the students in the classes. Column 5, y is the total number of students in classes of size x, or the product of x and f. Column 6 is a running total or cumulative total of students in classes of size less than or equal to x. The final column Py establishes a percentage of each figure in column 6 divided by the total sum of column 6.

As column Px indicates, 24.1 percent of all classes have five or fewer students in them and these classes contain 3.1 percent of the

Table 2. Classroom Use: Different Perspectives

(1) x	(2) f	(3) cum f	(4) Px	(5) y	(6) cum y	(7) Py
1	54	54	6.8%	54	54	0.3%
2	26	80	10.1	52	106	0.6
3	38	118	14.9	114	220	1.3
4	41	159	20.1	164	384	2.2
5	32	191	24.1	160	544	3.1
6	31	222	28.0	186	730	4.2
.	.	.	.	.	.	.
.	.	.	.	.	.	.
15	45	451	56.9	675	9,320	53.7
.	.	.	.	.	.	.
.	.	.	.	.	.	.
25	62	512	64.6	1,550	14,728	84.8
.	.	.	.	.	.	.
.	.	.	.	.	.	.
285	1	792	100.0	285	17,358	100.0

student body; as shown in column Py. Stated another way, 96.9 percent of the students must be in classes that have more than five students enrolled. At the same time, 56.9 percent of all classes have fifteen or fewer students enrolled, and these classes contain 53.7 percent of the student body. Space does not permit listing the total array of class sizes, but it can be readily seen that the institution shown in the example tends to have small classes. Nearly 85 percent of the students are in classes with an enrollment of twenty-five or less, and the largest class, of which there is only one, accommodates 285 students.

Another example might involve measuring the square footage of each classroom and office on campus. Dividing this footage by the students seated provides an index that can be compared with recommended state, federal, and institutional standards. From these comparisons can come recommendations of various kinds.

Student Retention. To turn to another area, let us assume that the problem is to determine the retention of students from term to term. (A recent national retention study by the American College Testing Program indicates that one fourth of the freshman class each fall tends to drop out by the beginning of the sophomore year.) Obviously, those students enrolled in the fall term become a source of enrollees for the spring term. By eliminating from the fall group those who graduated at the end of fall and others who are prevented from spring registration by reasons of academic, financial, or other "holds," one emerges with a pool of students eligible to return for spring. Following spring registration a comparison match is made, and dividing the registrants by the eligible group will give a percentage of retention from fall to spring. The summation of such data might be arranged in this order:

	Fresh.	Soph.	Jr.	Sr.	Grad.	Total
Fall eligibles	407	303	563	439	430	2,142
Spring enrollees	380	280	521	429	400	2,010
% of retention	93.4	92.4	92.5	97.7	93.0	93.8

Suppose, now, that one wants to find out why some of the eligible students chose not to return. One way to find out is simply to ask the students. However, the reasons given (personal, financial, illness, change of educational goal, or campus incompatibility) are almost always self-protective. No one, student or otherwise, wishes to make statements that are self-damaging. Consequently, the reasons given become difficult to convert into a program of corrective action. Moreover, not all dropouts are available for exit interviews; many students, at the conclusion of a term, simply elect not to register for the next term and hence are not available for interviewing. If a follow-up questionnaire is sent, the student will again tend to give the socially acceptable reasons. Therefore, efforts should be made to pinpoint those students who are "dropout prone," so that corrective measures can be initiated before the students make the decision to leave. One might, for instance, analyze freshman classes through graduation. Included in the data maintained on each class might be sex, honors at entrance, those on financial aid, those in remedial programs, ethnic background, test scores, geographical location, grade point average, and periods of enrollment. With each new term of enrollment, a matchup could be made against the original freshman class, so that retention percentage can be determined from year to year and also at graduation.

With these data available for analysis, one can answer such questions as these: Do women more than men survive through graduation? Do students who receive "honors at entrance" (because of prior outstanding academic achievements) graduate more consistently than those who do not receive such recognition? What happens to those who do not excel? Do remedial programs help students to succeed? Do these students succeed in about the same percentage as the other students in the class?

Majors and Nonmajors Served by Departments. Another area for research has to do with the number of majors and nonmajors served by the various departments. These relationships can be portrayed by again using a matrix type of display. Indicated horizontally on the top line are the various departments giving instruction. Listed vertically in the left-hand column or margin are the same department names, but in this instance they represent department "majors" who enroll in courses taught by the various departments. For example, in the simple matrix shown in Table 3, art majors develop 580 credits or units of study in the art department, 40 credits in biology, 90 credits in chemistry, and so forth, for a projected campus total of 2,000 credits of work generated by art

Table 3. Course Enrollments by Majors
in Various Departmental Offerings

| Student's | Teaching Departments | | | | | | | Total |
Major	Art	Biology	Chemistry	Drama	·	·	·	Credits
Art	580	40	90	150	·	·	·	2,000
Biology	40	2,200	1,800	400	·	·	·	8,000
Chemistry	60	1,600	3,400	10	·	·	·	6,000
Drama	300	50	75	3,300	·	·	·	4,000
·	·	·	·	·	·	·	·	·
·	·	·	·	·	·	·	·	·
·	·	·	·	·	·	·	·	·
Total credits	1,500	6,000	4,500	4,250	·	·	·	30,000

majors. Similarly, biology majors register for 40 credits of work in the art department, 2,200 in biology, 1,800 in chemistry, 400 in drama, with a projected total of 8,000 credits. The "Art Department" column shows a projected sum of 1,500 credits, which represents the total teaching effort expended by the art department. Likewise, biology has indicated a total teaching effort of 6,000 credits. Percentages can be determined in the rows and in the columns. The registrations by art majors in the art department (580) constitute 29 percent of their total registrations (2,000); and 38.7 percent of the art department's total teaching effort (1,500) is devoted to its own majors.

With the complete campus data arrayed for review, the ebbs and flows of student enrollment from term to term and to departments, colleges, and schools can be quickly related. A department that tends to serve only its own majors can be quickly observed. In contrast, a department that primarily serves students from one or more other departments can also be noted. The percentage can be related to departmental budgets and money amounts substituted for the percentages, thus providing some insight to help in developing realistic budget planning. The various relationships inferred from this type of study have significance for policy decisions in areas such as financial support, curriculum coordination, program or class scheduling patterns, and grading policies.

Grade Inflation. Another important subject for institutional researchers is grade inflation. In the last five to ten years, the average grade has risen from about a C+ (2.25) to a B (3.00). A number of studies—most notably a study developed by Michigan State University, which was based on data obtained from several hundred institutions—support this conclusion. In order to determine what can be done about grade inflation, the first step is to develop data that can be used for a review of the problem on one's own campus.

Every institution has a grade report form for each class on which the faculty indicates final grades for each student for the term. To establish grade distribution, one merely counts the number of different grades awarded in each class and computes percentages of each grade (A, B, C) given. Summations by level within a department (see Table 4), by division, by college or school, and by total campus can be developed. Presentations of this nature indicate whether certain instructors or departments are giving too many or too few grades of this or that kind, and whether one department or academic unit is more rigorous in its grading demands than another. Rates of withdrawals or incomplete grades also become evident in this type of array, and they too provide clues to grading and related instructional problems. These tabulations may be performed manually or by computer; in either case the summations or percentages can be portrayed in the form of a graph, so that relationships and comparisons between academic units or grading systems can be quickly assessed visually. Finally, an analysis of grade distribution patterns over a period of terms or years will provide excellent information on grading trends and grade inflation.

After final grades have been received, the registrar must determine which students have achieved an academic status of probation or disqualification. An interesting study can be made of these students. How many eventually, despite their marginal status, actually do graduate? How many do not? Do students with outside jobs have more academic difficulties than those who have financial assistance?

Drop/Adds. There is one area of concern that the registrar's office of almost every institution will discuss with considerable emphasis. That is the problem of drop/adds. The student, having just

Table 4. Summary of Grades Given by Bacteriology Department Faculty, Spring 1979

Grading Level and Academic Unit	Students Enrolled	Grade Distribution by Number and (Percent)								
		A	B	C	D	F	S	X[a]	W[a]	I[a]
Lower division										
Bact 101	296	43 (14.5)	87 (29.4)	74 (25.0)	37 (12.5)	36 (12.2)	0 (00.0)	0 (00.0)	6 (2.0)	13 (4.4)
Bact 201	89	13 (14.6)	39 (43.8)	25 (28.1)	4 (4.5)	3 (3.4)	0 (00.0)	0 (00.0)	5 (5.6)	0 (00.0)
.	.	.	.	.	.	.	.	.	.	.
Upper division										
Bact 301	68	13 (19.1)	25 (36.8)	17 (25.0)	9 (13.2)	2 (2.9)	0 (00.0)	0 (00.0)	1 (1.5)	1 (1.5)
Bact 401	65	15 (23.1)	32 (49.2)	13 (20.0)	5 (7.7)	0 (00.0)	0 (00.0)	0 (00.0)	0 (00.0)	0 (00.0)
.	.	.	.	.	.	.	.	.	.	.
Grad division										
Bact 501	21	6 (28.6)	13 (61.9)	2 (9.5)	0 (00.0)	0 (00.0)	0 (00.0)	0 (00.0)	0 (00.0)	0 (00.0)
Bact 601	7	4 (57.1)	3 (42.9)	0 (00.0)	0 (00.0)	0 (00.0)	0 (00.0)	0 (00.0)	0 (00.0)	0 (00.0)
.	.	.	.	.	.	.	.	.	.	.
Department total	709	130 (18.3)	250 (35.3)	169 (23.8)	56 (7.9)	43 (6.1)	33 (4.7)	0 (00.0)	13 (1.8)	15 (2.1)

[a]Symbol Key: X indicates grade withheld, W indicates withdrawal passing, I indicates a grade of incomplete.

completed registration, now wants to change courses for a variety of reasons—some seemingly justifiable, others not so. Yet for the student each is extremely important. For the office these changes add a tremendous work load. How can they be diminished? One could analyze the number of changes in order to determine which students, department, or faculty members appear to contribute most to the volume and what can be done to minimize the problem. One might find, for instance, that certain departmental programs lack clear description, so that students are uncertain about them, or that some advisers are so indeterminate in their suggestions that students are confused and need trial and error to establish their study programs.

Departmental Costs. Another area worthy of study is teaching load and cost perspectives, a sensitive subject from the faculty's point of view. Thus, it is imperative that the registrar work closely with the central administration in the development and use of these data. The analysis shown in Table 5 is an example of one method that might help the academic vice-president or dean project a more equitable way of adjusting and developing budgets. The "Registrations" column refers to students as they have enrolled in different classes; hence, a student can be counted as a "registration" as many times as the courses that the student is taking. The column headed "Units Generated" is a summary of the units (credits, hours) for which a student is enrolled for each course. The percent of units generated is the ratio of each department to the college total. The departmental budget is the total budget assignment to the depart-

Table 5. Sample Departmental Cost Analysis

| Dept. | Registrations | | | Units Generated | | | Dept. Budget | Unit Cost |
	Grad.	Undergrad.	Total	Grad.	Undergrad.	Total		
Art	0	808	808	0	2,666	2,666	$150,000	$56.26
Biology	88	1,807	1,807	279	7,214	7,493	288,398	38.49
Chemistry	40	1,169	1,209	124	6,514	6,638	383,970	57.84
.	.	.	.	.	.	.	.	.
.	.	.	.	.	.	.	.	.
Campus total	900	15,000	15,900	2,700	75,000	77,700	4,000,000	51.48

ment. Dividing the budget allocation by the total units generated provides an annual unit cost. Comparisons can be made by departments, by colleges, and with other institutions. If data from previous years are also used for comparison, trend indications will reveal relationships that may result in shifts in allocations to better serve the needs of the students. However, this information does not include consideration of areas of concern to the faculty, such as the time devoted to advising, to committee work, and to other administrative details for which no compensation is made.

Advising. An unusual research project might be in the area of advising. We mentioned earlier that advising is a debatable issue. Students criticize the advising by saying that advisers do not keep their office hours, do not know the requirements anyway, and are more interested in their own concerns than those of the students; therefore, the students complain, they must do their own advising and often feel that no one is interested in them as people. Faculty respond by saying that they must attend committee meetings which conflict with free advising periods; that students should assume a responsibility, since they must make their own decisions after graduation; and that advising seems to be little more than simply signing something the student has already worked out to fit his or her convenience.

It has been determined that about 75 percent of the usual advising routine is clerical in nature. That is, the courses completed must be matched against requirements to determine prospective enrollments for the future. If the academic record, which is usually shown in a chronological display, could instead be in a degree requirement completion array, there would be no need for the clerical activity. The adviser could quickly determine needed courses to meet the remaining requirements. The students would have the same display available at the end of each completed term and could not say that they did not know what remained to be completed. Both parties could eliminate the tediousness of matching requirements and completions and could concentrate instead on the actual field of study as a career option. Such advising would be more meaningful than the more common "check off and sign" procedure.

Presentation of Research Data

In the previous descriptions, some examples of research possibilities have been suggested. As important as the conclusions are in such studies, it is also necessary to present the findings concisely and in a form that makes them easily accessible to those who will use them. Pictorial presentations will usually make the salient and related points stand out more than written descriptions. For instance, if a grade distribution has been undertaken, the department, college, or all institution percentages can be converted into a visual display by the use of a line graph. Relationships will stand out for identification much more than from written descriptions. Similarly, retention study findings can be arrayed in visual form for much better portrayal of trend patterns. Brevity, the use of summary or pivotal points, and the use of color help attract the reader's interest and enhance a presentation. The techniques used in advertising are useful in catching and holding the interest of others. It is important to remember that research data are only as good as the ability to have them recognized and acted on. (Interesting papers on the presentation of research data were developed by Ruth Jass of Bradley University for the 1976 and 1977 annual AACRAO meetings and are reported in the summer 1976 and summer 1977 issues of *College and University.*)

A related concern in presenting data is that the results must be timely. A study whose findings have taken too long to assemble will not generate interest. Unfortunately, time has a way of robbing some studies of their significance. This delay occurs most often when the study involves a large mass of data and the work of analyzing and summarizing requires an inordinate amount of time. A number of institutions are using an optical scanning machine to expedite the input of data into the computer for analysis. If such a machine is not available in the office, a neighboring school district, insurance company, or corporation may have such a machine and may be willing to rent it or even loan it free of charge. While the procedure does have the limitation of forcing conformity of the questionnaire or research form to machine reading requirements, it is a cost-saving and time-conserving method of data input when one is using a computer. Whatever technique is used, the results will be most significant and useful if they are made available when the interest is at a high peak.

Sample Research Data

In order to stimulate further interest and to illustrate other research and reporting techniques, several exhibits (Tables 6–10 and Figures 1–2) are included here. These summary-type reports are included as examples only and should not be viewed as the last word in institutional research.

Table 6. Report of Geographical Distribution, Fall Semester 1978

| | *Washington by Counties* | | |
	Total	*(M–F)*	*(U–G)*
Adams	89	(61-28)	(87-2)
Asotin	137	(88-49)	(122-15)
Benton	650	(390-260)	(613-37)
Chelan	266	(153-113)	(257-9)
Clallam	88	(58-30)	(82-6)
Clark	418	(242-176)	(401-17)
Columbia	22	(15-7)	(19-3)
Cowlitz	188	(116-72)	(178-10)
Douglas	61	(41-20)	(59-2)
Ferry	8	(3-5)	(8-0)
Franklin	163	(99-64)	(148-15)
Garfield	30	(20-10)	(27-3)
Grant	271	(160-111)	(254-17)
Grays Harbor	153	(88-65)	(144-9)
Island	102	(61-41)	(99-3)
Jefferson	28	(18-10)	(27-1)
King	3,411	(1,765-1,646)	(3,283-128)
Kitsap	267	(153-114)	(260-7)
Kittitas	91	(65-26)	(76-15)
Klickitat	46	(28-18)	(44-2)
Lewis	134	(92-42)	(128-6)
Lincoln	80	(45-35)	(76-4)
Mason	41	(28-13)	(40-1)
Okanogan	157	(94-63)	(154-3)
Pacific	40	(23-17)	(35-5)
Pend Oreille	23	(16-7)	(20-3)
Pierce	1,457	(844-613)	(1,413-44)

Table 6. (Continued)

Washington by Counties	Total	(M–F)	(U–G)
San Juan	17	(10-7)	(17-0)
Skagit	187	(107-80)	(182-5)
Skamania	36	(22-14)	(35-1)
Snohomish	613	(331-282)	(593-20)
Spokane	1,595	(904-691)	(1,492-103)
Stevens	68	(43-25)	(63-5)
Thurston	465	(271-194)	(446-19)
Wahkiakum	2	(1-1)	(1-1)
Walla Walla	243	(149-94)	(221-22)
Whatcom	212	(109-103)	(203-9)
Whitman	1,343	(644-699)	(1,066-277)
Yakima	603	(358-245)	(585-18)
TOTAL	13,805	(7,715-6,090)	(12,958-847)

Territories & Possessions			
Canal Zone	1	(1-0)	(1-0)
Caroline Islands	1	(1-0)	(1-0)
Guam	4	(2-2)	(3-1)
Puerto Rico	3	(2-1)	(2-1)
TOTAL	9	(6-3)	(7-2)

Other States	Total	(M–F)	(U–G)
Alabama	7	(4-3)	(5-2)
Alaska	92	(51-41)	(80-12)
Arizona	41	(26-15)	(27-14)
Arkansas	8	(7-1)	(2-6)
California	468	(340-128)	(304-164)
Colorado	43	(29-14)	(20-23)
Connecticut	20	(15-5)	(13-7)
Delaware	4	(3-1)	(2-2)
District of Columbia	2	(0-2)	(0-2)
Florida	24	(19-5)	(9-15)
Georgia	11	(6-5)	(3-8)
Hawaii	118	(65-53)	(106-12)
Idaho	234	(137-97)	(159-75)
Illinois	75	(55-20)	(36-39)
Indiana	13	(11-2)	(5-8)
Iowa	7	(1-6)	(3-4)
Kansas	5	(3-2)	(1-4)
Kentucky	3	(0-3)	(1-2)

Table 6. (Continued)

| | *Other States* | | |
	Total	(M–F)	(U–G)
Louisiana	10	(5-5)	(5-5)
Maine	9	(7-2)	(4-5)
Maryland	16	(8-8)	(9-7)
Massachusetts	31	(22-9)	(14-17)
Michigan	27	(20-7)	(7-20)
Minnesota	35	(22-13)	(5-30)
Mississippi	2	(1-1)	(1-1)
Missouri	17	(11-6)	(7-10)
Montana	84	(56-28)	(64-20)
Nebraska	9	(6-3)	(2-7)
Nevada	30	(17-13)	(20-10)
New Hampshire	7	(3-4)	(4-3)
New Jersey	51	(34-17)	(30-21)
New Mexico	37	(26-11)	(18-19)
New York	84	(56-28)	(42-42)
North Carolina	10	(8-2)	(5-5)
North Dakota	15	(8-7)	(9-6)
Ohio	52	(38-14)	(30-22)
Oklahoma	11	(9-2)	(4-7)
Oregon	153	(103-50)	(106-47)
Pennsylvania	42	(31-11)	(17-25)
Rhode Island	8	(6-2)	(5-3)
South Carolina	9	(6-3)	(6-3)
South Dakota	6	(4-2)	(2-4)
Tennessee	9	(5-4)	(3-6)
Texas	54	(36-18)	(15-39)
Utah	31	(27-4)	(16-15)
Vermont	5	(4-1)	(2-3)
Virginia	34	(17-17)	(23-11)
West Virginia	4	(2-2)	(3-1)
Wisconsin	24	(17-7)	(8-16)
Wyoming	12	(7-5)	(9-3)
TOTAL	2,103	(1,394-709)	(1,271-832)

Table 7. Ethnic Enrollment Data by Class/Sex, Spring 1979

Class	Asian-American		Black/Afro-American		American Indian		Chicano/Mexican American		TOTAL
	Male	Female	Male	Female	Male	Female	Male	Female	
Freshman	19	19	38	25	24	16	25	17	183
Sophomore	32	18	33	19	12	13	19	19	165
Junior	25	19	36	26	9	6	10	5	136
Senior	35	24	26	13	12	7	10	10	137
Graduate	29	7	17	10	11	7	21	8	110
Other	4	3	1	6	1	2	0	3	20
Total	144	90	151	99	69	51	85	62	751
Grand Total	234		250		120		147		751

Table 8. Total Student Credit Hours, by Class, 1976–1978

	Spring 1976	SS 1976	Fall 1976	Spring 1977	SS 1977	Fall 1977	Spring 1978	SS 1978
Freshman	55,621	817	69,777	69,656	426	67,031	51,443	503
Sophomore	44,958	1,570	50,621	50,421	1,058	52,264	49,615	1,253
Junior	44,756	2,906	45,710	46,007	2,850	50,105	51,415	2,836
Senior	47,220	4,260	40,011	32,379	4,259	41,733	49,242	4,549
Class 5	3,892	1,100	4,377	4,690	968	4,899	5,240	914
Graduate	17,397	5,606	19,715	19,622	6,433	20,000	19,846	6,181
Professional	4,794	32	5,007	5,177	64	5,338	5,483	28
Other	571	2,665	612	517	2,571	644	704	2,492
Total	219,209	18,956	235,830	228,469	18,629	242,014	232,988	18,756
(enrollment)	(15,034)	(3,689)	(16,184)	(15,637)	(3,577)	(16,693)	(16,162)	(3,465)

Table 9. Student Course Enrollments, by Department, Spring 1978 to Spring 1979

Department	Course Enrollments		% Gain or loss
	Spr '78	Spr '79	
ACE (Ag Ext)	51	72	+41.2%
Aero	85	112	+31.8%
Agric (Gen)	121	100	−17.4%
Agric Econ	726	745	+2.6%
Agric Engr	159	227	+42.8%
Agric Mech	369	449	+21.7%
Agronomy	398	373	−6.3%
Animal Sci	833	876	+5.2%
Anthropology	1,078	819	−24.0%
Architecture	1,124	1,261	+12.2%
Asian Studies	10	31	+210.0%
Astronomy	188	246	+30.9%
Bact/Env H	709	683	−3.7%
BioCh/BioPh	170	217	+27.6%
Biological Sci	1,897	1,589	−16.2%
Biometry	314	314	—
Black Studies	126	109	−13.5%
Botany	464	439	−5.4%
Business Ad	6,312	5,702	−9.7%
Chemical Engr	258	348	+34.9%
Chemical Phys	8	21	+162.5%
Chemistry	2,460	2,187	−11.1%
Chicano Studies	210	117	−44.3%
Child & Fam St	1,099	1,033	−6.0%
Civil Engr	1,084	1,145	+5.6%
Cloth & Text	584	660	+13.0%
Communications	2,308	2,087	+10.6%
Computer Sci	1,246	1,278	+2.6%
Crim J	633	704	+11.2%
Economics	2,724	2,631	−3.4%
Education	2,402	2,421	+0.8%
Electr Engr	827	985	+19.1%
English	3,844	3,803	−1.1%
Entomology	238	242	+1.7%
Environ Sci	768	646	−15.9%
Fine Arts	1,983	1,593	−19.7%
Food Science	225	236	+4.9%
Foods & Nutr	850	918	+8.0%

Table 9. (Continued)

| Department | Course Enrollments | | % Gain or loss |
	Spr '78	Spr '79	
Foreign Lang	1,495	1,506	+0.7%
Forestry	1,066	1,140	+6.9%
Genetics	380	303	−20.3%
Geography	127	121	−4.7%
Geology	898	870	−3.1%
Health Educ	321	410	+27.7%
History	1,713	1,568	−8.5%
Home Economics	15	6	−60.0%
Horticulture	746	647	−13.3%
Hotel Admin	678	771	+13.7%
Humanities	273	271	−0.7%
Industrial Ed	266	220	−17.3%
Interior Desn	238	206	−13.4%
Landscape Arch	177	205	+15.8%
Library Sci	13	15	+15.4%
Mat Sci & Engr	195	239	+22.6%
Mathematics	3,785	3,677	−2.9%
Mechanical Engr	1,143	1,166	+2.0%
Med Sci	187	194	+3.7%
Men's P E	3,229	3,278	+1.5%
Military Sci	134	216	+61.2%
Music	1,646	2,002	+21.6%
Native Amer St	55	60	+9.1%
Nursing	807	1,011	+25.3%
Nutrition	—	22	—
Office Ad	386	380	−1.6%
Pharmacy	910	1,018	+11.9%
Philosophy	669	598	−10.6%
Physical Educ	1,377	1,392	+1.1%
Physics	1,270	1,259	−0.9%
Plant Path	199	164	−17.6%
Political Sci	1,365	1,192	−12.7%
Psychology	2,874	3,141	+9.3%
Rec & Park Ad	266	244	−8.3%
Sci & Math Tchg	58	79	+36.2%
Social Science	24	47	+95.8%

Table 9. (Continued)

Department	Course Enrollments Spr '78	Spr '79	% Gain or loss
Social Work	268	237	−11.6%
Sociology	2,786	2,697	−3.2%
Soils	388	333	−14.2%
Speech	2,846	2,719	−4.5%
Univ Honors	231	246	+6.5%
Vet Anatomy	292	297	+1.7%
Vet Clin Med	982	957	−2.5%
Vet Micro	285	173	−39.3%
Vet Pathology	289	228	−21.1%
Vet Pharm	257	273	+6.2%
Vo-Tech Educ	226	249	+10.2%
Women's P E	2,597	2,695	+3.8%
Zoology	1,540	1,316	−14.5%

**Table 10. Student Course Enrollments, by College,
Spring 1978 to Spring 1979**

College	Course Enrollments Spr '78	Spr '79	% Gain or Loss
Agriculture	6,010	6,145	+2.2%
Business & Economics	10,227	9,645	−5.7%
Education	10,649	10,924	+2.6%
Engineering	4,631	5,144	+11.1%
Home Economics	2,786	2,823	+1.3%
Nursing	807	1,011	+25.3%
Pharmacy	910	1,018	+11.9%
Sciences & Arts	41,893	39,438	−5.9%
Veterinary Medicine	2,105	1,928	−8.4%

Source of Data: Size of Class List (Tenth Day)

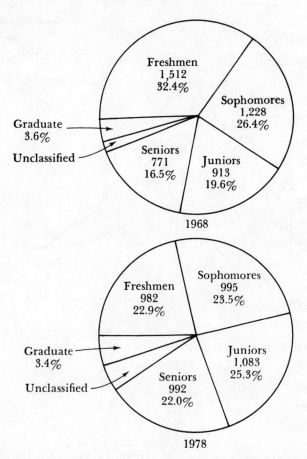

Figure 1. Student Mix by Class, Fall Terms 1968–1978

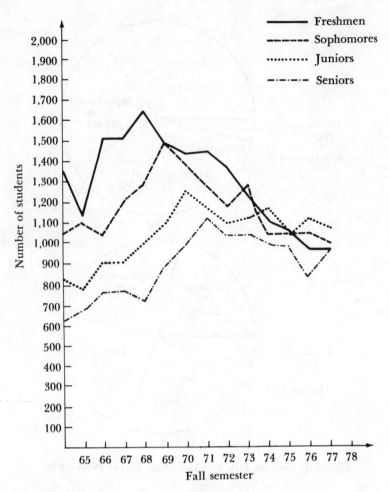

Figure 2. Undergraduate Enrollment—Student Mix by Class

Further Reading and Study

Paul Dressel's publication *Institutional Research in the University* (1971) is recommended reading for professionals involved in institutional research. Each chapter is written by an expert, and the array of topics provides an overview of various research possibilities. The American College Testing Program (ACT) has developed and published a series of monographs on research projects that can serve as departure points for further study. Another agency that has contributed greatly to the field of institutional research and management is the National Center for Higher Education Management Systems (NCHEMS). Located in Boulder, Colorado, NCHEMS is affiliated with the Western Interstate Commission for Higher Education (WICHE). The initial NCHEMS effort was in the identification of data elements that would permit analyses by a computer. More recent endeavors include budget analysis and allocation and campus facilities review. A current project is the determination of student outcomes as a way of measuring what an institution has accomplished for the student. This agency also conducts summer programs on institutional planning and research. The instructional handbooks provided for these programs supply a very important source of research procedures and findings.

Two other agencies have a special interest in institutional research. The Association for Institutional Research (AIR) is national in scope with affiliated regional associations. A national meeting is held each year, and the presentations are summarized for publication. The American Association of Collegiate Registrars and Admissions Officers (AACRAO) is also deeply committed to institutional research. Annual meetings are held at the national and regional levels, with pertinent research information published in the AACRAO quarterly, *College and University*. AACRAO also has a standing committee with the responsibility of developing programs and presentations on the various aspects of institutional research.

◙ ◙ ◙ ◙ ◙ ◙ ◙ 12

Preparing
for Commencement

◙ ◙ ◙ ◙ ◙ ◙ ◙ ◙ ◙ ◙ ◙ ◙ ◙ ◙ ◙ ◙

Margaret Ruthven Perry

Historical Background

In its commencement ceremony and academic attire, the modern university owes a substantial debt to its medieval predecessors. The universities that developed during the Middle Ages not only preserved what was best in civilization but formulated practices followed today. This medieval heritage has provided us with a teaching institution, the university; a method of measuring academic progress, degrees; and a structure for an appropriate ceremony recognizing the student's achievement, commencement.

The development of the universities in Western Europe around the middle of the twelfth century was the outgrowth of several influences in medieval life. One influence was the Catholic Church, which early had established monastic and cathedral schools to train churchmen and further the development of the Christian faith. Monasteries, which originated in the sixth century A.D., were the repositories of classical learning and the principal centers for copying, editing and writing books. As the Church developed, schools were often established at important cathedral centers to train clerics to assist the bishop in the administration of the diocese.

Because of their need for trained personnel, the royal courts also established schools and fostered education. Charlemagne called to his court many notable clerics and urged the establishment of schools.

Another basic structure of medieval life was the guild system. Every profession or trade had the basic right to form itself into a *collegium* (a supervisory executive committee or council of equally empowered members) and to elect its own magistrates. Around the middle of the twelfth century, teachers in Bologna and in Paris, having common interests and problems, organized themselves into guilds.

The first recognized *studium generale,* or university, in Western Europe was established at Bologna. Its Roman heritage and the rising demand for legal and commercial knowledge led to the study and teaching of civil law at Bologna around 1076 (see Durant, 1950). Its reputation spread throughout Europe, and somewhat later the faculties of arts and medicine were added. Around 1160 the doctors (from the Latin *doctoreum,* a learned person) at the various schools formed a guild, and the graduates of all schools received their license to teach from the archdeacon of Bologna. The system of degrees at Bologna is known to have been fully established by 1219. (For a detailed discussion of degree structures, see Spurr, 1970.)

The medieval university at Paris placed emphasis on the teaching of theology and the arts rather than on civil law. The concept of the teaching process as a special relationship between the master and the apprentice contributed to the idea and origin of the university. A master (from the Latin *magister,* teacher) in medieval times was a person licensed to teach by the chancellor of the Cathedral of Notre Dame. As the number of masters increased, they ultimately formed a guild. The word *universitas* was a common term applied to any collectivity, including that of guilds. The university probably took form around 1170 as a guild of teachers rather than as a union of faculties. It was sanctioned by Pope Innocent III in 1210 in a bull which recognized and approved the written statutes of the teachers' guild. By approximately 1250 the Parisian masters were divided into four faculties: theology, canon law, medicine, and the arts. The arts students, by far the greater number, correspond to our "undergraduates" of today. They ultimately organized themselves into "nations" based on the geographical regions of Europe from which they came. The universities, international in their appeal both to students and scholars, sought and received support from the papacy in their struggle with local authorities; thus, the conflict between town and gown was born.

Students attended classes and heard lectures and engaged in disputations, but there appears to have been no examination unless one ultimately determined to become a master. After four or five years of resident study, the student would indicate such an intention to "determine" and would be given a preliminary examination by the student's nation. The applicant was first given a private test—a *responsio* to questions—and then, in a public disputation, defended one or more theses; the examination concluded with a summation of the results, called *determinatio*. After passing these preliminary trials, the candidate would don a special gown and take a seat with the *bachalari*, or bachelors. This ceremony was often followed by a feast, with wine provided by the successful candidate. As Spurr (1970) suggests, perhaps from the symbolism of the feast of Bacchus and the laurel wreath of victory comes the term *baccalaureate*.

The bachelor could now hold a position as an assistant master or cursory lecturer. Within the guild organization, the student had moved from an apprentice (learner), who devoted full time to studies, to a journeyman (similar to our teaching fellow), whose time was divided between work (lecturing) and continued studying.

Between the baccalaureate and the master's degree, the student obtained a *licentiate*, an authorization to teach, granted by ecclesiastical authorities. At the University of Paris the license was usually conferred through the bishop's chancellor at Notre Dame or the abbot's chancellor at Ste. Geneviève du Mont. Again the candidate had to pass examinations on additional texts, swear to uphold the regulations of the nation and the statutes of the arts faculty, and pay the required fees. When all these obligations had been performed, the candidate came forward and knelt in front of the vice-chancellor at Ste. Geneviève, who licensed the graduate by intoning "I, by the authority invested in me by the apostles Peter and Paul, give you license for lecturing, reading, disputing, and determining and for exercising other scholastic and magisterial acts both in the faculty of arts at Paris and elsewhere, in the name of the Father and of the Son and of the Holy Ghost, Amen" (Daly, 1961, p. 135). By comparison, a degree at a modern commencement would be conferred with such a statement as "I have the honor as president of _____, under the authority of the board of trustees and upon the recommendation of the dean and the faculty, to confer upon you the degree of _____ with all rights, privileges, and obligations thereunto appertaining."

Although licensed to teach, the student was not considered a full-fledged teacher for the higher faculties until he was admitted into the masters' guild. Following another two or three years of study, if the master thought the student prepared and worthy, the master requested the chancellor to appoint examiners. If the student passed this final examination, he became a "master" or, in the Italian or German universities, a "doctor." He was then admitted into the guild of teachers by the master in a special ceremony and invested with the insignia of the office in the presence of others: "As a bachelor he had taught with uncovered head; now he was crowned with a biretta, received a kiss and a blessing from his master, and, seated in the magisterial chair, gave an inaugural lecture or held an inaugural disputation; this was his *inceptio*—called at Cambridge his 'commencement' as a master" (Durant, 1950, p. 929).

Graduates of Paris, Bologna, and Oxford, the oldest universities, were generally regarded as having a degree that entitled them to teach anywhere in Christendom—in accordance with the principle of *jus ubique docendi*, the "right of teaching everywhere" (Daly, 1961, p. 167). This principle was given imperial sanction by Emperor Frederick II when he established a *studium generale* at Naples in 1224 and papal sanction in 1237 by Pope Gregory IX with reference to the new University of Toulouse (founded 1229). As other universities gradually acquired or assumed this prerogative and conferred it on their graduates, the principle became universal for doctors and their English-French counterparts, masters.

In the Middle Ages, the terms *master, doctor,* and *professor* were used synonymously to indicate a teacher. The term *doctor* was more common at Bologna, and its use spread throughout Italy and into Germany; at Paris and later at Oxford, *master* was the more common designation for teacher, but the level of academic attainment was equivalent. Later, rather than signifying positions, the three terms came to be titles signifying levels of academic achievement or degrees. The term *professor* is now regarded universally as indicating a teacher of senior rank.

Until the Civil War, the American college system was based on the English model. Most colleges stood alone, rather than being part of a university, and the baccalaureate was the only earned degree awarded. The curriculum was invariably classical and essentially the same as in the Middle Ages. Daly's comparison of a medieval course of arts with the Bachelor of Arts program at a conservative American arts college reveals a remarkable similarity, except that in the medieval period philosophy received more attention than literary courses. "In the example chosen, the total of credit hours required for a B.A. is 128, one hour being equal to one hour of class study for a semester. The division breaks down to this: English and other languages, about 40 hours; science, 8 hours; history, 6 hours; philosophy, 20 hours; field of major concentration (this might be science, history, etc.), 30 hours; plus several hours of electives" (Daly, 1961, p. 85). A master's degree was offered in American colleges *in cursu* (as a matter of course) to the student who continued to study three years beyond the bachelor's degree and paid the customary fees.

Since there was little opportunity for postbaccalaureate study in the United States, students sought higher education abroad. After 1815, perhaps reflecting the nationalism born of the War of 1812, students increasingly attended German universities and returned with the concept of higher degrees as earned degrees based on a specified curriculum and embracing independent research.

In the 1830s the University of Virginia, Harvard College, and City University of New York attempted to offer an earned Master of Arts degree, but little came of these efforts. The University of Michigan was the first major university to establish the master's degree on an earned basis (in 1853; first awarded in 1859). Yale introduced the earned doctorate in 1860 (first awarded in 1861). (The development of the master's and doctor's degrees from the beginning to the 1930s is discussed in John, 1935.) Higher education based on the European model, with major emphasis on graduate programs, was achieved in America with the establishment of Johns Hopkins University in 1876. Other colleges and universities developed parallel programs, and by the turn of the century the doctorate had become almost essential for appointment to a professorship in a leading university.

The post–Civil War period received impetus from another direction also. The Morrill Act, adopted by Congress in 1862, established the land-grant-college system, which led to a rapid increase in public universities and an extension of graduate study. The expansion of the curriculum into new fields of specialization to meet the needs of an increasingly industrial society led to multiplication of degree titles to identify the area of educational experience and specialization.

In 1900 two thirds of the 2,400 degree titles recorded in the United States were still in use (Spurr, 1970, p. 14). For most purposes, however, five earned degree levels are generally recognized: (1) *associate*, awarded on the completion of two years of undergraduate studies in a college of liberal arts or in a community college; (2) *bachelor's*, awarded on the completion of a four-year program of undergraduate studies; (3) *master's*, the first postbaccalaureate or graduate degree, awarded on completion of one to two years of full-time study: (4) *doctorate*, the apex of scholarship, awarded after a minimum of three years of full-time graduate study and the demonstration of ability to do independent work; (5) *candidate, specialist,* or *engineer*—planned programs that involve at least one year beyond the master's but do not qualify as doctoral programs.

It is customary in America to add to the degree a designation of the faculty, school, or college in which the studies were carried out. While the term *arts* is sometimes applied to the broad spectrum of liberal arts, at other times it is limited to the humanities and social sciences, as distinct from the natural sciences. *Science* may embrace both theoretical and applied natural science, or it can be restricted to the former. *Philosophy*, in its broadest sense, embraces both arts and sciences. Some institutions further compound the multiplicity of degrees by adding the department or field of specialization to the name of the school or faculty: a Master of Science in Agriculture. Many professional schools also are moving from the Bachelor of Laws or Bachelor of Divinity to offering a doctorate, although the degree awarded is the first postbaccalaureate degree for that particular school.

The sixth level of degrees is the honorary degree *(honoris causa)*. It is a generally accepted principle in the United States that the same degree title should not be used for honorary degrees as for earned degrees. While this rule is violated occasionally with regard to the B.A. and M.A. degrees, the awarding of the Ph.D. as an honorary degree was largely eliminated after 1881. Some professional doctorates are awarded both as earned degrees and as honorary degrees. The Doctor of Science (D.Sc.), for example, is awarded by 221 institutions as an honorary degree and given by 8 as an earned degree, equal in rank with the Ph.D. (Spurr, 1970, p. 14).

For commencement purposes, the six degree levels indicated and certificates for terminal programs provided by two-year colleges represent the degree spectrum that must be dealt with at the end of the school year.

Commencement

Commencement is the special occasion that provides public recognition of the academic achievement of students after two, four, or more years of study by awarding a diploma specifying a degree. This diploma is an official document certifying the completion of past academic experience.

The typical commencement exercise begins and ends with an academic procession and may include the singing of the national anthem or a hymn, an invocation, remarks by the president of the senior class, a commencement address, the conferring of degrees and the hooding of advanced degree candidates, and possibly a message from the president or chancellor or the alumni director. Colleges and universities with large graduating classes have eliminated many of these components and reduced the program to its essential elements: the commencement address, the conferring of degrees, and the awarding of diplomas.

Plans for commencement are in a continuous state of preparation from the beginning of the school year in September through the commencement exercises in May or June. A commencement committee, elected by the faculty or selected by the administration, includes those actively involved in the production of commencement activities: president, registrar, deans, faculty marshals, music department, traffic or safety commission, alumni association, and the president of the senior class or student body. The committee devotes its attention to three main areas of responsibility: selection of the commencement speaker, selection of honorary degree recipients, and detailed coordinated planning of the procedures of the ceremony.

Since a key feature of most commencement ceremonies is the commencement address, special attention must be devoted to the selection of the commencement speaker. The method of selection varies from a decision by the president or chancellor to the recommendation of the commencement committee. Frequently the speaker is one of the recipients of an honorary degree, and 66 percent of the institutions select a person of state or national prominence.[1] Because the first selection might not be available, planning on this phase must begin early.

The next major decision is the selection of recipients for honorary degrees. The number awarded may relate to the size of the institution, but most institutions award only a limited number each year. Alumni who have achieved distinction in academic, religious, or public life are often selected. In large universities the recipient is usually an outstanding professional who is awarded the honorary degree in the discipline of his or her profession.

Various methods are used to solicit names for possible honorary degree recipients, but one that involves the academic community may follow these lines. The chief executive officer invites the faculty to submit a list of candidates, with résumés of their credentials. These nominations are reviewed by a special honors commit-

[1]The statistics derive from information gathered in a survey of commencement and examination practices (Perry, 1975) authorized and funded by AACRAO and conducted among its 1,896 members in 1975. Seventy-five percent of the institutions responded to the questionnaire, and percentages cited in the following pages are based on this survey.

tee, by the college or university senate, and by top administrative officers. Each reviewing committee assigns priorities and further reduces the list. After careful screening by these groups, a selected list is submitted to the board of trustees. The trustees return the final list to the administration. In larger institutions the selection process may be confined to administrators and the trustees. The selection and approval procedures may require six months.

The honorary degree recipient is notified of the award and invited to participate in the commencement ceremony by the chief executive officer. The university assumes the responsibility for providing appropriate academic attire and the cost of the hood given with the degree. The registrar orders the honorary degree diplomas, which usually follow the institutional format except that signatures of the highest administrators are used instead of those of faculty deans. A member of the faculty or board of trustees is designated to serve as host and sponsor of the recipient and places the hood on the candidate during the commencement ceremony. A citation extolling the achievements of the recipient is prepared by the secretary or registrar of the institution.

The most vital part of the commencement ceremony is the conferring of degrees and the awarding of diplomas, which is preceded by the certification of candidates for the associate, bachelor's, master's, or doctor's degrees. In 59 percent of all institutions, the registrar certifies that the candidates have completed degree requirements; 41 percent of the institutions distribute this responsibility among the vice-president for academic affairs, the provost, department heads, and the faculty.

The application for a certificate or degree, filed by the candidate for graduation, notifies the registrar that the student expects to complete all degree requirements by the next commencement date. The following items may be included on the application: division of the college or university; degree; major; ethnic background; local and permanent address; anticipated academic honors; summary of awards; social, professional, and religious memberships; campus activities; performing sports; publications; and interest groups.

Based on the information supplied by the student, the registrar compiles a master list of prospective candidates for graduation, checking off all requirements that may have been met and leaving only final grades as the missing element. The order for diplomas should be placed at least three months prior to the graduation date. If grade distinctions are determined at the end of the seventh semester or eleventh quarter, diplomas may be ordered with distinctions printed in Latin: *cum laude,* with honor; *magna cum laude,* with high honor; and *summa cum laude,* with highest honor. If the determination of honors and distinctions includes final term grades, the registrar makes a prediction of honors based on the past cumulative averages and delays the order for those whose distinction is borderline.

The inscription on the entire diploma was originally written in Latin, but only 9 percent of American institutions continue this format. Because of the high cost and inconsistent quality of sheepskin, most institutions now print the diploma on a good quality of parchment paper. The size of the diploma has been reduced, and many institutions provide a portfolio for protection of the document. A graduation fee, which includes the cost of the diploma and the renting of academic attire, is charged by 72 percent of AACRAO institutions.

The commencement program, usually compiled in the registrar's office, customarily includes an alphabetical list of candidates by degree title; a list of recipients of medals, prizes, awards, and honors; a short history of the institution; a brief explanation of academic heraldry; and the order of the ceremony. Most programs list the awarding of all degrees since the last printing of the commencement program. A majority of institutions require written permission for a candidate to be graduated in absentia (without being present). In institutions that hold commencement only once a year, the ceremony is usually held at the end of the spring term, and graduates who have completed degree requirements in previous terms are invited to return and participate in the commencement ceremonies; since this group of graduates have already received their diplomas, blank portfolios or blank diplomas are issued.

When formal invitations to graduation are issued, they are supplied for purchase through student groups or from a campus store. Disposable academic regalia usually is purchased through a campus store. Many institutions own and maintain a supply of fabric gowns, caps, and tassels for the convenience of graduates.

The celebration of commencement may include a baccalaureate service, alumni reunions, and the graduation ceremony. Institutions that have large graduating classes and extensive reunion activities often mail a miniprogram in advance, giving a topical summary of activities for degree candidates, alumni, and parents. The program may include a campus map and may indicate where visitors can find an information office, first-aid and comfort stations, and a lost-and-found desk.

The baccalaureate service, a more informal occasion than the graduation ceremony, is used by 27 percent of the AACRAO membership. It is usually held on Sunday evening of the commencement weekend. The processional proceeds with the platform party first, followed by the faculty and the degree candidates. The service varies according to the requirements of individual religious groups.

The format of the commencement ceremony is influenced by the nature and size of the institution and of the graduating class, the weather, the place of the ceremony, and other considerations. Institutions exercise a wide latitude in adapting the ceremony to particular facilities, climate, day of week, time of day, and length of the ceremony. A recent survey indicated the following preferences:

Day		Time	
Sunday	42%	midmorning	31%
Saturday	26%	midafternoon	39%
Friday	14%	early evening	28%

The variation in commencement ceremonial practices ranges from the delivery of a spray of red roses to each woman as she steps onto the platform to receive her diploma to the delivery of an official diploma to the president of the senior class, symbolic of the delivery of all diplomas.

An assistant vice-president of a large Canadian university has expressed the philosophy of his and many other institutions: "At commencement, everything is symbolic, nonlegal, noncompulsory, and a pain to get 3,000 names on seven different convocation programs moderately accurate. . . . The transcript is the legal document."

With the burgeoning enrollment of the large universities, only 4 percent of institutions in the 10,000 to 20,000 enrollment category are able to certify candidates prior to the actual graduation ceremony; 17 percent of all institutions permit all candidates for graduation to participate in the commencement ceremony. Diplomas are mailed later to those candidates who have met degree requirements. The registrar at a large midwestern institution summed up the modern dilemma: "We are certainly looking for innovative ideas to shorten the ceremony. With the increasing number of graduates, the delivery of the real diploma on stage, and the hooding of all M.A. and Ph.D. candidates, we are struggling with a ceremony that is too long, yet the administration and the students continue to demand these traditional elements in the ceremony." One solution to this problem might be found in the following reply to the questions on the survey: "Our innovative approach is to have name cards printed for each graduate. The cards are presented by the candidate to an official, who places them in front of a closed-circuit TV camera located at the foot of the steps leading to the stage. The dean reads the names from a small monitor inside the lectern on stage. Another monitor is placed on the opposite side of the stage where the diplomas are given out, to assist in locating the proper diploma. Candidates are presented two at a time, and the chancellor and vice-chancellor confer 400–500 degrees in 1½ hours."

In keeping with the literal meaning of the word *commencement,* one university plans a fall convocation for June and August graduates in order to generate a cohesive spirit within the entire university community. The fall ceremony affords the opportunity for the president to deliver a timely state-of-the-university message and for the university to bestow certain honors on its faculty, alumni, and friends.

Several institutions have reduced the united ceremony of massive numbers by having two or three convocations on the same day. The platform party visits each convocation, but the speaker for each convocation is chosen because of the special interest of the academic division. In a large two-year college, graduating students determine the format of the commencement exercise; however, the chief executive officer retains the right to overrule. In recent years, students at this institution have elected to eliminate the commencement speaker and to devote the time to the individual recognition of the graduates.

At least one large institution has combined the traditional elements of commencement, faculty procession, and the individual recognition of 3,000 graduates within a two-and-a-half-hour ceremony. The procession includes only faculty and the platform party. Graduates assemble in alphabetical order, within degree groups, and enter from side doors to sit in numbered seats, which match the sequential numerical order printed on their copy of the commencement program. The time saved by eliminating the student processional is devoted to individual recognition of graduates. Prior to the commencement date, $3'' \times 5''$ name cards, diploma tubes, and seats are numbered to match the numbers printed on the graduate's copy of the commencement program. Early on the morning of commencement day, the numbered name cards are attached to the numbered diploma tubes, and both are taped to the corresponding numbered seat. As the graduate marches to the platform to receive individual recognition, he or she presents the name card to a dean or other official stationed between the seating area and the official platform. The dean reads the name at the precise moment that the president congratulates the graduate. The diploma remains in the diploma tube attached to the seat until the conclusion of the ceremony. A modification of this procedure, used by many institutions, eliminates the need for placing diplomas and tubes on each chair. Instead, colorful diploma covers (empty) are presented to each candidate as part of the congratulatory ceremony. Diplomas may be picked up later or mailed to each student after the appropriate records have been checked and each student has been cleared for the degree.

A commencement procession is usually composed of degree candidates, faculty, administrative officers, commencement speakers, and trustees. It may also include a color guard, a college or university marshal, or a minister, or all three. If the color guard is used, it does not appear in academic attire and usually follows the leader of the procession—the mace bearer or faculty marshal.

The traditional order of the procession usually follows one of two patterns. The first is (1) faculty marshal or mace bearer, (2) degree candidates, (3) faculty, (4) deans of the various divisions, (5) platform party (led by a marshal or minister and including the president and/or chancellor and other administrative officers directly involved in the ceremony, the recipients of honorary degrees and their faculty or trustee sponsors, the student speaker, the commencement speaker, and other distinguished guests). The second pattern is reversing the above order, but degree candidates always appear in the order in which the degrees are to be awarded. Earned degrees are usually conferred in ascending order, with the baccalaureate degrees first and doctorates last. If honorary degrees are to be awarded, they are usually presented, with individual citations, after the earned degrees.

There are many customs for establishing the order of the faculty in the procession: (1) length of service, (2) teaching rank, (3) alphabetical arrangement by college or division. The procession usually is double file, except where a distinguished person is to be indicated or where a particular division is led by its own faculty marshal, who walks alone. The arrangement of individuals within the platform party may vary to suit the institution, but it should be remembered that the last person indicates the highest rank and the procession should reflect this position.

An unhurried pace by the procession lends dignity to the occasion. To ensure a smooth procession, it is well to provide a detailed plan of the building, or site, and the order of the procession, with each group's place in the ceremony indicated. In the actual march, approximately four feet should separate all marching pairs of individuals, to permit an even stride, with marshals of various groups following approximately ten feet behind the preceding group. Once the procession has arrived at its destination, all faculty remain standing until the president is seated, usually after the invocation or singing of a hymn.

During the ceremony, the president or dean of a college or school introduces the student speaker, who speaks for about five minutes. The president then introduces the person giving the commencement address, who normally speaks for no more than fifteen minutes. The conferring of degrees follows, beginning with the baccalaureate degrees and proceeding through the master's degrees, doctorates, and honorary degrees (if any). After the conferring of degrees, the president may speak briefly to the graduates. The ceremony usually is concluded with the singing of the alma mater and benediction by a guest minister. The order of the recessional is the reverse of the processional, except that the mace bearer or faculty marshal leads the recessional, followed by the highest-ranking member of the platform party.

Academic Attire[2]

Academic dress arose by a process of evolution and modification of the robes worn by medieval students, who were usually clerics in the cathedral schools and monasteries established by the church. As early as 1321, a statute required that all doctors, licentiates, and bachelors of the University of Coimbra (Portugal) wear gowns. (Gowns may have been necessary for warmth in the unheated medieval buildings; and hoods, until they were displaced by headdresses, may have been designed to cover tonsured heads.) Today, immediately after receiving a charter, most new institutions adopt a distinctive design for academic attire expressive of their individuality.

European institutions have continued to show much diversity in their specifications of academic dress. Oxford and Cambridge, where each college within the university has distinctive costumes for each of the higher degrees, have made academic dress a matter of university control and have issued extensive regulations governing minute details. The codification of dress and detail is so com-

[2]This discussion of academic attire is drawn principally from "An Academic Costume Code and an Academic Ceremony Guide" in *American Universities and Colleges* (Furniss, 1973). A more detailed discussion can be found in *Academic Heraldry in America* (Sheard, 1962), which provides a list of all institutions with hood designs and colors, based on responses to a questionnaire sent to all degree-granting institutions listed in the *Educational Directory* of the Office of Education. This volume also contains color illustrations of various hood designs, as well as a discussion of academic processions, commencement ceremony, academic seals, and flags. See also the article on "Academic Dress and Insignia" (Smith, 1977) in the *International Encyclopedia of Higher Education*.

plex that only faculty and students recognize the symbolism displayed by each other.

In the 1700s academic attire was imported from England and used at Columbia University (then King's College) and at other colleges founded in America during the colonial period. In keeping with British practices and the consciousness of the separateness of each colony, each college adopted its own designs, patterns, and customs, without regard to what other institutions had done. The passage of the Morrill Act in 1862, the development of an industrial society in the Midwest, and the extension of agriculture into the western plains states rapidly increased the number of colleges in the post–Civil War period. The older eastern colleges also expanded into universities, and the multiplicity of designs for academic attire threatened to become overwhelmingly conflicting and confusing.

Scholars and university personnel acquainted with European institutions sought to avoid the tangle of European customs by establishing guidelines for a system of academic apparel for American colleges. On May 26, 1895, a group of institutional representatives met at Columbia University to establish a uniform code for academic attire. They recommended "a By-Law, Regulations, or Statute" for establishing a suitable code of academic dress for all colleges and universities in the United States. In 1902 the regents of the University of the State of New York gave a charter to an organization named the International Bureau of Academic Costume to function as a source of information and guidance. The firm of Cotrell and Leonard of Albany, New York, manufacturers of academic costumes, was designated by the regents to act as a repository of information, a capacity in which they have continued to serve. Most American colleges and universities which have adopted academic attire have followed the standards prescribed.

In 1932 the American Council on Education appointed a committee to determine whether revision of the "Academic Costume Code" adopted in 1895 was desirable and, if so, to draft a revised code and submit it for consideration to the member institutions of the council. The committee reviewed and reaffirmed the code with only minor alterations in 1935. In 1959 the council appointed another committee on academic costumes and ceremonies, which again reviewed the code and made several significant changes. Academic attire which met the guidelines prior to the 1960 code changes is acceptable; however, attire manufactured after 1960 should follow the new guidelines.

The approved academic attire is composed of a cap, a gown, and a hood. The basic article of the attire is the gown, which is black in color for all degrees, baccalaureate and above. The basic design for gowns is similar for all degrees; the minor variations in fullness and length of sleeves and trimming are indicative of degree levels. Cotton poplin fabric is used for the bachelor's and master's gown, and ribbed rayon or silk material is reserved for the doctor's gown.

The hood, no longer worn for warmth, has become the colorful standard bearer of academic symbolism. By examining the hood, an informed observer should be able to identify the level of the degree, the academic field of learning in which the degree was earned, and the institution that conferred the degree. The hood is made of the same material as the gown and is invariably black on the outside. It varies in length from three feet, to three and a half feet, to four feet, representing the bachelor's, master's, and doctor's degrees, respectively. The color or colors of the lining of the hood indicate the institution that conferred the degree. The hood is trimmed or edged in a border of velvet either two inches, three inches, or five inches in width for the bachelor's, master's, and doctor's degrees. The border color represents the faculty or field of study in which the degree was awarded.

The approved cap of the academic costume is the mortarboard or Oxford cap—a stiff board nine inches square, usually covered in cotton poplin, Russell cord, or spun rayon, placed on a soft cap made of the same material and joined in a pointed design in front and back. The front of the cap is shorter than the back, but the color is always that of the gown and is uniformly black for the four-year degrees. Soft square-topped caps are permissible for women. The use of velvet material has been reserved for the cap for the doctor's degree. A silk cord with a tassel made of many strands of threads is attached to a button in the center of the board. The length of the cord and tassel may vary with the degree of the wearer. The tassel and cord may be black for any degree, but gold or metallic cord and tassel have been approved for the doctor's cap.

The tassel may reflect the color of the field of learning in which the degree was earned, and a few institutions use tassels of varied colors to indicate academic honors.

The committee of the American Council on Education in its "Academic Costume Code" (Furniss, 1973, p. 1756) states:

For all academic purposes—including trimming of doctor's gowns, edging of hoods, and tassels of caps—the colors associated with the different subjects are as follows:

Agriculture	Maize
Arts, Letters, Humanities	White
Commerce, Accountancy, Business	Drab
Dentistry	Lilac
Economics	Copper
Education	Light Blue
Engineering	Orange
Fine Arts, including Architecture	Brown
Forestry	Russet
Journalism	Crimson
Law	Purple
Library Science	Lemon
Medicine	Green
Music	Pink
Nursing	Apricot
Oratory (Speech)	Silver Gray
Pharmacy	Olive Green
Philosophy	Dark Blue
Physical Education	Sage Green
Public Administration, including Foreign Service	Peacock Blue
Public Health	Salmon Pink
Science	Golden Yellow
Social Work	Citron
Theology	Scarlet
Veterinary Science	Gray

The burgeoning development of community colleges and technical institutes has raised questions about the appropriate gowns and hoods to be worn in connection with the Associate in Arts degree. The committee has made a strong recommendation that "(a) the gown be of the same type as that worn by the recipients of the bachelor's degree; (b) the color of the gown be gray except for the small number in teacher education, for which light blue is recommended; (c) the hood be of the same shape as that worn by the Bachelor of Arts *except* that it have no velvet border and that the institutional colors be on the lining, and that the outside be black. If institutions prefer the flat shield hood, they are free to exercise the option, but it is not recommended" (Furniss, 1973, p. 1758).

The committee recommended that the master's gown be worn by graduates receiving six-year specialist degrees (such as M.A.T. or M.A.C.T.). It further recommended that "hoods be specially designed and intermediate in length between the master's and doctor's hoods, with a four-inch velvet border" and the colors distributed according to the established rules (p. 1758). The hood for the bachelor's and master's degrees in physical therapy should be white for the B.A. or M.A., and golden yellow if the degree is B.S. or M.S.

In general, since the basic academic attire is dark, it was recommended that faculty and students in academic attire wear auxiliary clothing that harmonizes with the basic color of the gown. As always, there are a few permissible variations from established procedures.

1. Members of the governing body of a college or university, and they only, whatever their degrees may be, are counted entitled to wear the doctor's gown (with black velvet), but their hoods may be only those of degrees actually held by the wearers or those especially prescribed for them by the institution.
2. In some colleges and universities, it is customary for the president, chancellor, or chief officer to wear a costume similar to that used by the head of a foreign university. This practice should be strictly limited.
3. The chief marshal may wear a specially designed costume approved by his or her institution.
4. It is customary in many large institutions for the hood to be dispensed with by those receiving bachelor's degrees.
5. Persons who hold degrees from foreign universities may wear the entire appropriate academic costume, including cap, gown, and hood.

6.   Members of religious orders and similar societies may suitably wear their customary habits. The same principle applies to persons wearing military uniforms or clad in special attire required by a civil office.

We have it on good authority that mankind does not live by bread—or, one may interpolate, by facts—alone. Symbols and pageantry are important, too, in epitomizing great moments in life. The medieval heritage of an appropriate ceremony for recognizing and honoring levels of academic achievement, in regalia both colorful and informative, is something to cherish. Its nearly 800 years of history indicates it has survived well beyond the normal test of time and is not likely soon to be discarded.

Further Reading and Study

In addition to the two references cited in the text (Furniss, 1973; Sheard, 1962), the most useful reference for anyone charged with the responsibility of planning and conducting a commencement or other academic ceremony is John S. Bailey's (1970) chapter, "Ceremonies and Special Events" in Volume 1 of the *Handbook of College and University Administration* (A. S. Knowles, editor). This chapter contains, among other things, a checklist for needed facilities, equipment, special services, and personnel; a calendar of dates during the academic year by which preparation for a commencement should be completed; and sample statements, sequences of events, and programs. A chapter in Volume 2 of the *Handbook,* "Degrees, Diplomas, and Academic Costume," by Everett Walters, also provides helpful information. It reviews the various types of degrees and includes a list of earned degrees most frequently awarded, the steps by which the awarding is authorized, and illustrations of various designs of diplomas. The "Academic Costume Code" is printed in its entirety. For an additional reference on degrees awarded, see Stephen H. Spurr's (1970) *Academic Degree Structures: Innovative Approaches, Principles of Reform in Degree Structures in the United States.*

□□□□□□□□13

History and Responsibilities of the American Association of Collegiate Registrars and Admissions Officers

□□□□□□□□□□□□□□□□□

J. Douglas Conner

Background and History

The American Association of Collegiate Registrars and Admissions Officers had its origin at a meeting on August 5, 1910, attended by twenty-four persons assembled in a Detroit High

School. These twenty-four included fifteen college registrars and nine college accountants or financial secretaries. Early in the meeting the college accountants decided that, since their work, problems, and methods differed greatly from those of college registrars, it would be more advantageous for them to form an independent association—later called the National Association of College and University Business Officers (NACUBO).

Following the departure of the college accountants, the first general conference of college registrars was organized. The conference was in session all that day. Topics and questions discussed at this first meeting included the duties or functions of a college registrar; the form and the content of an academic transfer from one college to another; the best and fairest method of reckoning the relative standing of students when the letter system of grading is used; how to secure from instructors a prompt report of students' grades; the new system of faculty advisers for students; how to get in touch with prospective students; the problem of late registration; and the question of whether grades should be disclosed to students (Smyser, 1960). Before adjournment the conference decided that a permanent national organization of college registrars should be formed and that it should hold its meetings once a year.

The history of the Association, for the first thirty years of its life, is written principally in the story of its annual meetings. It was chiefly a convention organization, holding extremely stimulating and fruitful meetings each year, but doing comparatively little in between. For the most part, the speakers at the conventions were drawn from the Association's membership. There were some notable exceptions: Nicholas Murray Butler addressed the seventh meeting, and there were papers by representatives of the U.S. Bureau of Education, the Carnegie Foundation, the American Council on Education, and similar educational bodies, as well as by several deans and presidents. But mostly programs consisted of registrars talking to, and with, registrars. Open Forum and Question Box sessions take up, year by year, a greater and greater part of the program [Smyser, 1960, p. 436].

According to Constance (1973, p. 18), "If the annual meetings were the principal fruit borne by the Association, they were happily not its only fruit." Very early in its history, AACRAO began to experiment with publications. As early as the second annual meeting, the *Proceedings* were printed and issued to members. In July 1925 a more general publication appeared: "New Series Number 1" of the *Bulletin,* as it was then named. This publication was announced as a quarterly, to be issued in January, April, July, and October; and all members were asked to send regular contributions of news material to the editor. The name of the quarterly was changed from *Bulletin* to *Journal* in October 1937. This quarterly, now named *College and University,* enjoys growing recognition as a leading educational journal and is one of the constructive contributions that AACRAO has made to the cause of higher education. AACRAO's publications now include a regular quarterly *Newsletter;* a forty-five-year-old guide, presently called *Transfer Credit Practices,* issued yearly and most often used by admissions officers and registrars in their day-to-day work of assessing credit transferability; the World Education Series, published with funding provided by the U.S. Department of State, books that explain the educational systems of foreign countries and assist in admitting and placing foreign students; and many other special publications for the general and specific need of the Association's membership.

Since its founding in 1910 as the Association of Collegiate Registrars, the organization has evolved from one with a singular scope to a multidimensional agency, in much the same way as the function of the registrar has changed since its founding in Europe in the Middle Ages. The role and record-keeping function of the earlier years underwent considerable change to meet the specialized needs of two- and four-year institutions, particularly following post–World War II enrollment increases. Administrative duties formerly performed solely by the registrar were expanded into several other areas, notably admissions. In 1949, in recognition of this extension of duties and responsibilities, the Association added "and Admissions Officers" to its name. As further specialization brought new areas within the older framework, the professional scope of AACRAO was redefined, by constitutional amendment in 1964, to include the offices of admissions, registration, records, financial aid, data management and research, institutional research, and international admissions and placement.

From its beginning in 1910 with fifteen registrars, the Association has grown in membership to nearly 2,000 institutions and over 6,800 active member representatives.

Development and Activities of the AACRAO Office

Association activity expanded considerably in the initial years until it produced an impact on higher education at the national level. AACRAO has long maintained constituent membership in the American Council on Education and was frequently consulted by the National Education Association and the U.S. Office of Education. In addition, because of various certification activities assigned to registrars and admissions officers, AACRAO provides a liaison function with many federal agencies, such as Selective Service, Social Security, and the Veterans Administration. The advent of contractual arrangements with additional federal agencies, such as the Agency for International Development and the Bureau of Educational and Cultural Affairs of the U.S. Department of State (now the International Communications Agency), emphasizes the responsibility of the Association in matters of international magnitude. Discussions concerning these important projects led to a plan to establish a national AACRAO office in Washington, D.C. The steps to this significant action occurred as follows:

1. In 1963 Past President Ted McCarrell proposed a reorganization plan for AACRAO, including a Washington office and a full-time executive secretary, which received strong support.

2. In June 1964 the executive committee approved the concept of an AACRAO office and established an office advisory committee to work out details to be voted on at the annual business meeting in April 1965.

3. The constitution committee proposed constitutional amendments (approved at the 1965 annual business meeting) that gave the executive committee broad authority to establish an office and employ an executive secretary and that increased membership dues to finance this far-reaching development.

4. In July 1965 the executive committee authorized the establishment of a central office committee to expedite the creation of the AACRAO office and the hiring of an executive secretary. This committee, chaired by Past President James Hitt, developed guidelines for the office and initiated a nationwide search for an executive secretary.

5. The search was completed on March 30, 1965, with the signing of a contract (tendered by AACRAO President Robert

Mahn) by J. Douglas Conner, registrar and director of admissions at Southern Methodist University.

The AACRAO office opened officially on August 1, 1966, at 1501 New Hampshire Avenue N.W., Washington, D.C., in space leased from the American Council on Education.

Restructuring Association Activities. The broad authority given to the executive committee in the initial establishment of the AACRAO office, "to employ an executive secretary and assign such duties as seem necessary and appropriate," was only a temporary step at best in developing the new alignment of association activities. Early in 1967 President Al Thomas charged the constitution committee to restructure the Association's professional activities in a manner that would more properly depict the wide range of administrative functions being performed by AACRAO members and relate these activities to professional committee efforts. In April of 1968 the membership passed a constitution and by-laws revision that provided the following realignment of the professional committee activity:

> The elected officers of the Association, together comprising the executive committee, shall include: (a) President; (b) President-Elect; (c) Immediate Past President; (d) Secretary-Treasurer; (e) Vice President for Admissions and Financial Aid; (f) Vice President for International Education; (g) Vice President for Records and Registration; (h) Vice President for Data Management and Research; (i) Vice President for Regional Associations.

Also included in the new constitution and by-laws was a specific outline of activities assigned to the executive secretary and AACRAO office, as follows (Constance, 1973, p. 147):

> The executive committee shall employ (with suitable bond) a full-time paid executive secretary. He shall assist the Association by staffing and maintaining an AACRAO Office. Duties and functions shall be assigned to this office by the executive committee as determined to be necessary and appropriate, including: (a) responsibility for preservation of the Association's permanent and historical records; (b) responsibility for reserving quantities of Association publications; (c) membership promotion and maintenance of AACRAO membership files, with records of AACRAO participation and personal data for each active member; (d) maintenance of the AACRAO placement service; (e) maintenance of AACRAO finan-

cial records and budget controls, handling of receipts and disbursements, and serving as custodian of all funds and investments as instructed by the executive committee through the secretary-treasurer; (f) assistance in AACRAO mail balloting procedures; (g) coordination of liaison activities between AACRAO representatives and other agencies in higher education; (h) service as coordinating office, when suitable, in projects of research and publication.

This restructuring placed AACRAO in consonance with the modern trends that had occurred administratively in higher education and lent direction to the development of the AACRAO office as a coordinative function for association activities and a professional support for its members to the various constituencies in higher education.

Role in Membership Support. The philosophical underpinnings of the Association's decision to develop an AACRAO office might best be summarized by a statement contained in the executive secretary's report to the membership *(College and University, 42* [4], 570) at the 1967 annual meeting: "The AACRAO office seeks to supplement but never supplant the professional voluntarism of its active members. It follows that the office must perform the general housekeeping chores for the Association, but its central role should be to reflect the professional personality of the membership and enhance that image in a way that will benefit the status of the admissions director and registrar as functioning professionals."

This theme has remained paramount in the ongoing direction of AACRAO office activity. The primary professional responsibility designated to the executive secretary is overseeing inter-association activities—that is, joint cooperative activities with some forty educational associations and federal agencies. Many significant joint projects have developed from this function. To delineate just a few:

1. The contractual arrangement with the Agency for International Development to provide consultants and foreign student admissions specialists who assist the agency in the selection, admission, and placement of AID-sponsored students.

2. A continuing grant from the Bureau of Educational and Cultural Affairs of the U.S. Department of State (now the International Communications Agency) to publish and distribute the

World Education Series booklets on the educational systems of foreign countries.

3. The joint sponsorship, with the National Association for Foreign Student Affairs, of foreign country workshops that bring together the top educational leaders of participating countries to further the cause of international student exchange.

4. The production of *Higher Education Facilities Planning and Management Manuals,* in cooperation with the Planning and Management Information Systems of the Western Interstate Commission on Higher Education (now the National Center for Higher Education Management Systems).

5. The sponsorship of national workshops for education data specialists in cooperation with the American Association of Community and Junior Colleges under a grant from the Education Professions Development Act of the Office of Education.

6. An ongoing relationship with the American Council on Education's Commission on Educational Credit (formerly the Commission on the Accreditation of Military Service Experience), which has produced three national *Guides to the Evaluation of Educational Experiences in the Armed Services,* publications which are utilized internationally to enhance the educational opportunities for armed services personnel.

Current Activities. Since 1975 the addition of an assistant executive secretary, to supplement the executive secretary and administrative assistant, has enabled AACRAO to participate more fully in the wide range of consultation that takes place among higher education associations concerning federal legislation, regulatory development, and governmental relations. This process is coordinated by the American Council on Education to provide as much consistency as possible in the way that higher education responds to the federal administration and Congress.

AACRAO has been in the forefront in areas of national interest and concern. In 1974 Congress passed legislation concerning the protection of students' rights and privacy and the release of information about students by educational institutions. AACRAO participated directly with the committees of the House and Senate in the development of the Buckley-Pell amendment, which modified the original legislation, and with the Department of Health,

Education and Welfare in drafting the final regulations for the Family Educational Rights and Privacy Act of 1974.

In 1977 AACRAO joined the higher education secretariat, composed of nineteen educational associations, convened by the American Council on Education. This group serves as a forum for the basic educational issues and affords members an opportunity to participate in issue discussions at the entry level, before policy lines are drawn and developed. In these and other meaningful ways the Association, through its office, provides service to the membership at the very basic level of professional concern.

AACRAO Regional Associations

The Association has always encouraged the organization of regional associations. At the 1922 meeting in St. Louis, when it was known that there would not be an annual meeting in 1923, the registrars were urged to organize by states and regions to meet in 1923 and discuss local problems. Thus, early in the beginning of its second decade, the Association began the practice of having state and regional meetings. The regional associations provide professional stimulation to members in the field, many of whom may not be able to attend the national meeting. AACRAO also has firmly established a policy of sending executive committee members to state and regional meetings at AACRAO expense to facilitate communication between the national and regional groups.

The authority for regional associations is contained in Article IV of the by-laws (Constance, 1973, p. 140): "The Association shall encourage the formation of regional associations. These associations shall determine their own constitutions consistent with the constitution of AACRAO, shall determine their own boundary lines in relation to other existing regional associations, and shall determine their own membership within the limits set forth by the national association. The regional associations shall elect their own offices, levy their own fees, and conduct their own meetings in accordance with regional interests and needs."

Recently the formation of regional associations has taken on international dimensions with the organization of an Association of Registrars of the Universities and Colleges of Canada and an Arab

ACRAO. An African ACRAO is being developed along the lines of AACRAO's regular domestic regional associations.

In 1970 AACRAO undertook a self-study, under the leadership of E. E. Oliver, which was published as *AACRAO in the 70s: A Program for Change.* This self-study led to numerous recommendations for improving and enhancing the Association's services to members and in particular called for specific effort to strengthen the organization's structure, improve communications, and increase the participatory base of AACRAO and the regional associations by establishing an AACRAO Regional Association Advisory Council. In 1973 the AACRAO executive committee approved the establishment of a Regional Association Advisory Council, comprising representatives of institutional members of AACRAO grouped according to geographical areas, with one representative for each 100 member institutions or major fraction thereof as listed in the current directory. The Regional Association Advisory Council has become the recognized medium for exchange of information between the national organization and the subdivisions of the regionals.

Further Reading and Study

The journal of the American Association of Collegiate Registrars and Admissions Officers, *College and University,* is replete with articles on the professional aspects of admissions and records. Robert Mahn's (1966) "Our Academic Role" and George Kramer's (1970) "Admissions as a Profession" discuss the professional roles of admissions officers and registrars. In addition, Metzger's (1976) "What Is a Profession" lays the groundwork for determining the distinctions of the profession. Finally, the AACRAO publication *Historical Review of the Association* (Constance, 1973) provides a comprehensive overview of the history and development of the American Association of Collegiate Registrars and Admissions Officers.

Appendix A

AACRAO Academic Record and Transcript Guide*

◙ ◙ ◙ ◙ ◙ ◙ ◙ ◙ ◙ ◙ ◙ ◙ ◙ ◙ ◙ ◙

I. Introduction

Since 1910 the American Association of Collegiate Registrars and Admissions Officers has had an abiding concern about the quality and adequacy of academic records and transcripts. During that time it has published several documents to guide its membership in the maintenance and production of records and transcripts; the last revision was published in 1971.

Since the 1971 edition, growth in the popularity of nontraditional modes of study, credit acquisition by examination, affirmation of "life experience," and the continuing education concept have brought new problems to those responsible for the production and maintenance of education records; passage of the Family Educational Rights and Privacy Act of 1974, as Amended, has required extensive changes in the handling of confidential information about students. These changes in postsecondary education are so significant that an update of *A Guide to an Adequate Perma-*

*Published by the American Association of Collegiate Registrars and Admissions Officers, 1977.

nent Record and Transcript is essential. That is the purpose of this document.

These guidelines have been prepared to serve those individuals who are charged with the responsibility for records in postsecondary institutions as they manage and maintain record systems. These record systems may vary from manual card to sophisticated computer systems but should contain the same basic information and adhere to the same good record-keeping practices.

Understanding key terms is essential to efficient record keeping; therefore, a glossary has been included in this guide for reference and convenience of the users of the document.

The American Association of Collegiate Registrars and Admissions Officers offers continued encouragement in the further development and improvement of academic records and transcripts to meet the changing needs of postsecondary education in America.

II. Historical Background

Historically, the American Association of Collegiate Registrars and Admissions Officers has devoted continuous and serious study to the question of academic records and transcripts. *College and University* and other publications of the Association reflect an abiding concern about record and transcript forms and procedures, their protection, their uses, and their interpretation. At the second annual meeting, held in Boston in 1911, the Association president appointed a committee to "give further consideration to the problem of devising a uniform blank for the transfer of a student's record." Discussions of the topic in those early years were devoted to a uniform transcript blank. Later discussions dealt with medical and dental blanks and state departments of education forms. The problem of false or forged transcripts also became an area of intense study and concern.

While these first efforts toward the improvement of transcripts emphasized a hope for a uniform transcript blank for most, if not all, colleges and universities, the aim since 1942 has been to agree on essential items of information which should be included on an academic record.

The transition from handwritten or typed transcripts to

present-day computer-generated copies of academic records has been influenced by a number of factors, including larger enrollments, increased student migration, varying transfer practices, and the significant advancement in mechanical and electronic procedures in academic recording and reporting. Many record systems were first adjusted for reproduction by the contact or tracing method. Later copying processes, as well as computer use in record keeping and reporting, further modernized transcript procedures.

The selection of essential items was initiated in 1942 and has been continually reviewed, updated, and revised since that time. Both the first *Guide,* issued in 1945, and the 1947 reprint listed the essential items. The 1949 *Supplement,* reissued in 1950, added brief explanations or definitions for each item. The revision of 1952 included discussions on transcript evaluation, forged transcripts, transcripts for teacher licensing needs, and a bibliography.

The 1959 *Guide* reflected advances made in cooperation with the National Association of State Directors of Teacher Education and Certification in the development of adequate transcripts that would serve more effectively those individuals responsible for academic records as well as state certification authorities. It also abstracted a report on "The Recording and Reporting of Student Disciplinary Records" that was developed jointly and adopted by the American Association of Collegiate Registrars and Admissions Officers, the American College Personnel Association, the National Association of Women Deans and Counselors, and the National Association of Student Personnel Administrators. The recommendations of the Association of Graduate Deans were considered in the arrangement of essential items.

A 1965 *Guide* included the formal resolution of the State Directors of Teacher Education and Certification related to the development of the transcript as an acceptable document to facilitate teacher certification. It also incorporated the recommendations of the Committee on Improvement of Student Personnel Records of the Council of Graduate Schools in the United States. A revised bibliography included modifications in the essential items as well as explanations and definitions. Attention was given to "Reproducing Equipment," with specific application to the reproduction of transcripts. "A Guide to Good Practices in the Recording and Reporting of Student Disciplinary Records," which appeared in the Appendix, was replaced by the 1970 AACRAO statement "Release of Information About Students: A Guide."

In 1971 the entire *Guide* was revised, omitting the bibliography and paying special attention to traditional as well as emerging policies and practices of good academic record-keeping and transcript procedures.

The 1977 *Guide* reflects the changes brought about by the passage of the Family Educational Rights and Privacy Act of 1974, as Amended, and also contains information and recommendations on continuing education and nontraditional education records.

III. Academic Records

The official educational record is referred to as the *academic record* to distinguish it from the personnel record, which is a record of the student's personal characteristics, experiences, family background, secondary school background, aptitudes, and interests. The academic record should be the complete, unabridged record of the student, indicating previous academic enrollment and all work pursued at the institution, although some institutions include only work completed or competencies achieved. Essential academic data should be completely and clearly recorded. Generally, admissions test scores, nonacademic awards, or honors should not be recorded on the academic record.

Recently a great deal of effort has been expended in the development of nontraditional educational experiences. This term may refer to the actual learning endeavor itself or to the manner in which the evaluation of such work is recorded. Since both quality and quantity recording techniques may vary substantially from traditional methods—narrative vs. grades, specified vs. unspecified academic term—the recording institution bears the responsibility to assure that quality evaluation and preparation of records will include all information required by the recipient of a transcript to make an informed and reasonable evaluation of the educational experience.

Academic records that are reproduced in their entirety *each term* by a computer should be well designed to insure that all necessary information is included, easily understood, and readily located.

The following data elements are categorized, for both traditional and nontraditional academic records, as either essential or optional:*

Data Elements	Essential	Optional
Identification of the Institution		
Name	X	
Location: City, State, ZIP Code	X	
Identification of the Student		
Name	X	
Address		X
Date of Birth	X	
Place of Birth		X
Identification Number		X
Basis of Admission		
Secondary School Graduation		
Name, Location of School	X	
Date of Graduation	X	
Previous Higher Education—		
Undergraduate		
Name, Location of Institution	X	
Period of Attendance	X	
Previous Higher Education—Graduate		
Name, Location of Institution	X	
Period of Attendance	X	
Date of Graduation	X	
Degree Received	X	
Other		
Examination		X
Individual Approval		X
Area of Study (at time of graduation)		
College, School, or Division	X	
Program or Major	X	
Minor		X
Record of Work Pursued		
Dates of Attendance	X	
Course Identification	X	
Amount of Credit	X	
Grades and Grade Points	X	
Narrative Evaluation	X	
Demonstrated Competencies	X	
Source or Type of Credit	X	
Termination Status*		
Statement of Graduation	X	
Status at Time of Last Attendance		
Good Standing		X
Academic Probation		X

*The reader is referred to the Glossary and Commentary (part VIII) for definition and/or supportive commentary for terms used.

Data Elements	Essential	Optional
Academic Suspension	X	
Academic Dismissal	X	
Supplemental Information for Graduate Students		
Graduate Examination Results		
Orals and Languages		X
Advancement and/or Admission to		
Candidacy		X
Title of Thesis and/or Dissertation		X

*Disciplinary action (such as probation, suspension, and/or dismissal) varies so greatly that institutions find it difficult to interpret such action taken on another campus; therefore, recording of disciplinary action on academic records is not recommended by this Task Force.

Note: 1. Correction of an erroneous entry on the academic record should be made promptly and carefully in a manner which would indicate official institutional action.

2. Institutional policy changes affecting academic records should not be applied retroactively.

IV. Continuing Education Unit Records

The concept of continuing education has been expanding rapidly during the past three decades. Millions of people participate each year in evening classes, short courses, workshops, seminars, conferences, institutes, and other forms of continuing education. Professional societies and organizations develop programs and award certificates to encourage members to update their knowledge and skills. In many occupational fields evidence of continued learning is required for maintenance of membership or certification, for occupational advancement and for recognition of personal and professional development.

Participants and their sponsoring organizations have found it increasingly difficult to accumulate and/or transfer records of continuing education experiences. Employers, professional groups, licensing agencies, and others who routinely examine and evaluate individual accomplishments have realized a need for uniformity in combining educational activities into a meaningful record. As a consequence, the Task Force of the National University Extension Association started a six-year research effort which culminated with the publication in 1974 of its comprehensive document entitled *The Continuing Education Unit—Criteria and Guidelines*. This publication defined the Continuing Education Unit (CEU) as the contact hours of participation in an organized continuing education experience under responsible sponsorship, capable direction, and qualified instruction. In addition, this publication reflects the expert judgment of thirty-four representatives from national organizations—government, business, labor, the professions, and education. Any institution or organization currently involved in or considering establishment of a continuing education program is urged to secure a copy of this publication from: National University Extension Association, Suite 360, One DuPont Circle, Washington, D.C. 20036.

Application of the CEU as a uniform and nationally accepted unit of measurement for continuing education provides:

1. Permanent records for individual participants for accumulating, updating, and transferring information concerning continuing education experiences.
2. A uniform system for accumulating data at the institutional or organizational level to assist in program planning and development and in administration and fiscal management.
3. A national system of measurement to facilitate the collection of data on a national basis and to provide valid statistical information necessary for legislative action and public policy determination relating to continuing education activities.

The CEU may be used for quantitative measuring, recording, reporting, accumulating, transferring, and recognizing participation in continuing education activities and is intended to serve all interests in continuing education, whether public or private and whether individual, institutional, organizational, governmental, or societal. The CEU may be used to measure all levels of continuing education without regard to age of participants, subject matter, program format, or instructional methodology.

Continuing Education Unit records serve essentially the same purpose as any other records of educational experience and should be designated to facilitate transcript production. An individual record for each participant must be maintained by the sponsoring organization or the institution's central record-keeping office. To provide a complete and accurate report of activity pursued and CEU(s) awarded, all essential data elements must be included on the record. Institutions are also encouraged to maintain comprehensive program information regarding instructional activities for which CEU's are awarded. For purposes of reporting and planning, institutions have the option of maintaining related information as well. The Continuing Education Unit record should be maintained in a format similar to that of an academic record. Record systems for maintaining Continuing Education Unit records and academic records may be integrated, but transcripts for each should be issued separately. (Special permission to reproduce the foregoing excerpts from *The Continuing Education Unit—Criteria and Guidelines* has been granted by Lloyd H. Davis, Executive Director, National University Extension Association.)

The following data elements are categorized, for purposes of maintaining a Continuing Education Unit record, as either essential or optional:

Data Elements	Essential	Optional
Identification of the Sponsoring Organization		
Name	X	
Location: City, State, ZIP Code	X	
Identification of the Participant		
Name	X	
Address		X
Date of Birth	X	
Place of Birth		X
Identification Number		X
Prior Education		X
Employment Status		X
Course Number	X	
Title or Brief Description of Program or Activity	X	
Location of Program or Activity		X
Date and/or Length of Program or Activity	X	
Qualitative or Quantitative Evaluation of Individual's Performance	X	
Number of CEU(s) Awarded	X	
Description of Program or Activity	(See Note 4 below)	

Note: 1. Course Number—Use any structured and/or codified series of numbers which will uniquely identify the CEU program or activity; codification structure should permit determination of type of program, i.e., class, institute, workshop, or seminar.

2. Date and/or Length of Program or Activity—Since the length of continuing education programs varies substantially according to the kind of activity, both the beginning and ending dates of such programs should be recorded on the record, and, if appropriate for certain shorter programs, the duration of the program should be noted on the record in terms of hours in session.

3. Qualitative or Quantitative Evaluation of Individual's Performance—The extensive variety of continuing education programs offered precludes the possiblity of a standardized evaluation system; however, appropriate qualita-

tive evaluation notations may be included on the record, either in terms of traditional letters/numerals or satisfactory/unsatisfactory designations.

4. Description of Program or Activity—In addition to the title, a brief description—including a record of program content, level, objective, format, instructor's name, as well as a brief syllabus of the program itself—should also be retained.

V. Record Security

Development and enforcement of security measures to protect educational records from accidental damage, destruction, and/or deliberate alteration are major responsibilities of the custodian of the records.

Recommended internal security measures include:

1. Limiting access to record storage areas.
2. Restricting the preparation and handling of records and transcripts to properly trained personnel.
3. Storing record stock, facsimile signature stamps, and official seals in restricted-access area.
4. Maintaining a backup system for auditing record entries to source documents.
5. Developing a microfilm system which includes storage of one copy in a secure area outside the records office.
6. Retaining the educational record in the appropriate records office at all times.

Computer-generated and stored records present unique security problems. Since these records may be located outside the records office in many institutions and are, therefore, more vulnerable to alteration or destruction by events or persons only indirectly responsible to the records custodian, special security measures are necessary to protect the data.

Maintenance of backup files will enable the data center to reconstruct a file in the event of accidental destruction. One of these files plus copies of change documents should be stored in a vault or fireproof cabinet in the records office. Backup files and the update documents should be audited periodically against the operational files as an added security measure.

Other recommended security measures for magnetic-based files include:

1. Using confidential access codes for computer terminal operation.
2. Maintaining a transaction register.
3. Developing an equally effective alternate program or procedure and a master program to compare the two and list differences.
4. Making random comparisons of computer output with source documents.

VI. Transcripts

A transcript is a reproduction of the complete, unabridged educational record at the issuing institution and must be an effective means of prompt and accurate communication of educational information. Institutions should require students to submit signed requests for transcripts of their academic records. It is recommended that an 8½-×-11-inch form be used for convenience in reading, interpreting, and filing. The quality of paper used should facilitate handling and insure permanency.

Authentication of Transcripts

Each official transcript must be authenticated with:

1. The signature and title of the certifying official.
2. The seal of the institution or issuing office.
3. The date of issue.
4. The statement informing parties to whom transcripts are sent that it is not permissible to release information from the transcripts to a third party as required by the Family Educational Rights and Privacy Act of 1974, as Amended.
5. The notation "Issued to Student," if this is the case.

Partial Transcripts

It is generally accepted that partial, incomplete, or supplemental transcripts should not be issued; however, if incomplete transcripts are released, they should be clearly and unmistakably identified. The foregoing should not be interpreted to preclude an institution from issuing separate transcripts of undergraduate or graduate academic work for the same individual. It is expected that transcripts of Continuing Education Unit records will be issued separately.

Transcript Key or Legend

A key or legend to the transcript containing a full statement of pertinent definitions should either be printed on the transcript, preferably on the reverse side, or attached as a separate document. The following items should be included to assist the recipient of the transcript in making the proper interpretation:

1. Calendar system and calendar system changes.
2. Definition of the credit unit.
3. Explanation of the course identification system.
4. Explanation of the grading system, including dates and details of changes in it.
5. Institutional name changes.
6. Special programs or transcript entries which may require clarification.
7. Statement of institutional policy whether or not all attempted or only all completed work appears on the record.

Copying Foreign Transcripts

Foreign transcripts present a unique problem, since there are countries where the student may receive only one official copy of the educational record and additional transcripts are not available from the issuing institution. A foreign transcript received directly from a student should be carefully examined to determine validity, and a certified copy should be made for the institutional file. The original should be returned to the student upon request.

Forged Transcripts

Under conditions lacking adequate security measures, the incidence of forged or altered transcripts increases because the opportunity for access to educational records is open to more individuals. It is essential that both the issuing and the receiving institutions maintain vigilance in order to prevent or at least detect forgery.

Transcript-issuing institutions can minimize opportunities for forgery by:

1. Maintaining internal security.
2. Auditing computer-generated transcripts against original input documents.
3. Stamping indelibly all transcripts issued to students with the notation "Issued to Student."
4. Reproducing official records by the photoreduction process.

Transcript-receiving institutions should:

1. Insist that official transcripts be sent directly from issuing institutions and that they bear appropriate seals and signatures.
2. Subject transcripts to careful scrutiny by experienced personnel.
3. Destroy all transcripts no longer needed.
4. Confer with the issuing institution when any irregularity is detected.
5. Report complete details of obviously forged transcripts to the issuing institution.
6. Maintain a local file on forged or altered transcripts, since institutional experience indicates a high frequency of repetition.
7. Exercise special care when evaluating credentials from foreign countries where the incidence of forged transcripts has been high.

A transcript is a legal document and should be treated accordingly.

VII. Release of Information About Students

The Family Educational Rights and Privacy Act of 1974, as Amended, prescribes the conditions under which information about students can be released. The provisions of the Act applicable to transcripts of academic records are basic to the following guidelines. For more detailed provisions of the Act and applicability to other education records, the reader is referred to the AAC-RAO publication of 1976 entitled *A Guide to Postsecondary Institutions for Implementation of the Family Educational Rights and Privacy Act of 1974, as Amended*. The written institutional policy required by the Act will further guide registrars, admissions officers, and other individuals in charge of educational records.

Disclosure to Students of Their Own Records

1. Students have the right to inspect their academic records and challenge the contents which they believe to be inaccurate or misleading. The institution may require that a staff member be present during the students' inspection and review.
2. Students have the right to transcripts of their own academic records. Such transcripts should be labeled "Issued to Student."
3. Institutions may refuse to provide transcripts of academic records for reasons such as nonpayment of financial obligation, but students cannot be denied the right to inspect and review their records.
4. Institutions should require students to submit signed requests for transcripts of their academic records. Although a record of such requests is not required, it is recommended for audit purposes.
5. Institutions are not obligated to provide students copies of original or source documents available elsewhere (for example, transcripts from other institutions).

Disclosure to Faculty and Administrative Officers of the Institution

Institutions may disclose academic records without written consent of students to those designated school officials within the institution as determined by the institution to have legitimate educational interest.

Disclosure to Parents and Other Educational Institutions

1. Information about students' academic records or transcripts of them may be disclosed to students' parents by either of two procedures:

a. Obtaining the students' written consent.
b. Having the parents establish the students' dependency as defined by Internal Revenue Code of 1954, Section 152. Another alternative is for institutions to declare all their students dependent and place the responsibility on the students to prove that they are not dependents. This should be stated in the written institutional policies.

2. Institutions may disclose the academic record of a student, without written consent, to officials of other institutions in which the student seeks to enroll on condition that the issuing institution makes a reasonable attempt to inform the student of the disclosure. A record of such disclosure must be kept.

Disclosure to Government Agencies

1. Institutions must disclose academic records without written consent of students to only the following government agencies:
    a. Comptroller General of the United States.
    b. The Secretary of the United States Department of Health, Education and Welfare.
    c. The United States Commissioner of Education, Director of National Institute of Education, or Assistant Secretary of Education.
    d. State educational authorities.
    e. State and local officials to whom disclosure is required by State Statute adopted prior to November 19, 1974.
    f. Veterans Administration (PL 94-502).

2. Institutions must also disclose academic records without written consent to persons in compliance with a judicial order or lawfully issued subpoena, provided that the institutions first make reasonable attempts to notify the students.

Disclosure to Other Individuals and Organizations

1. Institutions may release without written consent certain information identified by the institution as public or Directory Information, provided the following conditions are met prior to disclosure:

    a.   That institutions inform students of categories designated as Directory Information.

    b.   That students be given opportunity to refuse disclosure of any or all categories of Directory Information.

    c.   That students be given reasonable time in which to state such refusals in writing.

2.   Directory Information may include the following categories:

Category I.   Name, address, telephone number, dates of attendance, class.

Category II.   Previous institution(s) attended, major field(s) of study, awards, honors (includes dean's list), degree(s) conferred (including dates and any graduation honors).

Category III.   Past and present participation in officially recognized sports and activities, physical factors (height, weight of athletes), date and place of birth.

Note: 1.   Release of public or Directory Information by telephone is permissible; however, information released in this manner should be restricted to categories specified in the written institutional policy.

      2.   Institutions may disclose information about students without their written consent to persons in an emergency, if the knowledge of that information is necessary to protect the health or safety of the students or other persons.

Challenge of the Contents of Educational Records

1.   Institutions must provide students an opportunity to challenge the contents of their educational records which the students consider to be inaccurate, misleading, or otherwise in violation of their privacy or other rights.

2.   Students who are not provided full relief sought by their challenges must be informed by the appropriate officials of their rights to formal hearings on the matters. Decisions of the hearing panels will be final.

    a.   Institutions will correct or amend any educational records in accordance with the decisions of the hearing panels if the decisions are in favor of the students.

b. Should any decision be unsatisfactory to the student, the appropriate official must inform the student that:

(1) The student has the opportunity to place with the educational record a statement commenting on the information in the record or a statement setting forth any reason for disagreeing with the decision of the hearing panel.

(2) The statement placed in the educational record by the student will be maintained as part of the record for so long as the record is held by the institution.

(3) This educational record, when disclosed to an authorized party, must include the statement filed by the student.

Records of Requests and Disclosures

All institutions subject to the provisions of the Act are required to maintain records of requests and disclosures of personally identifiable information. The records of requests, whether granted or not, shall include the names and addresses of the person(s) who requested the information and their legitimate interests in the information. Records of requests and disclosures need not be maintained for:

1. Those requests made by students for their own use.
2. Those disclosures made in response to written requests from students.
3. Those made by school officials.
4. Those specified as Directory Information.

The records of disclosures and requests for disclosures are considered a part of students' educational records; therefore, they must be retained as long as the educational records to which they refer are retained by the institutions.

The records of requests and disclosures must be maintained in a form which permits students, responsible institutional officials, and federal auditors to inspect them.

VIII. Glossary and Commentary

The following list of definitions and/or supportive commentary is provided for the convenience and clarity in establishment and maintenance of educational records.

Academic Dismissal. Academic dismissal indicates an individual's involuntary separation from the institution for failure to maintain academic standards; the record notation need not specify a definite time when the student may apply for readmission. Academic dismissal should be permanently and clearly noted on the academic record.

Academic Probation. Probationary status denotes that a student's academic performance is below standard as delineated by the institution. Although many students, faculty, and academic advisers find it helpful for advisement purposes, it is recommended that academic probation notations, if recorded at all, not be retained on the academic record because of the irregular duration of this status, the lack of uniformity of application among institutions, and the frequent misinterpretation of its significance by recipients of transcripts.

Academic Record. The academic record is a chronological history of a student's entire quantitative and qualitative learning achievement and reflects the basis under which the individual entered and left the institution.

Academic Suspension. Involuntary termination without a degree for academic reasons may be identified as either suspension or dismissal. However, academic suspension differs from academic dismissal in that it implies or states a time limit after which return will be permitted. Academic suspension may be enforced for a specified period of time or until a stated condition is met.

Advancement and/or Admission to Candidacy in Graduate School Programs. The notation "advancement and/or admission to candidacy in graduate school programs" applies to the date when the student achieves advancement to candidacy.

Area of Study. The area of study denotes the college, school, division, and/or program in which the student was or is enrolled. In multidivisional institutions, the subordinate college, school, or division in which the student has been enrolled should be specified. The specific program of study that the student is following should also be shown.

Calendar System. The calendar system describes and defines the length of the academic session (semester, quarter, trimester, or term).

Contact Hour. The contact hour is a fifty-minute classroom instructional session or its equivalent.

Continuing Education. Continuing education includes all institutional and organizational learning experiences in organized formats that impart education to postsecondary-level learners but which do not apply toward degree programs.

Continuing Education Unit (CEU). A CEU is ten contact hours of participation in an organized continuing education experience under responsible sponsorship, capable direction, and qualified instruction.

Course Identification. The department name, course number, and descriptive title identify each course. An explanation of numerical distinctions—specifying basic, intermediate, advanced, and graduate-level courses, as well as lower- and upper-division offerings or other variations or classifications in local use, such as courses open to both undergraduate and graduate students—is important and should be included in the transcript key or legend. The specific descriptive title by which each course was designated in that year's catalog should be given. The level and subject of any practice teaching should be clearly indicated. It is understood that abbreviations often are necessary, but care should be taken to make them intelligible.

Credit Hour. The credit hour is the unit by which an institution measures its course work. The number of credit hours assigned to a course is usually determined by the number of hours per week in class, exclusive of laboratory periods and the number of weeks in the session. One credit hour is usually assigned to a class which meets fifty minutes a week over a period of a quarter, semester, or term.

Dates of Attendance. Dates of attendance are designated by the academic year (for example, fall or first semester 1980). Summer sessions are designated by the calendar year. When terms of the academic year are designated as first, second, and so forth, it is understood that they are numbered with the beginning of the academic year (the fall term). Some institutions have degree programs utilizing special terms or sessions that begin in one year and end in the next. In such cases the exact beginning and ending dates (day, month, year) should be indicated.

Good Standing. Good standing status denotes that a student is eligible to continue at or return to an institution.

Grade. A grade is a rating or evaluation of a student's achievement. Most frequently it is expressed on a letter scale or in percentages. Grades of A, B, C, D correspond in a general way to the terms excellent, good, fair, and lowest passing quality. The grade of F represents failure and is unacceptable for credit in a course. Some institutions use a plus or minus to further delineate a letter grade. Other grades sometimes used are Pass/Fail, Pass/No Record, Satisfactory/Unsatisfactory, Credit/No Credit. See: Narrative Evaluation.

Grade Points. Grade points are numerical values assigned to letter grades in order to provide a basis for quantitative determination of grade point averages; most common usage is the four-point system: A = 4, B = 3, C = 2, D = 1, F = 0.

Graduate Examination Results. Graduate examination results denote performance on comprehensive and language examinations required for the graduate degree.

Graduation, Statement of. The statement of graduation identifies the degree(s) awarded by the issuing institution, including date(s) and major(s).

Location of Institution. The location of the institution includes the street address, city, state, ZIP code, and country if applicable.

Name Changes. See: Name of Student.

Name of Institution. The name of the institution is its corporate or legal name. In complex institutions, separate administrative units and their locations may be different from the main campus.

Name of Student. The student's full name includes family name and all given names. Nicknames are not used for academic record purposes. Institutions have no obligation to record name changes for students not currently enrolled. Name changes for currently enrolled students should be recorded only when there is evidence of a legal basis for change.

Narrative Evaluation. A narrative evaluation is a faculty assessment, in written form, of the quality and characteristics of student performance. The narrative may stand alone or supplement the conventional evaluative information and usually includes a description of student performance and achievement.

Other Basis for Admissions. Admission by examination, individual approval, and conditional admission are typical "other basis" for admission.

Previous Higher Education. Previous higher education includes the name(s) and location(s) of all institution(s) previously attended, with periods of attendance, degrees earned, and transfer credits accepted.

Secondary School Graduation. Secondary school graduation denotes the name and location of the secondary school from which the individual received a diploma.

Source or Type of Credit. Credit derived from all types of study includes resident credit, extension, correspondence, credit by examination, military service, etc.

Student Identification Number. The identification number is any unique number assigned to the student by the institution.

Status at Time of Last Attendance. Status at time of last attendance refers to the last attendance not culminated by graduation.

Appendix B

Accrediting Agencies in Higher Education

▣ ▣ ▣ ▣ ▣ ▣ ▣ ▣ ▣ ▣ ▣ ▣ ▣ ▣ ▣ ▣ ▣ ▣

The Council on Postsecondary Accreditation (COPA) is a national, nonprofit organization whose purpose is to support, coordinate, and improve all nongovernmental accrediting activities conducted at the postsecondary educational level in the United States. Accrediting bodies vary greatly in sponsorship, organization, scope, and focus. They are regional and national in coverage, general (institutional) and specialized (programmatic) in perspective. They have a common commitment to the improvement of education through the evaluative process known as accreditation. Accrediting groups recognized by COPA are listed below. Those groups that accredit on an institutional basis are listed and described in that category; all others are listed by generic or specific discipline in alphabetical order under the programmatic heading. Regional groups are identified with their authorized area immediately following; all others are national in scope. The scope of accrediting activity and the address of each agency are also listed.

The American Council on Education publishes for COPA an annual directory of postsecondary institutions accredited by a recognized agency. Copies are available from the following: Publications Department, American Council on Education, One Dupont Circle N.W., Suite 818, Washington D.C. 20036.

Institutional Accreditation

American Association of Bible Colleges
Box 543
Wheaton, Illinois 60187
(Undergraduate Bible colleges that offer baccalaureate degrees and require Bible study as an essential part of their curricula.)

Association of Independent Colleges and Schools
Accrediting Commission
1730 M Street N.W.
Washington, D.C. 20036
(Private junior and senior colleges of business and private business schools.)

Middle States Association of Colleges and Schools
Commission on Higher Education
3624 Market Street
Philadelphia, Pennsylvania 19104
(Institutions of postsecondary education with programs of at least one academic year in Canal Zone, Delaware, District of Columbia, France, Maryland, New Jersey, New York, Pennsylvania, Puerto Rico, Switzerland, Virgin Islands.)

National Association of Trade and Technical Schools
2021 L Street N.W.
Washington, D.C. 20036
(Private trade and technical schools.)

National Home Study Council
Accrediting Commission
1601 Eighteenth Street N.W.
Washington, D.C. 20009
(Private and nonprivate home study institutions.)

New England Association of Schools and Colleges
Commission on Institutions of Higher Education and Commission on Vocational, Technical, Career Institutions
131 Middlesex Turnpike

Burlington, Massachusetts 01803
(Degree- and non-degree-granting institutions of higher education in Connecticut, Maine, Massachusetts, New Hampshire, Rhode Island, Vermont.)

North Central Association of Colleges and Schools
Commission on Institutions of Higher Education
1221 University Avenue
Boulder, Colorado 80302
    and
820 Davis Street
Evanston, Illinois 60201
(Institutions of higher education in Arizona, Arkansas, Colorado, Illinois, Indiana, Iowa, Kansas, Michigan, Minnesota, Missouri, Nebraska, New Mexico, North Dakota, Ohio, Oklahoma, South Dakota, West Virginia, Wisconsin, Wyoming.)

Northwest Association of Schools and Colleges
Commission on Colleges
3700-B University Way N.E.
Seattle, Washington 98105
(Institutions of postsecondary education with programs of at least one academic year in Alaska, Idaho, Montana, Nevada, Oregon, Utah, Washington.)

Southern Association of Colleges and Schools
Commission on Colleges and Commission on Occupational Education Institutions
795 Peachtree Street N.E.
Atlanta, Georgia 30308
(Degree-granting institutions of postsecondary education and non-degree-granting occupational education institutions in Alabama, Florida, Georgia, Kentucky, Louisiana, Mexico, Mississippi, North Carolina, South America, South Carolina, Tennessee, Texas, Virginia.)

Western Association of Schools and Colleges
Accrediting Commission for Senior Colleges and Universities
c/o Mills College, Box 9990
Oakland, California 94613

and
Accrediting Commission for Community and Junior Colleges
9053 Soquel Drive
Aptos, California 95003
(Senior colleges and universities and community and junior colleges, as well as certain private specialized institutions in California, Guam, Hawaii, and such other areas of the Pacific Trust Territories as may apply.)

Programmatic Accreditation

ALLIED HEALTH:

American Medical Association
Committee on Allied Health Education and Accreditation
535 North Dearborn Street
Chicago, Illinois 60610
(Recognition is extended to the AMA and its Committee on Allied Health Education and Accreditation as an "umbrella" agency—in collaboration with appropriate health/medical societies, associations, or organizations—for accrediting programs training for the following occupational titles: Blood Bank Technology Specialist, Cytotechnologist, Medical Assistant, Medical Record Administrator and Medical Record Technician, Medical Technologist, Nuclear Medicine Technologist, Occupational Therapist, Physical Therapist, Physician's Assistant (assistant to the primary-care physician and the surgeon's assistant), Radiation Therapy Technologist and Radiologic Technologist, Respiratory Therapist and Respiratory Therapy Technician.)

ARCHITECTURE:

National Architectural Accrediting Board
1735 New York Avenue N.W.
Washington, D.C. 20036
(First professional programs.)

ART:

National Association of Schools of Art
Commission on Accreditation and Membership

11250 Roger Bacon Drive, No. 5
Reston, Virginia 22090
(Institutions offering professional preparation.)

BUSINESS:

American Assembly of Collegiate Schools of Business
750 Office Parkway, Suite 50
St. Louis, Missouri 63141
(Bachelor's and master's degree programs.)

CHEMISTRY:

American Chemical Society
Committee on Professional Training
1155 Sixteenth Street N.W.
Washington, D.C. 20036
(Undergraduate professional programs.)

CHIROPRACTIC EDUCATION:

Council on Chiropractic Education
3209 Ingersoll Avenue
Des Moines, Iowa 50312
(Schools and programs leading to the Doctor of Chiropractic degree.)

CLINICAL PASTORAL EDUCATION:

Association for Clinical Pastoral Education, Inc.
Interchurch Center, Suite 450
475 Riverside Drive
New York, New York 10027
(Professional training centers.)

CONSTRUCTION EDUCATION:

American Council for Construction Education
P. O. Box 1266
Manhattan, Kansas 66502
(Baccalaureate programs.)

DENTISTRY AND DENTAL AUXILIARY PROGRAMS:

American Dental Association
Commission on Accreditation of Dental and Dental Auxiliary Educational Programs
211 East Chicago Avenue
Chicago, Illinois, 60611
(Programs leading to D.D.S. or D.M.D. degrees; professional programs in Dental Hygiene, Dental Assisting, and Dental Technology.)

DIETETICS:

American Dietetic Association
Commission on Evaluation of Dietetic Education
430 North Michigan Avenue
Chicago, Illinois 60611
(Coordinated baccalaureate programs.)

ENGINEERING AND ENGINEERING TECHNOLOGY:

Engineers' Council for Professional Development
345 East Forty-Seventh Street
New York, New York 10017
(Professional engineering programs at the baccalaureate and master's level; baccalaureate programs in engineering technology; and two-year associate degree programs in engineering technology.)

FORESTRY:

Society of American Foresters
5400 Grosvenor Lane
Washington, D.C. 20014
(Professional schools.)

HEALTH SERVICES ADMINISTRATION:

Accrediting Commission on Education for Health Services Administration
One Dupont Circle N.W., Suite 420
Washington, D.C. 20036
(Graduate programs.)

HOME ECONOMICS:

American Home Economics Association
Office of Professional Education
2010 Massachusetts Avenue N.W.
Washington, D.C. 20036
(Undergraduate programs.)

INDUSTRIAL TECHNOLOGY:

National Association for Industrial Technology
P. O. Box 17074, Pottsburg Station
University of North Florida
Jacksonville, Florida 32216
(Baccalaureate programs.)

INTERIOR DESIGN:

Foundation for Interior Design Education Research
730 Fifth Avenue
New York, New York 10019
(Interior design programs at two-year, three-year, baccalaureate,
and master's levels.)

JOURNALISM:

American Council on Education for Journalism
Accrediting Committee
563 Essex Court
Deerfield, Illinois 60015
(Program sequences used in acquiring the first professional degree
in journalism.)

LANDSCAPE ARCHITECTURE:

American Society of Landscape Architects
Landscape Architectural Accreditation Board
1900 M Street N.W., Suite 750
Washington, D.C. 20036
(Professional programs.)

LAW:

American Bar Association
Indiana University
355 North Lansing Street
Indianapolis, Indiana 46202

Association of American Law Schools
One Dupont Circle N.W., Suite 370
Washington, D.C. 20036
(Professional Schools.)

LIBRARIANSHIP:

American Library Association
Committee on Accreditation
50 East Huron Street
Chicago, Illinois 60611
(Master's degree programs.)

MEDICAL ASSISTANT AND MEDICAL LABORATORY TECHNICIAN:

Accrediting Bureau of Medical Laboratory Schools
Oak Manor Offices
29089 U.S. 20 West
Elkhart, Indiana 46514
(Private medical assistant educational institutions and programs
and schools and programs for the medical laboratory technician.)

MEDICINE:

In odd-numbered years, beginning each July 1, contact:

American Medical Association
Council on Medical Education
535 North Dearborn Street
Chicago, Illinois 60610

In even-numbered years, beginning each July 1, contact:

Association of American Medical Colleges
Liaison Committee on Medical Education
One Dupont Circle N.W., Suite 200

Washington, D.C. 20036
(Programs leading to M.D. degree and programs in the basic medical sciences.)

MUSIC:

National Association of Schools of Music
11250 Roger Bacon Drive, No. 5
Reston, Virginia 22090
(Postsecondary schools of music.)

NURSING:

National League for Nursing
10 Columbus Circle
New York, New York 10019
(Baccalaureate and higher degree programs, technical associate degree programs, diploma programs, and practical nursing programs.

National Association for Practical Nurse Education and Service
122 East Forty-Second Street
New York, New York 10017
(Practical nursing programs only.)

OPTOMETRY:

American Optometric Association
Council on Optometric Education
7000 Chippewa Street
St. Louis, Missouri 63119
(Professional schools.)

OSTEOPATHIC MEDICINE:

American Osteopathic Association
Office of Osteopathic Education
212 East Ohio Street
Chicago, Illinois 60611
(Programs leading to D.O. degree.)

PHARMACY:

American Council on Pharmaceutical Education
One East Wacker Drive
Chicago, Illinois 60601
(Programs leading to baccalaureate and doctor of pharmacy degrees.)

PHYSICAL THERAPY:

American Physical Therapy Association
Department of Educational Affairs
1156 Fifteenth Street N.W.
Washington, D.C. 20005
(Professional programs in physical therapy.)

PODIATRY:

American Podiatry Association
Council on Podiatry Education
20 Chevy Chase Circle N.W.
Washington, D.C. 20015
(Professional schools.)

PSYCHOLOGY:

American Psychological Association
1200 Seventeenth Street N.W.
Washington, D.C. 20036
(Doctoral programs leading to the professional practice of psychology.)

PUBLIC HEALTH:

Council on Education for Public Health
1015 Eighteenth Street N.W.
Washington, D.C. 20036
(Graduate schools of public health and master's degree programs in community health education.)

REHABILITATION COUNSELING EDUCATION:

Council on Rehabilitation Education
Rehabilitation Institute
Southern Illinois University
1001 South Elizabeth
Carbondale, Illinois 62901

Natresources, Inc. (Consultant to CORE)
520 North Michigan Avenue
Chicago, Illinois 60611
(Master's degree programs.)

SOCIAL WORK:

Council on Social Work Education
Division of Educational Standards and Accreditation
345 East Forty-Sixth Street
New York, New York 10017
(Master's and baccalaureate degree programs.)

SPEECH PATHOLOGY AND AUDIOLOGY:

American Speech and Hearing Association
Education and Training Board
10801 Rockville Pike
Rockville, Maryland 20852
(Master's degree programs.)

TEACHER EDUCATION:

National Council for Accreditation of Teacher Education
1750 Pennsylvania Avenue N.W.
Washington, D.C. 20006
(Bachelor's and higher degree programs.)

THEOLOGY:

Association of Theological Schools in the United States and Canada
P. O. Box 130
Vandalia, Ohio 45377
(Graduate professional schools.)

VETERINARY MEDICINE:

American Veterinary Medical Association
Scientific Activities
930 North Meacham Road
Schaumburg, Illinois 60196
(Schools offering D.V.M. or V.M.D. degree programs.)

Appendix C

Higher Education Associations

▣ ▣ ▣ ▣ ▣ ▣ ▣ ▣ ▣ ▣ ▣ ▣ ▣ ▣ ▣ ▣ ▣ ▣ ▣

Adult Education Association of the U.S.A.
810 Eighteenth Street N.W., Suite 500
Washington, D.C. 20006

American Association of Colleges for Teacher Education
One Dupont Circle N.W., Suite 610
Washington, D.C. 20036

American Association of Collegiate Registrars and Admissions Officers
One Dupont Circle N.W., Suite 330
Washington, D.C. 20036

American Association of Community and Junior Colleges
One Dupont Circle N.W., Suite 410
Washington, D.C. 20036

American Association for Higher Education
One Dupont Circle N.W., Suite 780
Washington, D.C. 20036

American Association of Nurse Anesthetists
111 East Wacker Drive, Suite 929
Chicago, Illinois 60601

American Association of State Colleges and Universities
One Dupont Circle N.W., Suite 700
Washington, D.C. 20036

American Association of University Administrators
P.O. Box 6, Bidwell Station
Buffalo, New York 14222

American Association of University Professors
One Dupont Circle N.W., Suite 500
Washington, D.C. 20036

American Bar Association
Professional Service Activities
1155 East Sixtieth Street
Chicago, Illinois 60637

American Board of Funeral Service Education, Inc.
201 Columbia Street
Fairmont, West Virginia 26554

American Chemical Society, Committee on Professional Training
1155 Sixteenth Street N.W.
Washington, D.C. 20036

American Council on Education
One Dupont Circle N.W., Suite 800
Washington, D.C. 20036

American Council on Pharmaceutical Education
1 East Wacker Drive, Suite 2210
Chicago, Illinois 60601

American Dental Association
Council on Dental Education
211 East Chicago Avenue
Chicago, Illinois 60611

American Dietetic Association
430 North Michigan Avenue
Chicago, Illinois 60611

American Medical Association
Council on Medical Education
535 North Dearborn Street
Chicago, Illinois 60610

American Optometric Association
Council on Optometric Education
7000 Chippewa Street
Saint Louis, Missouri 63119

American Osteopathic Association
Office of Osteopathic Education
212 East Ohio Street
Chicago, Illinois 60611

American Podiatry Association
Council on Podiatry Education
20 Chevy Chase Circle N.W.
Washington, D.C. 20015

American Psychological Association
1200 Seventeenth Street N.W.
Washington, D.C. 20036

American Public Health Association
1015 Eighteenth Street N.W.
Washington, D.C. 20036

American Society of Allied Health Professions
One Dupont Circle N.W., Suite 300
Washington, D.C. 20036

American Society for Engineering Education
One Dupont Circle N.W., Suite 400
Washington, D.C. 20036

American Society of Landscape Architects
1900 M Street N.W., Suite 750
Washington, D.C. 20036

American Speech and Hearing Association
10801 Rockville Pike
Rockville, Maryland 20852

American Veterinary Medical Association
930 North Meacham Road
Schaumburg, Illinois 60196

Association of Advanced Rabbinical and Talmudical Schools
175 Fifth Avenue, Room 711
New York, New York 10010

Association of American Colleges
1818 R Street N.W.
Washington, D.C. 20009

Association of American Law Schools
One Dupont Circle N.W., Suite 370
Washington, D.C. 20036

Association of American Medical Colleges
Liaison
One Dupont Circle N.W., Suite 200
Washington, D.C. 20036

Association of American Universities
One Dupont Circle N.W., Suite 730
Washington, D.C. 20036

Association for Continuing Higher Education
1700 Asp Avenue
Norman, Oklahoma 73037

Association of Governing Boards of Universities and Colleges
One Dupont Circle N.W., Suite 720
Washington, D.C. 20036

Association for Innovation in Higher Education
P. O. Box 12560
St. Petersburg, Florida 33733

Association for Institutional Research
314 Stone Building
Florida State University
Tallahassee, Florida 32306

Association of Physical Plant Administrators of Universities and Colleges
Eleven Dupont Circle N.W., Suite 250
Washington, D.C. 20036

Association of Theological Schools in the United States and Canada
P. O. Box 130
Bandalia, Ohio 45377

Association of University Programs in Health Administration
One Dupont Circle N.W., Suite 420
Washington, D.C. 20036

CAUSE
737 Twenty-Ninth Street
Boulder, Colorado 80303

Coalition of Adult Education Organization
New York City Community College
300 Jay Street
Brooklyn, New York 11201

College and University Personnel Association
Eleven Dupont Circle N.W.
Washington, D.C. 20036

Commission on Independent Colleges and Universities
37 Elk Street
Albany, New York 12224

Council for the Advancement of Small Colleges
One Dupont Circle N.W., Suite 320
Washington, D.C. 20036

Council for Advancement and Support of Education
One Dupont Circle N.W., Suite 530/600
Washington, D.C. 20036

Council on Education for Public Health
1015 Eighteenth Street N.W., 9th Floor
Washington, D.C. 20036

Council of Graduate Schools in the United States
One Dupont Circle N.W., Suite 740
Washington, D.C. 20036

Council of Independent Kentucky Colleges and Universities
Box 668
Danville, Kentucky 40422

Council on Postsecondary Accreditation
One Dupont Circle N.W., Suite 760
Washington, D.C. 20036

Council on Social Work Education
Division of Standards and Accreditation
345 East Forty-Sixth Street
New York, New York 10017

Education Commission of the States
1860 Lincoln Street, Suite 300
Denver, Colorado 80295

Engineers' Council for Professional Development
345 East Forty-Seventh Street
New York, New York 10017

Foundation for Interior Design Education Research
730 Fifth Avenue
New York, New York 10019

Institute for Services to Education
2001 S Street N.W.
Washington, D.C. 20009

National Association of College Admissions Counselors
9933 Lawler Avenue, Suite 500
Skokie, Illinois 60076

National Association of College and University Attorneys
One Dupont Circle N.W., Suite 650
Washington, D.C. 20036

National Association of College and University Business Officers
One Dupont Circle N.W., Suite 510
Washington, D.C. 20036

National Association for Foreign Student Affairs
1860 Nineteenth Street N.W.
Washington, D.C. 20009

National Association of Independent Colleges and Universities
1717 Massachusetts Avenue N.W., Suite 503
Washington, D.C. 20036

National Association for Practical Nurse Education and Service, Inc.
122 East Forty-Second Street, Suite 800
New York, New York 10017

National Association for Public Continuing and Adult Education
NEA Building
1201 Sixteenth Street, N.W., Suite 429
Washington, D.C. 20036

National Association of Schools of Music
11250 Roger Bacon Drive, #5
Reston, Virginia 22090

National Association of State Universities and Land-Grant Colleges
One Dupont Circle N.W., Suite 710
Washington, D.C. 20036

*National Catholic Educational Association, College and University
Department*
One Dupont Circle N.W., Suite 770
Washington, D.C. 20036

National Education Association, Division of Affiliate Services
1201 Sixteenth Street N.W.
Washington, D.C. 20036

National League for Nursing
10 Columbus Circle
New York, New York 10019

National University Extension Association
One Dupont Circle N.W., Suite 360
Washington, D.C. 20036

New England Board of Higher Education
40 Grove Street
Wellesley, Massachusetts 02181

Society of American Foresters
5400 Grosvenor Lane
Washington, D.C. 20014

Society for College and University Planning
3 Washington Square Village, Suite 1A
New York, New York 10012

Southern Regional Education Board
130 Sixth Street N.W.
Atlanta, Georgia 30313

State Higher Education Executive Officers Association
1301 West Seventh Street
Little Rock, Arkansas 72201

Western Interstate Commission for Higher Education
P. O. Drawer P
Boulder, Colorado 80302

Appendix D

Statement of Principles of Good Practice with Reference to College Admissions

◨◨◨◨◨◨◨◨◨◨◨◨◨◨◨◨

The American Association of Collegiate Registrars and Admissions Officers, the College Entrance Examination Board, and the National Association of College Admissions Counselors recognize the following statement of Principles of Good Practice with Reference to College Admissions.

1. Admissions Promotion and Recruitment
1.1 Principles Relating to Colleges and Universities
    A. Admissions counselors are professional members of their institution's staff. As professionals, they receive remuneration on a fixed salary, rather than commission or bonus based on the number of students recruited.

B. When admissions counselors are responsible for the development of publications used for their institution's promotional and recruitment activities designed to elicit the interests of prospective students, these publications should:
- state clearly and precisely requirements for secondary school preparation, admissions tests, and transfer-student admissions requirements;
- include a current and accurate admissions calendar;
- give precise information about opportunities and requirements for financial aid;
- describe in detail any special programs such as overseas study, early decision, early admission, credit by examination, or advanced placement;
- contain descriptions of the campus and community that are current and realistic.

C. Colleges and universities are responsible for all people whom they involve in admissions, promotional, and recruitment activities (including their alumni, coaches, students, faculty) and for educating them about the principles outlined in this statement. Colleges and universities that engage the services of admissions management firms or consulting firms are responsible for assuring that such firms adhere to the principles stated herein.

D. Admissions counselors are forthright and accurate and give comprehensive information in presenting their institutions to high school personnel, prospective students, and their parents. They:
- state clearly the admissions and other requirements of their institutions;
- make clear all dates concerning application, notification, and candidates' reply requirements, for both admissions and financial aid;
- furnish data descriptive of currently enrolled classes;
- avoid unfavorable comparisons with other institutions.

E. Admissions counselors avoid unprofessional promotional tactics, such as:

- contracting with high school personnel for remuneration for referred students;
- contracting with placement services that require a fee from the institution for each student enrolled;
- encouraging students to transfer if they have shown no interest in doing so.

F. Admissions counselors do not recruit students enrolled and registered at other colleges or universities unless the students initiate inquiries themselves, or unless cooperation is sought from institutions that provide transfer programs.

1.2 Principles Relating to Schools. Schools will:

A. Provide a program of counseling that is accurate and comprehensive with respect to the college opportunities sought by students and available to them.

B. Encourage students and their parents to take the initiative in learning about colleges and universities.

C. Invite college and university representatives to assist in counseling candidates about college opportunities.

D. Avoid unfavorable comparisons with other institutions.

E. Refuse unethical or unprofessional requests (for lists of top students, lists of athletes, etc.) from college or university representatives (alumni, coaches, etc.).

F. Refuse any reward or remuneration from a college, university, or private counseling service for placement of their school's students.

1.3 Principles Relating to Community Agencies. Such agencies will:

A. Provide accurate descriptions for schools and colleges of the services available through their agencies, since it is the responsibility of community agencies to make such services known to students, parents, secondary schools, and colleges.

B. Provide students with up-to-date information on post-secondary institutions and processes.

C. Assist students in discovering the colleges that meet their abilities, needs, and interests.

  D. Counsel students on all postsecondary options: college, vocational education, job opportunities.

  E. Report to secondary schools on their respective students so that accurate files can be maintained in the schools.

1.4 College fairs, clearinghouses, and matching services that provide liaison between colleges and universities and students shall be considered a positive part of the admissions process if they effectively supplement other high school guidance activities and adhere to the principles of good practice stated herein.

2. Application Procedures

2.1 Principles Relating to Colleges and Universities. Colleges and universities will:

  A. Accept full responsibility for admissions decisions and for proper notification of those decisions to candidates and, when possible, to secondary schools.

  B. Receive information about candidates in confidence and respect completely, within the confines of federal and/or state laws, the confidential nature of such data.

  C. Not apply newly revised requirements to the disadvantage of a candidate whose secondary school course has been established in accordance with earlier requirements.

  D. Notify candidates as soon as possible if they are clearly inadmissible.

  E. Not deny admission to a candidate on the grounds that their institution does not have aid funds to meet the candidate's apparent financial need, except for foreign students.

  F. Not require candidates or their schools to indicate the order of candidates' college or university preferences, except under early decision plans.

  G. Permit candidates to choose without penalty among offers of admission until they have heard from all colleges to which they have applied, or until the date established under the Candidates Reply Date Agreement.

  H. Maintain a waiting list of reasonable length and only for a reasonable period of time.

    I.   State clearly the application procedures for transfer students by informing candidates of deadlines, documents required, courses accepted, and course equivalency.

2.2   Principles Relating to Secondary Schools. Schools will:

    A. Provide for colleges and universities accurate, legible, and complete transcripts for their school's candidates.

    B. Describe their school's marking system and method of determining rank in class.

    C. Describe clearly special curricular opportunities (honors, advanced placement courses, seminars, etc.).

    D. Provide accurate descriptions of the candidates' personal qualities that are relevant to the admissions process.

    E. Report any significant change in candidates' status or qualifications between the time of recommendation and graduation.

    F. Urge candidates to recognize and discharge their responsibilities in the admissions process by:

- complying with requests for additional information in a timely manner;
- responding to institutional deadlines on admissions and refraining from stockpiling acceptances;
- responding to institutional deadlines on room reservations, financial aid, health record, and prescheduling where all or any of these are applicable.

    G. Not, without permission of candidates, reveal the candidates' college preference.

    H. Advise students not to sign any contractual agreement with an institution without examining the provisions of the contract.

    I. Advise students to notify other institutions when they have accepted an admissions offer.

2.3   Principles Relating to Community Agencies. Such agencies will:

    A. Exercise their responsibility to the entire educational community.

    B. Discourage unnecessary multiple applications.

    C. Discourage students from stockpiling offers of admission.

3. Financial Assistance (where such assistance is based on need). Financial assistance consists of scholarships, grants, loans, and employment, which may be offered to all students singly or in various forms.

3.1 Principles Relating to Colleges and Universities. Colleges and universities will:

A. Strive, through their publications and communications, to provide schools, parents, and students with factual information about their institution's aid opportunities, programs, and practices.

B. View financial assistance from colleges and other sources as supplementary to the efforts of a student's family when the student is not self-supporting.

C. In determining the financial contribution of a candidate's family, use methods that assess ability to pay in a consistent and equitable manner, such as those developed by the College Scholarship Service and the American College Testing Program.

D. Clearly state the total yearly cost of attending their institution and outline estimates of need for students seeking assistance.

E. Permit candidates to choose, without penalty, among offers of financial assistance until they have heard from all colleges to which they have applied, or until the date established under the Candidates Reply Date Agreement.

F. Clearly state policies on renewals of aid awards.

G. Not announce publicly the amount of financial award to an individual candidate, and thus avoid revealing the candidate's family financial situation.

H. Not consider a student's need for financial aid as a criterion for admissions selection.

I. Notify applicants of institutional financial aid decisions before the date by which they must reply to the institution's offer of admission.

J. Meet the full need of students to the extent possible within the institution's capabilities.

K. Make awards to students who apply for renewal of aid by reviewing each student's financial circumstances and establishing the amount of aid needed with full consideration of the student's current need.

3.2 Principles Relating to Secondary Schools. Schools will:

A. Refrain, in public announcements, from giving the amounts of financial aid received by students.

B. Advise students who have been awarded aid by sources outside colleges that it is their responsibility to notify the colleges to which they have applied of the type and amount of such outside assistance.

4. Advanced Standing Students and the Awarding of Credit

4.1 Principles Relating to Colleges and Universities. Colleges and universities agree that:

A. Placement, credit, and exemption policies that are designed principally to recruit students are inimical to the best interests of students.

B. Student achievement should be evaluated through use of validated methods and techniques.

C. Policies and procedures for granting credit should be defined and published as part of an institution's preadmissions information.

D. The evaluation of previously earned credit should be done in a manner that ensures the integrity of academic standards published by the admitting college or university.

4.2 Principles Relating to Secondary School Personnel. Such personnel agree that they will:

A. Alert students to the full implications of college and university placement, credit, and exemption policies for the students' educational planning and goals.

B. Make students aware of the importance of accreditation.

C. Make students aware of the possibilities of earning credit through nontraditional educational experience and through examinations and alternative methods of instruction.

Appendix E

Standards and Responsibilities in International Educational Interchange*

◙ ◙ ◙ ◙ ◙ ◙ ◙ ◙ ◙ ◙ ◙ ◙ ◙ ◙ ◙ ◙ ◙ ◙

Introduction

In a world of increasing global interdependence, international education has become an essential part of United States higher education, whether in the small, private college or the public university. It is, however, a component often left to chance for development, refinement, review, and direction by individual institutions. Institutional services that support international educational interchange are among those often left to develop without policy direction and management coordination.

*Published by the Field Service Program, National Association for Foreign Student Affairs, 1860 19th St., N.W., Washington, D.C. 20009. This statement was adopted by the NAFSA Board of Directors on June 10, 1978, and is a revision of the original statement issued by the board on October 21, 1970, and May 2, 1964.

In response to the need for comprehensive guidance for establishing and for maintaining programs in international student education, the NAFSA Field Service Program published its first *Guideline on Responsibilities and Standards in Work with Foreign Students* in 1964. That document was designed for use by professionals involved in foreign student affairs, administrative officers of colleges and universities, career guidance counselors working with foreign students, and others.

This is the first revision of that earlier document and reflects many important developments in higher education as well as the evolution of NAFSA as the single national agency concerned with professional standards for those involved with educational interchanges. This publication includes, for the first time, special attention to the importance of study-abroad advising as a distinctive professional role.

This *Guideline* is designed for the policymaker and policy implementer. It advocates a set of standards that will guide and direct the effective execution of responsibilities in international student education by competent and well-trained professional or volunteer staff, whether full time or part time. More importantly, however, this statement presumes to be a set of principles based on the consensus and common experience of those who deal with foreign student affairs at colleges and universities in this country as well as abroad. To this end, NAFSA expects this statement to be useful as a sourcebook for those who develop policy for institutions and organizations, a statement of professional conduct for staff, and a guide for the continuing development of a dynamic field of educational endeavor.

NAFSA's Growth and Professionalism

NAFSA is a professional association of institutions and individuals committed to international educational interchange. Its membership includes public and private educational institutions, private organizations, and individuals, both employees and volunteers, who work with students and scholars either coming to the United States from abroad or going from the United States to other countries.

The association consists of five professional sections:

• Council of Advisers to Foreign Students and Scholars (CAFSS), which is made up of staff members and administrators of institutions and organizations concerned with the advising of foreign students, scholars, and trainees in the United States.

• Admissions Section (ADSEC), whose members are staff and administrators involved in the selection, admission, and academic placement of foreign students at undergraduate, graduate, and professional levels, and in the assessment of credit for studies completed by United States students abroad.

• Association of Teachers of English as a Second Language (ATESL), which includes teachers and administrators of programs in the teaching of English as a foreign language.

• Community Section (COMSEC), which consists of volunteers and salaried staff involved in programs and services for foreign students and scholars in United States community life.

• Section on U.S. Students Abroad (SECUSSA), for administrators, faculty, and staff involved in the advising of students interested in study, travel, short-term employment, or volunteer service in other countries, and in organizing and operating formal programs in these fields.

Professionalism in Educational Interchanges

In American higher education, many thousands of people on a full-time, part-time, or occasional basis, salaried or unsalaried, take part in some aspect of interchanges or deal with participants in such programs. Regardless of the nature or the extent of the involvement, they can be effective participants only with knowledge of accepted principles and practices developed over many years of experience with international interchanges.

NAFSA's objectives as a professional organization are:

• To assure that all individuals participating in international educational interchanges* between the United States and other

---

*The phrase *international educational interchange* is used in this publication to describe the increasing two-way flow of students and scholars across international boundaries for educational purposes.

countries achieve the educational and personal goals envisioned for their sojourn in the United States.

  • To assure that those professional people who come in contact with participants in interchanges are guided by a firm belief in the worth, dignity, and potential of every human being, regardless of national or ethnic origin, cultural or linguistic background, sex, race, social status, political affiliation, or religious belief.

  • To assure that participants in educational interchanges learn as effectively and freely as possible, recognizing that the learning achieved in one culture is to be applied in others.

  • To promote the larger goals of educational interchanges, reflecting the increasing need for people of all countries to learn about one another and understand the conditions for interdependence. More specifically, the American people are urged to learn about the world and the ways in which it affects us, while people of other countries are expected to learn about us, our ways of life, and the ways in which our decisions and policies affect them.

This *Guideline* is designed to encourage those working professionally in international interchange to carry out and stimulate wide public discussion, understanding, and practice of these standards and responsibilities. NAFSA requests its members to collect and distribute case studies bearing on responsibilities, ethical principles, professional standards, and resolution of difficult problems for wide discussion in professional conferences and workshops. These efforts will assist members of the profession in improving their professional competence and in resolving conflicts arising out of the application of these standards.

In the meantime, this *Guideline* is offered to the members of the profession and to officials of their institutions and organizations for serious study and implementation.

1. Educational Interchange Policy Considerations

Establishment of clearly stated policies for international educational interchanges which are accepted and well understood by those who direct or implement institutional purposes is an essential ingredient in the international education process. Such policy must draw on and relate to the fundamental mission of the institution, recognize and direct sufficient resources for carrying out the policy, and carry the authority of the highest level in the institutional governance structure.

A meaningful institutional policy develops from the understanding of the obligation to provide international dimensions in the institution's educational programs in relation to the educational mission of a college or university in today's interdependent world; international interchange as a factor in attracting staff and students for whom international interests are of particular importance; international involvements as a means of securing special funding for educational programs; mechanisms for funding which can be more carefully planned and administered within stated policies; recognition of the student expectation for first-hand experiences with other cultures as a part of their own educational experience; and maintaining international educational interchanges as an educational priority against competing and often transitory interests.

Possible Effect of Not Having Policy

In the absence of policy:
• Individual faculty with enthusiasm for international interests, but little knowledge of how to develop them, are likely to start activity by inviting foreign scholars or students to the campus or by setting up a study-abroad program. Such well-meant attempts not only can conflict with one another but they can also become costly fiascos that harm both the participants and the institution.

• Students and staff may leave the institution to find outlets elsewhere for their international interests.

• Unqualified and poorly financed foreign students may be accepted, with harmful results both to the students and the institution, and in possible violation of legal requirements under United States law.

• Students and faculty coming from or going to another country may have totally unrealistic expectations and may not only be disappointed in their experience but may be involved in serious academic, financial, or legal difficulties.

Elements of a Comprehensive Policy

Institutional decision makers have a number of choices to make in determining a satisfactory policy on international educational interchanges. Attention to the following considerations is pertinent:

Directional Flow of Students and Scholars. An institution may accept foreign students or foreign scholars and allow or encourage its own domestic students and faculty to study and carry on research or service outside the United States, or it may decide to engage in only some or none of these programs.

Nature and Scope of Interchanges. Institutional objectives for educational interchanges must be carefully weighed, with specific attention to the nature and scope of those interchanges—faculty exchanges, language and area studies, desirable mix of foreign and American students, the means to ensure credible study-abroad experience for American students, and teaching and research that deals with international, intercultural, and comparative topics. A comprehensive program that involves most of those elements may be highly satisfactory for one institution and wholly inappropriate for another.

Once the scope of involvement is decided, an institution must determine the nature and extent of services needed for international interchanges. Competent services must be provided both for foreign students and scholars coming to the campus and for United States students and scholars going abroad. The services required vary according to the goals of the institution, but a certain number are prerequisites to any international involvement. A foreign student program on a United States campus needs admissions services and evaluation of foreign credentials. The admission of foreign students and scholars also involves certain commitments to advising them on aspects of their legal status in the United States. Many other desirable programs for high-quality education include orientation to the United States, training in English as a foreign language, personal counseling, and opportunities for nonformal learning and interaction with United States culture off campus.

While staffing for a program is dependent upon what services an institution chooses to offer, experience has shown that an institution which enrolls 350 foreign students should have the equivalent of one full-time foreign student adviser with clerical assistance and at least one admissions person who specializes in foreign admissions and credentials evaluation. For fewer foreign admissions, an institution may consider contracting its credentials evaluation to another institution or agency. Larger foreign student programs can adjust their ratios of students to staff, depending upon their goals, taking advantage of economies of scale.

In the case of study-abroad programs, staffing depends upon whether an institution operates its own programs, contracts with others for these programs, or is in a consortium operating joint programs. As a minimum, an institution must have a person designated as a contact point for possible entry into a program. It is highly desirable also to have an academic adviser, an orientation program, and an adviser on cost information. Clerical support for these functions, of course, is necessary. If the program is to be operated by the institution itself, then provisions must be made for program planning, academic content, participant selection and orientation, transportation, supervision and instruction abroad, experience in the host country culture, and a range of other needs.

Administrative Location of Services. Institutions vary widely in the administrative location and level assigned to services for foreign student and study-abroad programs. Either or both may be located in the president's or vice-president's office, in academic affairs, in student affairs, in an international program unit, in the registrar's office, or as independent units. The placement of such responsibility within the institutional hierarchy will determine its emphasis. The rationale for setting the responsibility within the institution's accountability structure must be considered carefully in each institution.

Decisions About the Foreign Student Population

Ratio Between U.S. and Foreign Students. Policymakers are urged to decide what they consider is an appropriate and feasible cultural mix (ratio) of the United States and foreign students in the institution as a whole, at each academic level, in particular schools or departments, and for what purposes.

Geographical Origin. The institution may wish to accept students from one or more countries or world areas or seek broad geographical representation in its foreign student population. Financial aid policies must recognize and deal with the foreign student population and the objectives for international educational interchange.

Socioeconomic Background. Depending upon financial aid resources available, a decision must be made as to the extent to which financial aid will be provided to academically qualified but financially needy students.

Admissions Qualifications. Decisions must be made on acceptable admissions qualifications, including:

1. Academic level and quality of work undertaken in a foreign educational system, which requires a knowledgeable individual to determine equivalence.
2. English-language proficiency through acceptable methods of measurement.
3. Educational objectives which can be fulfilled by instruction offered at the institution.
4. Adequate financial resources. Prior to authorizing the student to enter the United States for study or transfer from another institution, the institution is obliged to determine the adequacy of the student's financial resources for the program of study. These resources may be any combination of personal, family, sponsor, or institutional funds—including those which the institution may develop specifically for foreign student education. This provision must include adequate health and accident insurance for both students and dependents, travel costs, and financial support in the event of emergencies.
5. Legal obligations. By accepting foreign students, an institution assumes obligations involved in admission and enrollment of foreign students. These obligations result chiefly from federal legislation and regulation with respect to entry and sojourn of aliens, but also from laws governing taxes, social security, and other requirements for aliens. Decisions must be made as to who will be responsible for carrying out institutional obligations within the institution.

2. Standards and Principles for
Professional Staffs and Volunteers

General Principles

Professionally, all who work in any phase of international educational interchange of people are expected to develop and maintain competence in their fields as described below. This expectation applies equally to part-time and full-time workers, salaried or unsalaried.

1. *Primary responsibility.* The basic responsibility of professionals is to the foreign and United States students and scholars with whom they work and to their institutions.

2. *Job setting or environment.* All professionals should be thoroughly familiar with their institutions and their obligations to students, with the responsibilities assigned to their positions, and with the prerogatives, facilities, and resources which are or are not available for carrying out the responsibilities.

3. *Preparation and continued growth.* Professionals should strive to go beyond minimal academic credentials in relevant disciplines required for entry level positions. They should seek continuing professional development opportunities and assist others to do so in areas such as acquiring additional formal study or reading; maintaining liaison with counterparts at other institutions; attending professional conferences, seminars, and workshops; conducting and cooperating in relevant research in accordance with established ethics and methodologies for cross-cultural research; gaining first-hand experience and understanding of other cultures through international study and travel whenever possible.

4. *Representation of the field.* Professionals in the field of international interchange have the responsibility to represent and interpret the entire field, including unique needs of participants to concerned people in and outside educational institutions.

5. *Representation of qualifications.* Professionals in the field must restrict themselves to the performance of duties for which they are professionally trained and qualified.

6. *Responsibility for ethical action.* Professionals must always act in a responsible and ethical manner and abide by the standards of the academic and professional community and of NAFSA.

7. *Self-enhancement or profit.* Professionals do not seek self-enhancement through comparisons or evaluations damaging to others. Neither should they seek personal profits through influence upon or association with students or staff with whom they work. Acceptance of free trips, services, or personal gifts without appropriate accountability and awareness of cultural implications may result in implicit reciprocal obligations and damage the reputation of professionals and their field.

8. *Reports and evaluations.* The individual in a professional position should report regularly to superiors and undertake regular self-evaluation of work accomplished while at the same time seeking evaluation of others.

9. *Development of professionalism.* Professionals, salaried or unsalaried, should seek to foster the development of their field by acquiring, contributing to, and applying specialized and systematic knowledge, skills, and attitudes relevant to the field; working for higher standards of performance and effectiveness; fostering a set of professional standards and ethics; developing broader institutional and community support for the field; joining, supporting, and participating in active leadership in NAFSA as the professional association in the field; working toward better understanding between the people of the United States and the world; promoting the development of other countries and the welfare and betterment of their citizens through education and training; creating the awareness of global perspectives.

10. *Advising.* Professionals should develop an effective advising relationship through dealing with all persons with patience, understanding, and respect for their individuality and culture; informing and describing alternatives and helping the individual decide the action to be taken, (except in matters of law or institutional regulation, final decisions are the responsibility of the individual foreign student or scholar); striving to assure that the information provided is accurate, clearly stated, and as complete as possible, so that each student or staff member will be fully aware of the alternatives available in determining a course of action; interpreting to foreign students and staff the academic practices and regulations of the institution; local, state, and national laws; accepted standards of conduct; and expectations and reactions of those they meet in

the United States (this should be done, insofar as possible, on the basis of background knowledge of the students' and scholars' own cultures); maintaining confidentiality and personal information about students and scholars and their personal problems within prescribed and institutional policy; referring students and scholars to other colleagues for assistance whenever their problems require knowledge, training, or authority not possessed by the person initially providing advice.

11. *Obligations in administration.* Professionals with administrative responsibilities have the following obligations: *Planning and evaluation.* Administrators must assess the needs in their areas of responsibility, make adequate plans to meet these needs, provide necessary leadership in carrying out the plans successfully, avoid duplication, assure coordination of services, make periodic reports, and evaluate their total programs. *Staffing.* Administrators must select the most competent people available for staff responsibilities; provide staff with adequate orientation to the institution and its international education program; assign them to tasks best suited to their skills, experience, and interests; provide appropriate in-service training opportunities to increase their competence; encourage them to take advantage of professional growth opportunities provided by the institution or outside agencies and professional associations; and provide them with as much administrative support and encouragement as possible to enable them to work with effectiveness and satisfaction.

Responsibilities of Foreign Student Advisers

In addition to the general principles and obligations noted, the foreign student adviser (FSA) has the following responsibilities:

1. *Leadership and coordination.* In most United States colleges and universities the FSA is the originator and/or coordinator of various policies, services, and programs related to foreign students and scholars.

2. *Identification and mobilization of resources.* The FSA should develop close relations with a broad range of people who may be able to assist foreign students and staff in their life in the institution and the community. Close liaison should be maintained with faculty

and staff who are responsible for academic advising, student records, financial aid, housing, food and health services, student activities, career counseling, and placement.

3. *Interpretation of background and needs.* The FSA must often provide two-way interpretation of objectives, needs, educational backgrounds, cultural differences, and problems between foreign students and scholars and their sponsors on the one hand and administrators, faculty, United States students, and the community on the other. It is desirable not only to facilitate the expeditious completion of foreign students' academic programs, but also to enable them to learn as much as they wish to about the United States and its culture and problems.

4. *Appropriateness to academic programs.* It is a responsibility of the FSA to encourage foreign students and their academic advisers and professors to keep in mind that the foreign students will be using their education in their home countries after graduation. Constant attention should be given to adapting or supplementing the United States educational experience to make it applicable to home-country needs.

5. *Learning with foreign students.* The FSA should provide or encourage the development of programs through which the American campus or community can benefit educationally from the presence of foreign students.

6. *Responsibility for staff.* Advisers should ascertain that all office staff and volunteers are trained to understand and practice the principles and obligations described in this document, and especially those regarding attitude, accuracy, and confidentiality.

7. *Responsibility to sponsors.* Although professionals on United States campuses should be aware of the needs and requirements of foreign students' sponsors and home governments, they should not assume responsibility for relationships between the students and their sponsors or governments.

8. *Immigration regulations.* Major obligations of FSAs are providing information to foreign students and scholars about their legal rights and responsibilities as temporary residents in the United States; assuring institutional adherence to regulations of the United States government, especially those of the Immigration and Naturalization Service; providing accurate, up-to-date information to students and scholars about such regulations.

9. *Dependents.* The FSA must assure that foreign students are aware of the costs and problems they will encounter if they bring dependents with them to the United States. To be of greatest benefit, this information must reach them well in advance of their departure from their home countries. Provision must be made for assistance to those who do bring dependents in such matters as housing, health services and insurance, schooling for children, etc.

10. *Community programs.* FSAs usually serve as liaison between the foreign student and scholar group and the local community. They often are leaders in encouraging community interest in foreign students. Meaningful contacts and associations with the American communities are important to the social and educational experiences of foreign students in the United States. In these endeavors the FSA also plays an important role in interpreting foreign cultures to Americans.

11. *Emergency action.* In case of emergency, such as severe medical or psychological problems, death, or other crises, the FSA should take appropriate and decisive measures and assume leadership in utilization of available campus and community resources. These crisis situations are some of the tests of the FSA's professional competence and allow no margin for error.

Responsibilities of Foreign Student Admissions Officers

Foreign student admissions officers, in addition to the general responsibilities noted have the following specific responsibilities:

1. *Selection and admission.* The admissions officer must assure that foreign students have the requisites for potential success, are screened and selected intelligently, and are given appropriate academic placement. Close cooperation between the admissions officer and the FSA is indispensable to the accomplishment of these tasks in an efficient, effective, and sensitive manner. Specifically, the admissions officer must assure that the following steps have been taken in the case of each foreign application:

a. Information. Each applicant should receive fully adequate, up-to-date information about the institution, its academic offerings, its facilities, and its arrangements for foreign students.

b. Curriculum and instructional facilities. The institution

should offer admission to a foreign student only when a suitable curriculum is available at that institution.

c. Academic background. Foreign applicants' academic backgrounds must be thoroughly checked to assure that they are academically prepared to undertake their proposed programs of study. If the applicants are admitted, their departments or academic advisers must be given sufficient information on their academic backgrounds to provide a proper basis for academic advising and placement.

d. Language proficiency. The admissions officer should assure insofar as possible that admitted foreign students have adequate proficiency in English to enable them to perform successfully in the proposed academic program or, if the students are applying to an intensive English-language program initially or exclusively, that they have sufficient ability, aptitude, and motivation to succeed.

e. Financial support. Since the admissions office is usually the first point of contact for foreign students, it is crucial that a realistic picture of finances be communicated to each foreign applicant. The admissions office, in cooperation with the FSA and/or the financial aids officer, should put together an accurate estimate of the minimum resources necessary for the complete academic and nonacademic costs students will incur. Admissions offices should furnish prospective foreign students with *complete and detailed information on costs,* including transportation to the institution from usual ports of entry, tuition and fees, room, meals, books and supplies, winter clothing, health and accident insurance, local transportation, vacation expense, summer maintenance and/or summer school costs, costs of dissertations, costs for dependents, incidentals, and any other items required for realistic cost estimates. A schedule of payments must also be given to enable admitted foreign students to make suitable arrangements for the necessary financial resources. If costs are likely to increase, this should also be stated. The admissions office also has the responsibility of verifying that all prospective students have the total resources necessary for the full periods of study for which they are admitted.

f. Health. There must also be positive evidence that each foreign applicant is in good physical and mental health.

2. *Test use.* The admissions officer should understand and explain to others the proper use of standardized tests as applied to foreign students. It should be recognized that such tests are useful indicators, but that they are less reliable and valid for students from other cultural and linguistic backgrounds than for United States students. While tests, including those for English proficiency, may be employed as aids in the admission process, they should not be used as the sole or most important criterion in the selection of foreign students for admission. With reference to evaluating foreign applicants' performance on standardized external English proficiency tests, close cooperation between the admissions officer and the institution's teacher(s) of English as a second language and/or the FSA is indispensable.

3. *Foreign student recruitment.* Responsible recruitment of foreign students should be in accordance with established and tested standards regularly applied to United States and foreign students. This is especially important when an institution finds the recruitment of foreign students attractive as a means of building up declining enrollments or otherwise meeting institutional goals. Statements describing and supporting these standards have been prepared by such professional organizations as the College Entrance Examination Board, the American Association of Collegiate Registrars and Admissions Officers, and NAFSA.

Responsibilities of Teachers of English as a Second Language

In addition to the general obligations noted, teachers of English as a second language (ESL) have the following responsibilities:

1. *Training.* Teachers must be adequately and specifically trained and proficient in the special academic discipline of teaching English as a second language.

2. *Attitude.* The teachers must deal with the second-language learner with the patience and understanding necessary to the student's success but not with undue sympathy, which may jeopardize academic standards and the student's ultimate academic success.

3. *Instruction.* The teachers must assure, insofar as possible, that students receive instruction in all aspects of the English language necessary to their success in the intended academic situation,

recognizing that language competence involves a high degree of acculturation and a great deal of knowledge above and beyond vocabulary and grammar.

4. *Interpretation.* Teachers of ESL must understand and interpret to faculty and administrative colleagues the realities of language acquisition, including those linguistic areas which students may justifiably be expected to master and those which they are not likely to acquire.

5. *Communication.* Teachers, through their special relationship developed with students, may receive significant information concerning problems and needs of foreign students and may communicate this information to the foreign student adviser or other appropriate campus official in a confidential and professional manner when it would be in the students' interest to do so.

6. *Referral.* Teachers of ESL should not become involved in trying to solve the personal or academic problems of foreign students but should encourage students to seek assistance from other appropriate people and agencies on the campus and should help support those people or agencies in their relationships with students.

7. *Professional relationships.* The teachers should work closely with other people and agencies on the campus and in the community to help them understand the nature and extent of foreign students' linguistic problems and to advise them of ways in which they can appropriately assist students to overcome their language handicaps without lowering academic standards.

8. *Research and professional development.* Teachers should constantly maintain their own levels of professional preparation and scholarship intended to increase knowledge concerning language acquisition and other aspects of international educational interchanges.

Responsibilities of Community Activities Programmers

In addition to the general obligations noted, community activities programmers, whether paid or unpaid, full or part time, have the following obligations:

1. *Community access.* Community activities programmers help facilitate access to the community for foreign students and scholars by providing opportunities for relationships with local families and participation in a variety of social, cultural, governmental, religious, educational, commercial, or industrial institutions and activities in the society.

2. *Coordination of campus and community programs.* Community activities and services should be carefully coordinated with campus programs, so that they will complement rather than compete with each other and so that students and scholars may be referred from campus to community, and vice versa, to obtain the most appropriate and effective services and experiences.

3. *Knowledge of the educational institution and learning process.* Community activities programmers should familiarize themselves thoroughly with the work and functions of those campus agencies and offices with whom they work most closely, especially the foreign student adviser and the English-language programs. In this way, they will know when problems or situations should be resolved primarily on the campus or community level.

4. *Training.* Community program representatives should be adequately trained to ensure that they deal patiently and sensitively with all foreign students and scholars, respecting the individuality and cultural background of each student. In addition, they should serve as educators, working with both foreign students and United States community people, so that each may derive maximum benefits and understanding from contact with each other.

5. *Support services for dependents.* Community activities programmers should be aware that many foreign students and scholars are married and either leave the members of their immediate families in their home countries or strive to bring them with them to the United States. Community groups have unique opportunities to provide to this group additional support services, homes-away-from-homes, and programs and learning opportunities for "dependents."

6. *Professional growth and development.* Whether they are a part of university structures or maintain their own independent identities, community activities programmers, whether paid or unpaid,

are discharging their functions in a professional manner. Therefore, they should explore, and be aided in this effort, further opportunities for personal and professional growth. For this purpose,
they should acquaint themselves with all available campus, community, and national resources from which they can obtain additional training in community leadership and self-actualization
which community involvement brings. In return, they should assist
newcomers with their personal and professional growth.

7. *Confidentiality.* Community activities programmers and
their associates obtain considerable personal information about
foreign students and scholars through community contact. The
confidentiality of such information must be protected. Urgent
problems and needs of these foreign students and scholars should
be communicated to the foreign student advisers or other appropriate campus officials.

8. *Flexibility and innovativeness.* Community activities programmers should be aware that the needs of visitors and programs
may change from time to time due to changing international relations, changing needs of visitors over duration of stay, or changing
needs due to variety of cultural backgrounds. Community services
and programs should be sufficiently flexible and innovative to meet
these changing needs.

9. *Responsibility to entire community.* Although their functions
may be limited, community activities programmers have a special
and unique responsibility to assure that the entire community from
which they come is aware of the unique opportunities which this
community has in learning about the world and other countries
and cultures.

10. *Research and evaluation.* As professionals, community activities programmers should strive to add to available knowledge
about the field and its dynamics through research, evaluation of
programs, writing of program descriptions, and collecting of case
studies.

11. *Religious and political groups.* Community workers related
to religious and political groups must recognize that the religions
and political beliefs of any foreign people in the United States are
important parts of their cultural heritage and merit the respect of
Americans and the effort by Americans to learn about and under-

stand them. Religious and political groups can perform a service by providing opportunities for foreign students and scholars to observe and join in mutual inquiry into beliefs and practices. However, there must never be any attempt to proselyte, and any invitation to a foreign student or scholar to an event sponsored by a religious or political group should clearly indicate the nature of the event and its sponsorship.

Responsibilities of Advisers to U.S. Students, Staff on Study, Travel, Employment, Service Abroad

In addition to the general obligations noted, the advisers of United States students and staff going abroad have the following responsibilities:

1. *Information.* The advisers are responsible for collecting, organizing, and making available current information on study, independent and group travel, short- or long-term employment, volunteer service, exchange traineeships, home-stay programs, and other opportunities for meaningful experiences outside the United States available to students and staff. Information should include all programs and opportunities offered by or available through the home campus or other institutions and organizations. Insofar as possible, information should be available on programs and opportunities known to be of acceptable quality in content and management. In cases where students are interested in programs of doubtful or unknown quality, the adviser should be prepared to assist them in an honest and fruitful evaluation of the program to determine the extent to which the students' objectives will be met if they participate.

2. *Student Advising.*

a. Objectives. The objectives of advising should be to encourage students to undertake opportunities in other countries which will be educationally and culturally beneficial, and to help them judge the quality, value, and appropriateness of overseas opportunities and services they are considering.

b. Preparation. It is essential that the adviser be familiar with the curricula and requirements of the home campus to be able to advise students desiring to interrupt their studies for nonacademic experiences in other countries. Knowledge of relevant on-campus resources, such as library materials, foreign students and faculty, and United States students and faculty returned from overseas experiences, is very desirable. The adviser must also know the basic criteria for evaluating study programs and other opportunities in other countries and be familiar with the nature, content, sponsorship, and reputation of a wide range of those available.

c. Advance planning. Students should be encouraged and helped to begin their investigation and planning processes as early as possible.

d. Factors to be considered. In making choices, factors to be considered include location, institutional sponsorship or connection, language requirements, orientation, academic content and standards, available supervision, acceptability of credits, cost, financial aids, living arrangements, accident and health insurance, transportation, the country's entry requirements, degree of cultural difference and student's adjustment capability, and contact with host-country nationals.

e. Income-producing services. Advising offices may legitimately become involved in sales of International Student Identity Cards, Youth Hostel memberships, charter flights for large groups of students or alumni, or relevant books and publications.

3. *Faculty and staff advising.* Although most overseas opportunities offices are focused on students, they should also provide services to faculty and staff interested in study, research, employment, or travel abroad.

4. *Publicity.* Although the advisers should be involved in encouraging and publicizing overseas opportunities and programs, they should avoid innocently publicizing undesirable programs through such devices as posters on department bulletin boards, advertising in student newspapers, or hired student representatives.

5. *Study-abroad programming and standards.* Whether or not advisers are administratively responsible for the institution's study-abroad program planning, development, operation, evaluation, and establishment of standards, they should be actively involved in and familiar with these aspects and should cooperate with others concerned to strengthen, extend, and diversify quality study-abroad opportunities for students.

3. Standards and Principles For Nonformal Education

Foreign students come to the United States for a variety of objectives. Their primary purpose is academic education and training, often needed in their countries. This is also the primary objective of most of our educational institutions, of sponsoring agencies, and of policies and legislation of governments that encourage international educational interchanges. However, informal, out-of-class experiences, if well planned and executed, can have high educational value in their own right and should be encouraged as an integral part of an international educational program. These programs should be guided by standards and principles described in the following pages.

Needs for Nonformal Education

Four factors are emerging which indicate significant adjustments are needed in the traditional thinking about the nature of cross-cultural educational experiences:

1. "Incidental learning" obtained from nonclassroom education is often as important to the individuals as traditional academic education.

2. In many fields foreign students need meaningful nonclassroom experiences in order to understand their educational program in relation to the United States cultural setting, and thereby more readily adapt it to conditions in their home countries.

3. United States students need increasing exposure to persons of other cultures in order to enrich their own educational experiences for their careers in this and the next century.

4. Research and experiences continue to document that meaningful interpersonal contact with members of other countries and cultures can lead to understanding of social, educational, economic, cultural, and political interactions and ultimately to improved international relations.

Purposes

Although many activities develop spontaneously, there is an area of responsibility which professional personnel in international educational interchanges should accept for the following purposes:

1. To provide, through the presence of foreign students on our campuses, a unique opportunity for students of various cultures to have mutually beneficial experiences together, thus simulating conditions of real international relations among states and peoples.

2. To enable both foreign and United States students to develop meaningful and supportive relationships and friendships.

3. To give foreign students an opportunity for participation in campus life, including student organizations, student governance, university governance, and educational, cultural, and recreational activities. For many foreign students, this may be the only leadership training opportunity in the United States. As participants and leaders, foreign students should maintain the same standards of effectiveness and responsibility as United States students.

4. To offer foreign students, on the other hand, an opportunity to organize themselves in ways which would permit them to maintain their national and cultural identities and facilitate reentry into their home countries.

5. To provide these specific and unique educational benefits through meaningful and sophisticated programs of intercultural exposure, presently not available in typical academic programs of our educational institutions:

a. For foreign students:

Development of leadership skills.

Synthesis of their education in the United States.

Perspective on conditions in the home countries.

Building of long-lasting relationships with Americans and other foreign students.

Acquisition of practical skills of cross-cultural communication and relations needed both here and upon return home.

b. For United States students:

First-hand experiences in dealing with members of other cultures.

Development of skills in cross-cultural communication and relations needed to relate to people of other cultures, as well as to varied subcultural groups within the United States.

Experiences in comparative thinking and analysis.

Understanding cultural dimensions of their fields of study.

Realistic retrospect and perspective of how others see us, which has a bearing on the future tasks and problems facing young Americans.

Principles

In the pursuit of these goals, the following principles should be considered:

1. Universities and colleges should strive to create an atmosphere conducive to meaningful intercultural experiences for all students. Research indicates that chance encounters are inadequate and often detrimental.

2. Sponsors should plan campus programs in ways which will assure *mutual* benefits for both foreign and United States students.

3. Social activities should be balanced with a variety of other educational, cultural, and intellectual programs.

4. Sponsored events should assure that wide public participation is not only tolerated but welcome.

5. Leadership and membership in campus organizations should be open to all interested students, with United States student hosts urged to invite foreign student participation.

6. Relationships between officers of student organizations and members of the staff and faculty of our colleges and universities should be clearly defined.

7. Purposes of public meetings should be clearly publicized and articulated, and efforts should be made, where necessary, to interpret these purposes cross-culturally, especially in cases of political or religious activities.

8. Expected outcomes of participation in campus programs should be equally well defined and articulated.

9. Careful and meaningful advance consultation should take place when programs are being planned for a specific group of students by another group or agency.

10. Campus programs and activities should be conducted in accordance with principles of cultural sensitivity and prevailing university rules and standards of accountability.

11. Sponsors of programs should be encouraged to strive for high quality, good taste, and equal time for opposing points of view.

12. The institution regularly should provide meaningful

training in leadership skills and dynamics of cross-cultural groups whenever necessary.

13. There should be active encouragement to foreign students to run for student offices and share in the responsibilities for student organization activities and participation in institutional governance.

14. Student programs should be evaluated against their stated objectives, especially where funds raised from others have been used in the programs.

15. Above all, the universities should assure that student activities, like academic activities, are conducted in an atmosphere of full academic freedom. Free inquiry and free expression must be assured. As members of the academic community, both United States and foreign students should be encouraged to practice and develop capacity for critical judgment and engage in the search for truth. Neither individuals nor organizations must interfere in the pursuit of the academic freedom of other individuals or groups.

Special Activities

In addition to traditional social, educational, cultural, and sports events and programs, festivals, and dramatic presentations, professional staff should be involved in a variety of new, innovative, or experimental programs involving foreign and United States students. In these rapidly changing fields in which modern social and behavioral sciences make constant contributions, experimentation and innovation should be encouraged, and application of new methods attempted even in traditional programs. A great deal of activity with exciting potential exists in orientation and campus programs for:

1. Foreign students to adjust to American education.

2. Foreign students to learn about American life and culture.

3. United States students to learn about the dynamics of living and adjusting to other cultures.

4. United States students to study and learn about other countries, cultures, and languages.

5. Training both United States and foreign students in cultural awareness.

6. Training both groups in cross-cultural communication.

7. Training both groups in global awareness and interdependence.

8. Training both groups in understanding the processes of national development.

Curricular Activities

Research and experience indicate that understanding other cultures is a result of a combination of cognitive and experiential learning. Foreign students have the advantage of being taught cognitively about the United States, while they at the same time experience living here. The vast majority of United States students not only do not receive academic training in other cultures, but they also infrequently have opportunities for meaningful cross-cultural experiences.

Where possible, faculty and administrators should be encouraged to:

1. Encourage faculty members to utilize the presence of foreign students for cross-cultural education of their United States students, and vice versa, through curricular experiences, new courses, practica, fieldwork, or laboratories.

2. Assure that such experiences include meaningful interpersonal interaction through interviews, simulation games, task participation, and other appropriate techniques.

3. Encourage foreign students to volunteer their time and knowledge for the education of United States students.

4. External Relations

Professional standards discussed earlier in this publication have related to individual professional people as they deal with students, staff, and faculty within their institutions. It is also important to have a body of standards which addresses the relations of the professionals and their institutions to those outside, such as governments, organizations, foundations, corporations, home country universities, and families. In the area of international interchange, there are many significant extrainstitutional people and organizations with which the professionals in the field must establish and maintain relationships.

Many of the foreign students and staff with whom institutional or local professionals in the field deal are also in direct or indirect contact with outside, often non–United States, organizations which have their own goals and professional standards. Since both may directly be involved in a situation involving the same student, there is a potential source for conflict of two standards of ethics. In the case of conflict, the *Guidelines* which institutions and professional people should follow are listed below.

Self-Determination

Foreign students and faculty must be responsible for their own actions and behavior. Individuals must decide their own goals and objectives and how they best should be advanced. Students and faculty also have a right to determine for themselves their own goals and objectives and to work towards these goals.

Free Inquiry and Expression

Free inquiry and expression are indispensable and inseparable. Students, whether from the United States or other countries, are encouraged to develop a capacity for critical judgment and an independent search for truth. This means specifically that foreign students are full participants in academic pursuits and have the right to seek formal and informal knowledge, verbal or written, in whatever direction and with whatever legitimately appropriate associations are necessary, without fear of reprisal.

Freedom of Association

An individual should have the right to choose any social, cultural, or political action or activity, as long as these activities do not infringe on or abridge the rights and freedoms of other individuals or groups.

Institutional Rights

An educational institution reserves for itself the following rights:

1. Determination of its educational programs and degree requirements.

2. Determination of admission requirements as to (a) who should be admitted, (b) what requirements are necessary, (c) how an education should be paid for, (d) how diversified a student population should be.

3. Developing policies ensuring that foreign students will be sufficiently financed, with or without institutional participation.

4. Developing policies ensuring that entering foreign students not only can meet admission requirements but also can complete degree requirements.

5. Governance of itself, including enforcement of educational policies.

6. Individuals, as students in academic institutions, have the right to seek total personal growth and development, rather than restricting their growth to academic activities leading to a degree.

7. An institution may choose to withhold cooperation with an outside agency which does not have legitimate governmental authority mandating such cooperation.

Right to Privacy

As outlined in federal, state, and institutional legislation, students enrolled at United States educational institutions have a guaranteed right to privacy. This right to privacy cannot be abridged by the institution or any outside agency.

Additional Expectations

In addition to these *Guidelines* for interaction with outside organizations or individuals, institutions enrolling foreign students have expectations which are held important:

1. Agreements between students, governments, sponsors, and others should be open and fully disclosed.

2. Arbitrary changes in agreements with students should not be made.

5. Student Responsibilities in International Interchanges

Most of the principles and responsibilities described in this *Guideline* relate to the work done by professional people involved in international educational interchange. These principles are within the control of professional people and United States institutions. This is not the case, however, with responsibilities incumbent on the students themselves when they are studying outside of their home countries. These responsibilities can only be hoped for and encouraged by professionals, whose influence in eliciting their observance must be limited to persuasion and education. Professionals can expect that all participants in the international interchange of persons will:

1. Strive to understand and tolerate a host country's educational and cultural setting, including standards of conduct, law, respect for others, honesty, and integrity.

2. Respect rights of self-determination of others.

3. Observe the laws and respect the culture of the host country.

4. Participate as fully as possible in the life of the host university and country.

5. Seek to participate in joint and cooperative ventures of an educational, social, or cultural nature with citizens and students of the host country and with other international students and scholars.

6. Individually and in groups, act with respect for the rights of persons from other countries, cultures, and subcultures, without abridging those rights even in the pursuit of one's own rights.

7. In general, by actions and deeds, accept responsibility for the best interests of international educational interchange programs, so as to gain the largest amount of public support for them, and the widest possible involvement in them.

6. Decisions with Respect to Study-Abroad Programs

Desirable Percentage of Students to Study Abroad

Each institution must decide the degree to which study abroad can contribute to its educational objectives. Involvements may vary from one single program to a required academic experience abroad.

Operational Pattern

Options for operational patterns are numerous and should be determined by the character of teaching of the institutional mode. Some institutions prefer to operate their own study-abroad programs, while others join consortia of United States institutions, contract with foreign universities to accept their students, use programs of private commercial organizations, encourage their students to apply directly to institutions, or approve independent study projects of individual students.

Group Programs Operated by a U.S. Campus

If an institution elects to operate its own study-abroad programs, many decisions must be made and considerable advance planning undertaken.

1. *Instructional pattern.* Students may enroll in regular classes of a foreign university or in universities or private institutions for foreign students. The program may be managed by a home-campus faculty director with instruction by qualified locally hired instructors at the program site, or home-campus faculty may be sent to do all the instruction.

2. *Subject fields.* While foreign languages still play a strong part in study abroad, they no longer dominate curricula abroad. Virtually every field has its international and comparative dimensions and might advantageously be studied in some other part of the world.

3. *Program length.* Study programs for academic credit vary

from one week to one year or more in length. Academic year, semester, six to eight weeks in the summer, and two- to four-week interim terms are common patterns. Value to participants is usually greater in the longer programs.

4. *Program size.* Experience suggests that the optimum group size is 25 to 35 students to maximize cultural interaction for the group in a host country, to allow for effective administration by a single program director, and to facilitate group travel.

5. *Supervision patterns.* A home-campus faculty director accompanying the group or visiting them several times during their foreign sojourn is common, but foreign student advisers of host institutions, host country nationals employed for the purpose, or even graduate students are possible alternatives.

6. *Funding.* A common practice is for the sponsoring United States institution to fund instruction and supervision as part of its regular budget, or use participants' tuition payments for that purpose. Some prorate the cost among participants, thus confining the opportunity to relatively affluent students. In any case, the students are usually responsible for paying their home-campus tuition and their costs of transportation, housing, health and accident insurance, meals, books, and incidentals while abroad.

7. *Credits and grading.* Decisions must be made as to how many credits will be granted and how and by whom grades will be determined. If grades are given by a foreign institution, translation, certification, and transmission must also be arranged.

8. *Financial aids.* If study-abroad participants are enrolled at their home campuses while earning credits abroad toward their degrees, they should be eligible for virtually any financial aid for which they might qualify if they remained at home.

Appendix F

Joint Statement: Transfer and Award of Academic Credit*

◙ ◙ ◙ ◙ ◙ ◙ ◙ ◙ ◙ ◙ ◙ ◙ ◙ ◙ ◙ ◙ ◙ ◙

This statement is directed to institutions of postsecondary education and others concerned with the transfer of academic credit among institutions and award of academic credit for extrainstitutional learning. Basic to this statement is the principle that each institution is responsible for determining its own policies and practices with regard to the transfer and award of credit. Institutions are encouraged to review their policies and practices periodically to assure that they accomplish the institution's objectives and that they function in a manner that is fair and equitable to students. Any statements, this one or others referred to, should be used as guides, not as substitutes, for institutional policies and practices.

Transfer of credit is a concept that now involves transfer between dissimilar institutions and curricula and recognition of extrainstitutional learning, as well as transfer between institutions and curricula of similar characteristics. As their personal circumstances and educational objectives change, students seek to

*From Wermers (1979).

437

have their learning, wherever and however attained, recognized by institutions where they enroll for further study. It is important for reasons of social equity and educational effectiveness, as well as the wise use of resources, for all institutions to develop reasonable and definitive policies and procedures for acceptance of transfer credit. Such policies and procedures should provide maximum consideration for the individual student who has changed institutions or objectives. It is the receiving institution's responsibility to provide reasonable and definitive policies and procedures for determining a student's knowledge in required subject areas. All institutions have a responsibility to furnish transcripts and other documents necessary for a receiving institution to judge the quality and quantity of the work. Institutions also have a responsibility to advise the students that the work *reflected* on the transcript *may or may not* be accepted by a receiving institution.

Interinstitutional Transfer of Credit

Transfer of credit from one institution to another involves at least three considerations: (1) the educational quality of the institution from which the student transfers; (2) the comparability of the nature, content, and level of credit earned to that offered by the receiving institution; and (3) the appropriateness and applicability of the credit earned to the programs offered by the receiving institution, in light of the student's educational goals.

Accredited Institutions

Accreditation speaks primarily to the first of these considerations, serving as the basic indicator that an institution meets certain minimum standards. Users of accreditation are urged to give careful attention to the accreditation conferred by accrediting bodies recognized by the Council on Postsecondary Accreditation (COPA). COPA has a formal process of recognition which requires that any accrediting body so recognized must meet the same standards. Under these standards, COPA has recognized a number of accrediting bodies, including: (1) regional accrediting commissions (which historically accredited the more traditional colleges and universities but which now accredit proprietary, vocational-technical, and single-purpose institutions as well); (2) national accrediting bodies that accredit various kinds of specialized institutions; and (3) certain professional organizations that accredit free-standing professional schools, in addition to programs within multipurpose institutions. (COPA annually publishes a list of recognized accrediting bodies, as well as a directory of institutions accredited by these organizations.)

Although accrediting agencies vary in the ways they are organized and in their statements of scope and mission, all accrediting bodies that meet COPA's standards for recognition function to assure that the institutions or programs they accredit have met generally accepted minimum standards for accreditation.

Accreditation affords reason for confidence in an institution's or a program's purposes, in the appropriateness of its resources and plans for carrying out these purposes, and in its effectiveness in accomplishing its goals, insofar as these things can be judged. Accrediation speaks to the probability, but does not guarantee, that students have met acceptable standards of educational accomplishment.

Comparability and Applicability

Comparability of the nature, content, and level of transfer credit and the appropriateness and applicability of the credit earned to programs offered by the receiving institution are as important in the evaluation process as the accreditation status of the institution at which the transfer credit was awarded. Since accreditation does not address these questions, this information must be obtained from catalog and other materials and from direct contact between knowledgeable and experienced faculty and staff at both the receiving and sending institutions. When such considerations as comparability and appropriateness of credit are satisfied, however, the receiving institution should have reasonable confidence that students from accredited institutions are qualified to undertake the receiving institution's educational program.

Admissions and Degree Purposes

At some institutions there may be differences between the acceptance of credit for admission purposes and the applicability of credit for degree purposes. A receiving institution may accept previous work, place a credit value on it, and enter it on the transcript. However, that previous work, because of its nature and not its inherent quality, may be determined to have no applicability to a specific degree to be pursued by the student. Institutions have a responsibility to make this distinction, and its implications, clear to students before they decide to enroll. This should be a matter of full disclosure, with the best interests of the student in mind. Institutions also should make every reasonable effort to reduce the gap between credits accepted and credit applied toward an educational credential.

Unaccredited Institutions

Institutions of postsecondary education that are not accredited by COPA-recognized accrediting bodies may lack that status for reasons unrelated to questions of quality. Such institutions, however, cannot provide a reliable, third-party assurance that they meet or exceed minimum standards. That being the case, students transferring from such institutions may encounter special problems in gaining acceptance and transferring credits to accredited institutions. Institutions admitting students from unaccredited institutions should take special steps to validate credits previously earned.

Foreign Institutions

In most cases, foreign institutions are chartered and authorized by their national governments, usually through a ministry of education. Although this provides for a standardization within a country, it does not produce useful information about comparability from one country to another. No other nation has a system comparable to voluntary accreditation. The Division of Higher Education of the United Nations Educational, Scientific, and Cultural Organization (UNESCO) is engaged in a project to develop international compacts for the acceptance of educational credentials. At the operational level, four organizations—the Council on International Educational Exchange (CIEE), the National Council on Evaluation of Foreign Student Credentials (CEC), the National Association for Foreign Affairs (NAFA), and the National Liaison Committee on Foreign Student Admissions (NLC)—often can assist institutions by distributing general guidelines on admission and placement of foreign students. Equivalency or placement recommendations are to be evaluated in terms of the programs and policies of the individual receiving institution.

Validation of Extrainstitutional and Experiental Learning for Transfer Purposes

Transfer-of-credit policies should encompass educational accomplishment attained in extrainstitutional settings as well as at accredited postsecondary institutions. In deciding on the award of credit for extrainstitutional learning, institutions will find the services of the American Council on Education's Office of Educational Credit helpful. One of the office's functions is to operate and foster programs to determine credit equivalencies for various modes of extrainstitutional learning. The office maintains evaluation programs for formally structured courses offered by the military and by civilian noncollegiate sponsors such as businesses, corporations, government agencies, and labor unions. Evaluation services are also available for examination programs, for occupations with validated job proficiency evaluation systems, and for correspondence courses offered by schools accredited by the National Home Study Council. The results are published in a Guide series. Another resource is the General Educational Development (GED) Testing Program, which provides a means for assessing high school equivalency.

For learning that has not been validated through the ACE formal credit recommendation process or through credit-by-examination programs, institutions are urged to explore the Council for Advancement of Experiential Learning (CAEL) procedures and processes. Pertinent CAEL publications designed for this purpose are also listed.

Uses of this Statement

This statement has been endorsed by the three national associations most concerned with practices in the area of transfer and award of credit: the American Association of Collegiate Registrars and Admissions Officers, the American Council on Education/ Commission on Educational Credit, and the Council of Postsecondary Accreditation.

Institutions are encouraged to use this statement as a basis for discussions in developing or reviewing institutional policies with regard to transfer. If the statement reflects an institution's policies, that institution might want to use this publication to inform faculty, staff, and students.

It is recommended that accrediting bodies reflect the essential precepts of this statement in their criteria.

AACRAO
Code of Ethics

◻ ◻ ◻ ◻ ◻ ◻ ◻ ◻ ◻ ◻ ◻ ◻ ◻ ◻ ◻ ◻ ◻ ◻

The American Association of Collegiate Registrars and Admissions Officers, vitally concerned with the advancement of postsecondary education, has adopted the following code of ethics, exemplifying those qualities and attributes which have distinguished members of the Association both past and present:

1. A belief in, and loyalty to, the philosophy and goals of the profession and the institutions we serve.
2. An understanding of, and respect for, the rights and responsibilities of those who serve and are served by postsecondary education.
3. Courage to experiment with procedures and to initiate policies which will support the goals of our profession.
4. Willingness to assert ourselves when policies or practices are proposed which seem to be contrary to the philosophy and goals of our profession and our institutions.
5. Responsive participation in professional activities and their development to ensure effective and efficient management of data and personnel.
6. Presentation of an accurate interpretation of our institutions' admission criteria, educational costs, and major offerings to

assist prospective students and their parents in making a wise choice.

7. A sincere effort to assist in the improvement of the educational standards and evaluative methods of courses and grading which are meaningful in reflecting the academic achievement of students.

8. A sensitive appreciation of the dynamics of interpersonal relationships when dealing with students, parents, faculty, administration, associates, and the public.

9. A commitment to the development of data systems which will ensure the integrity of institutional records and the accurate interpretation of resulting data.

10. A dedication to ideals which will serve in the development of students' talents and interests in order that they may become responsible contributors to the improvement of society.

11. The practice of honesty and integrity in all our activities.

Bibliography

□ □ □ □ □ □ □ □ □ □ □ □ □ □ □ □ □

Abernathy, L. "Highlighting What's New in Admissions." *College Board Review*, 1976, *100*, 29–35.

Ainsworth, W. "The Primacy of the User." *Infosystems*, April 1977, pp. 46–48.

Allison, V. M., Schmidt, R. P., and Sperry, F. E. "The Use of Computer Output Microfilm at the University of Wisconsin— Milwaukee." Paper presented at College and University Machine Records Conference, May 1970.

Almond, M. "An Algorithm for Constructing University Timetables." Paper presented at Queen Mary College, University of London, 1965.

Alter, S. L. "How Effective Managers Use Information Systems." *Harvard Business Review*, Sept.–Oct. 1976, pp. 97–104.

American Association of Collegiate Registrars and Admissions Officers. *Professional Training Recommended for the Registrar and Admissions Officer.* Washington, D.C.: American Association of Collegiate Registrars and Admissions Officers, 1954.

American Association of Collegiate Registrars and Admissions Officers. *Retention of Records: A Guide for Registrars and Admissions Officers in Collegiate Institutions.* Washington, D.C.: American Association of Collegiate Registrars and Admissions Officers, 1960.

American Association of Collegiate Registrars and Admissions Officers. *The University Calendar.* Washington, D.C.: American Association of Collegiate Registrars and Admissions Officers, 1961.

American Association of Collegiate Registrars and Admissions

Officers. *Optical Scanning Applications in Higher Education.* Washington, D.C.: American Association of Collegiate Registrars and Admissions Officers, 1972.

American Association of Collegiate Registrars and Admissions Officers. *A Guide to Postsecondary Institutions for Implementation of the Family Educational Rights and Privacy Act of 1974, as Amended.* Washington, D.C.: American Association of Collegiate Registrars and Admissions Officers, 1976.

American Association of Collegiate Registrars and Admissions Officers. *Academic Record and Transcript Guide.* Washington, D.C.: American Association of Collegiate Registrars and Admissions Officers, 1977.

American Association of Collegiate Registrars and Admissions Officers and American Council on Education. *Recruitment, Admissions and Handicapped Students: A Guide for Compliance with Section 504 of the Rehabilitation Act of 1973.* Washington, D.C.: American Association of Collegiate Registrars and Admissions Officers and American Council on Education, 1978.

American Association of Collegiate Registrars and Admissions Officers and National Association of College Admissions Counselors. *Professional Audit for Admissions Officers.* Washington, D.C.: American Association of Collegiate Registrars and Admissions Officers, 1977.

"American Association of Collegiate Registrars and Admissions Officers Code of Ethics." *College and University,* 1975, *50* (4), 807–808.

American College Testing Program. "The ACT-APP Concept." In *Good Users of ACT Data and Services.* Iowa City, Iowa: American College Testing Program, 1975.

American College Testing Program. *Handbook for Financial Aid Administrators for the 1979–80 Academic Year.* Iowa City, Iowa: American College Testing Program, 1978.

American Council on Education. *A Fact Book on Higher Education.* (3rd ed.) Washington, D.C. American Council on Education, 1971.

American Council on Education. "An Academic Costume Code and an Academic Ceremony Guide." In *American Universities and Colleges* (11th ed.) Washington, D.C.: American Council on Education, 1973.

American Council on Education. *Guide to the Evaluation of Educational Experiences in the Armed Services.* Washington, D.C.: American Council on Education, 1976.

American Council on Education. *Recommendations on Credentialing Educational Accomplishment.* Washington, D.C.: American Council on Education, 1978a.

American Council on Education. *The Bakke Decision: Implications for Higher Education Admissions.* Washington, D.C.: American Council on Education, 1978b.

American National Standards Committee and Computer and Business Equipment Manufacturers Association. *American National Dictionary for Information Processing.* Washington, D.C.: American National Standards Committee and Computer and Business Equipment Manufacturers Association, 1977.

American National Standards Institute. *American National Standards for Information Processing.* New York: American National Standards Institute, 1970.

Astin, A. W. *Preventing Students from Dropping Out.* San Francisco: Jossey-Bass, 1975.

Avedon, D. M. *National Standard Glossary of Micrographics.* Silver Spring, Md.: National Microfilm Association, 1971.

Awad, E. M. *Automatic Data Processing Principles and Procedures.* Englewood Cliffs, N.J.: Prentice-Hall, 1966.

Babbott, E. F. "A Year Early: What 378 Colleges Say About Admitting Students Right After Their Junior Year of High School." *College Board Review,* 1973, *1* (10), 32–33.

Baehne, G. W. *Practical Applications of the Punched Card Method in Colleges and Universities.* New York: Columbia University Press, 1935.

Bailey, J. S. "Ceremonies and Special Events." In A. S. Knowles (Ed.), *Handbook of College and University Administration. Vol. 1: General.* New York: McGraw-Hill, 1970.

Barnett, A. "The Systems Man's Role in Systems Development." *Barnett Data Systems,* 1971, pp. 1–12.

Bell, D. J., Melott, R., and Wooley, D. R. "Three Operational On-Line Registration Systems." *College and University,* 1977, *52* (4), 434–448.

Benedict, B. N., and O'Connell, J. W. "Attacking the Data Management Problem: Selecting a Minicomputer to Manage Student

Data at Berkeley." Paper presented at College and University Machine Records Conference, May 1978.

Benson, A. G., and Kovach, J. (Eds.). *A Guide to the Education of Foreign Students*. Washington, D.C.: National Association for Foreign Student Affairs, 1974.

Biehl, G. R. *Guide to the Section 504 Self-Evaluation for Colleges and Universities*. Washington, D.C.: National Association of College and University Business Officers, 1978.

Blakesley, J. F. "A Data Processing System for Scheduling University Students to Classes Using an Intermediate-Speed Digital Computer." Unpublished master's dissertation, Purdue University, 1960.

Bocchino, W. A. *Management Information Systems*. Englewood Cliffs, N.J.: Prentice-Hall, 1972.

Bogard, K., Patterson, R. A., and Scriven, J. "Building a Class Schedule and Space Assignment: A Computer Assisted System." *College and University*, 1977, *52* (4), 430–434.

Bouwman, C. H. "History of the 4-1-4 Program." *College and University*, 1970, *45* (4), 625–640.

Bowen, W. G. "Admissions and the Relevance of Race." *Educational Record*, 1977, *58* (4), 333–349.

Bradley, W. P. "Is Virtual Memory for Real?" *Infosystems*, Sept. 1973, pp. 80–82.

Broder, S. "Final Examination Scheduling." *Communications of the ACM*, 1964, 7 (8), 494–495.

Bruker, R. M. *A Survey of Salary Levels in the Admissions and Records Profession*. Washington, D.C.: American Association of Collegiate Registrars and Admissions Officers, 1977.

Bureau of the Budget. *Automatic Data Processing Glossary*. Washington, D.C.: Bureau of the Budget, 1962.

Buros, O. K. (Ed.). *The Seventh Mental Measurements Yearbook*. (3 vols.) Highland Park, N.J.: Gryphon Press, 1972.

Bury, J. B. *The Cambridge Medieval History*. Cambridge, England: Cambridge University Press, 1964.

Caffery, J., and Mosmann, C. J. *Computers on Campus*. Washington, D.C.: American Council on Education, 1967.

Carbone, R. F. *Students and State Borders*. ACT Special Report 7. Iowa City, Iowa: American College Testing Program, 1973.

Carnegie Commission on Higher Education. *Less Time, More Options.* New York: McGraw-Hill, 1971.

Carnegie Commission on Higher Education. *The More Effective Use of Resources.* New York: McGraw-Hill, 1972.

Carnegie Council on Policy Studies in Higher Education. *Selective Admissions in Higher Education: Comment and Recommendations and Two Reports.* San Francisco: Jossey-Bass, 1977.

Cashwell, R. "What's So Sacred About May 1 and November 1?" *College Board Review,* 1976, *101,* 20–22.

Cass, J., and Birnbaum, M. *Comparative Guide to American Colleges.* New York: Harper & Row, 1977.

Chalmers, J. A. "The Effective Admissions Officer." *College and University,* 1975, *50* (4), 647–657.

"The Changing Academic Calendars." *Chronicle of Higher Education,* 1978, *15* (18), 13.

Cleary, T. A., and others. "Educational Uses of Tests with Disadvantaged Students." *American Psychologist,* 1975, *30* (1), 15–41.

Cleveland, H. "The Education of Administrators for Higher Education." Fourth David D. Henry Lecture, University of Illinois, Urbana, April 1977.

Cole, A. J. "The Preparation of Examination Timetables Using a Small Store Computer." *Computer Journal,* 1964, *7* (2), 117.

College Entrance Examination Board. *A Chance to Go to College.* New York: College Entrance Examination Board, 1971.

College Entrance Examination Board. *A Role for Marketing in College Admissions.* New York: College Entrance Examination Board, 1976.

College Entrance Examination Board. *On Further Examination: Report of the Advisory Panel on the Scholastic Aptitude Test Score Decline.* New York: College Entrance Examination Board, 1977.

College Entrance Examination Board. *The Bakke Decision: Retrospect and Prospect.* New York: College Entrance Examination Board, 1978.

College Scholarship Service. *Perspective on Financial Aid.* New York: College Entrance Examination Board, 1975.

College Scholarship Service. *Principles of Student Financial Aid Administration.* New York: College Entrance Examination Board, 1976a.

College Scholarship Service. *Practices of Student Financial Aid Administration.* New York: College Entrance Examination Board, 1976b.

College Scholarship Service. *CSS Need Analysis: Theory and Computation Procedures for the 1977–78 PCS* [Parents' Confidential Statement] *and FAF* [Financial Aid Form], *Including Sample Cases and Tables.* New York: College Entrance Examination Board, 1976c.

Committee on Code of Ethics, American Association of Collegiate Registrars. "A Code of Ethics for Registrars." *Proceedings of the American Association of Collegiate Registrars, 13th National Meeting,* 1925, *1,* 259–260.

Constance, C. L. (Ed.). *Historical Review of the Association.* Washington, D.C.: American Association of Collegiate Registrars and Admissions Officers, 1973.

Corson, J. J. *The Governance of Colleges and Universities.* New York: McGraw-Hill, 1975.

Council on Postsecondary Accreditation. *The Balance Wheel for Accreditation.* Washington, D.C.: Council on Postsecondary Accreditation, 1977.

Council on Postsecondary Accreditation. *Accredited Institutions of Postsecondary Education and Programs.* Washington, D.C.: American Council on Education, 1978. (Published annually.)

Cowley, W. H. *A Study of the Relative Merits of the Quarter and Semester Systems.* Columbus: Ohio State University, 1932.

Crawford, A. R. "Publications for Key Audiences." In A. W. Rowland (Ed.), *Handbook of Institutional Advancement: A Practical Guide to College and University Relations, Fund Raising, Alumni Relations, Government Relations, Publications, and Executive Management for Continued Advancement.* San Francisco: Jossey-Bass, 1977.

Daly, L. J. *The Medieval University 1200–1400.* New York: Sheed and Ward, 1961.

Dearden, J. "MIS Is a Mirage." *Harvard Business Review,* Jan.–Feb. 1972, pp. 92–99.

Dexter, F. B. *The Literary Diary of Ezra Stiles.* Vol. 1. New York: Scribner's, 1901.

Dewey, J. *Experience and Education.* New York: Macmillan, 1938.

Dickens, R. L., and Rogers, C. H. "The Duke University Exam Scheduling Program." *College and University,* 1967, *42* (2), 105–116.

Dressel, P. L., and others. *Institutional Research in the University: A Handbook.* San Francisco: Jossey-Bass, 1971.

Drucker, P. "Peter Drucker on Performance and Planning." *Modern Office Procedures,* Oct. 1977, pp. 101–106.

Durant, W. *The Story of Civilization.* Vol. 4: *The Age of Faith: A History of Medieval Civilization—Christian, Islamic, and Judaic—from Constantine to Dante: A.D. 325–1300.* New York: Simon and Schuster, 1950.

Eells, W. C., and Haswell, H. A. *Academic Degrees Earned and Honorary Degrees Conferred by Institutions of Higher Education in the United States.* U.S. Office of Education Bulletin No. 28. Washington, D.C.: U.S. Government Printing Office, 1961.

Ehrensberger, M. "Data Base—The Solution to the Impossible Dream." In *College and University Machine Records Conference Proceedings.* Waco, Texas: Baylor University Press, 1974.

Ekstrom, V. R., and others. *Management of Data for Students II.* Washington, D.C.: American Association of Collegiate Registrars and Admissions Officers, 1972.

El-Khawas, E. H. "A Guide to Fair Practice." *AGB Report,* July-Aug. 1977a, pp. 38–44.

El-Khawas, E.H. *Better Information for Student Choice: Report on a National Task Force.* Washington, D.C.: National Task Force on Better Information for Student Choice, Fund for the Improvement of Postsecondary Education, 1977b.

Fellows, J. E. "Manual of Office Procedure." *College and University,* 1950, *25* (4), 607–610.

Fincher, C. "Standardized Tests, Group Differences, and Public Policy." *College Board Review,* 1977, *103,* 19–31.

Fine, B. *Barron's Profiles of American Colleges.* (10th ed.) Woodbury, N.Y.: Barron's Educational Series, 1976.

Fredenburgh, F. A. "Maximal Utilization of Instructional Time." *College and University,* 1968, *44* (1), 29–34.

Freeman, P. "The Context of Design." In P. Freeman and A. I. Wasserman (Eds.), *Software Design Techniques, IEE/Computer Society.* Long Beach, Calif.: Institute of Electrical and Electronic Engineers, 1977.

Furniss, W. T. (Ed.). "An Academic Costume Code and an Academic Ceremony Guide." In *American Universities and Col-*

leges. (11th ed.) Washington, D.C.: American Council on Education, 1973.

Gerritz, E. M., and Thomas, A., Jr. "The Admissions Office in Twenty-Eight Selected Colleges and Universities." *College and University,* 1953, *29* (1), 65–68.

Giampetro, G., and Rooney, R. "The Use of Direct Mail in Recruitment." *College and University,* 1977, *52* (4), 614–624.

Gillis, E. L. "The Evolution and Development of the Registrar's Office." *Registrar's Journal,* 1939, *14* (2), 114–117.

Goddard, S., Martin, J. S., and Romney, L. C. *Data Element Dictionary.* Boulder, Colo.: National Center for Higher Education Management Systems, 1973.

Green, J. E. "Minicomputers with Vendor Software." *Information & Records Management,* June 1977, p. 10.

Grindley, K., and Humble, J. *The Effective Computer.* New York: McGraw-Hill, 1974.

"Guaranteed Loan Program." *Federal Register,* 1975, *40* (35), III, 7586–7599.

Haines, R. W. "Student Recruitment Practices: A Survey Yields Some Surprises." *National ACAC Journal,* 1975, *20* (1), 35–37.

Halstead, D. K. "Space Management and Projection." In *Statewide Planning in Higher Education.* Washington, D.C.: U.S. Department of Health, Education and Welfare, 1974.

Harris, J. J., III, Pyles, M. H., and Carter, D. G. "The Culturally Different: An Analysis of Factors Influencing Educational Success." *The Clearing House,* 1976, *50,* 39–43.

Harvard University. *Statement of the Treasurer of Harvard College.* Cambridge, Mass: Harvard, Dec. 1824.

Hauser, J., and Lazarsfeld, P. *The Admissions Officer.* New York: College Entrance Examination Board, 1964.

Hefferlin, JB. "Intensive Courses—An Old Idea Whose Time for Testing Has Come." *Journal of Research and Development in Education,* 1972, *6* (1), 83–98.

Higham, R. *The Compleat Academic.* New York: St. Martin's Press, 1974.

Hills, J. R. "Use of Measurement in Selection and Placement." In R. L. Thorndike (Ed.), *Educational Measurement.* (2nd ed.) Washington, D.C.: American Council on Education, 1971.

Hoffman, B. B., and Smith, E. D. *Registration Roulette: A National Study of Schedule Changing with Emphasis on Approaches to Student Behavior and the Involvement of Systems of Registration and Scheduling.* Syracuse, N.Y.: Syracuse University, 1967.

Hopperton, J.D. "Registration Can Be Fun; A Small Computer Can Do It All." *The Journal: Technological Horizons in Education,* Dec. 1975, pp. 23–27.

Hoppner, O. J. (Ed.). *Academic Costume in America.* Albany, N.Y.: Cotrell and Leonard, 1959.

Huffman, D. "Why Optical Character Recognition?" *OCR Today,* 1977, *1* (2), 15–17.

Ihlanfeldt, W. "A Management Approach to the Buyer's Market." *College Board Review,* 1975, *96,* 22–25, 28–32.

International Business Machines Corporation. *Data Processing Glossary.* Poughkeepsie, N.Y.: Programming Systems Publications, 1972.

Jarman, B. H. "The Registrar in Institutions Accredited by the Association of American Universities." *College and University,* 1947, *23* (1), 96–113.

Jass, R. "Build on Strengths—Focus on Contribution." Paper presented at Illinois Association of Collegiate Registrars and Admissions Officers, July 1978.

Jencks, C., and Riesman, D. *The Academic Revolution.* New York: Doubleday, 1969.

John, W. C. *Graduate Studies in Universities and Colleges in the United States.* U.S. Office of Education Bulletin No. 20. Washington, D.C.: U.S. Office of Education, 1935.

Johnston, W. E., Jr. "The Registrar in English Universities." *Association of American Colleges Bulletin,* 1949, *35* (2), 295–301.

Kaplan, A. C., and Veri, C. C. *The Continuing Education Unit.* Information Series No. 1. DeKalb, Ill.: ERIC Clearinghouse in Career Education, 1974.

Kastner, E. C. "The Registrar and Director of Admissions." In G. P. Burns (Ed.), *Administrators in Higher Education: Their Functions and Coordination.* New York: Harper & Row, 1962.

Keller, R. E., and others. "From Admissions to Archives—A Comprehensive Student Information System." *College and University,* 1974, *49* (4), 471–487.

Kentucky Association of Collegiate Registrars and Admissions Officers. *Self-Audit Manual for Registrars.* (2nd ed.) Louisville: Kentucky Association of Collegiate Registrars and Admissions Officers, 1975.

Knowles, A. S. *Handbook of College and University Administration.* Vol. 1: *General;* Vol. 2: *Academic.* New York: McGraw-Hill, 1970.

Kotler, P. *Marketing for Nonprofit Organizations.* Englewood Cliffs, N.J.: Prentice-Hall, 1975.

Kozachok, P. "Brigham Young University: S.C.O.U.T." *Scanning the Educational World,* 1977, *1* (3), 1.

Kramer, G. A. "Admissions as a Profession." *College and University,* 1970, *45* (3), 273–280.

Kuhns, E. P. "Modular Calendar." *College and University,* 1971, *46* (4), 311–317.

Lenning, O. T., and Cooper, E. M. *Guidebook for Colleges and Universities: Presenting Information to Prospective Students.* Boulder, Colo: National Center for Higher Education Management Systems, 1978.

Lindsey, E. E., and Holland, E. O. *College and University Administration.* New York: Macmillan, 1930.

Lovejoy, C. E. *Lovejoy's College Guide.* New York: Simon and Schuster, 1979.

Mahn, R. E. "The Registrar's Primer." *College and University,* 1949, *24* (2), 239–243.

Mahn, R. E. "Our Academic Role." *College and University,* 1966, *42* (1), 93–101.

Mallet, C. E. *A History of the University of Oxford.* London: Methuen, 1924.

Malott, F. S., Mensel, R. F., and Royer, J. T. *Administrative Compensation Survey, 1975–76.* Washington, D.C.: College and University Personnel Association, 1976.

Manning, W. H. "The Pursuit of Fairness in Admissions to Higher Education." In Carnegie Council on Policy Studies in Higher Education, *Selective Admissions in Higher Education,* San Francisco: Jossey-Bass, 1977.

Martorana, S. V., and Kuhns, E. *Managing Academic Change: Interactive Forces and Leadership in Higher Education.* San Francisco: Jossey-Bass, 1975.

McFadden, F. R., and Suver, J. D. "Cost and Benefits of a Data

Base System." *Harvard Business Review,* Jan.–Feb. 1978, pp. 131–139.

McGrath, E. J. "The Evolution of Administrative Offices in Institutions of Higher Education in the United States from 1860 to 1933." Unpublished doctoral dissertation, University of Chicago, 1938.

Menacker, J. *From School to College: Articulation and Transfer.* Washington, D.C.: American Council on Education, 1975.

Metzger, W. P. "What Is a Profession." *College and University,* 1976, *52* (1), 42–55.

Meyer, P. *Awarding College Credit for Non-College Learning: A Guide to Current Practices.* San Francisco: Jossey-Bass, 1975.

Miller, J. E. *Building the Master Schedule of Classes.* University Park: Pennsylvania State University Press, 1968.

Morgan, G. E., and Blakesley, J. F. "A Comprehensive University Scheduling System." Paper presented at the 10th College and University Machine Records Conference, May 1965.

Murdick, R. G., and Ross, J. E. *Information Systems for Modern Management.* Englewood Cliffs, N.J.: Prentice-Hall, 1971.

National Association for Foreign Student Affairs. *A Guide to the Admission of Foreign Students.* Washington, D.C.: National Association for Foreign Student Affairs, 1965.

National Association for Foreign Student Affairs. *Standards and Responsibilities in International Educational Exchange.* Washington, D.C.: National Association for Foreign Student Affairs, 1979.

National Association of College Admissions Counselors. *Statement of Principles of Good Practice.* Skokie, Ill.: National Association of College Admissions Counselors, 1976.

National Association of College and University Business Officers. *A Student Records Manual.* Washington, D.C.: National Association of College and University Business Officers, 1970.

National Association of Secondary School Principals. *Rank-in-Class.* Reston, Va.: National Association of Secondary School Principals, 1972.

National Association of Secondary School Principals. "Guidelines for School-to-College Transcript Content." *Curriculum Report,* 1974, *3* (5).

National Association of Student Financial Aid Administrators. *Statement of Good Practices.* Washington, D.C.: National Association of Student Financial Aid Administrators, n.d.

National Association of Student Personnel Administrators. *Questions and Answers on Regulations Implementing Sec. 504, Rehabilitation Act of 1973 (29 U.S.C. 706).* Portland, Ore.: National Association of Student Personnel Administrators, 1977.

National Bureau of Standards. *Guidelines for Automatic Data Processing, Physical Security and Risk Management.* Washington, D.C.: U.S. Government Printing Office, 1974.

National Center for Education Statistics, U.S. Department of Health, Education and Welfare. *Definitions of Student Personnel Terms in Higher Education.* Washington, D.C.: U.S. Department of Health, Education and Welfare, 1968.

National Task Force on the Continuing Education Unit. *The Continuing Education Unit: Criteria and Guidelines.* Washington, D.C.: National University Extension Association, 1974.

Nolan, R. L. "Computer Data Bases: The Future Is Now." *Harvard Business Review,* Sept.–Oct. 1973, pp. 98-114.

Nolan, R. L. "Controlling the Costs of Data Services." *Harvard Business Review,* July–Aug. 1977, pp. 114-124.

"Nondiscrimination on the Basis of Handicap." *Federal Register,* 1977, *42* (86), IV, 22676-22702.

"Nondiscrimination on Basis of Sex." *Federal Register,* 1975, *40* (108), II, 24128-24145.

Oleson, L. C. *A Report on Academic Calendars.* Washington, D.C.: American Association of Collegiate Registrars and Admissions Officers, 1971.

Oleson, L. C. "Calendar Changes Effective 1974–75." *Newsletter of the American Association of Collegiate Registrars and Admissions Officers,* 1975, *18* (1), 28-33.

Oleson, L. C. "Academic Calendars." In A. S. Knowles (Ed.), *International Encyclopedia of Higher Education.* Vol. 2. San Francisco: Jossey-Bass, 1977a.

Oleson, L. C. "1977 Academic Calendar Survey." Unpublished report. Crete, Neb., Doane College, 1977b.

Oregon State System of Higher Education. *Proposed 1978–79 Admissions Policies for State System Institutions.* Portland: Office of Academic Affairs, Oregon State System of Higher Education, 1977.

Parrott, A. H. "The Genesis of a Registrar." *Registrar's Journal,*

1946, *21* (2), 231–238.

Partridge, F. A. "The Evolution of Administrative Offices in Liberal Arts Colleges from 1875 to 1933." Unpublished master's dissertation, University of Chicago, 1934.

Patrick, W. S. "Nonresident Student Practices." *College and University*, 1976, *51* (3), 291–321.

Perry, M. R. "Commencement and Examination Practices." *College and University*, 1975, *50* (4), 786-793.

Perry, R. R. "The Office of Admissions—Role of the Administrator." In A. S. Knowles (Ed.), *Handbook of College and University Administration*. Vol. 2: *Academic*. New York: McGraw-Hill, 1970.

Peterson, E. D., and Spencer, R. W. "On-Line Admissions and Registrar Systems." A seminar sponsored by EDUCOM and the American Association of Collegiate Registrars and Admissions Officers, 1978.

Peterson, R. G. "The College Catalog as a Contract." *Educational Record*, 1970, *51* (3), 260–266.

Presser, L. "Designing Out the Bugs." *Data Processing Management*, 1977, *2* (1), 5–6.

Price, W. C. "Electronic Data Processing in Collegiate Admissions and Registration Programs." Unpublished doctoral dissertation, University of Missouri-Columbia, 1966.

Price, W. C. "A Computer User Defines the Problem." Unpublished position paper, University of Oklahoma, Norman, 1968.

Price, W. C. "Computer Output Microfilm—A New Management Tool." Paper presented at Microfilm Seminar, Illinois Association of Collegiate Registrars and Admissions Officers, 1972.

Price, W. C., and others. "Systems That Failed." *College and University*, 1973, *48* (4), 378–387.

Privacy Protection Study Commission. *Personal Privacy in an Information Society.* Washington, D.C.: U.S. Government Printing Office, 1977.

Rashdall, H. *The Universities of Europe in the Middle Ages.* Vol. 1. Oxford: Clarendon Press, 1895.

Reynolds, R. L. *List of School Opening and Other Dates.* Oberlin, Ohio: National Association of College Stores, 1972 through 1976. (Mimeographed.)

Rich, C. R. (Ed.). *Problems of Registrars and Admissions Officers in*

Higher Education. Washington, D.C.: Catholic University of America Press, 1955.

Roller, F. E., Edwards, W. M., and Bruker, R. M. "Summer Sessions Are a Part of the Calendar, Too." *College and University,* 1973, *48* (4), 363–378.

Rosenthal, C., McIvor, A. G., and Meadows, G. "How Can Admissions Officers Select Commercial Agencies." *College and University,* 1977, *52* (4), 575–590.

Rowland, A. W. (Ed.). *Handbook of Institutional Advancement: A Practical Guide to College and University Relations, Fund Raising, Alumni Relations, Government Relations, Publications, and Executive Management for Continued Advancement.* San Francisco: Jossey-Bass, 1977.

Rowray, R. D., and others. *Professional Audit for Admissions Officers.* Washington, D.C.: American Association of Collegiate Registrars and Admissions Officers; Skokie, Ill.: National Association of College Admissions Counselors, 1977.

Rudolph, F. *The American College and University.* New York: Knopf, 1962.

Salmen, S. *Duties of Administrators in Higher Education.* New York: Macmillan, 1971.

Sanders, D. H. *Computers and Management in a Changing Society.* New York: McGraw-Hill, 1974.

Shaw, G. W. *Academical Dress of British Universities.* Cambridge, England: W. Heffer & Sons, 1966.

Sheard, K. *Academic Heraldry in America.* Marquette: Northern Michigan College Press, 1962.

Shield, R. "Registration, Scheduling, and Student Records." In A. S. Knowles (Ed.), *Handbook of College and University Administration.* Vol. 2: *Academic.* New York: McGraw-Hill, 1970.

Shoor, R. "Close Encounters of the First Kind: Technician vs. User." *Computerworld,* 1978, *12* (20), 15–19.

Shulman, C. H. *University Admissions: Dilemmas and Potential.* ERIC/Higher Education Report No. 5. Washington, D.C.: American Association for Higher Education, 1977.

Simpson, C. "Computer Sectioning." *College and University,* 1968, *44* (1), 38–46.

Smallwood, M. L. *An Historical Study of Examinations and Grading Systems in Early American Universities.* Cambridge, Mass.: Harvard University Press, 1935.

Smerling, W. H. "The Registrar: Changing Aspects." *College and University,* 1960, *35* (2), 180–186.

Smith, H. H. "Academic Dress and Insignia." In A. S. Knowles (Ed.), *International Encyclopedia of Higher Education.* Vol. 2. San Francisco: Jossey-Bass, 1977.

Smyser, W. C. "Our First Fifty Years." *College and University,* 1960, *35* (4), 435–451.

Southern Association of Colleges and Schools. *The Continuing Education Unit: Guidelines and Other Information.* Atlanta, Ga.: Southern Association of Colleges and Schools, 1973.

Spencer, D. D. *Introduction to Information Processing.* Columbus, Ohio: Merrill, 1974.

Spurr, S. H. *Academic Degree Structures: Innovative Approaches, Principles of Reform in Degree Structures in the United States, Report of the Carnegie Commission on Higher Education.* New York: McGraw-Hill, 1970.

Stout, E. M. "The Origin of the Registrar." *College and University,* 1954, *29* (3), 415–418.

Strassmann, P. A. "Managing the Costs of Information." *Harvard Business Review,* Sept.–Oct. 1976, pp. 133–142.

"Student Consumer Information Services." *Federal Register,* 1977, *42* (231), 61043-61047.

Temmer, H. "A Manager's Bill of Rights." *College and University,* 1970, *45* (4), 328–335.

Temmer, H. "Facilities Utilization Analysis, Classroom Allocation, and Course Scheduling." *College and University,* 1972, *48* (1), 10–20.

Thomason, R. F. "The Origin, Background, and Philosophy of the Office of Admissions and Records." *College and University,* 1953, *29* (1), 100–109.

Thorndike, L. *University Records and Life in the Middle Ages.* New York: Columbia University Press, 1944.

Thornton, J. W., Jr. *The Community Junior College.* (2nd ed.) New York: Wiley, 1966.

Thresher, B. A. *College Admissions and the Public Interest.* New York: College Entrance Examination Board, 1966.

Thresher, B. A. "Admissions in Perspective." In A. S. Knowles (Ed.), *Handbook of College and University Administration.* Vol. 2: *Academic.* New York: McGraw-Hill, 1970.

Tombaugh, R. L. *Financial Aid Administrators Handbook.* Denver, Colo.: Education Methods, 1977.

Treadwell, D. R., Jr. "In Admissions, the Ideal Director Boasts the Speech of Demosthenes and the Patience of Job." *Chronicle of Higher Education,* 1977, *14* (7), 18.

Turner, William L. "The Continuing Education Unit of Measure in Review." *College and University,* 1973, *48* (4), 262–271.

U.S. Department of Health, Education and Welfare. *Report on Higher Education.* Washington, D.C.: U.S. Department of Health, Education and Welfare, 1971.

U.S. Department of Health, Education and Welfare. *Records, Computers and the Rights of Citizens.* Washington, D.C.: U.S. Department of Health, Education and Welfare, 1973.

U.S. Department of Health, Education and Welfare. *Title IX: Selected Resources.* Washington, D.C.: U.S. Department of Health, Education and Welfare, 1977.

U.S. Department of Health, Education and Welfare. *Keeping Your School or College Catalog in Compliance with Federal Laws and Regulations.* Washington, D.C.: U.S. Department of Health, Education and Welfare, 1978.

Van Antwerp, E. S., MacCorkle, D. B., and Wermers, D. J. "Council on Postsecondary Accreditation." *College and University,* 1976, *51* (4), 388–398.

Vinson, D. E. *The Admissions Officer: A Decade of Change.* Dissertation Copy 77–08, 122. Ann Arbor: University Microfilms, 1976.

Volkmann, M. F. "Cost-Saving Devices." In A. W. Rowland (Ed.), *Handbook of Institutional Advancement: A Practical Guide to College and University Relations, Fund Raising, Alumni Relations, Government Relations, Publications, and Executive Management for Continued Advancement.* San Francisco: Jossey-Bass, 1977.

Wagner, E. "Group IV: Data Management and Research." *Newsletter of the American Association of Collegiate Registrars and Admissions Officers,* 1977, *20* (2), 10–11.

Wagner, J. J. "Hierarchical Management Information Systems: A Decentralized Approach for University Administration." *College and University*, 1977, *53* (1), 65–76.

Walker, C. U. "The Functional Structuring of Stanford University." Unpublished doctoral dissertation, Stanford University, 1964.

Walters, E. "Degrees, Diplomas, and Academic Costume." In A. S. Knowles (Ed.), *Handbook of College and University Administration.* Vol. 2: *Academic.* New York: McGraw-Hill, 1970.

Walz, O. C. "A Study of Major Calendar Changes in Selected Institutions of Higher Education in the United States, 1969–1972." Unpublished doctoral dissertation, University of Nebraska, 1972.

Ward, L. B. "The Interview as an Assessment Technique." In *College Admissions 2: The Great Sorting.* New York: College Entrance Examination Board, 1955.

Watson, S. R. "An Approach to the Drop/Add Problem." *College and University*, 1974, *49* (3), 299–304.

Watts, S. F. (Ed.). *The College Handbook* and *The College Handbook Index of Majors.* New York: College Entrance Examination Board, 1977.

Wermers, D. J. "The Use of Commercial Guidance Agency Publications in College Counseling by High School Counselors." Unpublished research memorandum 74-3, University Office of School and College Relations, University of Illinois, 1974.

Wermers, D. J. (Ed.). *Transfer Credit Practices of Selected Educational Institutions.* Washington, D.C.: American Association of Collegiate Registrars and Admissions Officers, 1979. (Published annually.)

Wert, R. "The Impact of Three Nineteenth Century Reorganizations Upon Harvard University." Unpublished doctoral dissertation, Stanford University, 1955.

Western Interstate Commission for Higher Education (in cooperation with American Association of Collegiate Registrars and Admissions Officers). *Higher Education Facilities Planning and Management Manuals.* Boulder, Colo.: Western Interstate Commission for Higher Education, 1971.

Willingham, W. W. *Free Access Higher Education.* New York: College Entrance Examination Board, 1970.

Willingham, W. W. *The Source Book for Higher Education.* New York: College Entrance Examination Board, 1973.

Willingham, W. W. "Some Educational and Social Implications of *University of California* v. *Bakke.*" New York: College Entrance Examination Board, 1978.

Willingham, W. W., and Breland, H. M. "The Status of Selective Admissions." In Carnegie Council on Policy Studies in Higher Education, *Selective Admissions in Higher Education: Comment and Recommendations and Two Reports.* San Francisco: Jossey-Bass, 1977.

Wright, O. R., Jr. "Summary of Research on the Selection Interview Since 1964." *Personnel Psychology,* 1969, *22,* 391–413.

X, Professor (pseud.). *This Beats Working for a Living.* New Rochelle, N.Y.: Arlington House, 1973.

Yaw, E. J., and Eyestone, T. A. "1974–75 NACAC Salary Survey." *National ACAC Journal,* 1975, *20* (1), 1–4.

Young, K. E., Oliver, E. E., and Loeb, J. W. "Institutional Transfer Credit Policies: A Postsecondary Education Issue." *College and University,* 1977, *52* (4), 364–375.

Yourdon, E. "The Emergence of Structured Analysis." *Computer Decisions,* 1976, pp. 58–59.

Zoars, A., and others. *Online Admissions System.* Chicago: Office of Admissions and Records, University of Illinois at Chicago Circle, 1977.

Index

□ □ □ □ □ □ □ □ □ □ □ □ □ □ □ □ □ □ □